Volume 4
by Natsumi Mukai

HAMBURG // LONDON // LOS ANGELES // TOKYO

+ A N I M A

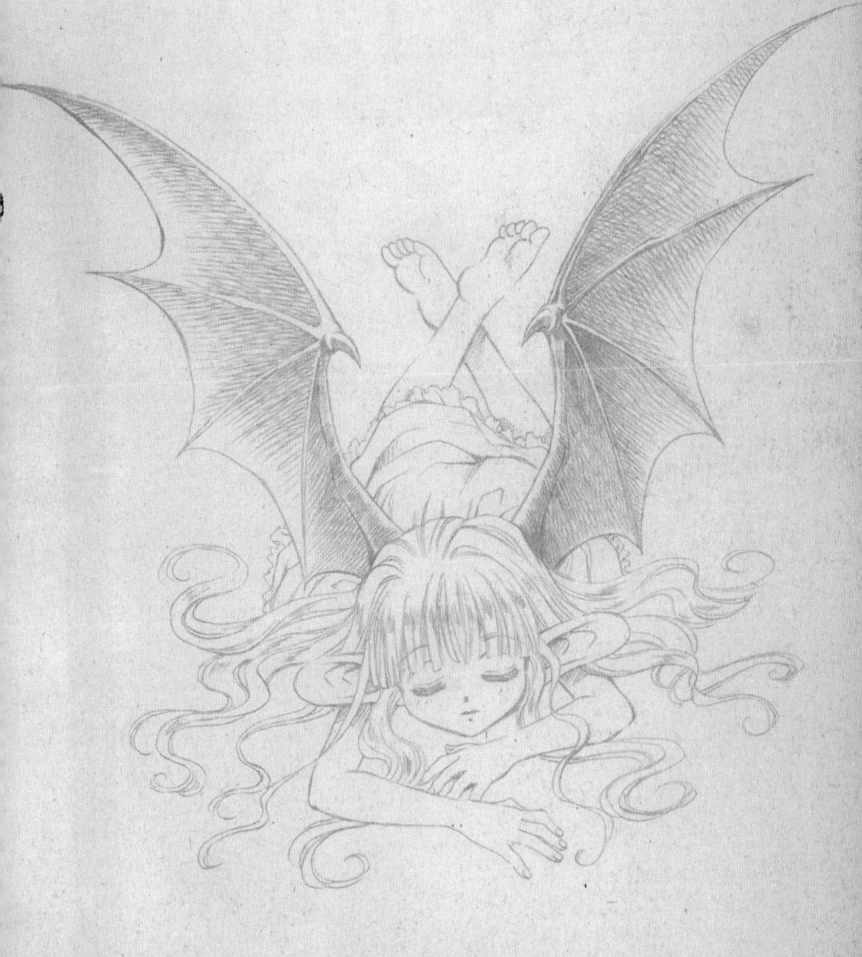

+ANIMA

プラスアニマ

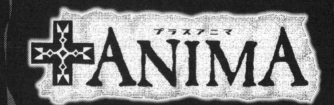

迎夏生

NATSUMI MUKAI

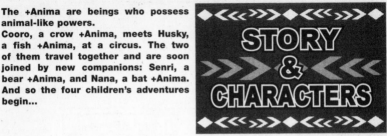

STORY & CHARACTERS

The +Anima are beings who possess animal-like powers.
Cooro, a crow +Anima, meets Husky, a fish +Anima, at a circus. The two of them travel together and are soon joined by new companions: Senri, a bear +Anima, and Nana, a bat +Anima. And so the four children's adventures begin...

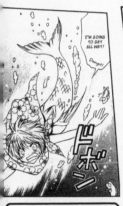

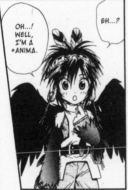

The four cross the mountains with Rose, a peddler whom they met along the path. The narrow mountain pass is thrown into confusion when they clash with an army troop led by Igneous, an Astarian soldier who hates the Kim-un-kur mountain people (Senri's clan).
With the help of Rose, who turns out to be a cat +Anima, they manage to settle the uproar and safely arrive in town.

I'M GOING TO GET ALL WET!
Dang!!
ドボン

ハスキー[Husky]

Fish +Anima. He can swim freely through water like a merman. He's a little stubborn, and he hates girls.

EH...?
OH...! WELL, I'M A +ANIMA.

クーロ[Cooro]

Crow +Anima. When he spreads his pitch-black wings, he can fly freely in the sky. He is a bit of a glutton!

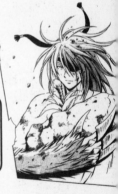

センリ[Senri]

Bear +Anima. With his arm bearing sharp claws, he has amazing strength. He doesn't talk very much.

I CAME TO GET YOU.

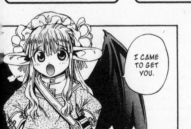

ナナ[Nana]

Bat +Anima. She can fly and use an ultrasonic screech. A fashion-conscious girl, she is scared of forests at night.

ローズ[Rose]

Cat +Anima. A girl Cooro and the others met on their journey. She meets them again in another town, and is now traveling with them.

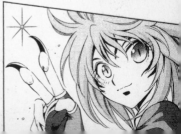

Later, a storm hits the village, and the roads become impassable. At the same time, Shadow's beloved goats fall ill at the top of the mountain.

Shadow takes some medicine and aims his glider at the mountain peak, but the glider is caught up in a strong wind. Just when it seems Shadow will run into a cliff, Cooro arrives to help, and Shadow arrives safely at the mountain peak.

Cooro and the others look for work to raise a little money, but they run into the Astarian troops led by Igneous again.

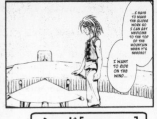

...I HAVE TO MAKE THE GLIDER WORK SO I CAN GET MEDICINE TO THE TOP OF THE MOUNTAIN WHEN IT'S NEEDED!
I WANT TO RIDE ON THE WIND...

シャド[Shadow]

Cooro becomes friends with Shadow, a young man who wishes to fly like a bird. Cooro takes interest in Shadow's homemade glider, and decides to help him with his experiment.

Husky is hurt, and things look tense between Igneous and Senri, but Harden, a skilled artisan, intervenes. Harden invites Cooro and the others into his home, and tells them that he will no longer forge swords for the Astarian army. Hearing his story, Nana devises a plan to help Harden.

Unfortunately, her plan fails, and Nana is captured by Igneous. Harden promises to forge swords in exchange for Nana's safety, but decides to turn the swords into scissors and kitchen knives instead. Even so, Igneous takes the goods Harden forged and reluctantly puts the incident behind him.

Cooro and company also say goodbye to Harden and set out on their journey.

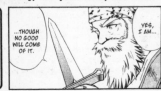

ハーデン[Harden]

YES, I AM...
...THOUGH NO GOOD WILL COME OF IT.

ANYWAY, I HEARD THAT YOU WERE COMING BACK FROM YOUR OFFICIAL TRIP, IGNEOUS.
SOMETHING ABOUT YOUR SWORDS BEING TRANSFORMED INTO SCISSORS AND KITCHEN KNIVES...?

フライ[Fly]

After leaving Cooro and the others, Igneous returns to the capital, Astar. There his childhood friend, the researcher Fly, comes to ask him about his journey. Hearing his story, Fly is interested in the +Anima. It seems that he is especially interested in Cooro.

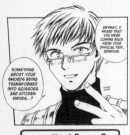

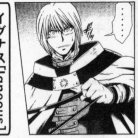

イグナス[Igneous]

......

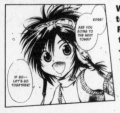

ROSE!
ARE YOU GOING TO THE NEXT TOWN?
IF SO-- LET'S GO TOGETHER!

When the four enter the hot springs town Bubbly, they are reunited with Rose. The inn they stay at appears to be losing customers because of a +Anima, and the innkeeper is ready to have a mountain hunt to kill it. Cooro and the others volunteer to intervene, and succeed in persuading the injured bison +Anima to leave the hot spring, and there's no great trouble.

Rose joins them, and they become a party of five. What adventures await them at the next stop on their journey?

Meanwhile, the party camps out yet again. Husky doesn't bathe with the others, and Nana suspects that he may actually be a girl. Husky shows her his body however, and proves beyond all doubt that he actually is a boy.

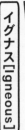

CONTENTS

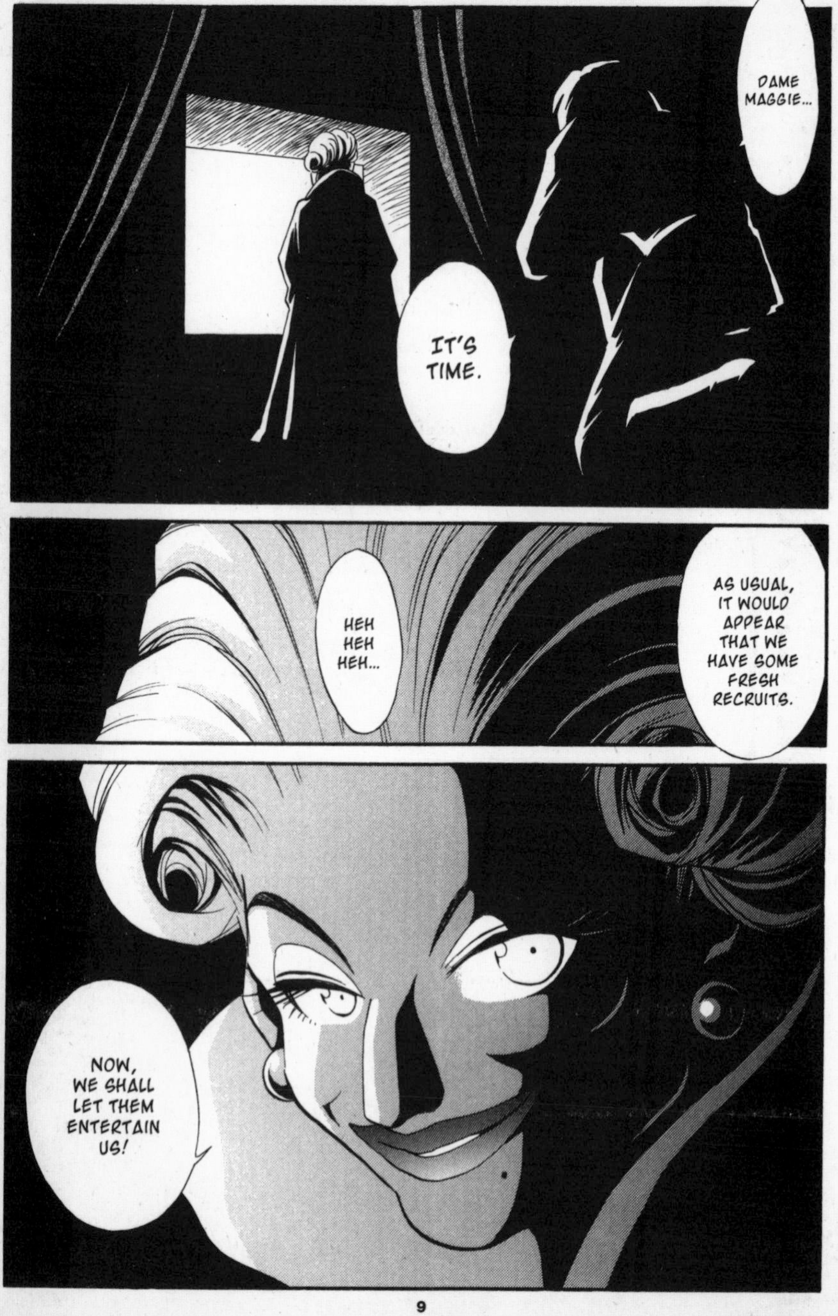
DAME MAGGIE...
IT'S TIME.
AS USUAL, IT WOULD APPEAR THAT WE HAVE SOME FRESH RECRUITS.
HEH HEH HEH...
NOW, WE SHALL LET THEM ENTERTAIN US!

Chapter 15: Maggie Coliseum—Part 1

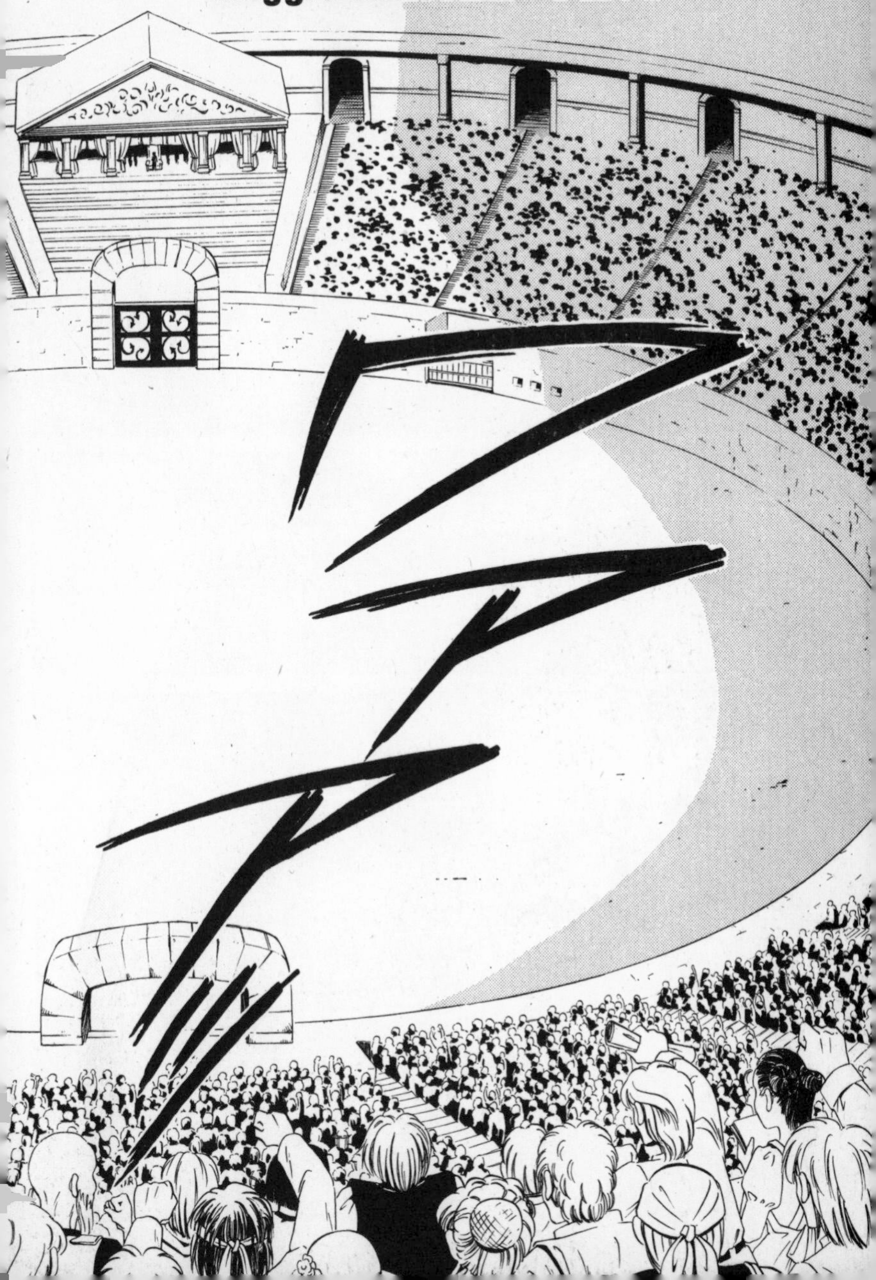

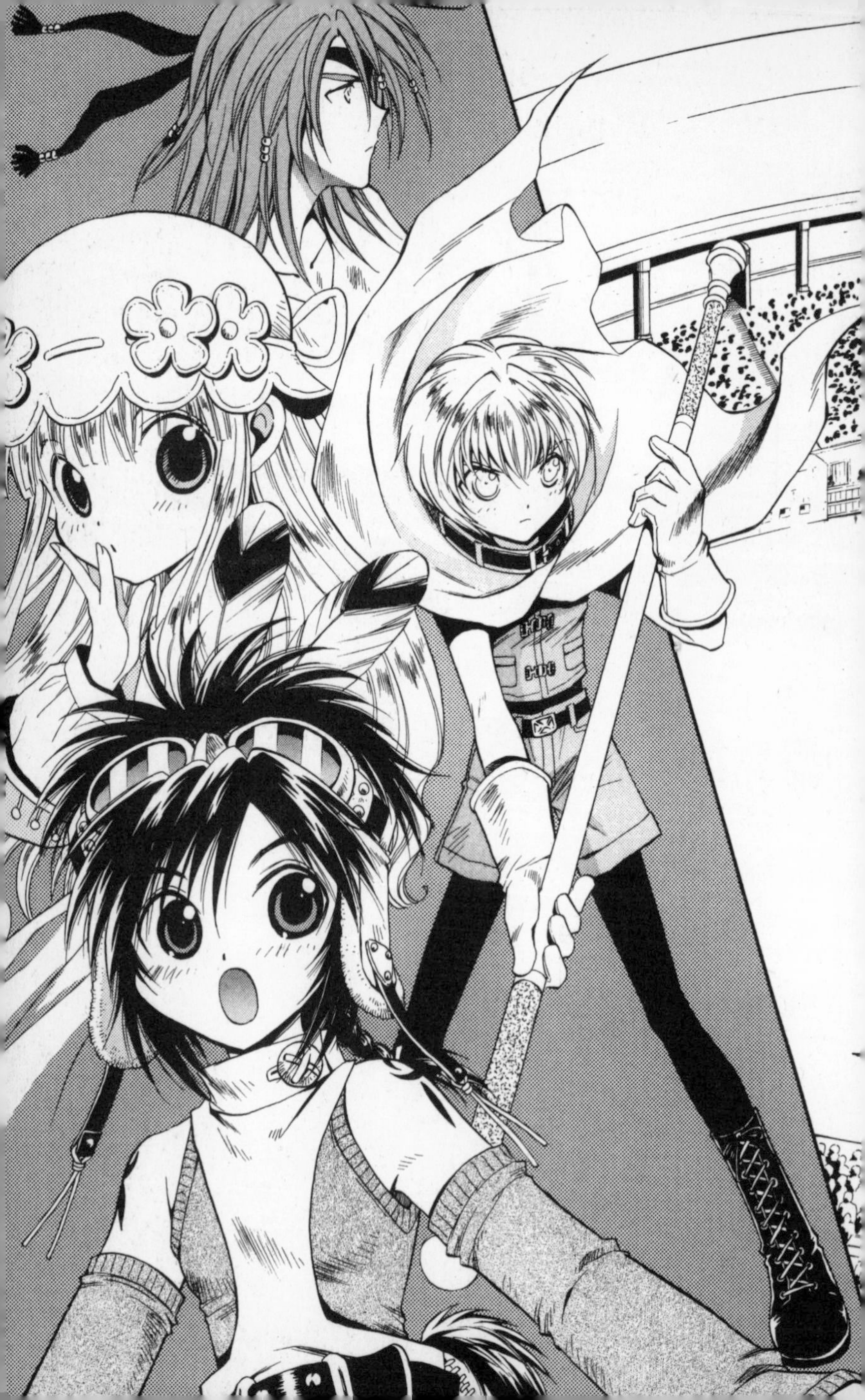

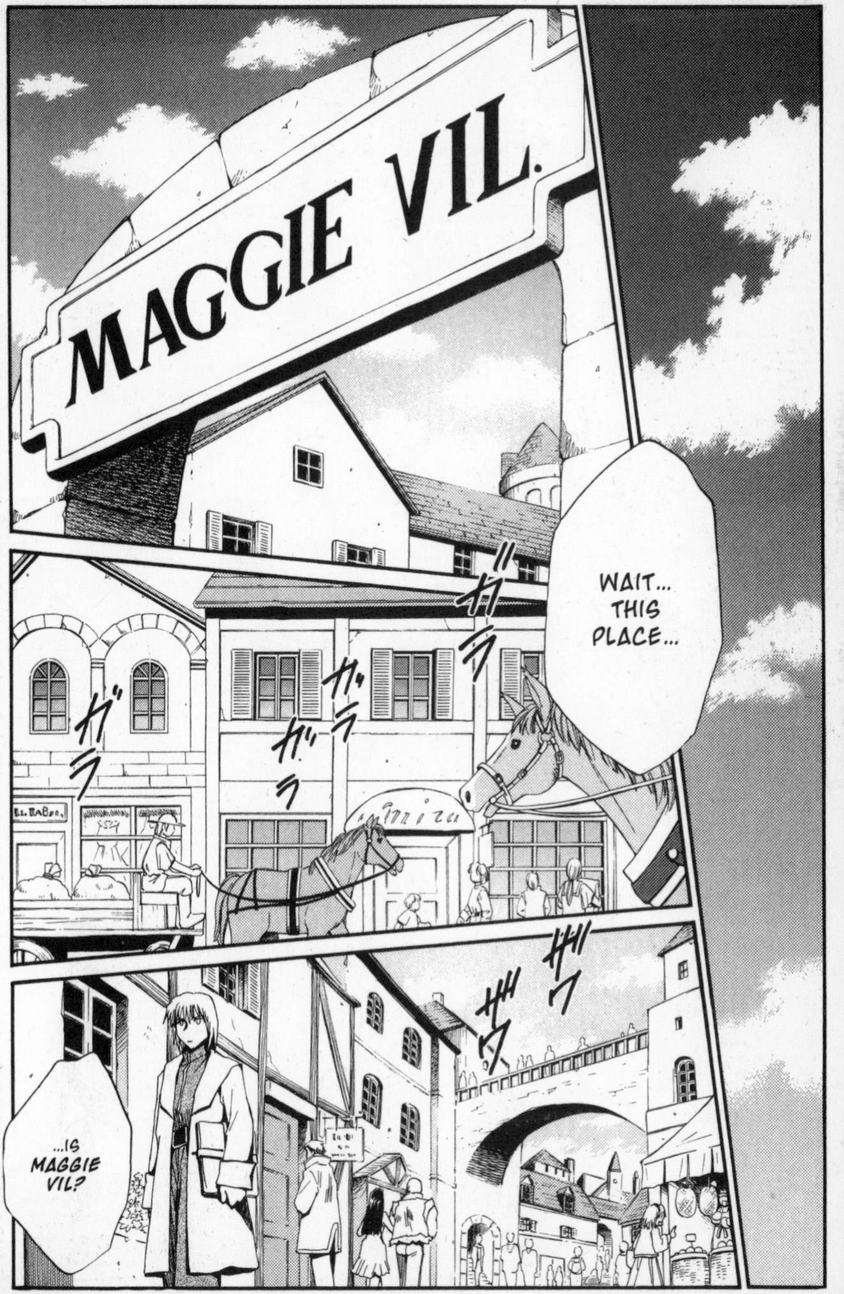
MAGGIE VIL.
WAIT... THIS PLACE...
ガラ
ガラ
ガラ
ガラ
ザワ
ザワ
...IS MAGGIE VIL?

Vil = Village

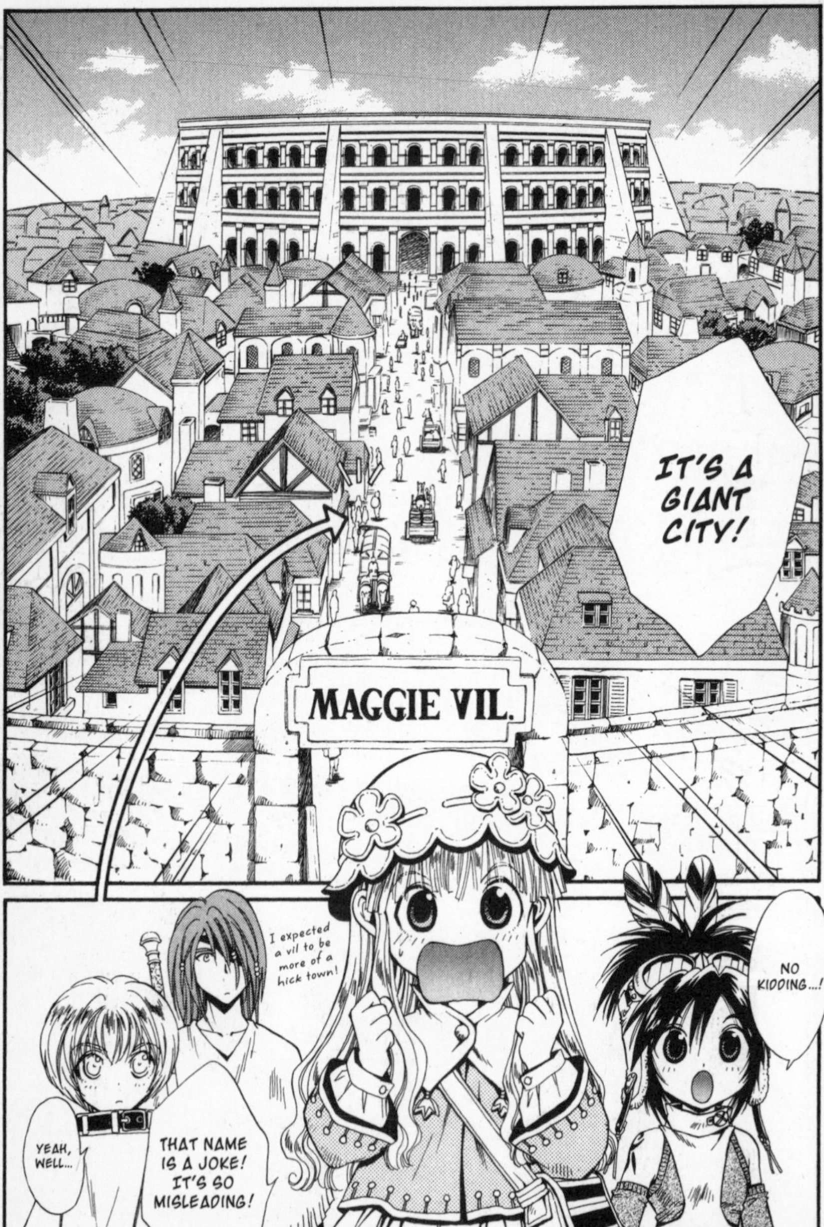
IT'S A GIANT CITY!
MAGGIE VIL.
NO KIDDING...!
I expected a vil to be more of a hick town!
THAT NAME IS A JOKE! IT'S SO MISLEADING!
YEAH, WELL...

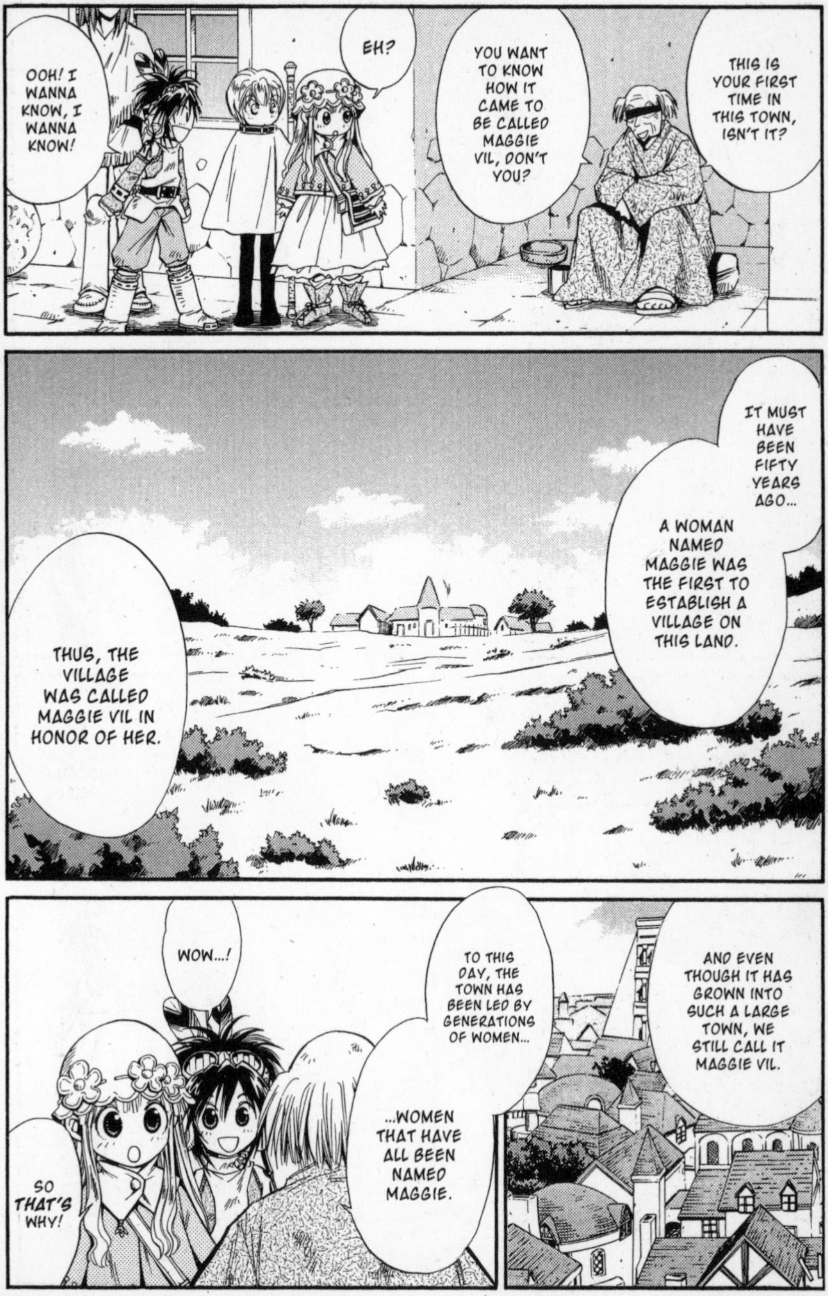
THIS IS YOUR FIRST TIME IN THIS TOWN, ISN'T IT?
YOU WANT TO KNOW HOW IT CAME TO BE CALLED MAGGIE VIL, DON'T YOU?
EH?
OOH! I WANNA KNOW, I WANNA KNOW!
IT MUST HAVE BEEN FIFTY YEARS AGO...
A WOMAN NAMED MAGGIE WAS THE FIRST TO ESTABLISH A VILLAGE ON THIS LAND.
THUS, THE VILLAGE WAS CALLED MAGGIE VIL IN HONOR OF HER.
AND EVEN THOUGH IT HAS GROWN INTO SUCH A LARGE TOWN, WE STILL CALL IT MAGGIE VIL.
TO THIS DAY, THE TOWN HAS BEEN LED BY GENERATIONS OF WOMEN...
WOW...!
...WOMEN THAT HAVE ALL BEEN NAMED MAGGIE.
SO THAT'S WHY!

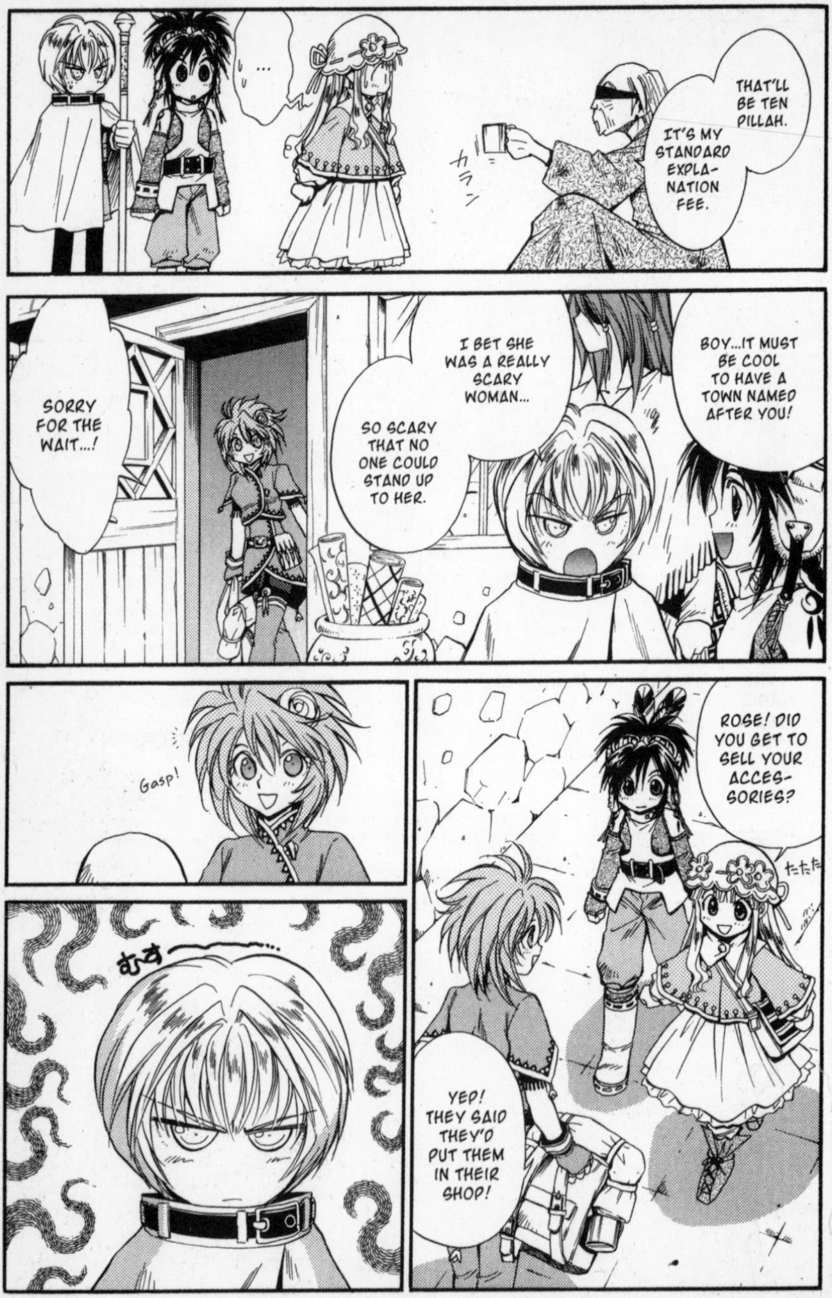
THAT'LL BE TEN PILLAH. IT'S MY STANDARD EXPLANATION FEE.
カラン
...
BOY...IT MUST BE COOL TO HAVE A TOWN NAMED AFTER YOU!
I BET SHE WAS A REALLY SCARY WOMAN... SO SCARY THAT NO ONE COULD STAND UP TO HER.
SORRY FOR THE WAIT...!
ROSE! DID YOU GET TO SELL YOUR ACCESSORIES?
たたた
YEP! THEY SAID THEY'D PUT THEM IN THEIR SHOP!
Gasp!
むすーーー...

* 1 pillah = app. 1 cent
100 pillah = 1 gillah

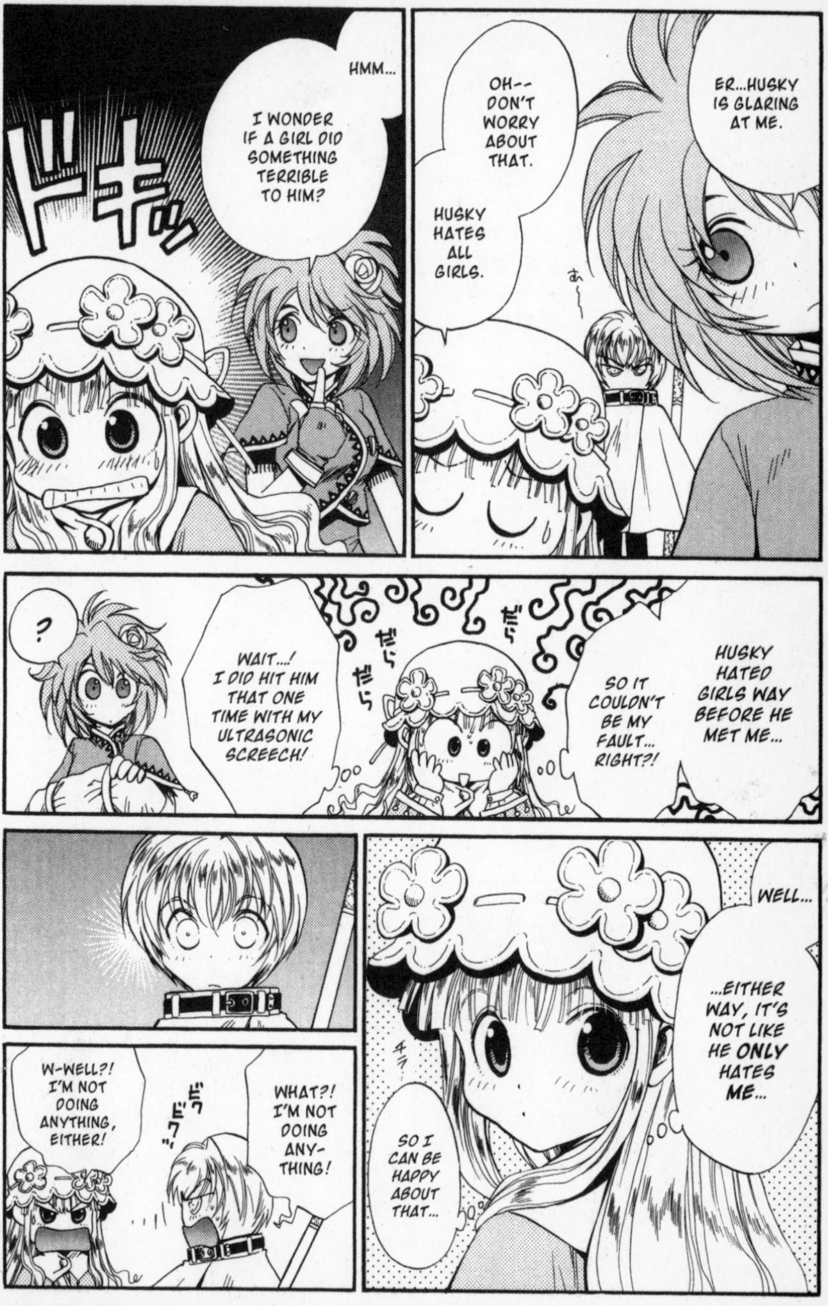
ER...HUSKY IS GLARING AT ME.
OH-- DON'T WORRY ABOUT THAT.
HUSKY HATES ALL GIRLS.
HMM...
I WONDER IF A GIRL DID SOMETHING TERRIBLE TO HIM?
ドキッ
HUSKY HATED GIRLS WAY BEFORE HE MET ME...
SO IT COULDN'T BE MY FAULT... RIGHT?!
だら
だら
だら
WAIT...! I DID HIT HIM THAT ONE TIME WITH MY ULTRASONIC SCREECH!
?
WELL...
...EITHER WAY, IT'S NOT LIKE HE ONLY HATES ME...
SO I CAN BE HAPPY ABOUT THAT...
チラ
WHAT?! I'M NOT DOING ANY-THING!
W-WELL?! I'M NOT DOING ANYTHING, EITHER!

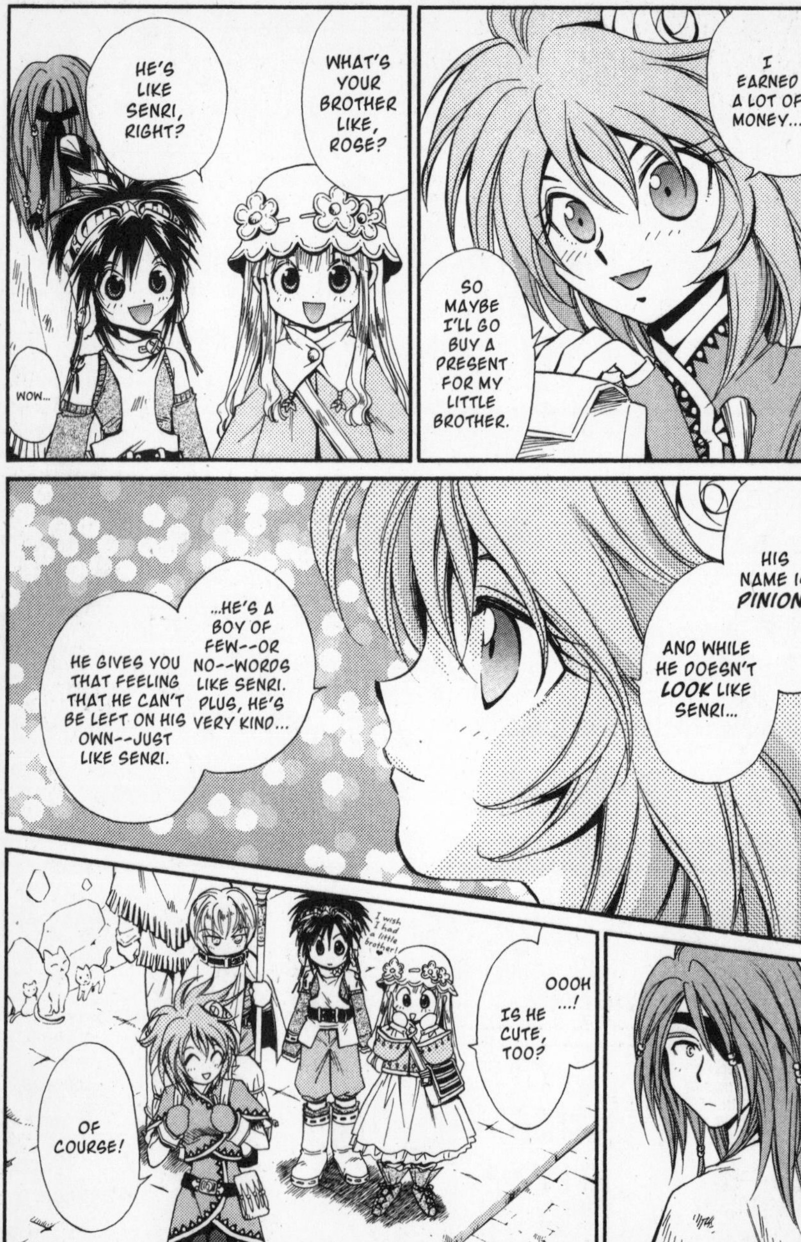
I EARNED A LOT OF MONEY...
SO MAYBE I'LL GO BUY A PRESENT FOR MY LITTLE BROTHER.
WHAT'S YOUR BROTHER LIKE, ROSE?
HE'S LIKE SENRI, RIGHT?
WOW...
HIS NAME IS PINION.
AND WHILE HE DOESN'T LOOK LIKE SENRI...
...HE'S A BOY OF FEW--OR NO--WORDS LIKE SENRI. PLUS, HE'S VERY KIND...
HE GIVES YOU THAT FEELING THAT HE CAN'T BE LEFT ON HIS OWN--JUST LIKE SENRI.
OOOH...!
IS HE CUTE, TOO?
I wish I had a little brother!
OF COURSE!

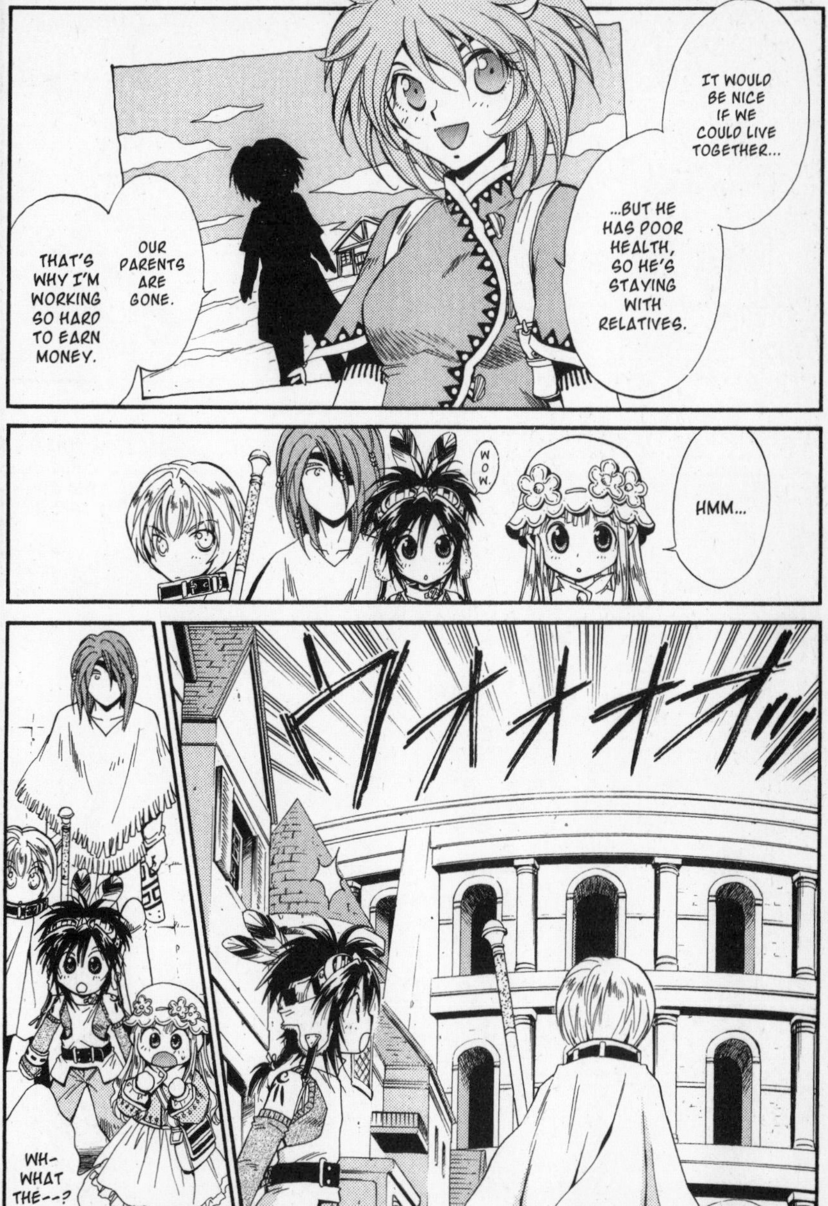
IT WOULD BE NICE IF WE COULD LIVE TOGETHER...
...BUT HE HAS POOR HEALTH, SO HE'S STAYING WITH RELATIVES.
OUR PARENTS ARE GONE.
THAT'S WHY I'M WORKING SO HARD TO EARN MONEY.
HMM...
WOW.
WH- WHAT THE--?

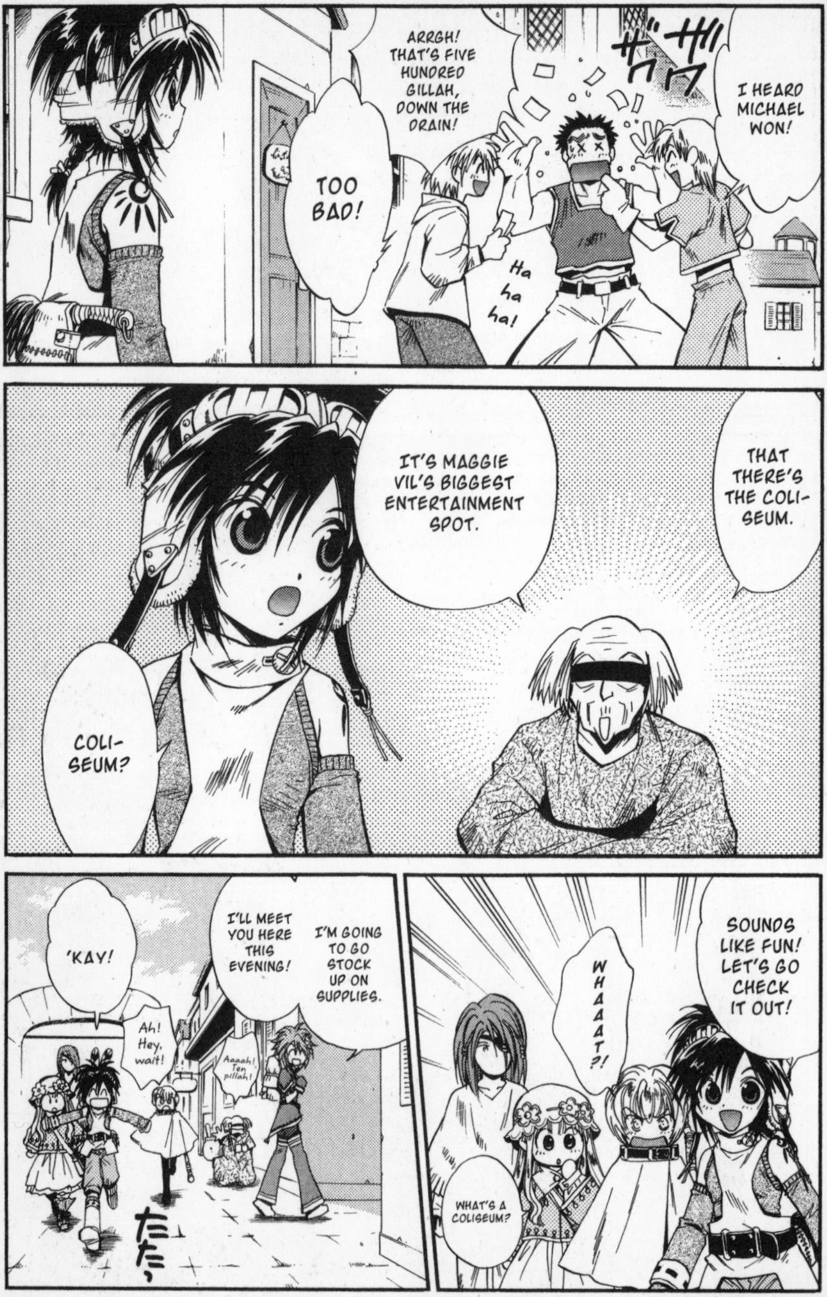
I HEARD MICHAEL WON!
ザワ ザワ
ARRGH! THAT'S FIVE HUNDRED GILLAH, DOWN THE DRAIN!
TOO BAD!
Ha ha ha!
THAT THERE'S THE COLI-SEUM.
IT'S MAGGIE VIL'S BIGGEST ENTERTAINMENT SPOT.
COLI-SEUM?
SOUNDS LIKE FUN! LET'S GO CHECK IT OUT!
WHAAAAT?!
WHAT'S A COLISEUM?
I'M GOING TO GO STOCK UP ON SUPPLIES.
I'LL MEET YOU HERE THIS EVENING!
Aaaah! Ten pillah!
'KAY!
Ah! Hey, wait!
たた

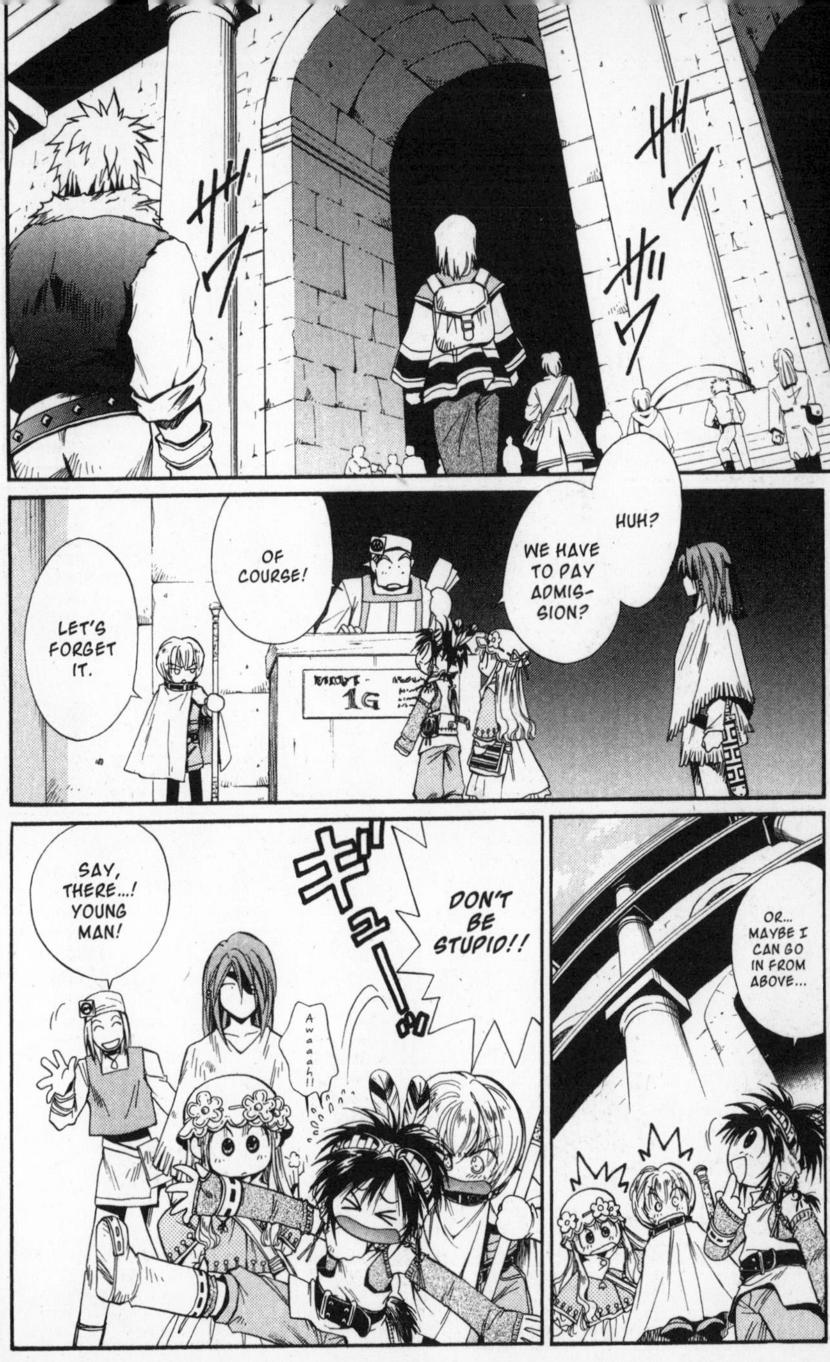
ザワ
ザワ
ザワ
HUH?
WE HAVE TO PAY ADMIS-SION?
OF COURSE!
LET'S FORGET IT.
1G
OR... MAYBE I CAN GO IN FROM ABOVE...
DON'T BE STUPID!!
Awaaah!!
SAY, THERE...! YOUNG MAN!

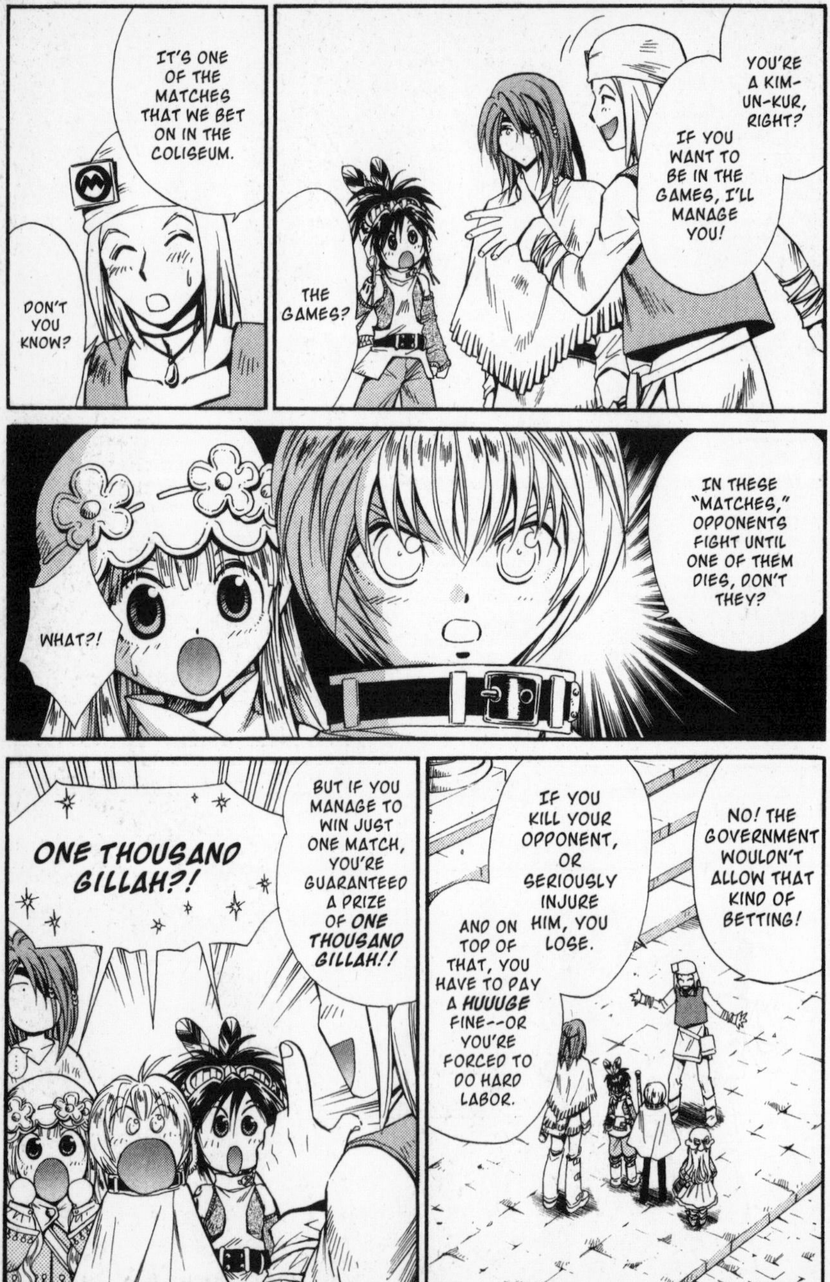
YOU'RE A KIM-UN-KUR, RIGHT?
IF YOU WANT TO BE IN THE GAMES, I'LL MANAGE YOU!
THE GAMES?
IT'S ONE OF THE MATCHES THAT WE BET ON IN THE COLISEUM.
DON'T YOU KNOW?
IN THESE "MATCHES," OPPONENTS FIGHT UNTIL ONE OF THEM DIES, DON'T THEY?
WHAT?!
NO! THE GOVERNMENT WOULDN'T ALLOW THAT KIND OF BETTING!
IF YOU KILL YOUR OPPONENT, OR SERIOUSLY INJURE HIM, YOU LOSE.
AND ON TOP OF THAT, YOU HAVE TO PAY A *HUUUGE* FINE--OR YOU'RE FORCED TO DO HARD LABOR.
BUT IF YOU MANAGE TO WIN JUST ONE MATCH, YOU'RE GUARANTEED A PRIZE OF *ONE THOUSAND GILLAH!!*
ONE THOUSAND GILLAH?!

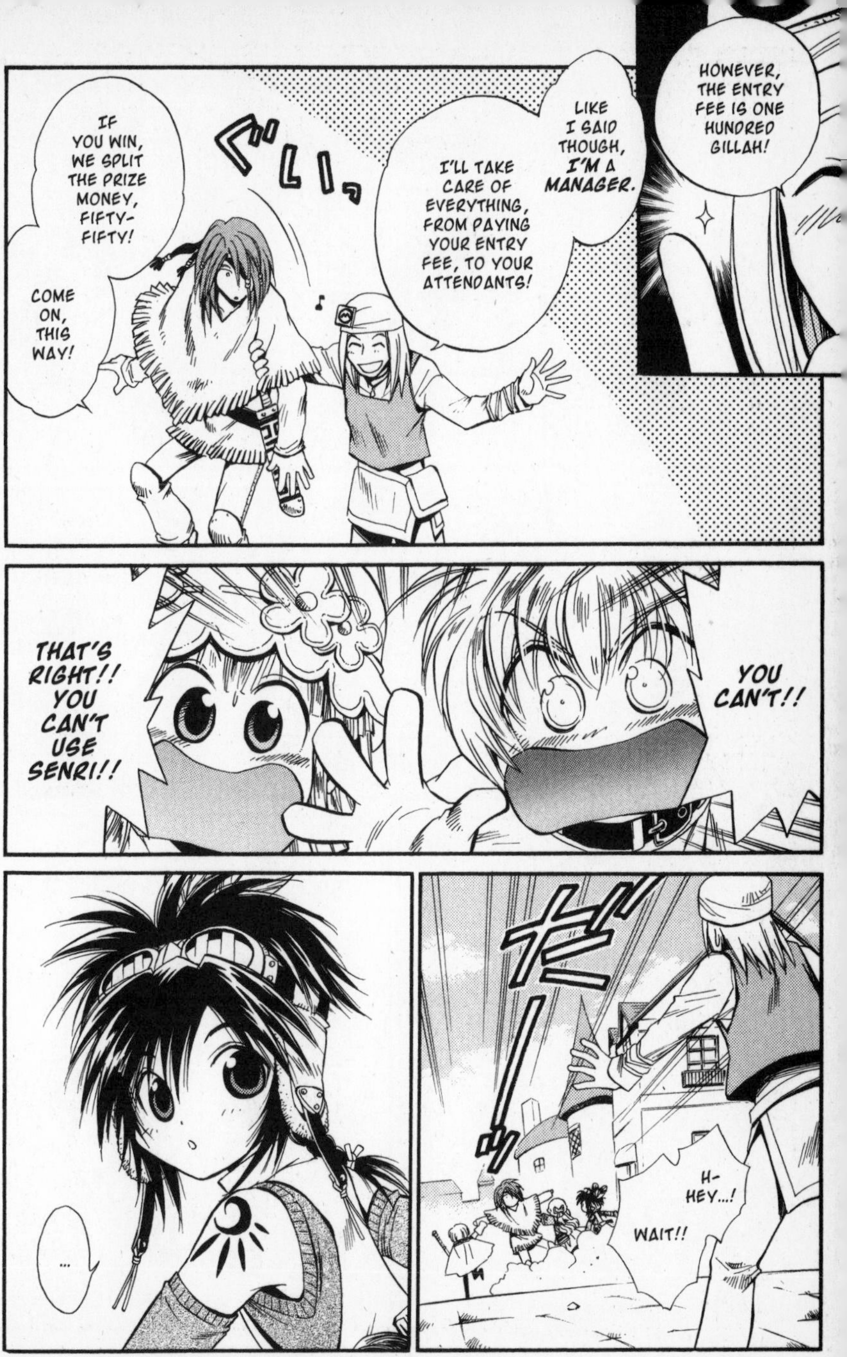
HOWEVER, THE ENTRY FEE IS ONE HUNDRED GILLAH!
LIKE I SAID THOUGH, I'M A MANAGER.
I'LL TAKE CARE OF EVERYTHING, FROM PAYING YOUR ENTRY FEE, TO YOUR ATTENDANTS!
IF YOU WIN, WE SPLIT THE PRIZE MONEY, FIFTY-FIFTY!
COME ON, THIS WAY!
YOU CAN'T!!
THAT'S RIGHT!! YOU CAN'T USE SENRI!!
H-HEY...!
WAIT!!
...

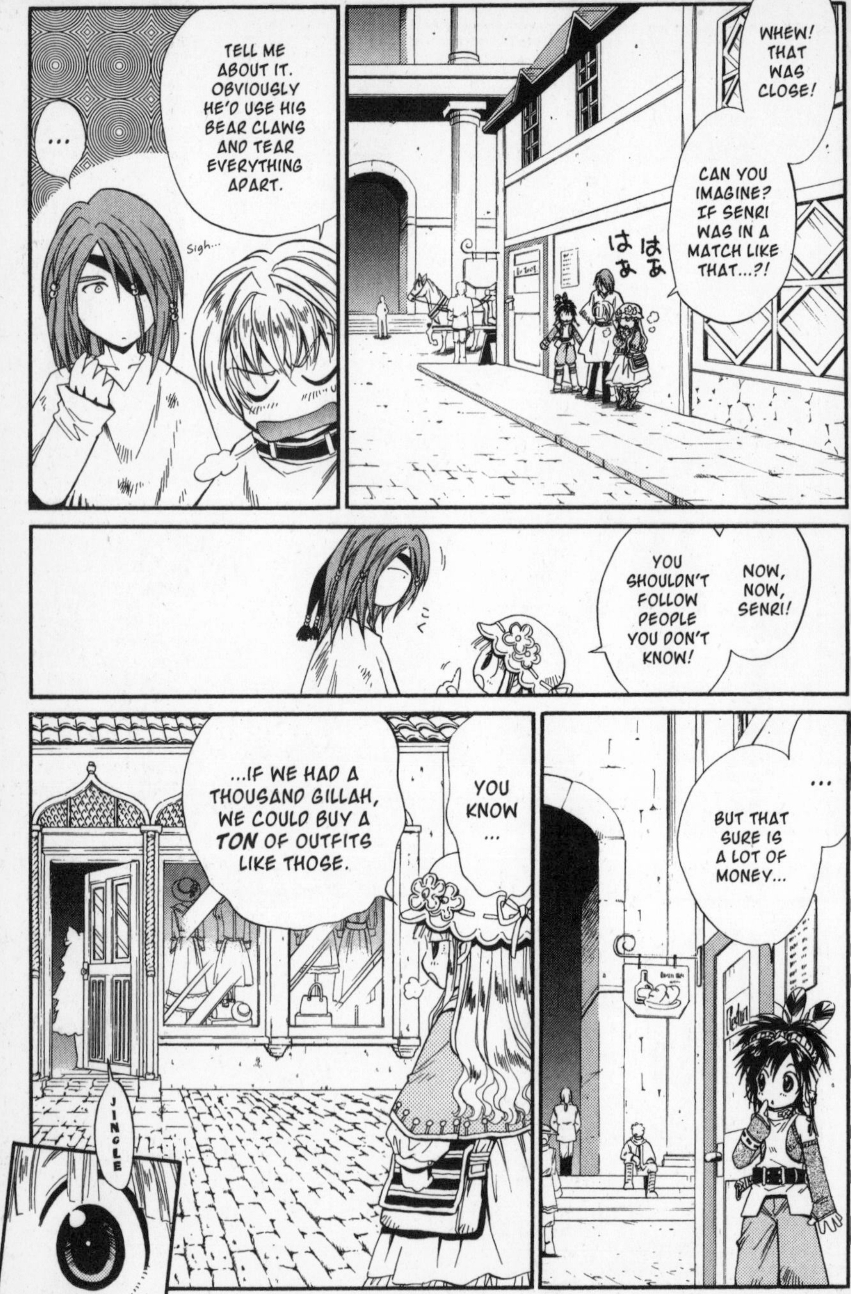
WHEW! THAT WAS CLOSE!
CAN YOU IMAGINE? IF SENRI WAS IN A MATCH LIKE THAT...?!
はあ はあ
TELL ME ABOUT IT. OBVIOUSLY HE'D USE HIS BEAR CLAWS AND TEAR EVERYTHING APART.
...
Sigh...
NOW, NOW, SENRI!
YOU SHOULDN'T FOLLOW PEOPLE YOU DON'T KNOW!
...
BUT THAT SURE IS A LOT OF MONEY...
YOU KNOW ...
...IF WE HAD A THOUSAND GILLAH, WE COULD BUY A **TON** OF OUTFITS LIKE THOSE.
JINGLE

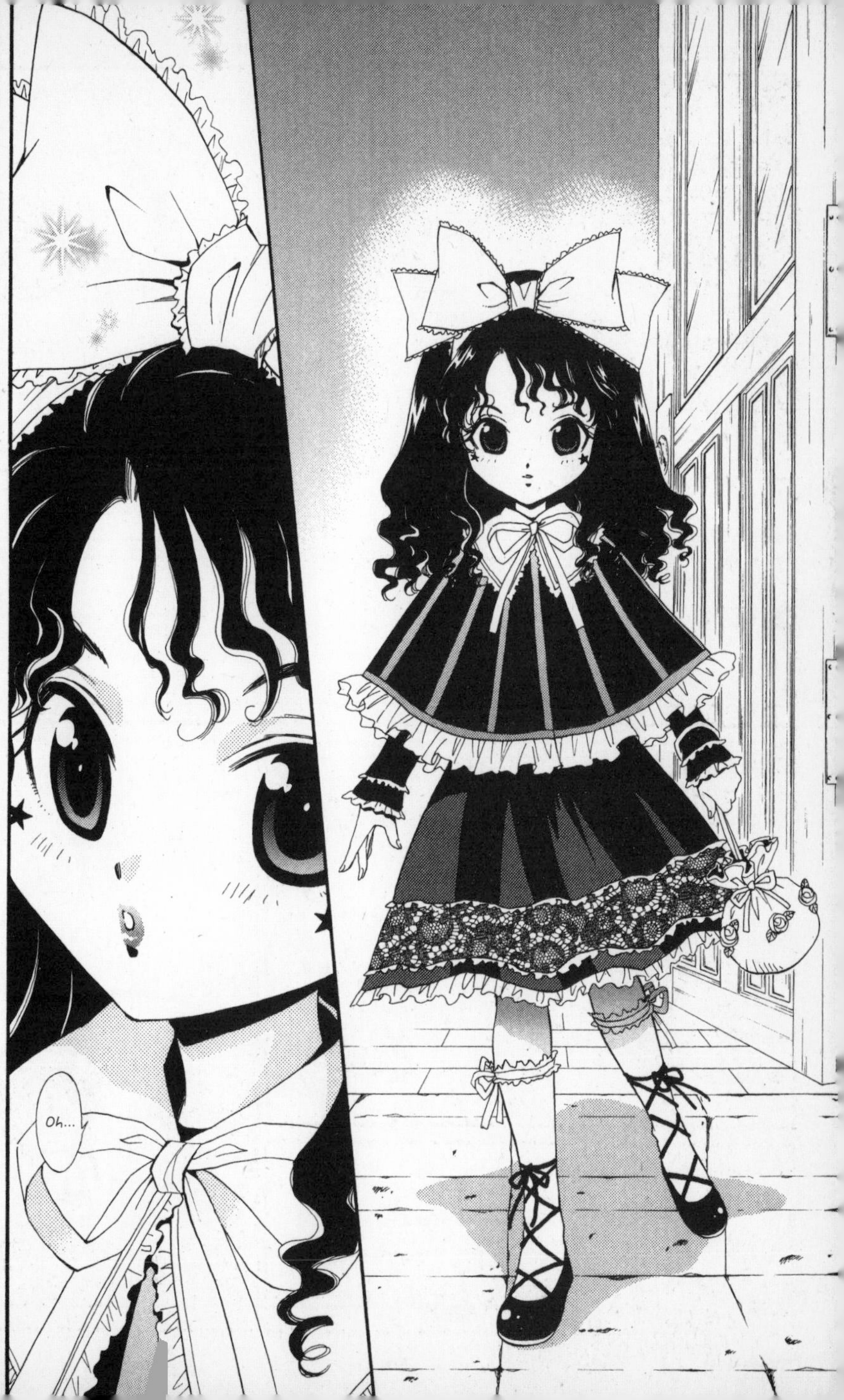
Oh...

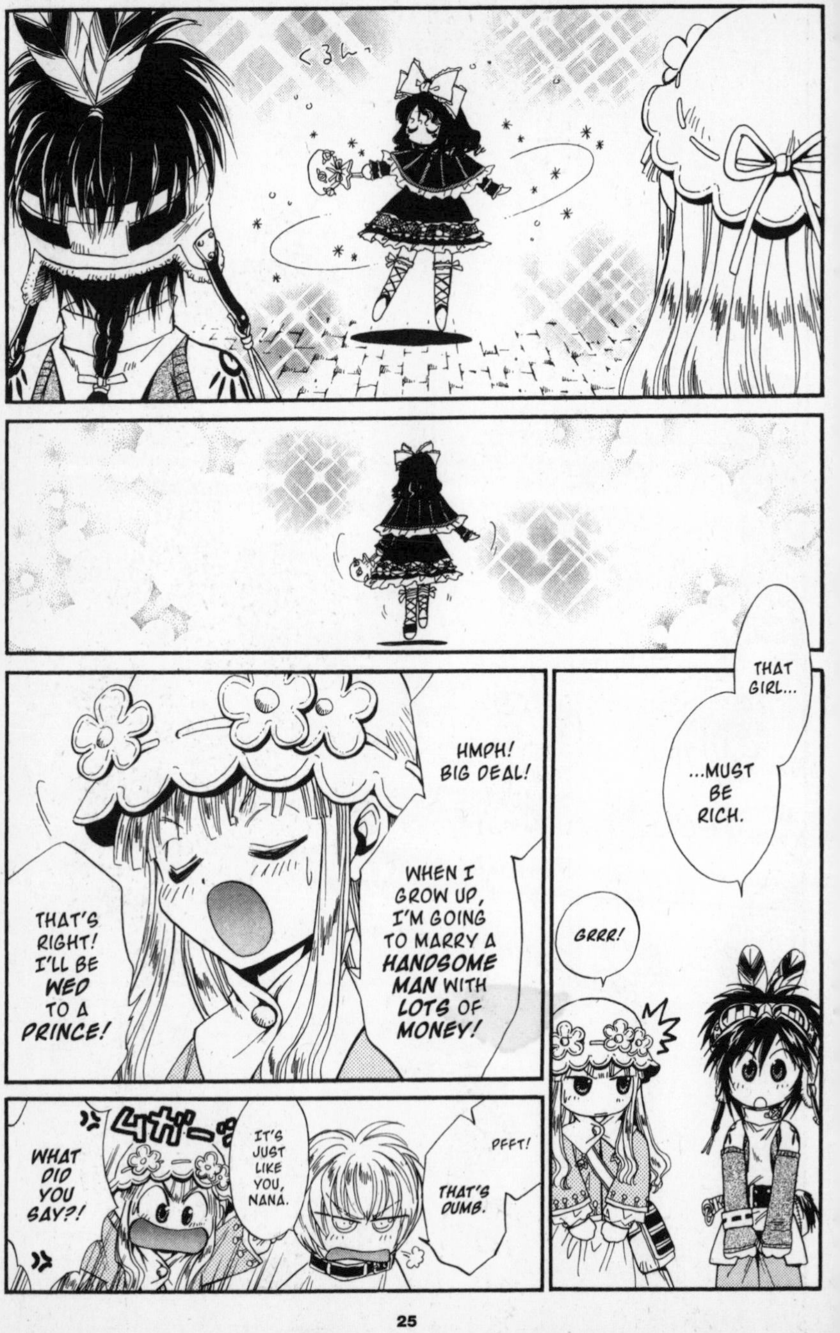

くるん
THAT GIRL...
...MUST BE RICH.
GRRR!
HMPH! BIG DEAL!
WHEN I GROW UP, I'M GOING TO MARRY A HANDSOME MAN WITH LOTS OF MONEY!
THAT'S RIGHT! I'LL BE WED TO A PRINCE!
PFFT! THAT'S DUMB.
IT'S JUST LIKE YOU, NANA.
ムガー
WHAT DID YOU SAY?!

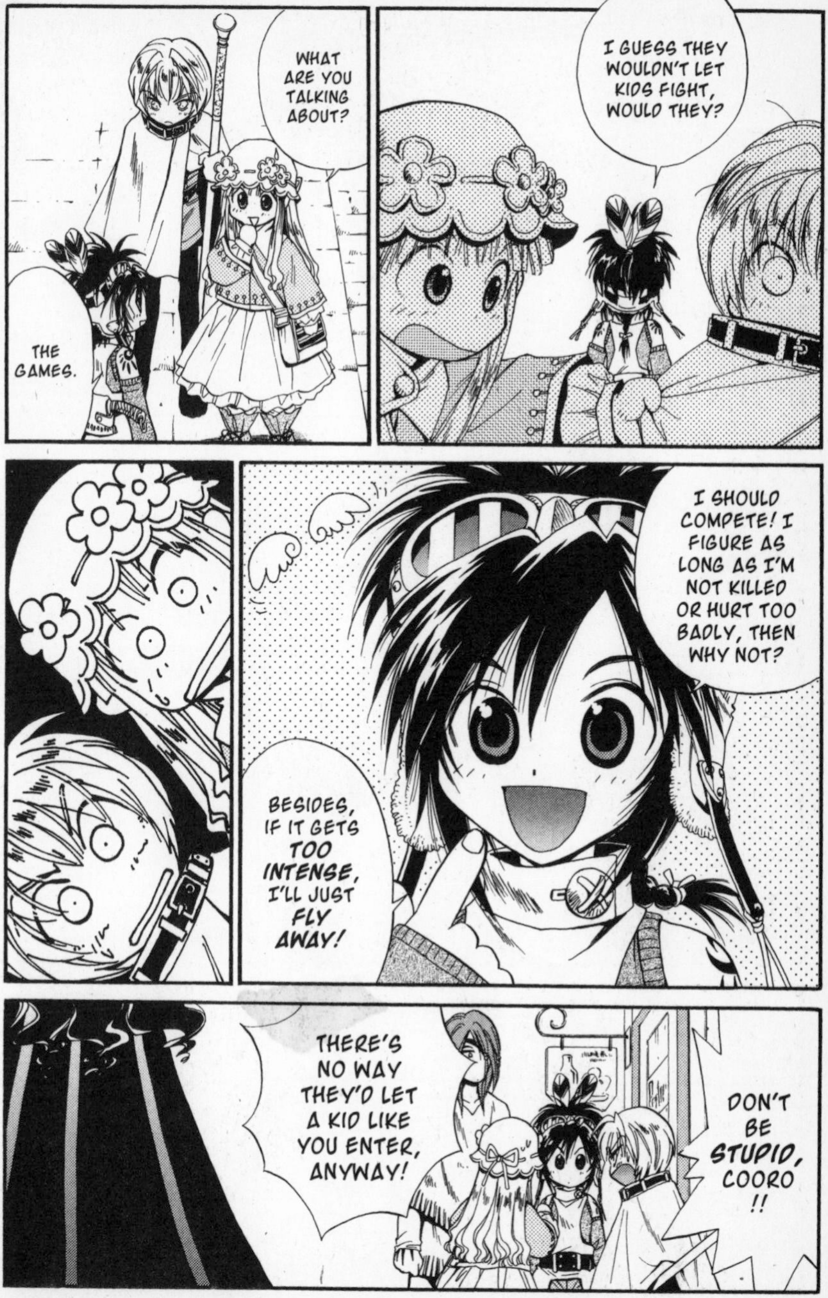
I GUESS THEY WOULDN'T LET KIDS FIGHT, WOULD THEY?
WHAT ARE YOU TALKING ABOUT?
THE GAMES.
I SHOULD COMPETE! I FIGURE AS LONG AS I'M NOT KILLED OR HURT TOO BADLY, THEN WHY NOT?
BESIDES, IF IT GETS TOO INTENSE, I'LL JUST FLY AWAY!
DON'T BE STUPID, COORO!!
THERE'S NO WAY THEY'D LET A KID LIKE YOU ENTER, ANYWAY!

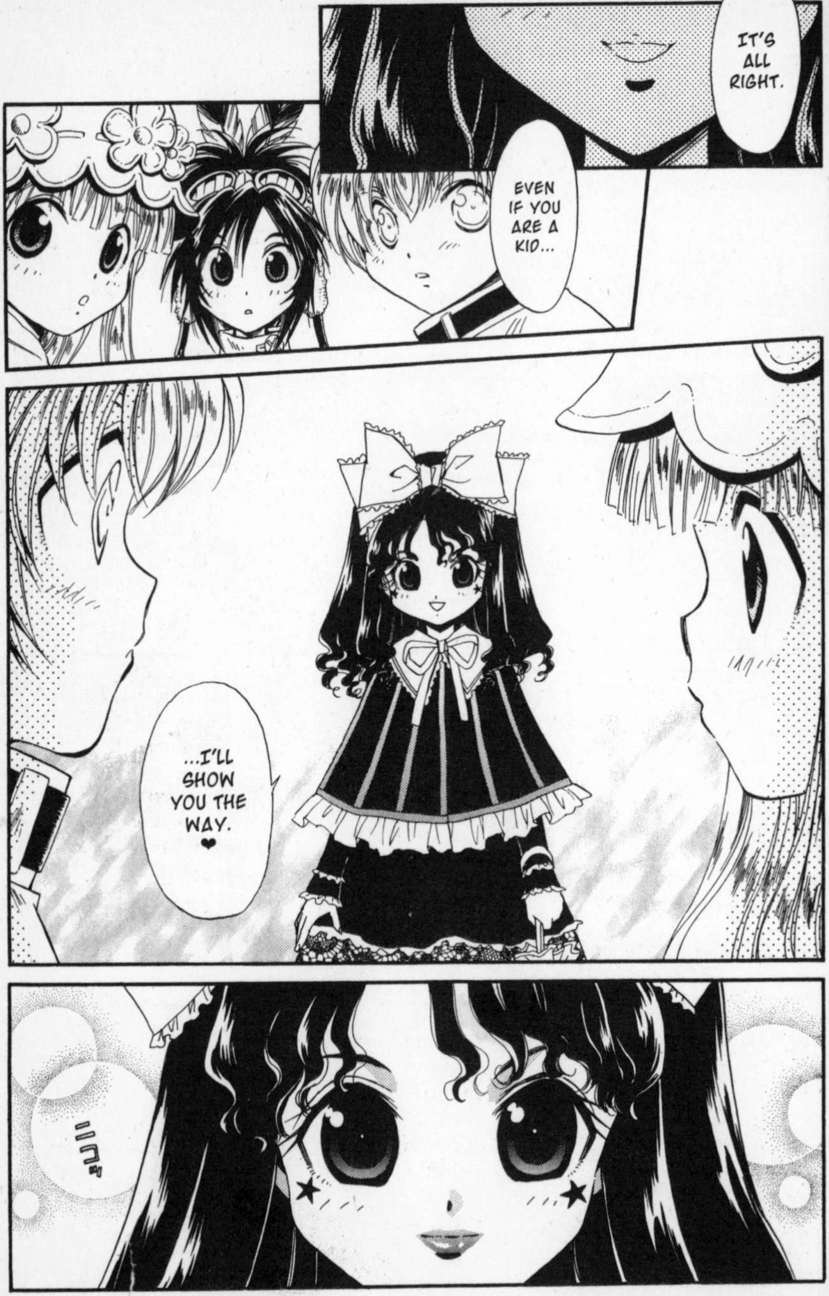
IT'S ALL RIGHT.
EVEN IF YOU ARE A KID...
...I'LL SHOW YOU THE WAY. ❤

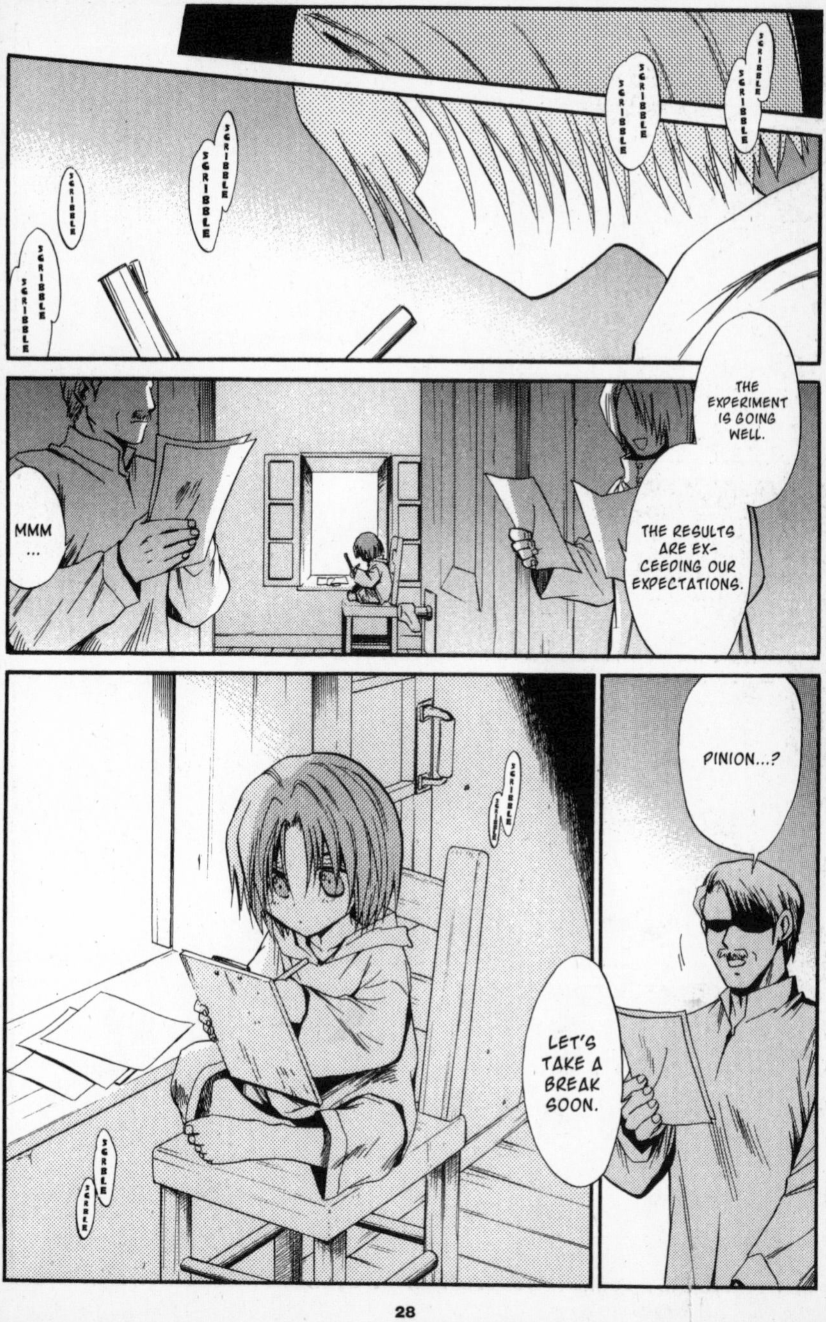

SCRIBBLE
SCRIBBLE
SCRIBBLE
SCRIBBLE
SCRIBBLE
SCRIBBLE
SCRIBBLE
SCRIBBLE
THE EXPERIMENT IS GOING WELL.
THE RESULTS ARE EXCEEDING OUR EXPECTATIONS.
MMM ...
PINION...?
LET'S TAKE A BREAK SOON.
SCRIBBLE
SCRBLE
SCRBLE

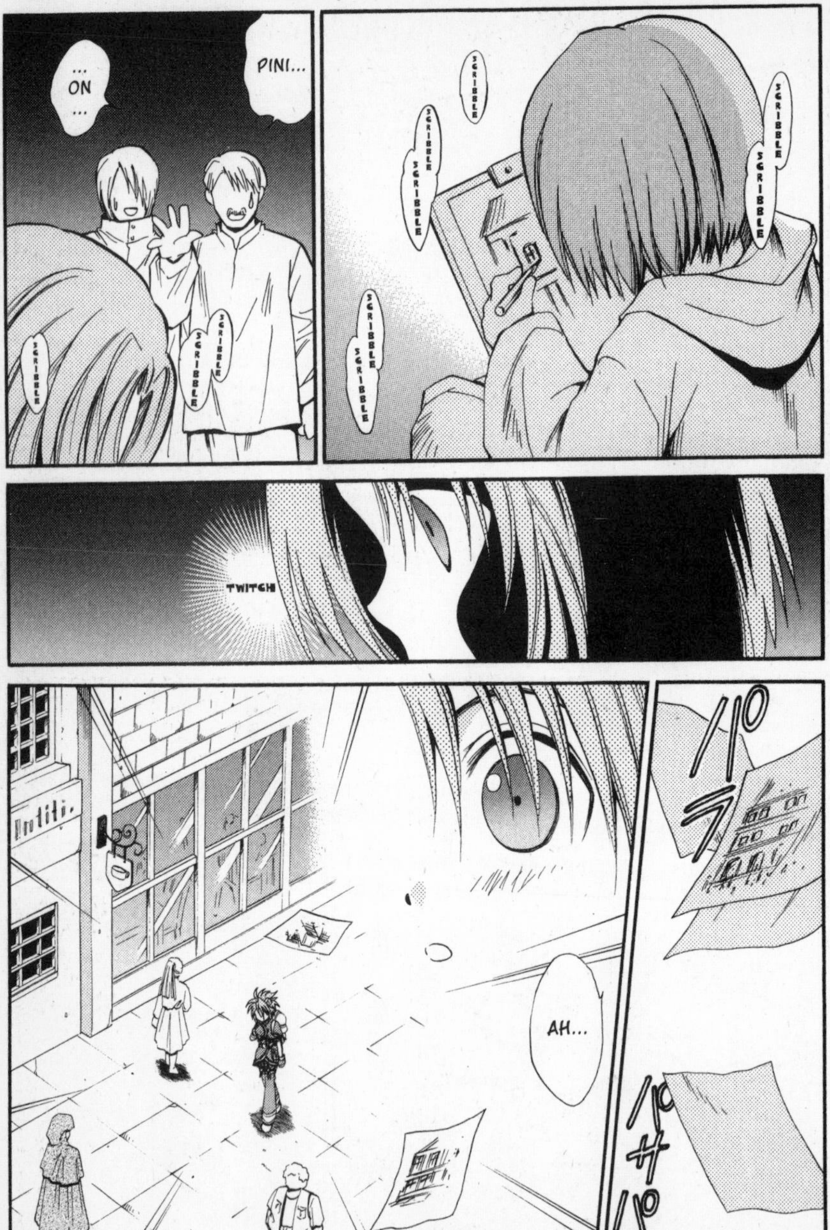
SCRIBBLE
SCRIBBLE
SCRIBBLE
SCRIBBLE
SCRIBBLE
SCRIBBLE
SCRIBBLE
PINI...
... ON ...
SCRIBBLE
SCRIBBLE
SCRIBBLE
TWITCH
パラ
パサパサ
AH...

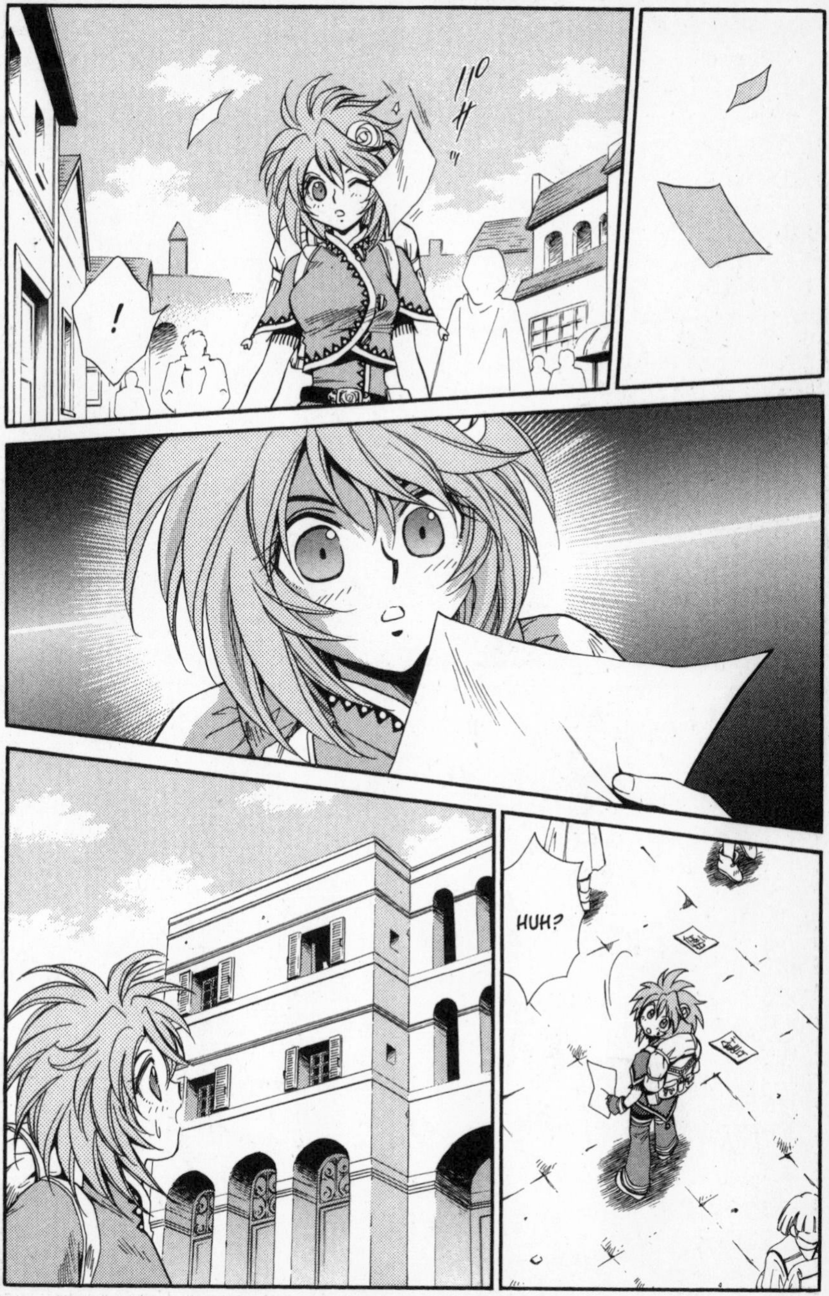
バサッ
!
HUH?

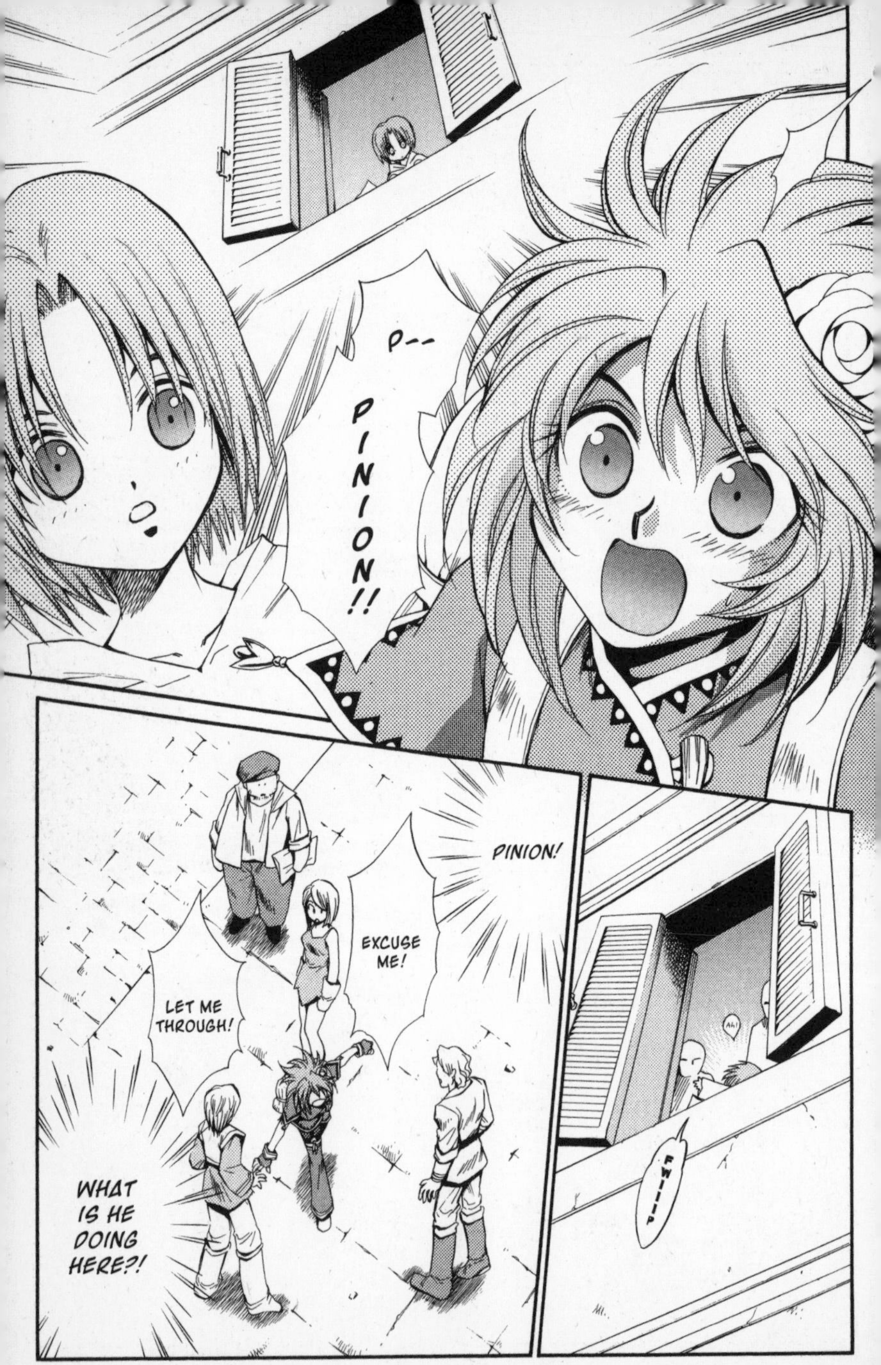
P--
PINION!!
Ah!
FWIIIP
PINION!
EXCUSE ME!
LET ME THROUGH!
WHAT IS HE DOING HERE?!

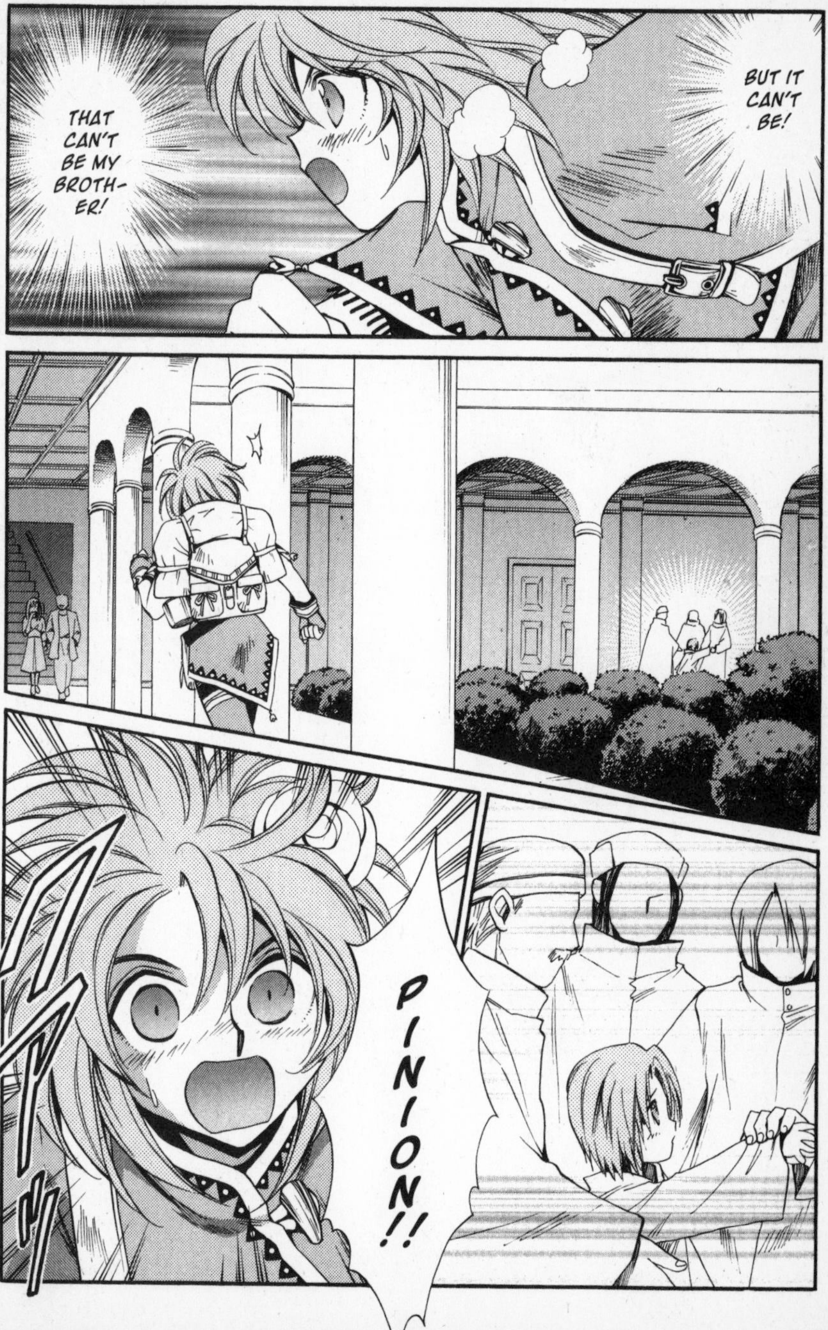
BUT IT CAN'T BE!
THAT CAN'T BE MY BROTHER!
PINION!!

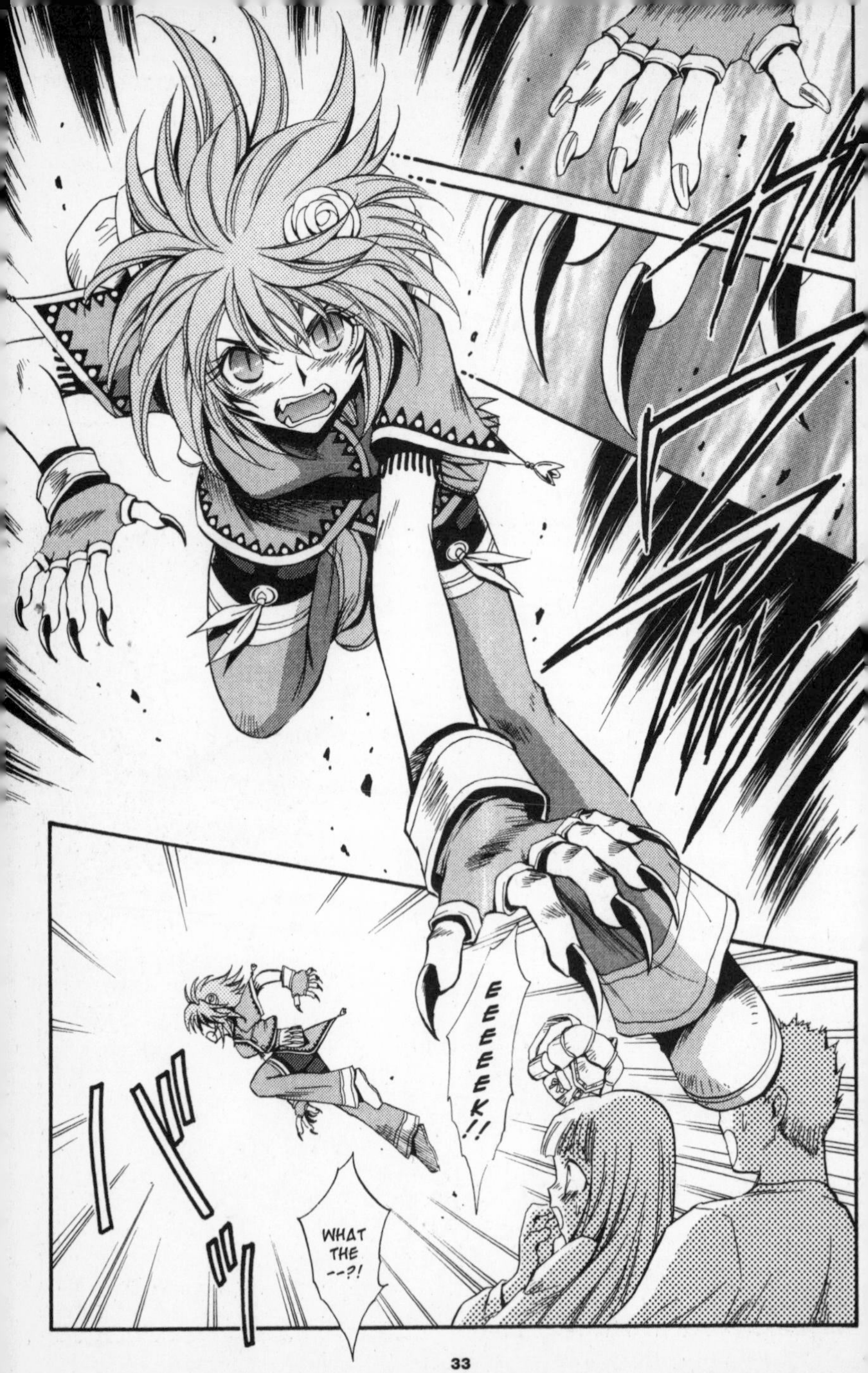
EEEEEEK!!
WHAT THE --?!

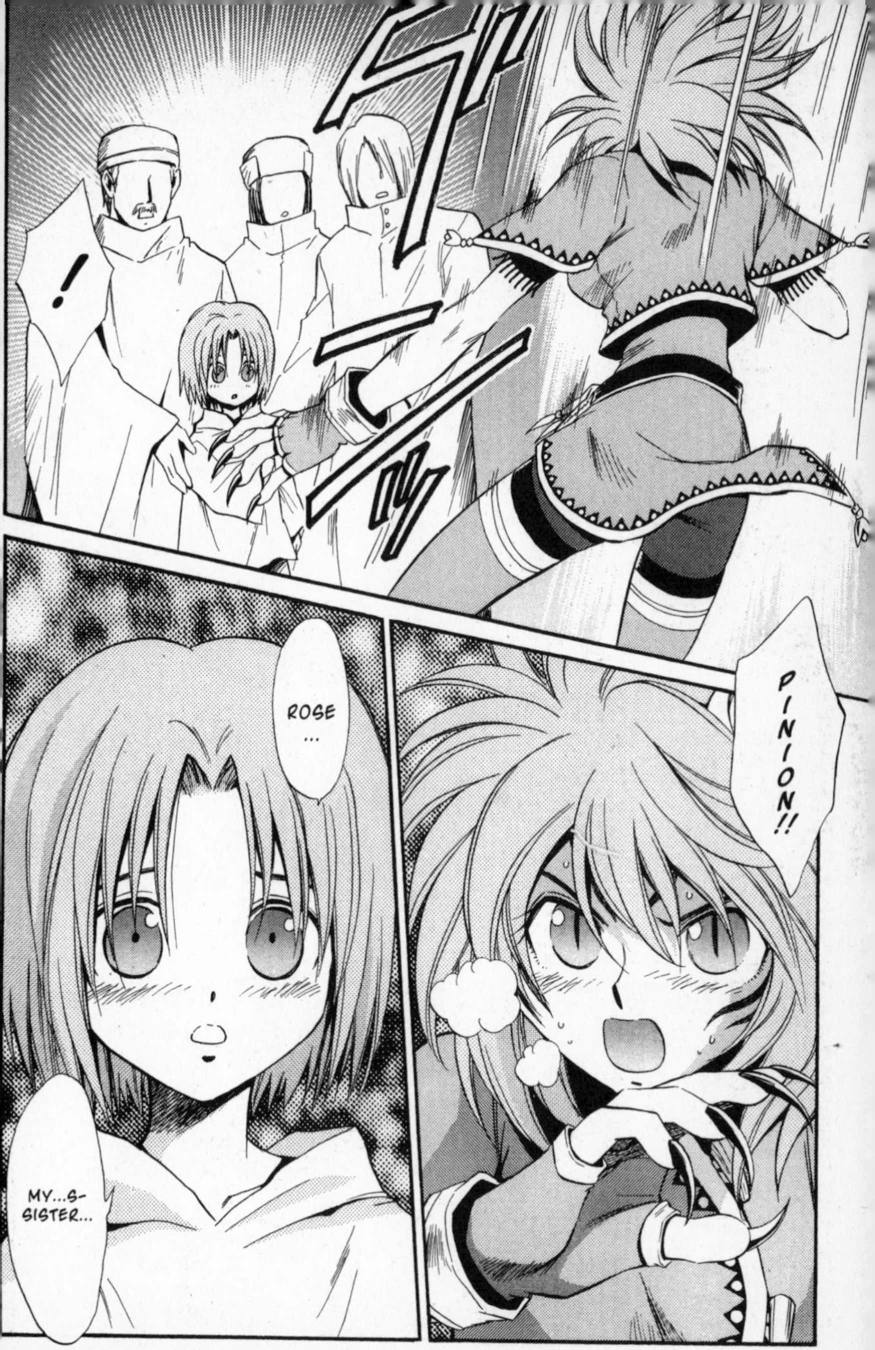
!
PINION!!
ROSE ...
MY...S-SISTER...

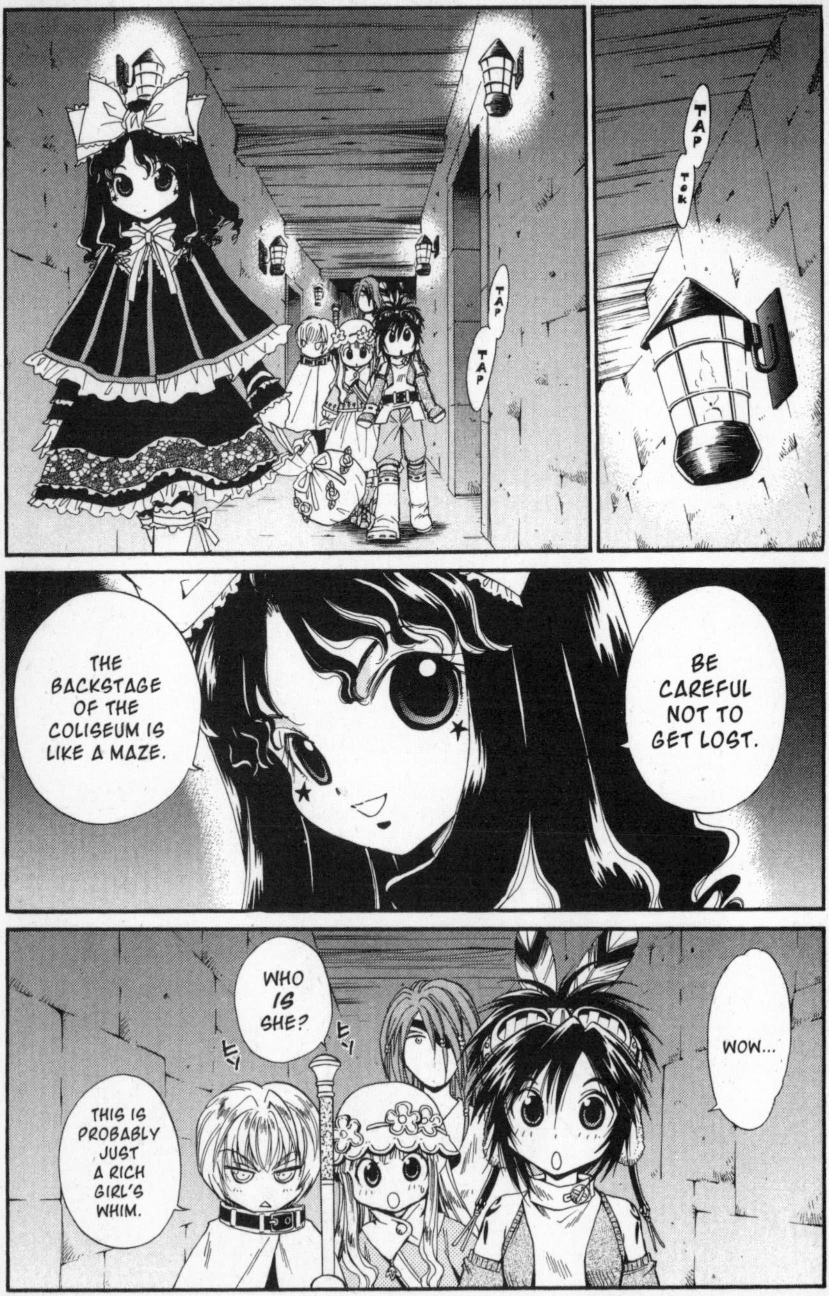
TAP
Tok
TAP
TAP
BE CAREFUL NOT TO GET LOST.
THE BACKSTAGE OF THE COLISEUM IS LIKE A MAZE.
WOW...
WHO *IS* SHE?
THIS IS PROBABLY JUST A RICH GIRL'S WHIM.

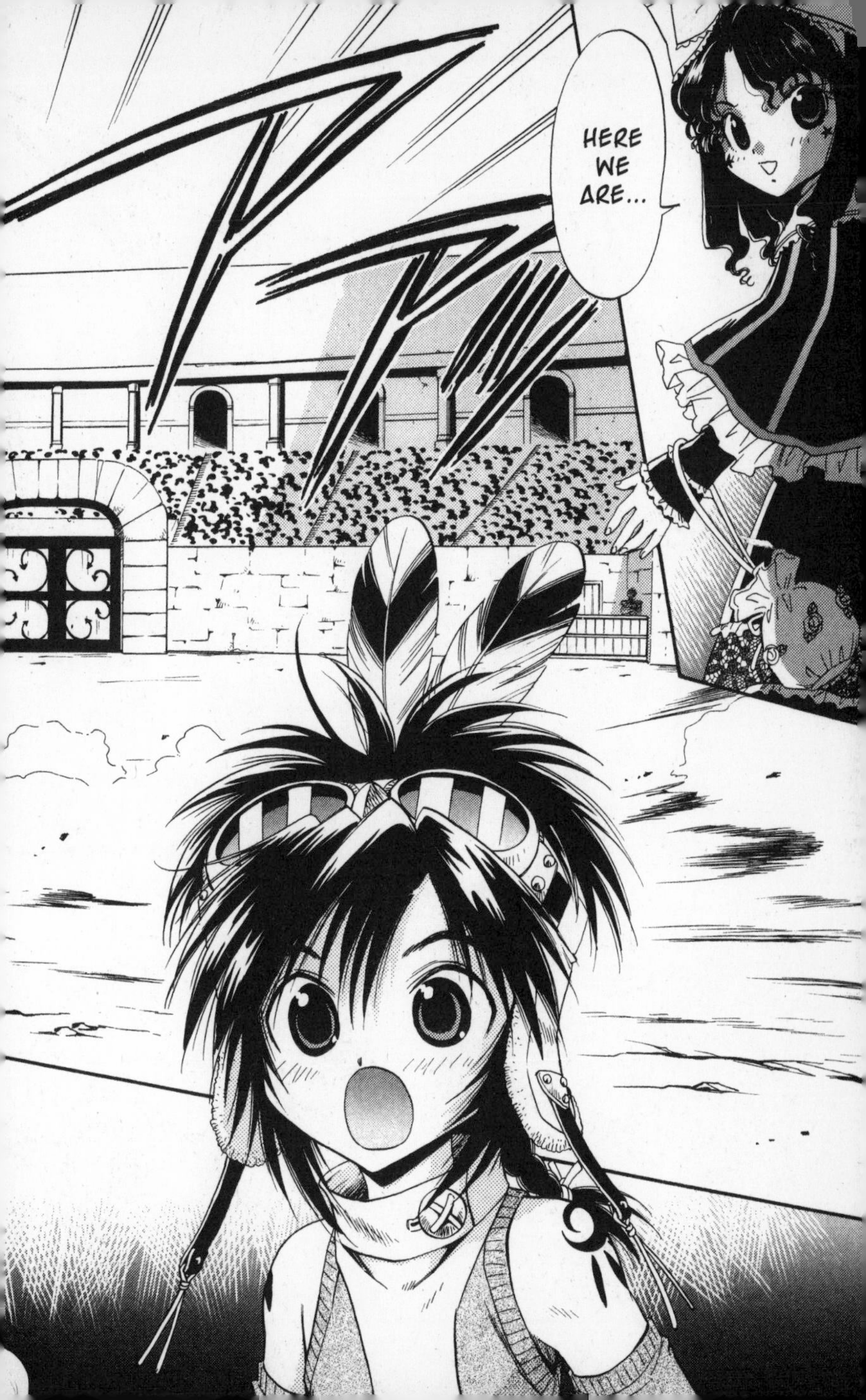
HERE WE ARE...

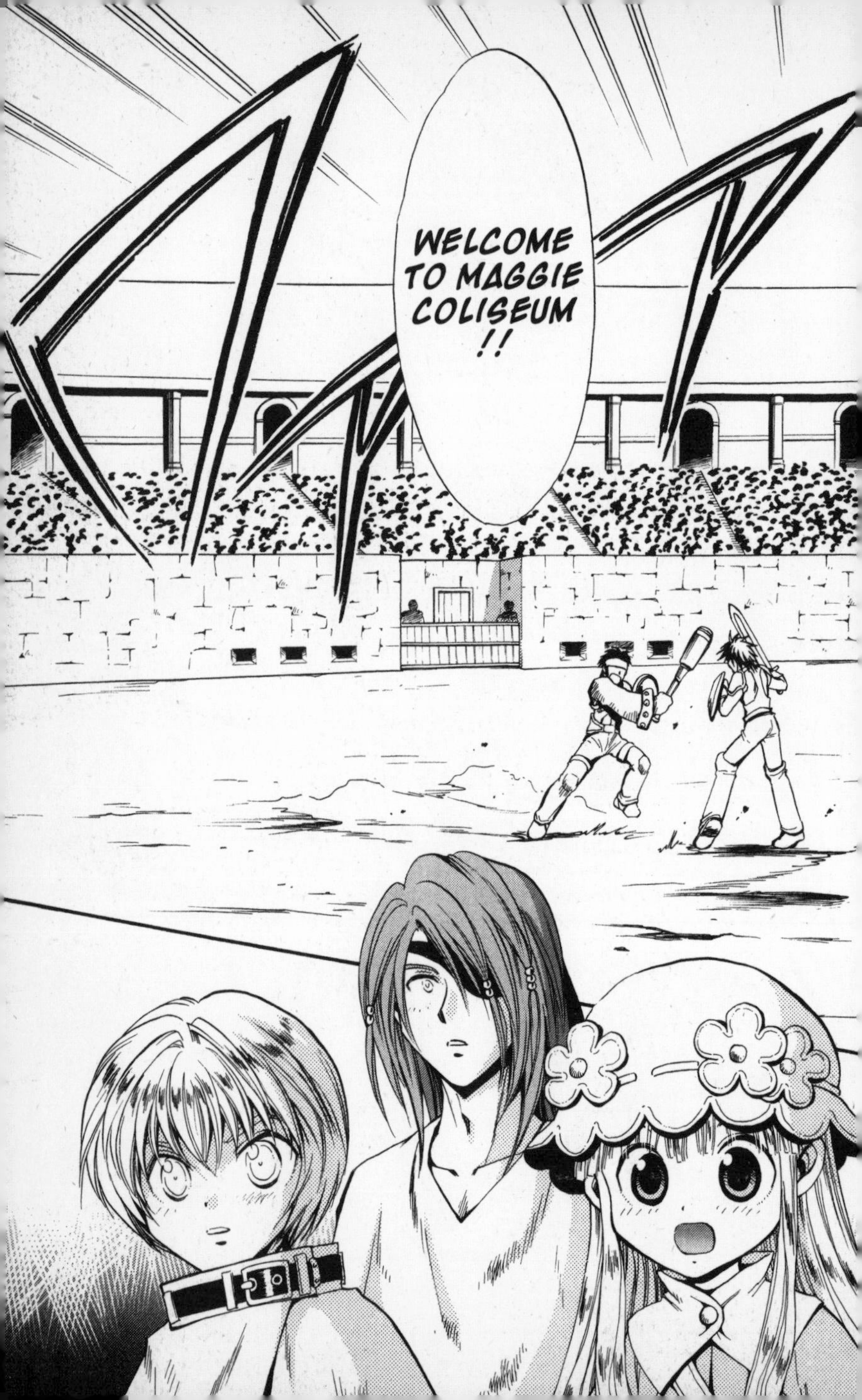
WELCOME TO MAGGIE COLISEUM !!

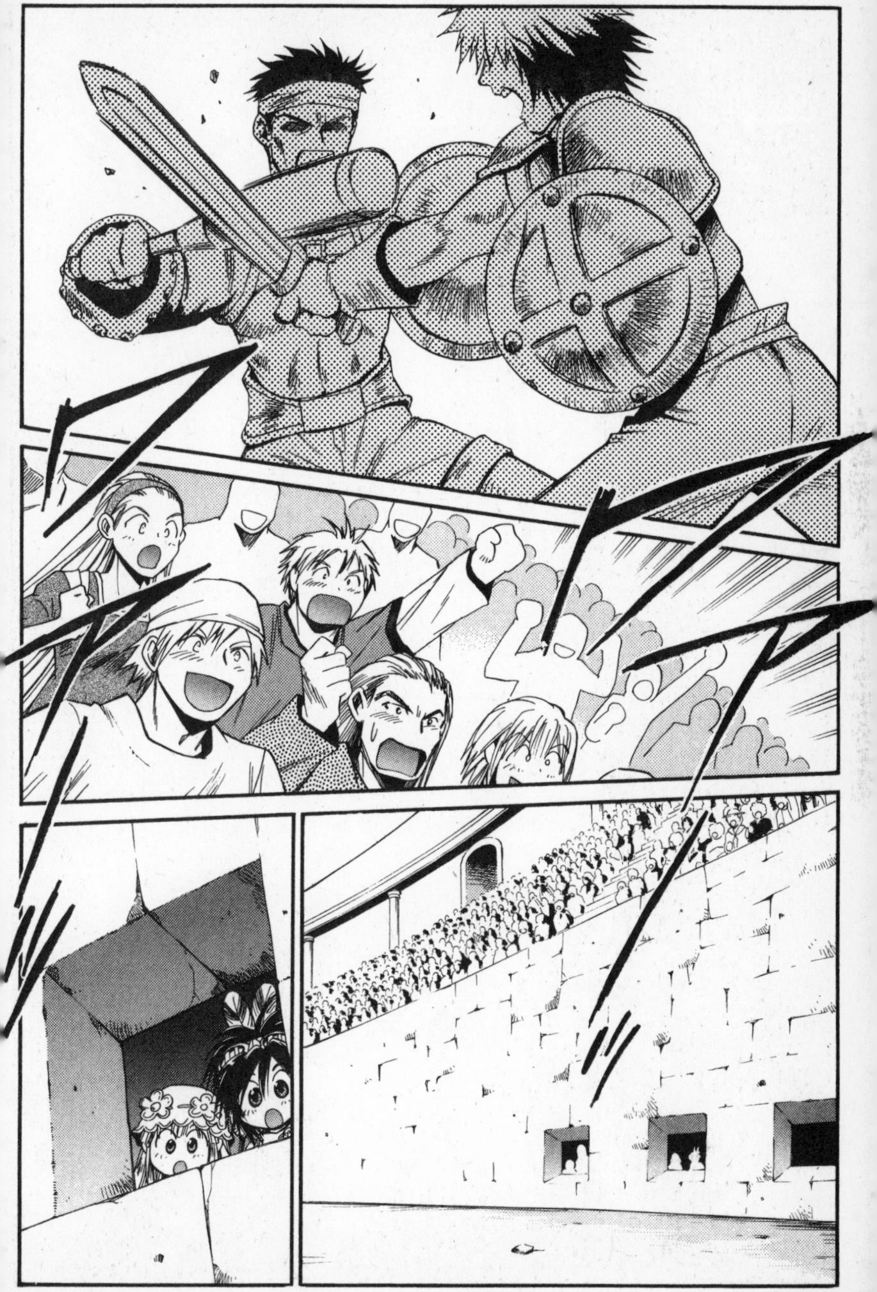

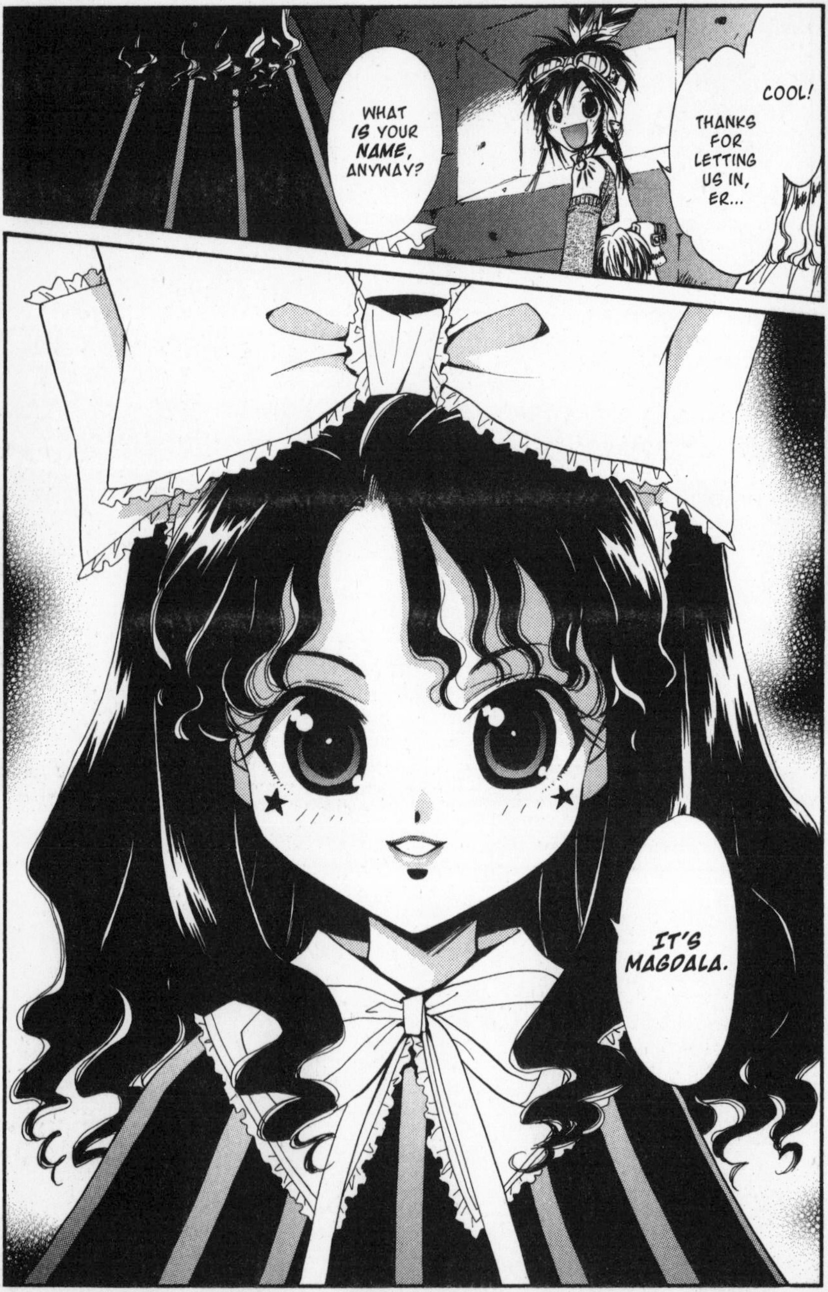
COOL!
THANKS FOR LETTING US IN, ER...
WHAT *IS* YOUR *NAME*, ANYWAY?
IT'S MAGDALA.

Please don't forget me!

Chapter 16: Maggie Coliseum—Part 2

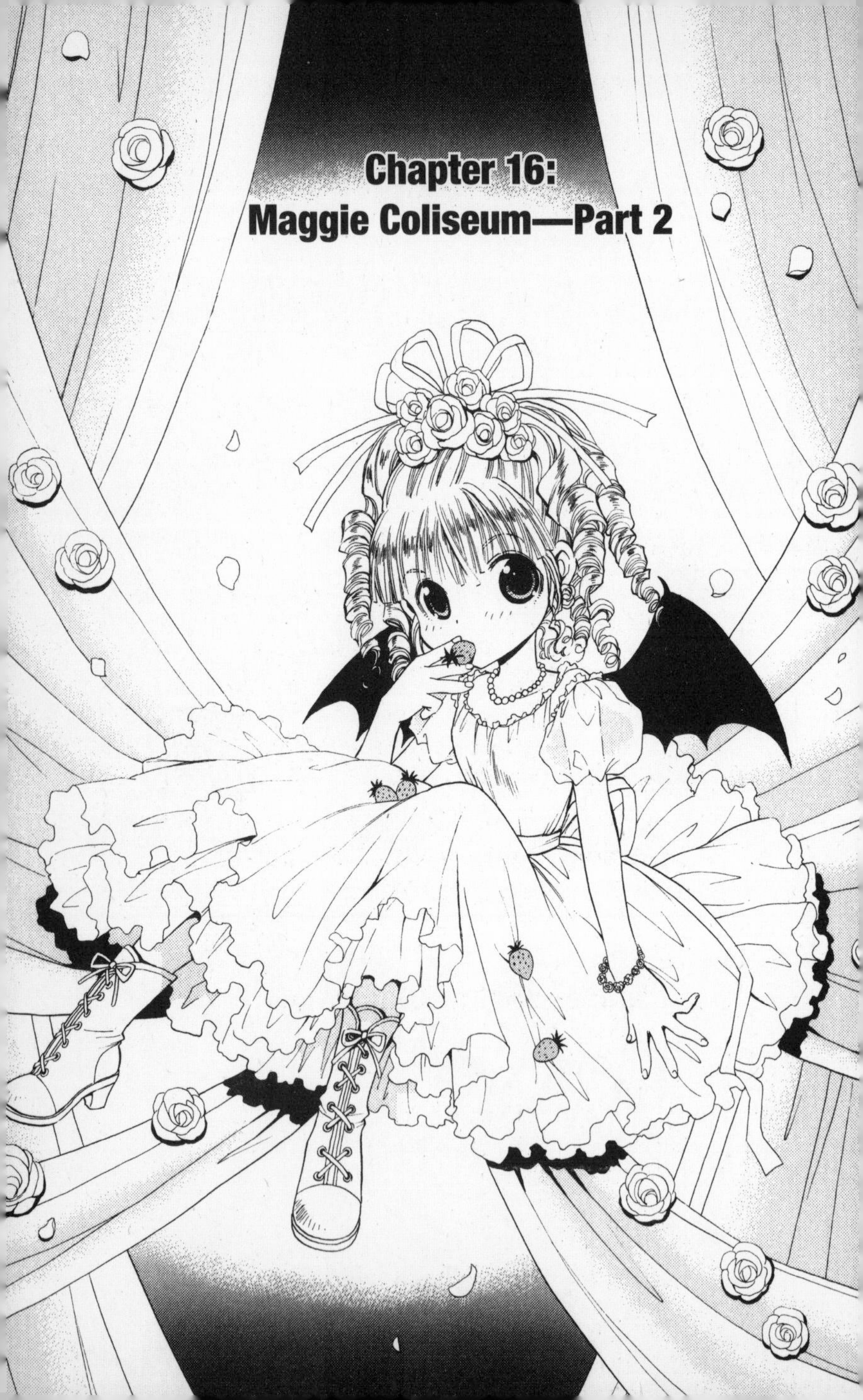

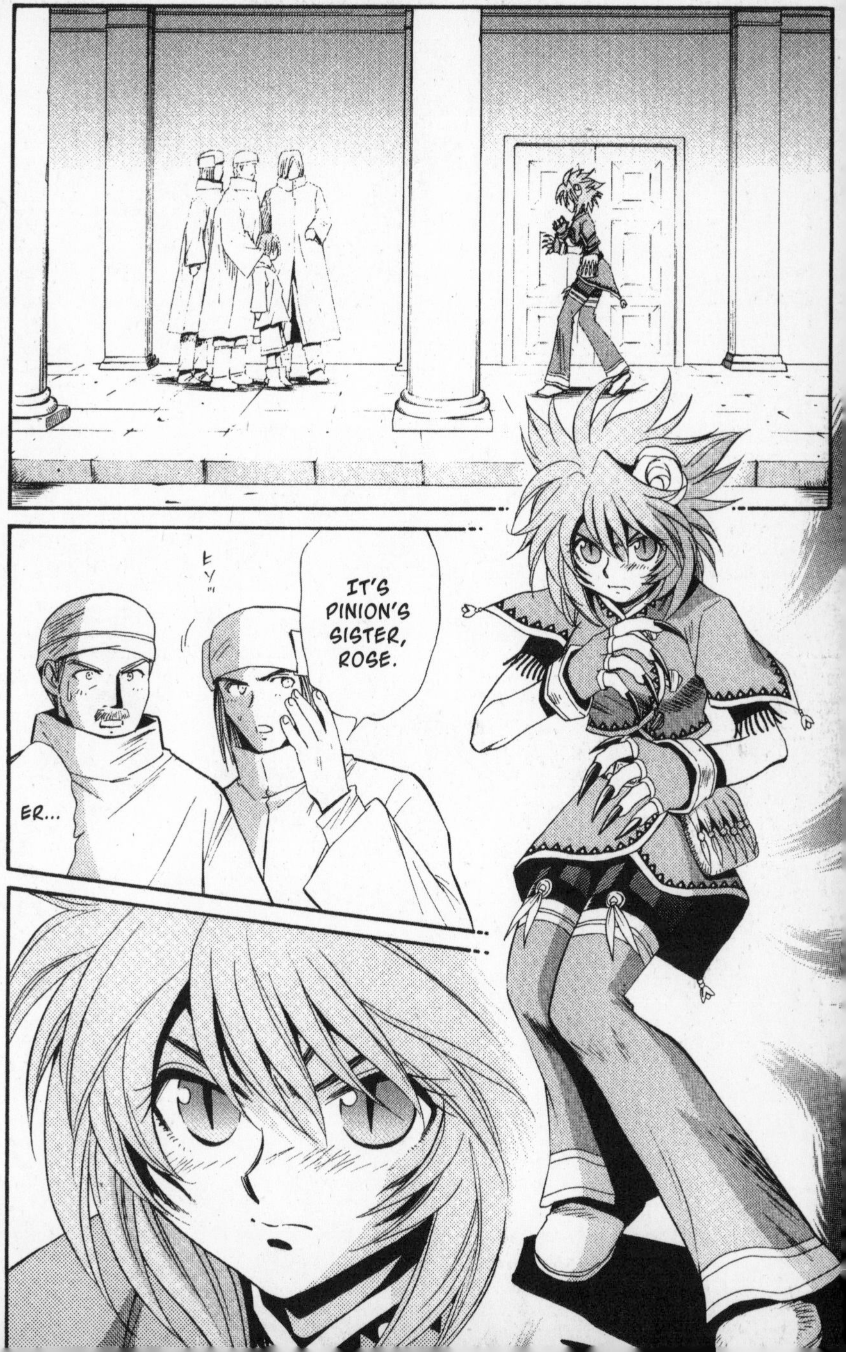
IT'S PINION'S SISTER, ROSE.
ヒソ
ER...

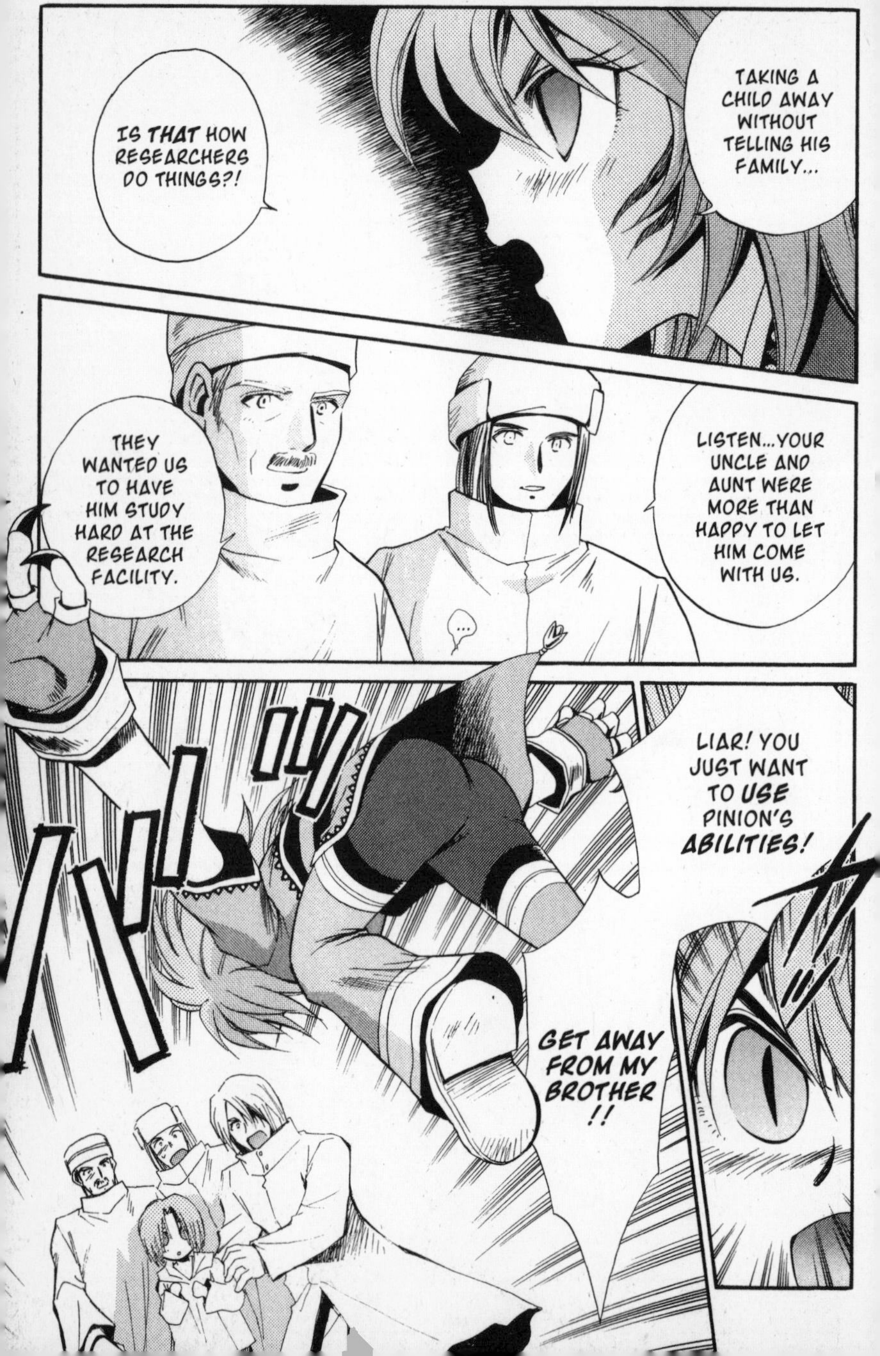
TAKING A CHILD AWAY WITHOUT TELLING HIS FAMILY...
IS THAT HOW RESEARCHERS DO THINGS?!
LISTEN...YOUR UNCLE AND AUNT WERE MORE THAN HAPPY TO LET HIM COME WITH US.
THEY WANTED US TO HAVE HIM STUDY HARD AT THE RESEARCH FACILITY.
...
LIAR! YOU JUST WANT TO USE PINION'S ABILITIES!
GET AWAY FROM MY BROTHER !!

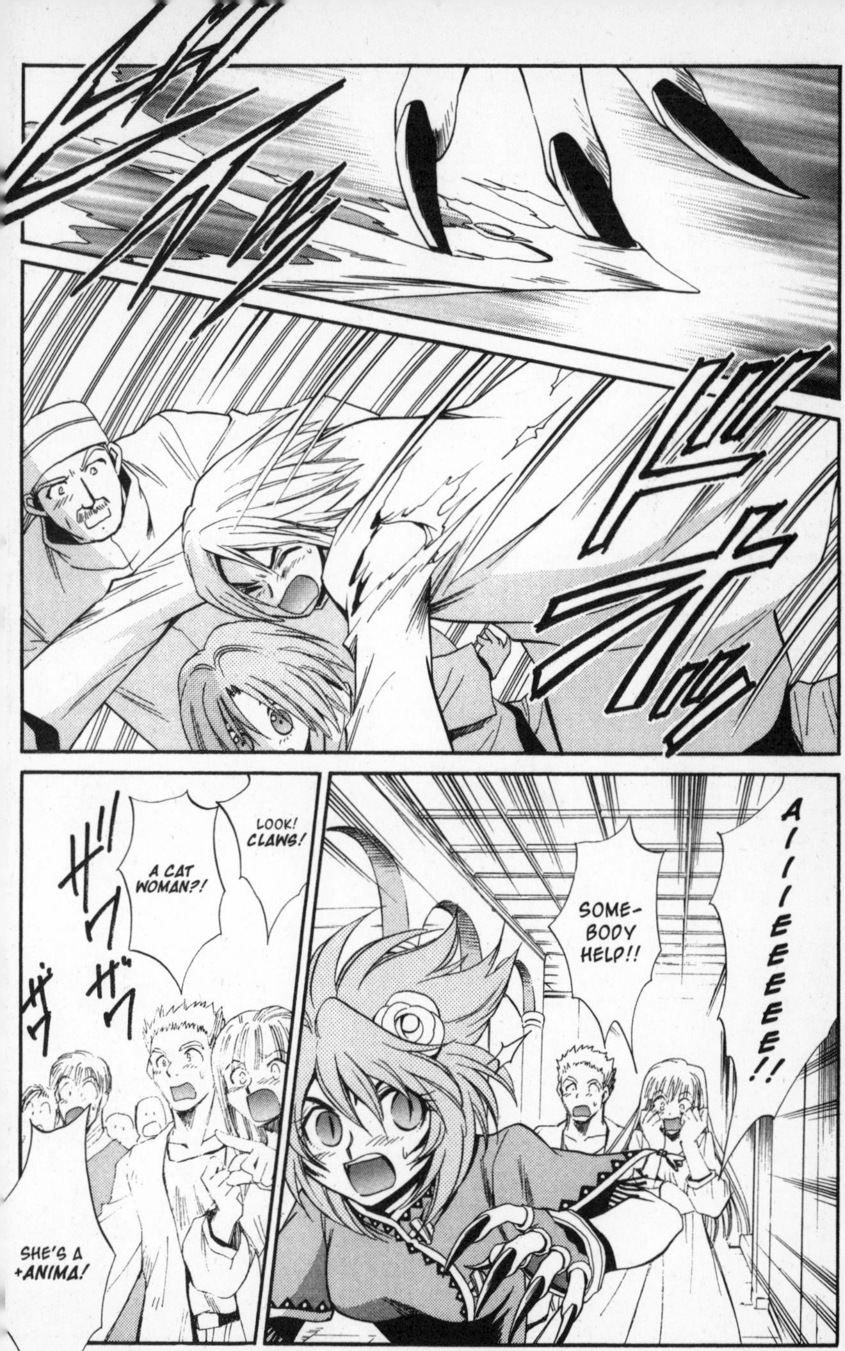
AIIIEEEEEE!!
SOME-BODY HELP!!
LOOK! CLAWS!
A CAT WOMAN?!
SHE'S A +ANIMA!

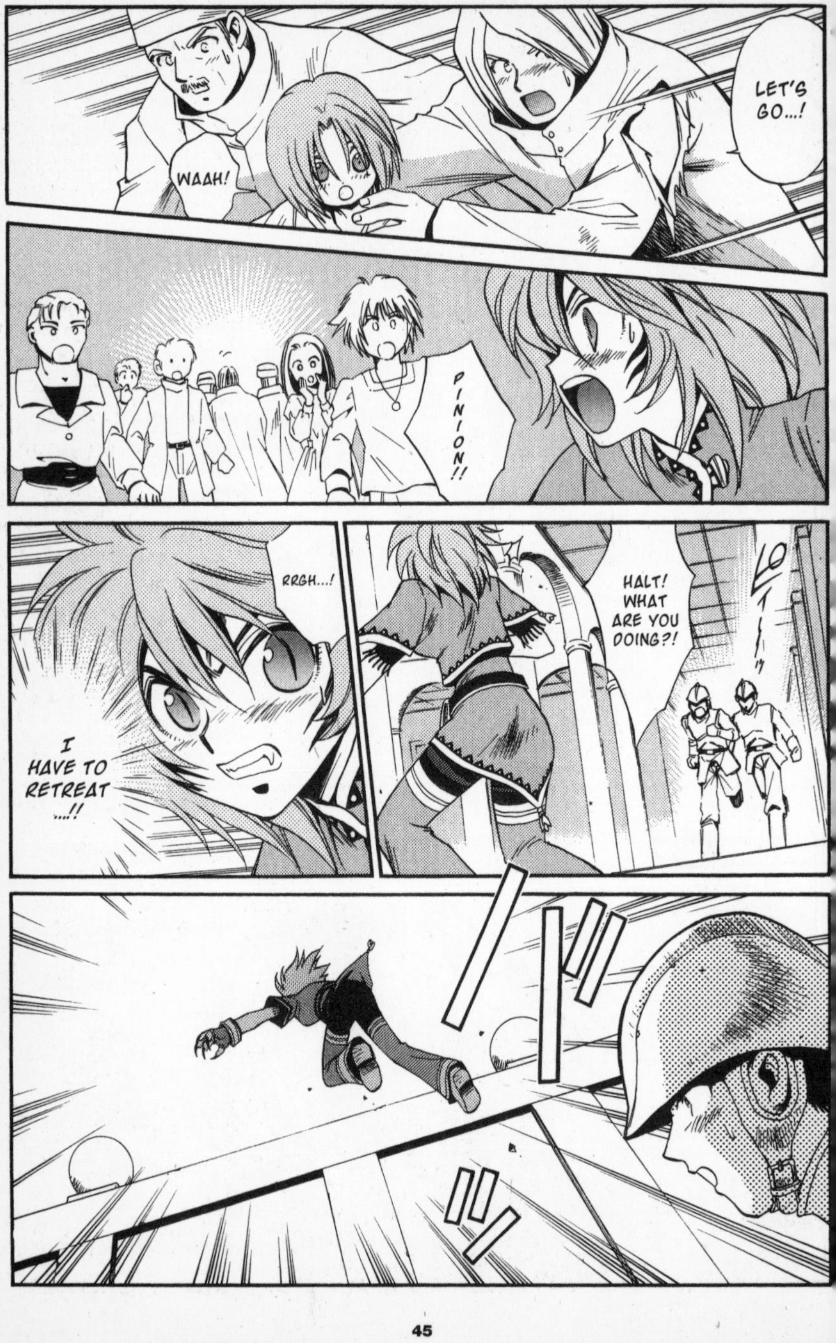
LET'S GO...!
WAAH!
PINION!!
HALT! WHAT ARE YOU DOING?!
RRGH...!
I HAVE TO RETREAT...!!

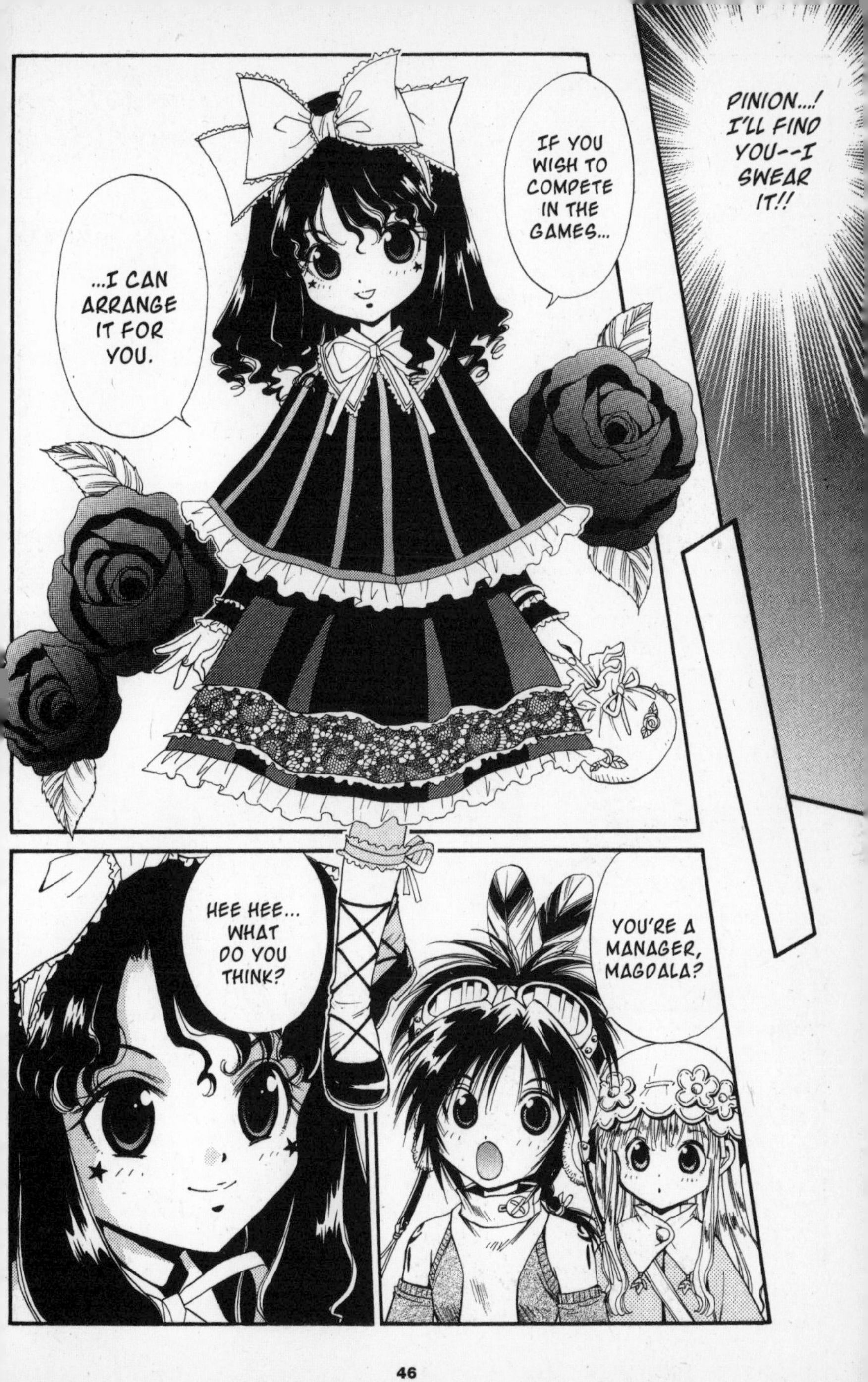
PINION...! I'LL FIND YOU--I SWEAR IT!!
IF YOU WISH TO COMPETE IN THE GAMES...
...I CAN ARRANGE IT FOR YOU.
YOU'RE A MANAGER, MAGDALA?
HEE HEE... WHAT DO YOU THINK?

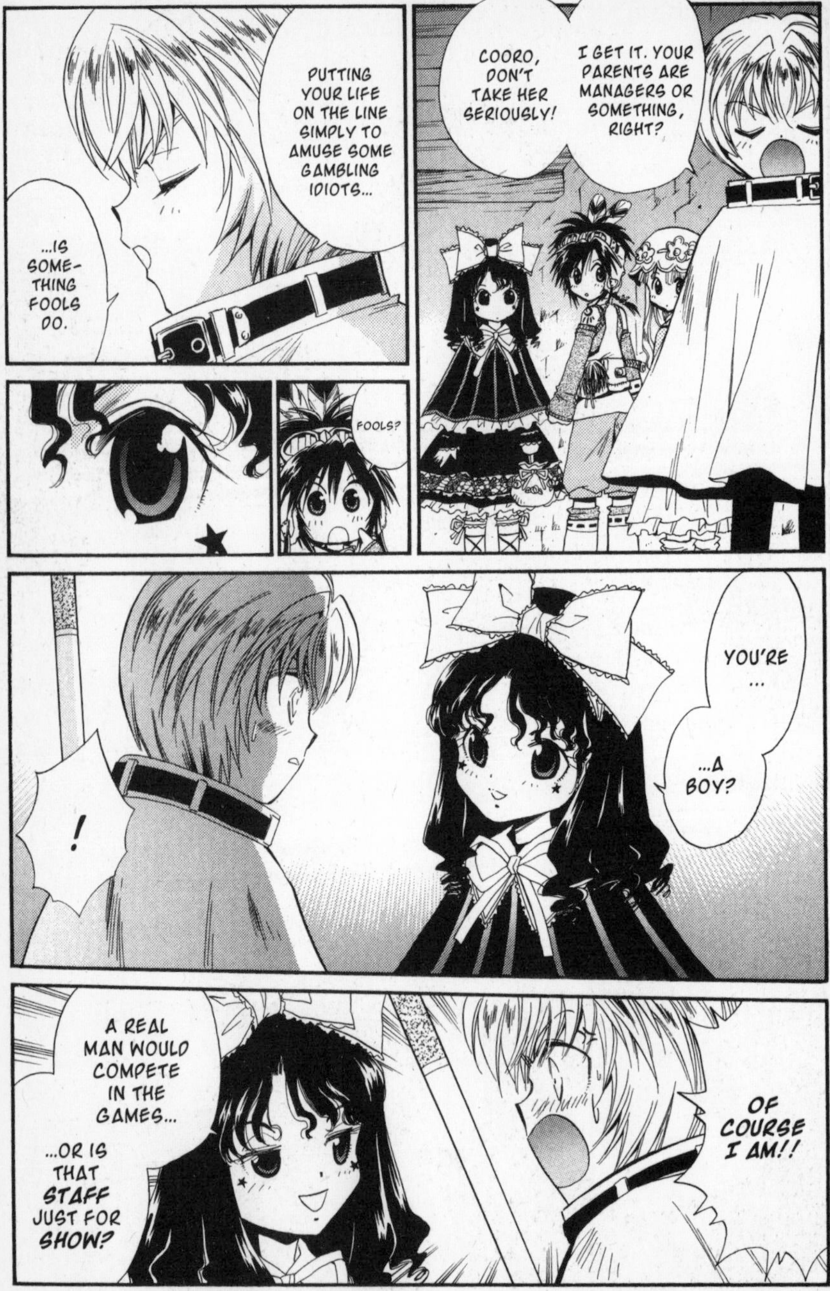
I GET IT. YOUR PARENTS ARE MANAGERS OR SOMETHING, RIGHT?
COORO, DON'T TAKE HER SERIOUSLY!
PUTTING YOUR LIFE ON THE LINE SIMPLY TO AMUSE SOME GAMBLING IDIOTS...
...IS SOMETHING FOOLS DO.
FOOLS?
YOU'RE ...
...A BOY?
!
OF COURSE I AM!!
A REAL MAN WOULD COMPETE IN THE GAMES...
...OR IS THAT STAFF JUST FOR SHOW?

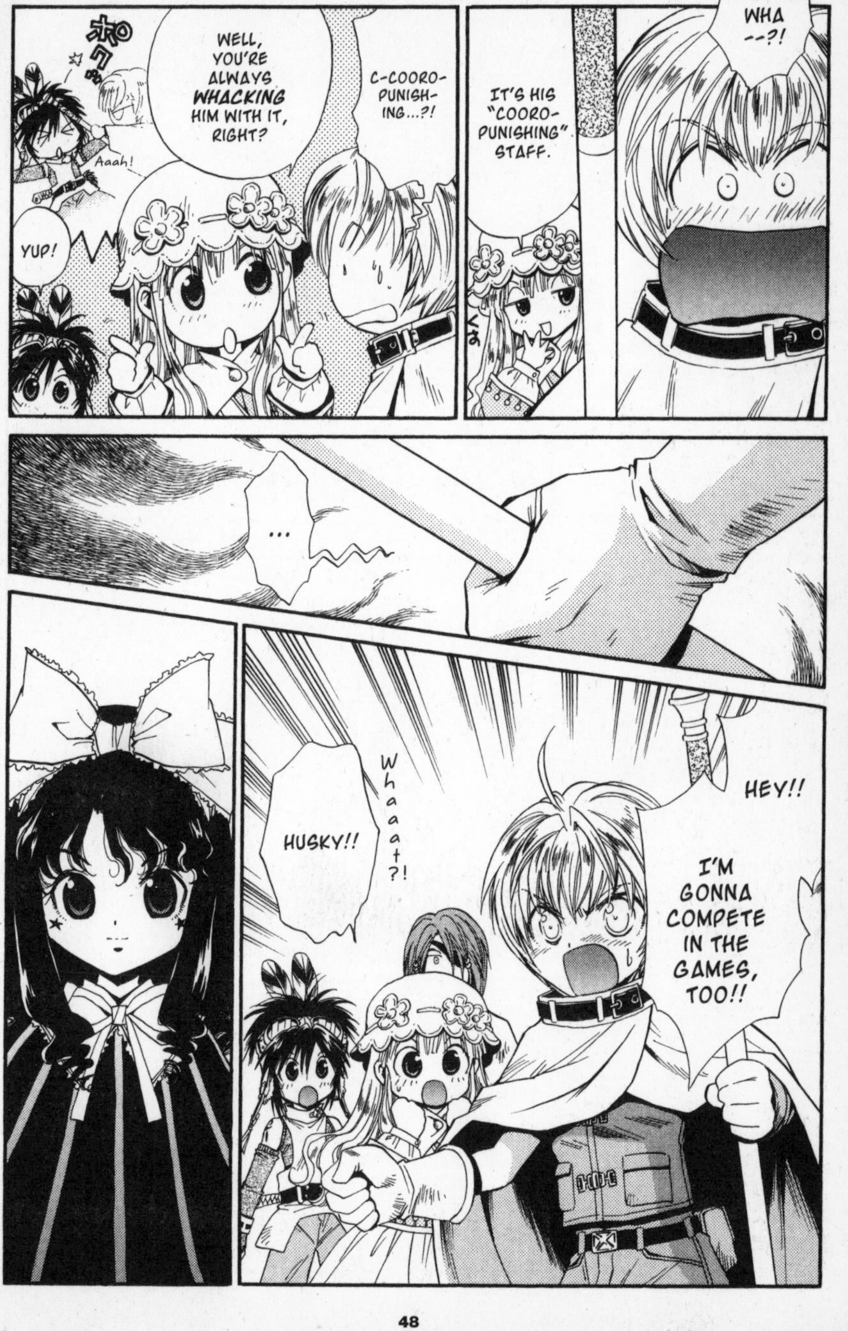
WHA --?!
IT'S HIS "COORO-PUNISHING" STAFF.
C-COORO-PUNISHING...?!
WELL, YOU'RE ALWAYS WHACKING HIM WITH IT, RIGHT?
Aaah!
YUP!
...
HEY!!
I'M GONNA COMPETE IN THE GAMES, TOO!!
HUSKY!!
Whaaaat?!

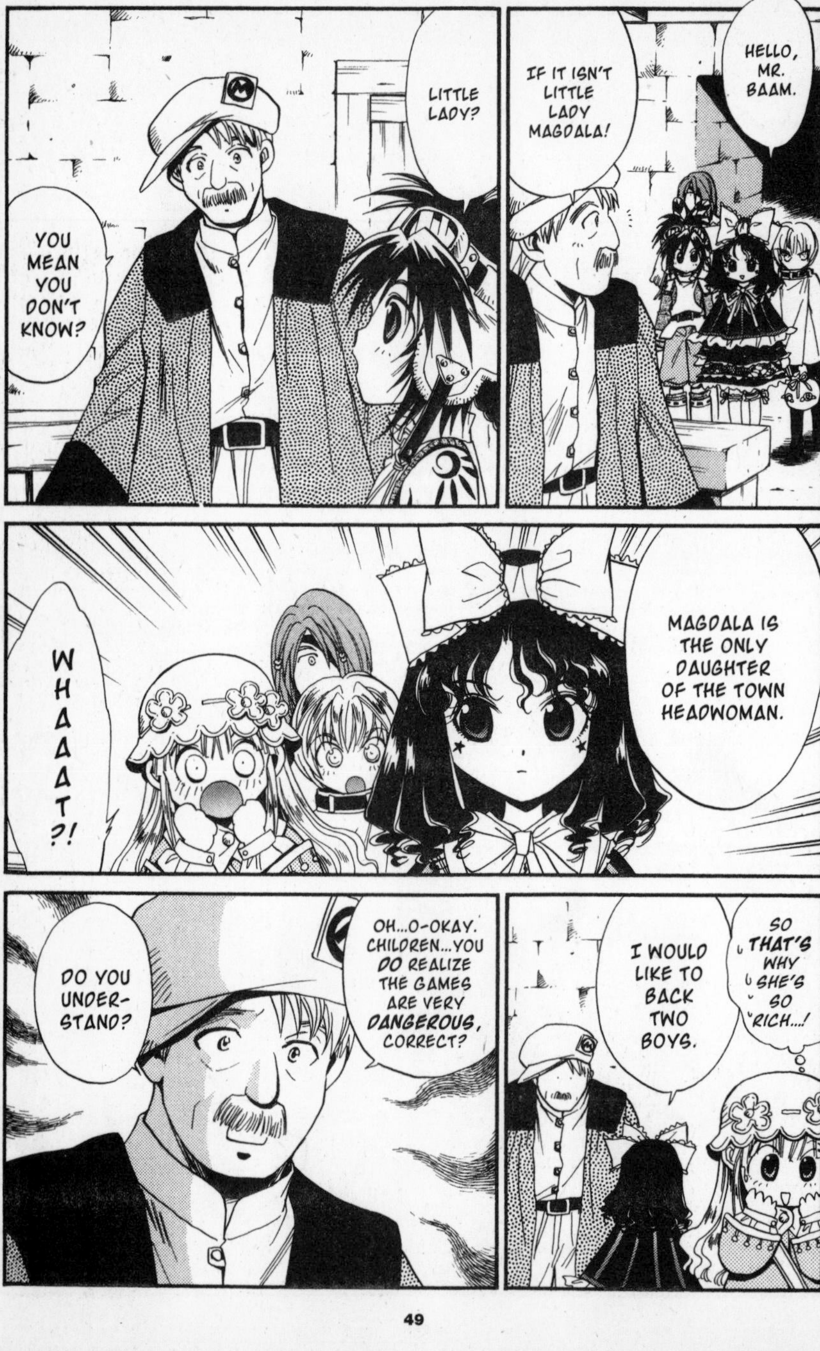
HELLO, MR. BAAM.
IF IT ISN'T LITTLE LADY MAGDALA!
LITTLE LADY?
YOU MEAN YOU DON'T KNOW?
MAGDALA IS THE ONLY DAUGHTER OF THE TOWN HEADWOMAN.
WHAAAAT?!
SO **THAT'S** WHY SHE'S SO RICH...!
I WOULD LIKE TO BACK TWO BOYS.
OH...O-OKAY. CHILDREN...YOU **DO** REALIZE THE GAMES ARE VERY **DANGEROUS**, CORRECT?
DO YOU UNDER-STAND?

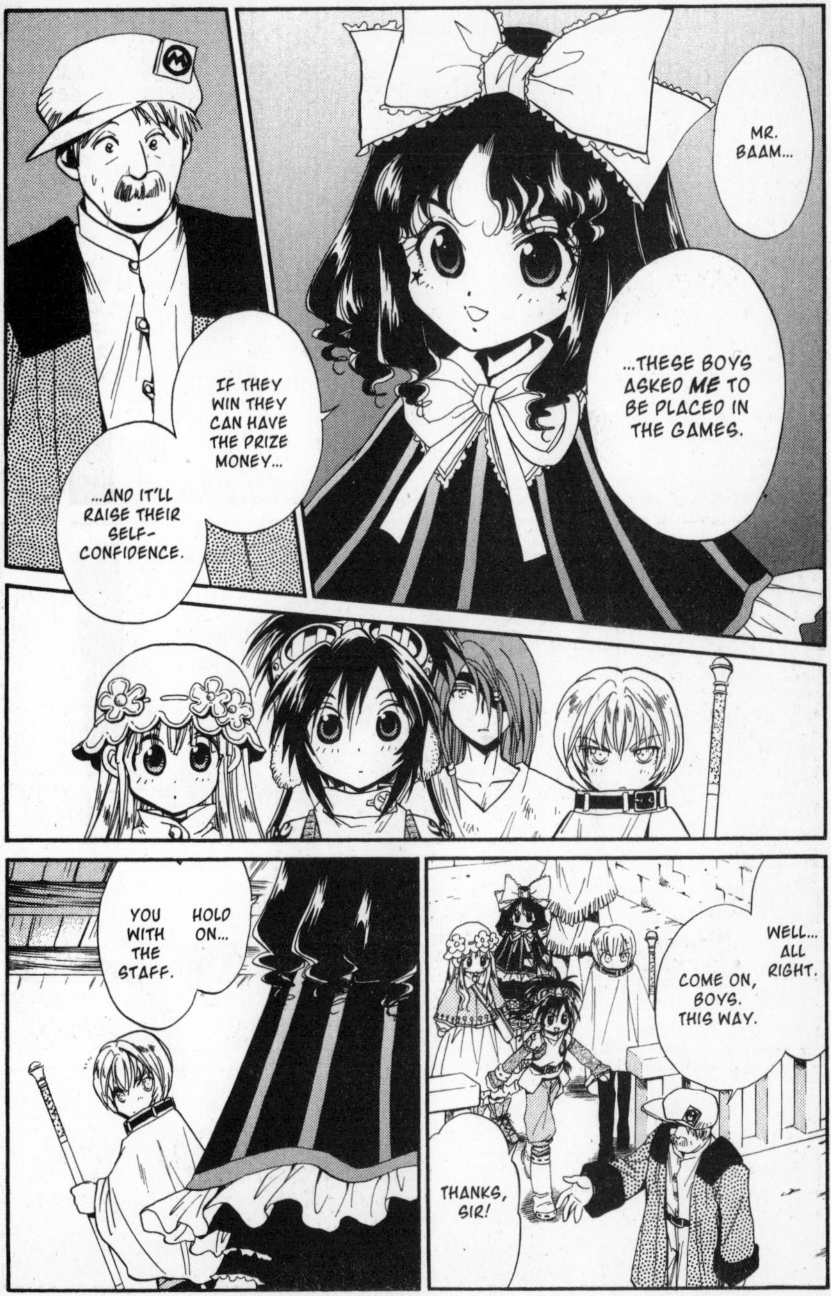
MR. BAAM...
...THESE BOYS ASKED **ME** TO BE PLACED IN THE GAMES.
IF THEY WIN THEY CAN HAVE THE PRIZE MONEY...
...AND IT'LL RAISE THEIR SELF-CONFIDENCE.
WELL... ALL RIGHT.
COME ON, BOYS. THIS WAY.
THANKS, SIR!
HOLD ON...
YOU WITH THE STAFF.

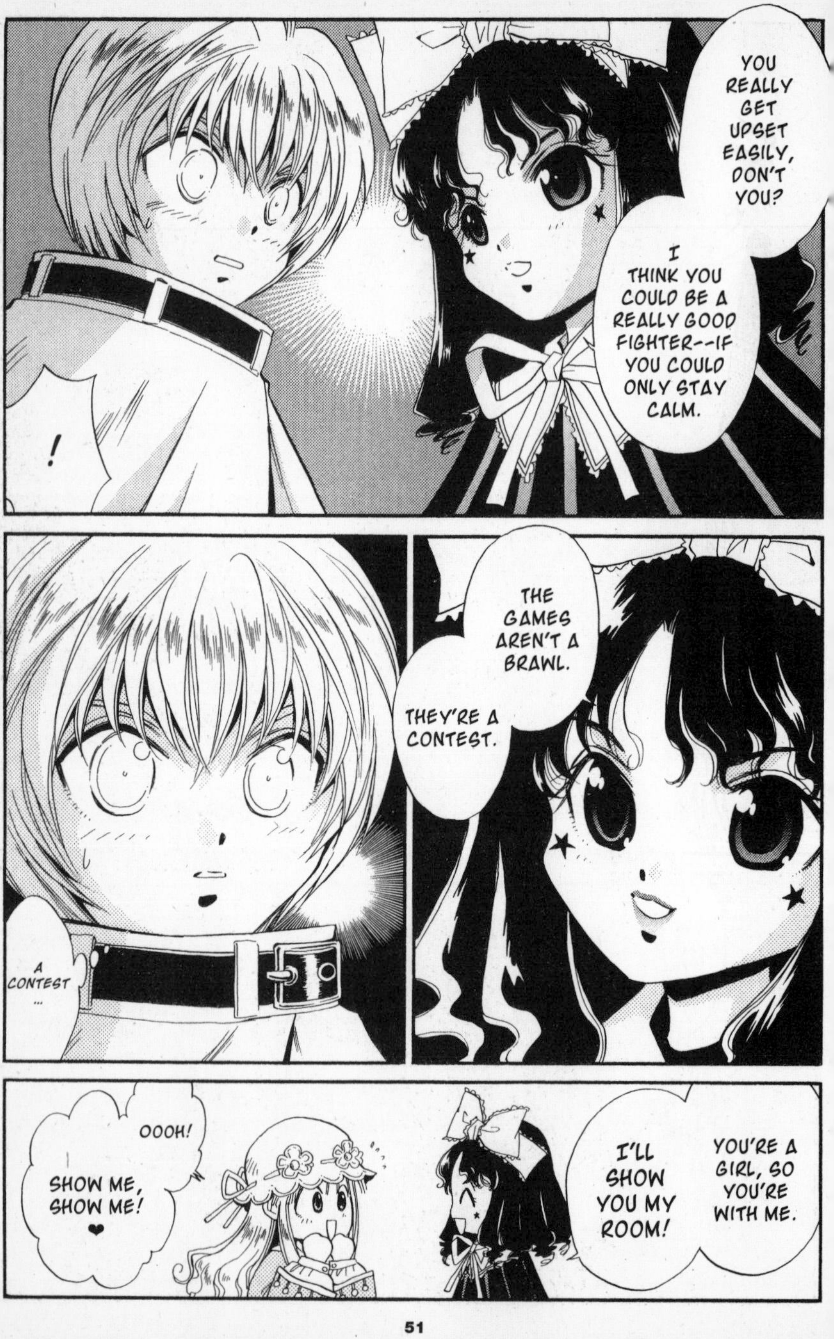
YOU REALLY GET UPSET EASILY, DON'T YOU?
I THINK YOU COULD BE A REALLY GOOD FIGHTER--IF YOU COULD ONLY STAY CALM.
!
THE GAMES AREN'T A BRAWL.
THEY'RE A CONTEST.
A CONTEST ...
YOU'RE A GIRL, SO YOU'RE WITH ME.
I'LL SHOW YOU MY ROOM!
OOOH!
SHOW ME, SHOW ME! ❤

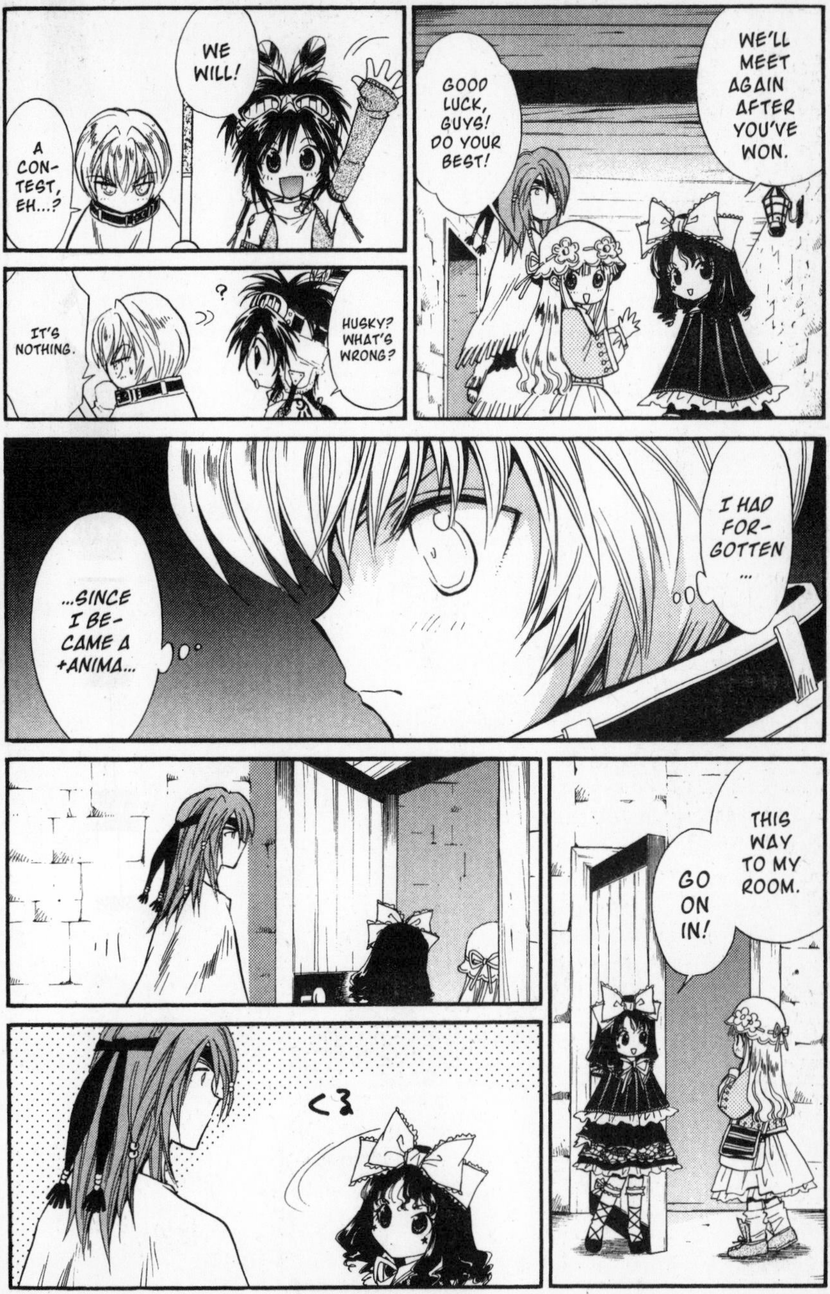
WE'LL MEET AGAIN AFTER YOU'VE WON.
GOOD LUCK, GUYS! DO YOUR BEST!
WE WILL!
A CONTEST, EH...?
HUSKY? WHAT'S WRONG?
IT'S NOTHING.
I HAD FORGOTTEN...
...SINCE I BECAME A +ANIMA...
THIS WAY TO MY ROOM.
GO ON IN!
くる

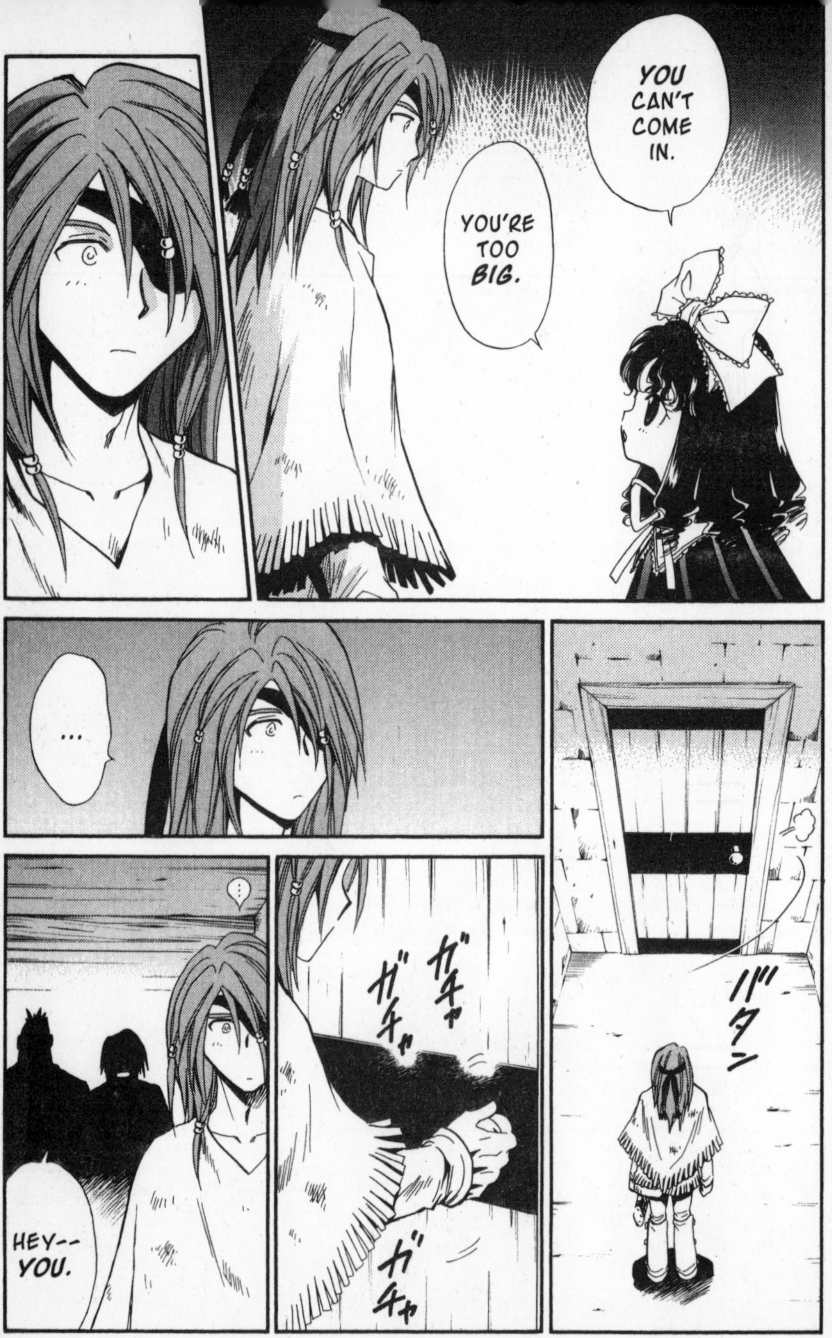
YOU CAN'T COME IN.
YOU'RE TOO BIG.
バタン
...
ガチャ
ガチャ
ガチャ
...
HEY-- YOU.

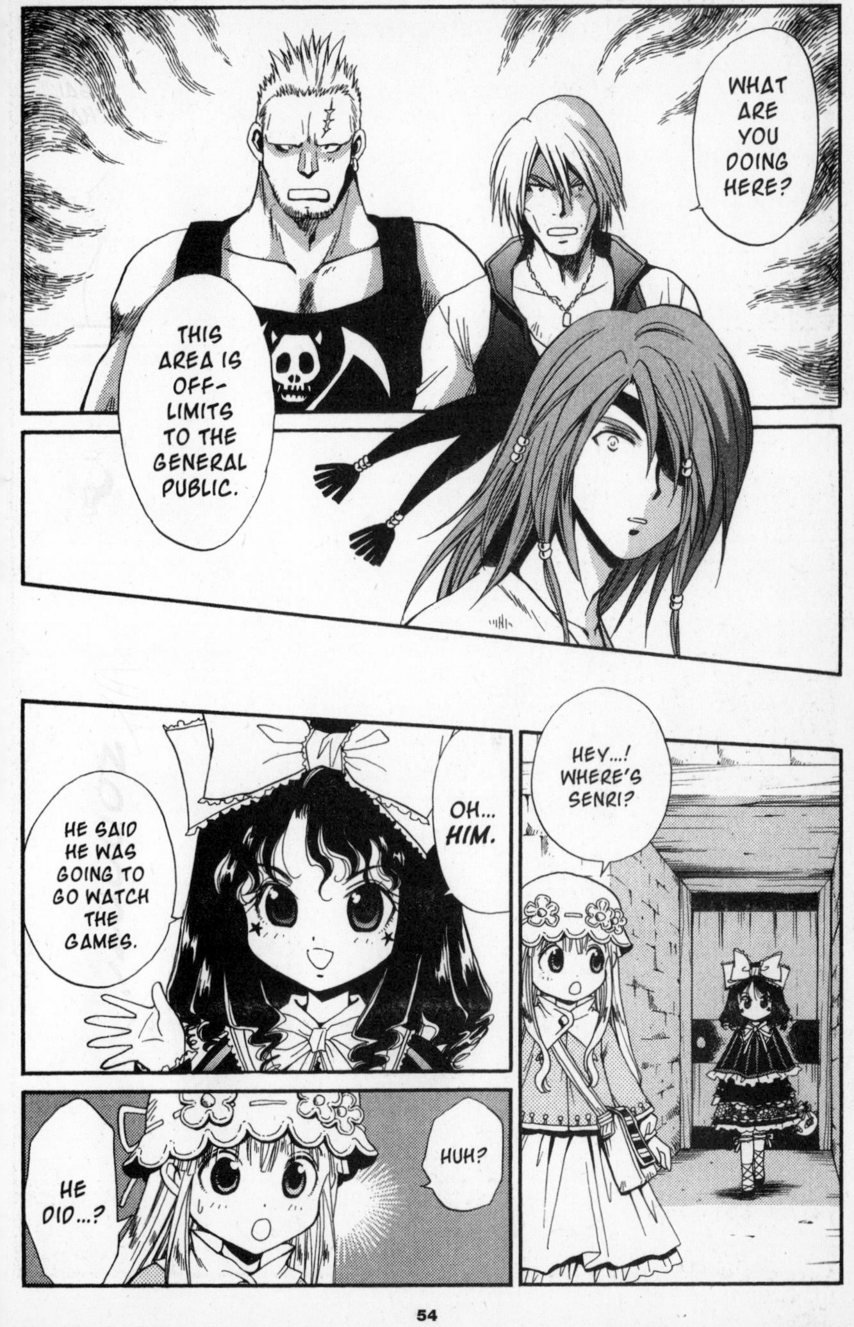
WHAT ARE YOU DOING HERE?
THIS AREA IS OFF-LIMITS TO THE GENERAL PUBLIC.
HEY...! WHERE'S SENRI?
OH... HIM.
HE SAID HE WAS GOING TO GO WATCH THE GAMES.
HUH?
HE DID...?

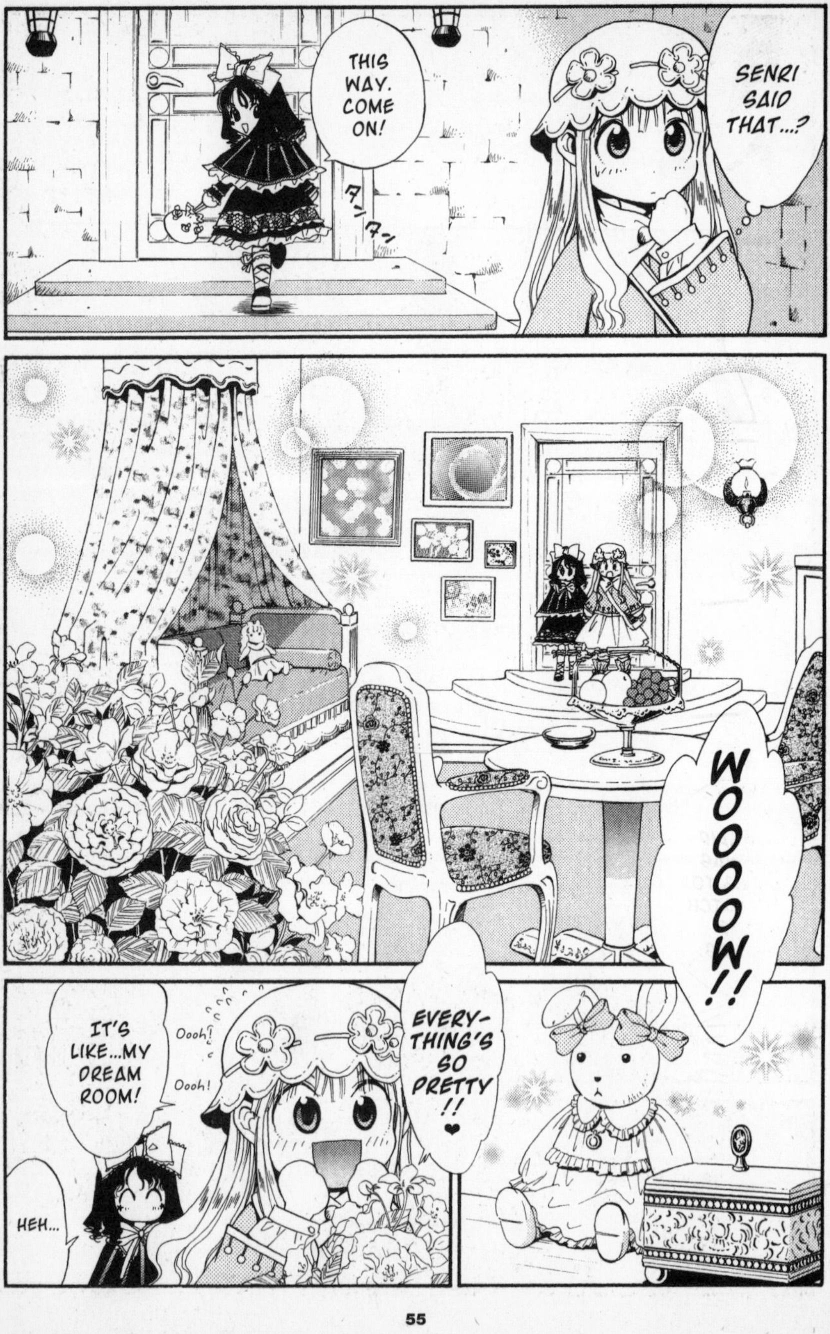
SENRI SAID THAT...?
THIS WAY. COME ON!
タッ タッ
WOOOOOW!!
EVERY-THING'S SO PRETTY!! ❤
Oooh! Oooh!
IT'S LIKE...MY DREAM ROOM!
HEH...

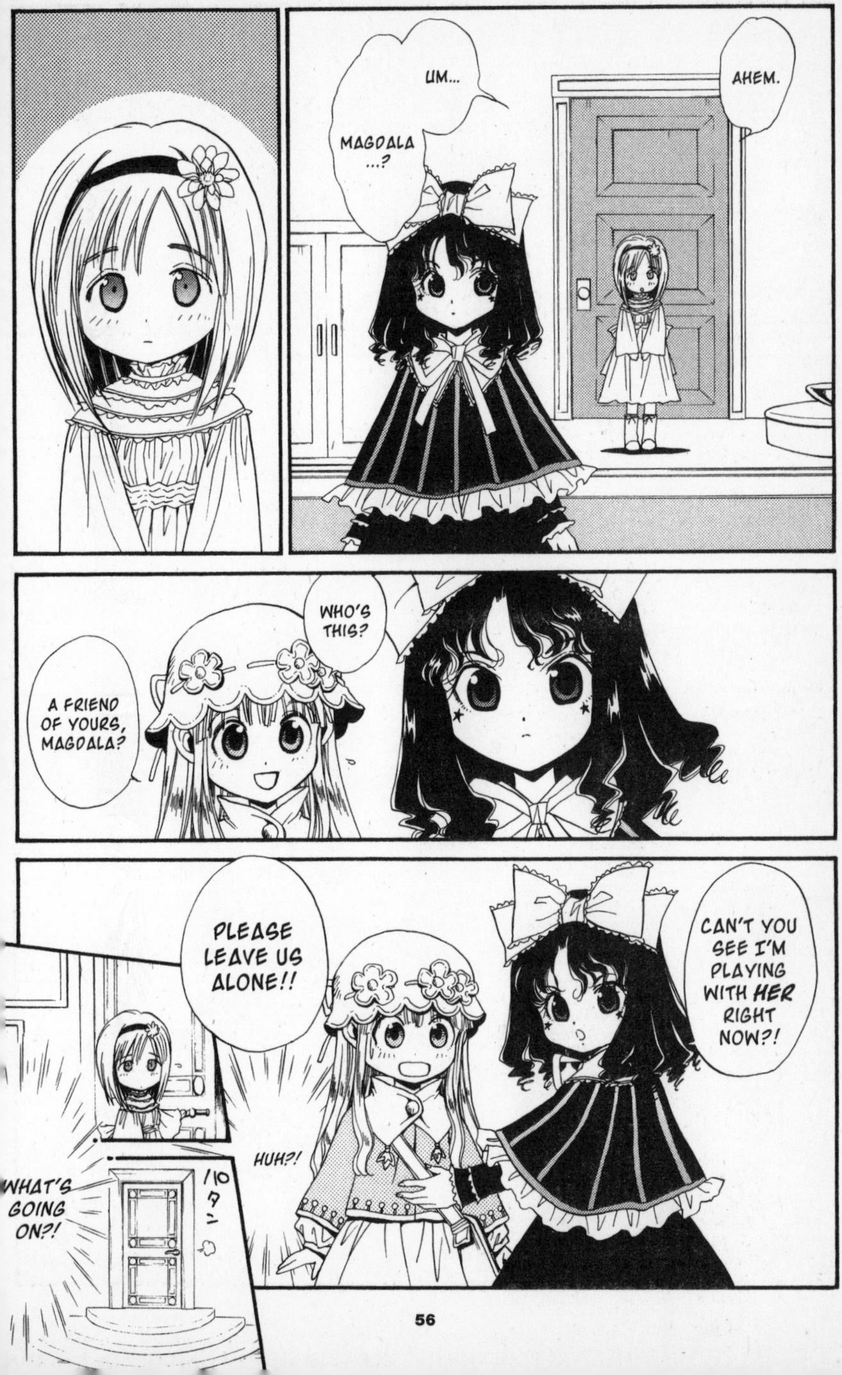
AHEM.
UM...
MAGOALA ...?
WHO'S THIS?
A FRIEND OF YOURS, MAGOALA?
CAN'T YOU SEE I'M PLAYING WITH HER RIGHT NOW?!
PLEASE LEAVE US ALONE!!
HUH?!
WHAT'S GOING ON?!

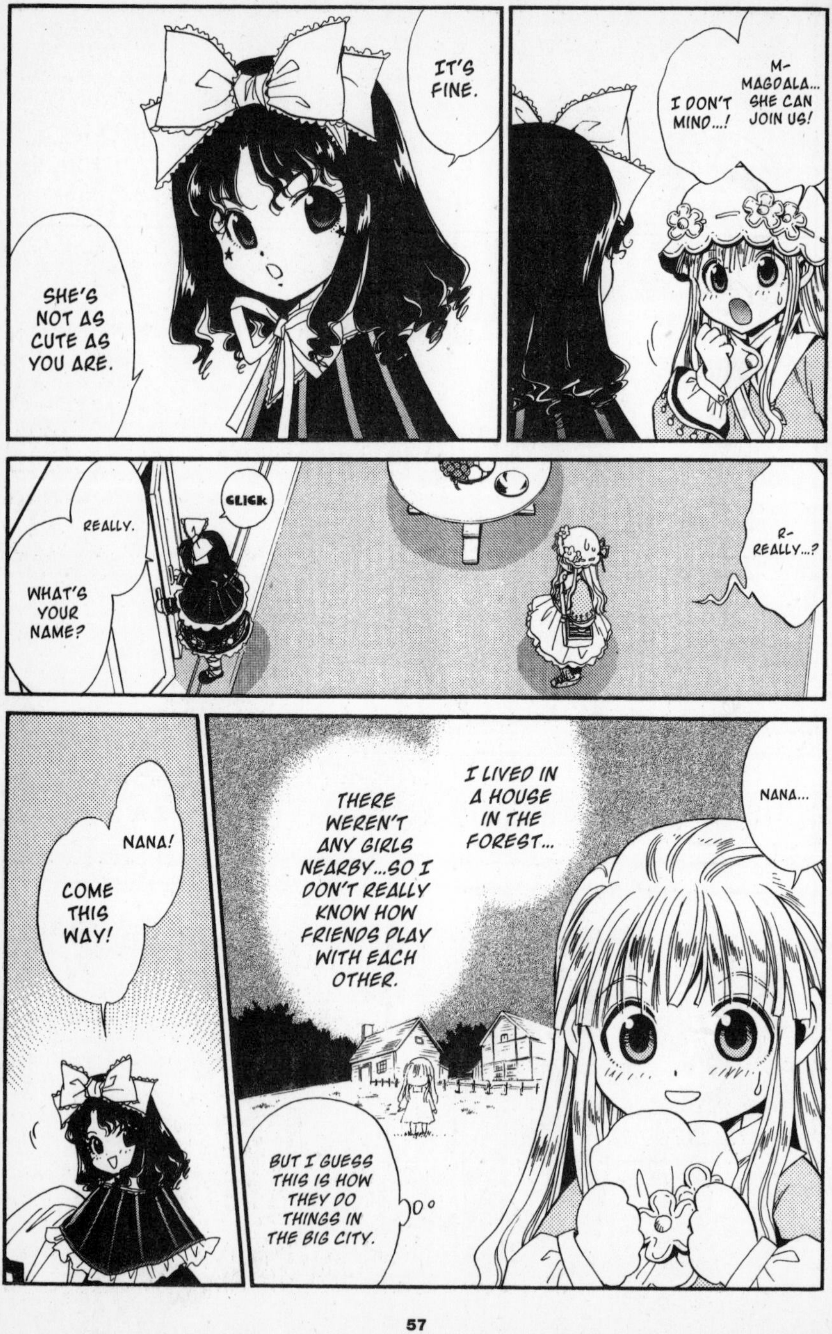
M-MAGDALA... SHE CAN JOIN US!
I DON'T MIND...!
IT'S FINE.
SHE'S NOT AS CUTE AS YOU ARE.
R-REALLY...?
CLICK
REALLY.
WHAT'S YOUR NAME?
NANA...
I LIVED IN A HOUSE IN THE FOREST...
THERE WEREN'T ANY GIRLS NEARBY...SO I DON'T REALLY KNOW HOW FRIENDS PLAY WITH EACH OTHER.
BUT I GUESS THIS IS HOW THEY DO THINGS IN THE BIG CITY.
NANA!
COME THIS WAY!

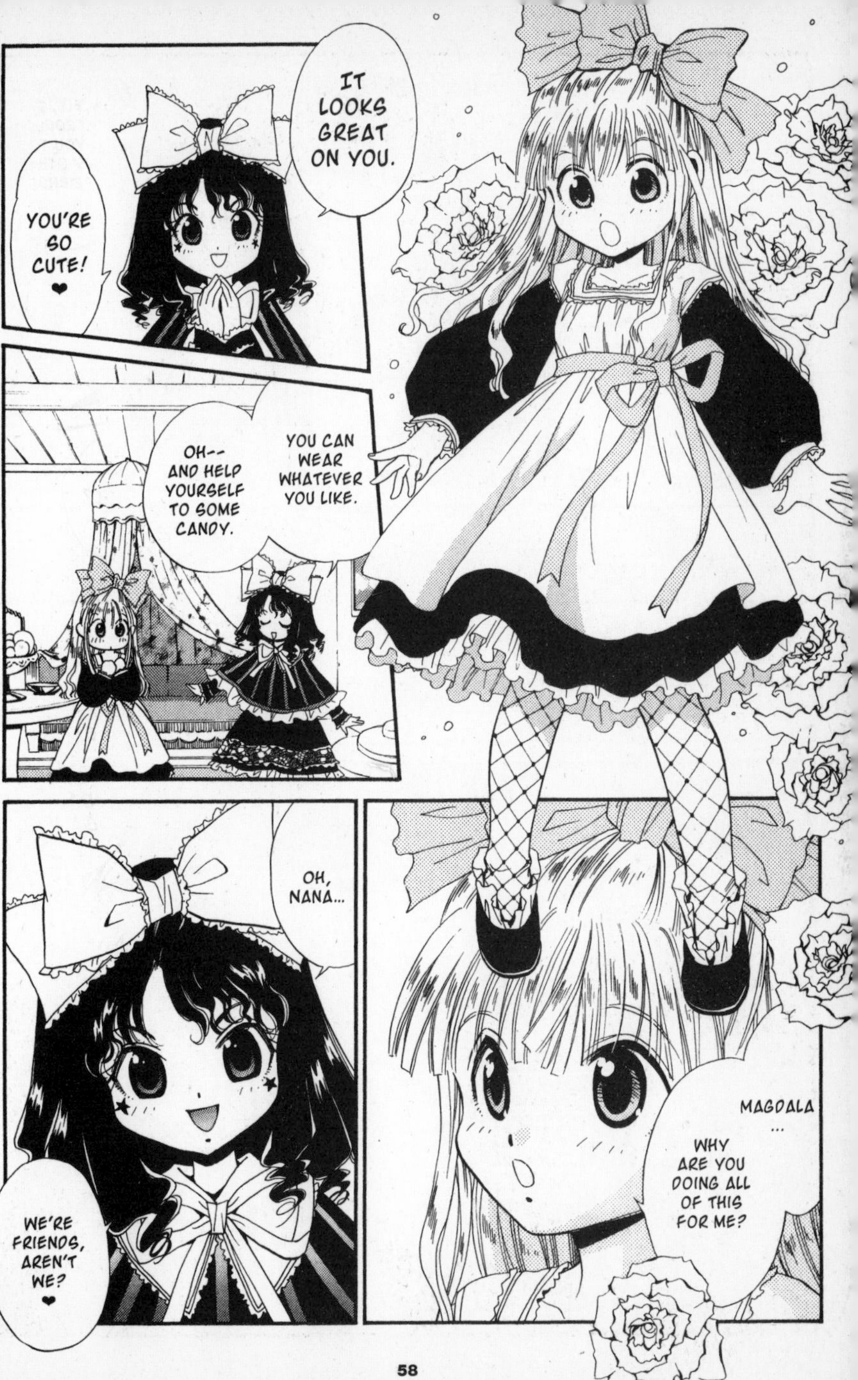
IT LOOKS GREAT ON YOU.
YOU'RE SO CUTE! ❤
YOU CAN WEAR WHATEVER YOU LIKE.
OH-- AND HELP YOURSELF TO SOME CANDY.
MAGOALA ...
WHY ARE YOU DOING ALL OF THIS FOR ME?
OH, NANA...
WE'RE FRIENDS, AREN'T WE? ❤

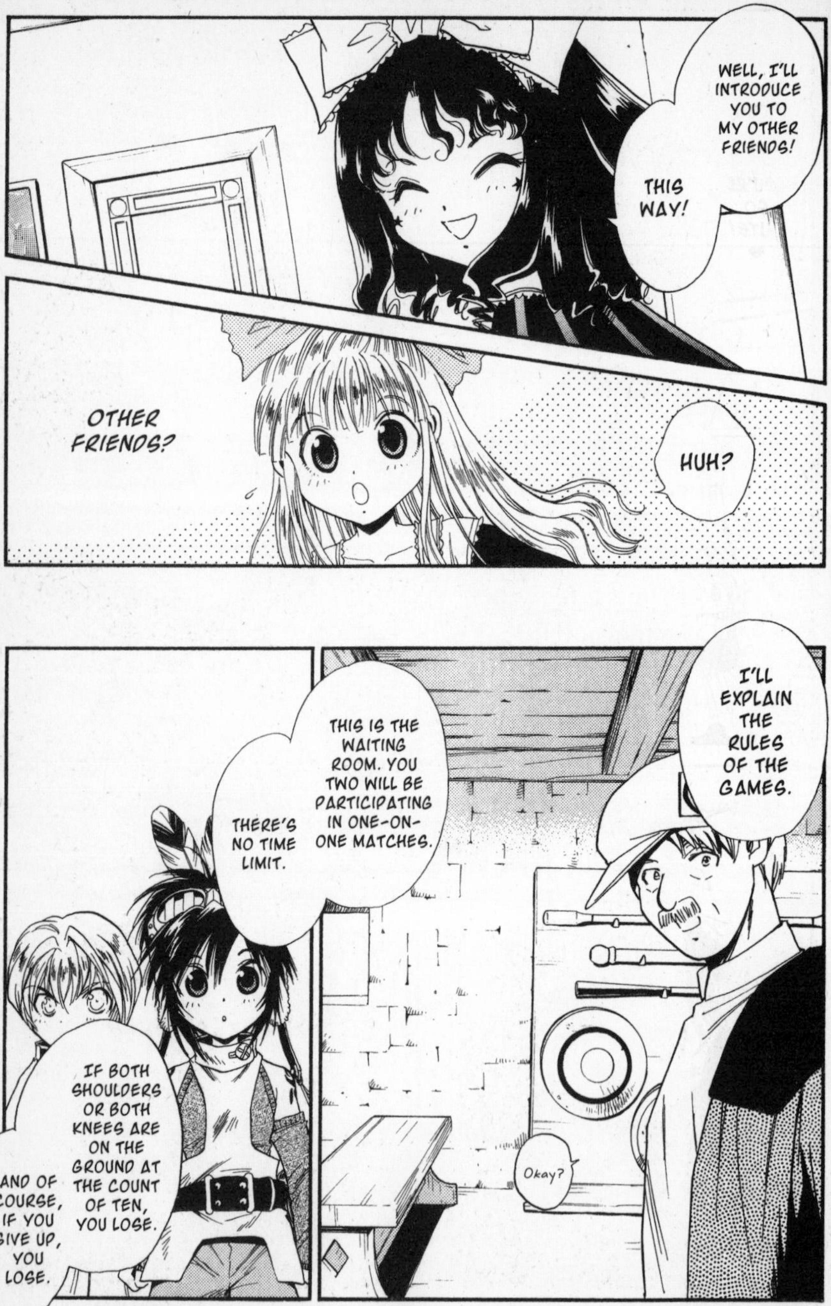
WELL, I'LL INTRODUCE YOU TO MY OTHER FRIENDS!
THIS WAY!
HUH?
OTHER FRIENDS?
I'LL EXPLAIN THE RULES OF THE GAMES.
Okay?
THIS IS THE WAITING ROOM. YOU TWO WILL BE PARTICIPATING IN ONE-ON-ONE MATCHES.
THERE'S NO TIME LIMIT.
IF BOTH SHOULDERS OR BOTH KNEES ARE ON THE GROUND AT THE COUNT OF TEN, YOU LOSE.
AND OF COURSE, IF YOU GIVE UP, YOU LOSE.

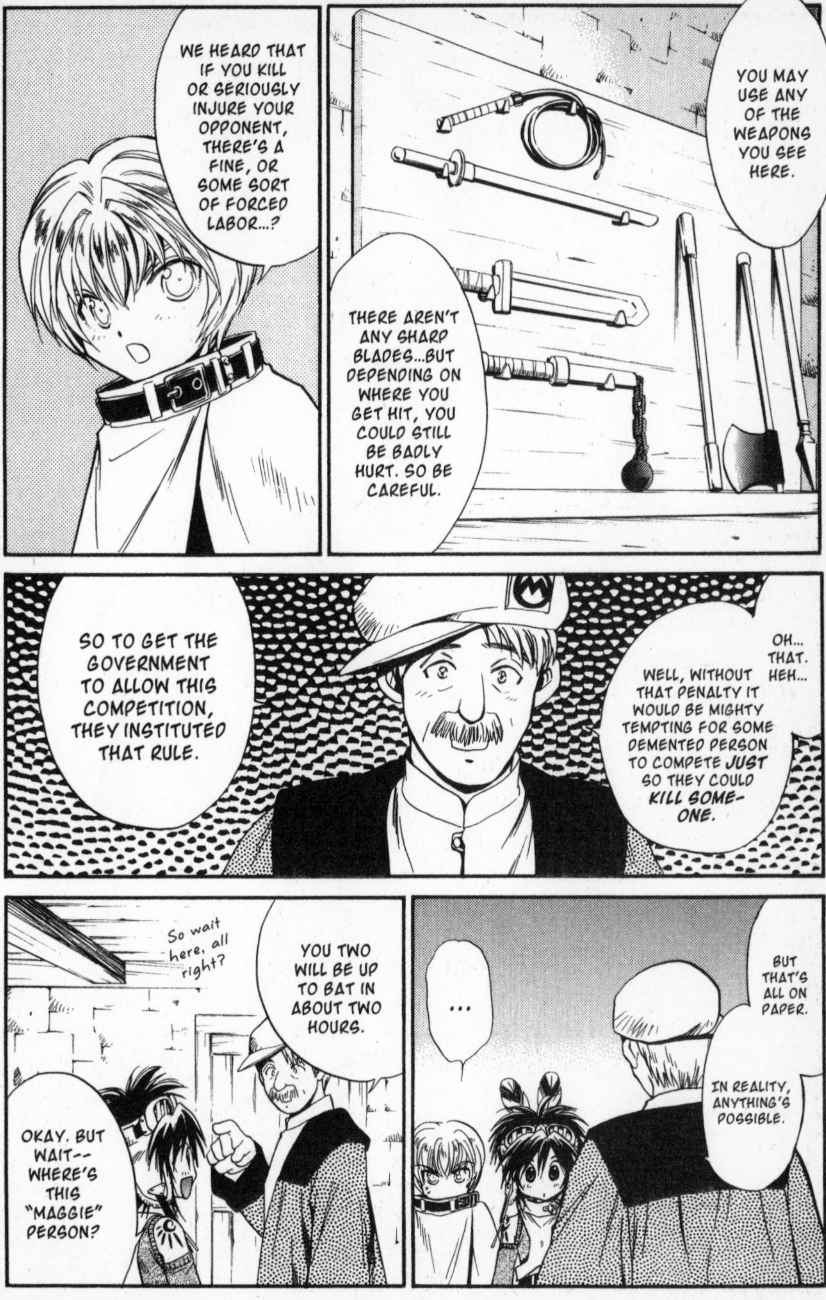
YOU MAY USE ANY OF THE WEAPONS YOU SEE HERE.
THERE AREN'T ANY SHARP BLADES...BUT DEPENDING ON WHERE YOU GET HIT, YOU COULD STILL BE BADLY HURT. SO BE CAREFUL.
WE HEARD THAT IF YOU KILL OR SERIOUSLY INJURE YOUR OPPONENT, THERE'S A FINE, OR SOME SORT OF FORCED LABOR...?
OH... THAT. HEH...
WELL, WITHOUT THAT PENALTY IT WOULD BE MIGHTY TEMPTING FOR SOME DEMENTED PERSON TO COMPETE JUST SO THEY COULD KILL SOME-ONE.
SO TO GET THE GOVERNMENT TO ALLOW THIS COMPETITION, THEY INSTITUTED THAT RULE.
BUT THAT'S ALL ON PAPER.
IN REALITY, ANYTHING'S POSSIBLE.
...
YOU TWO WILL BE UP TO BAT IN ABOUT TWO HOURS.
So wait here, all right?
OKAY. BUT WAIT-- WHERE'S THIS "MAGGIE" PERSON?

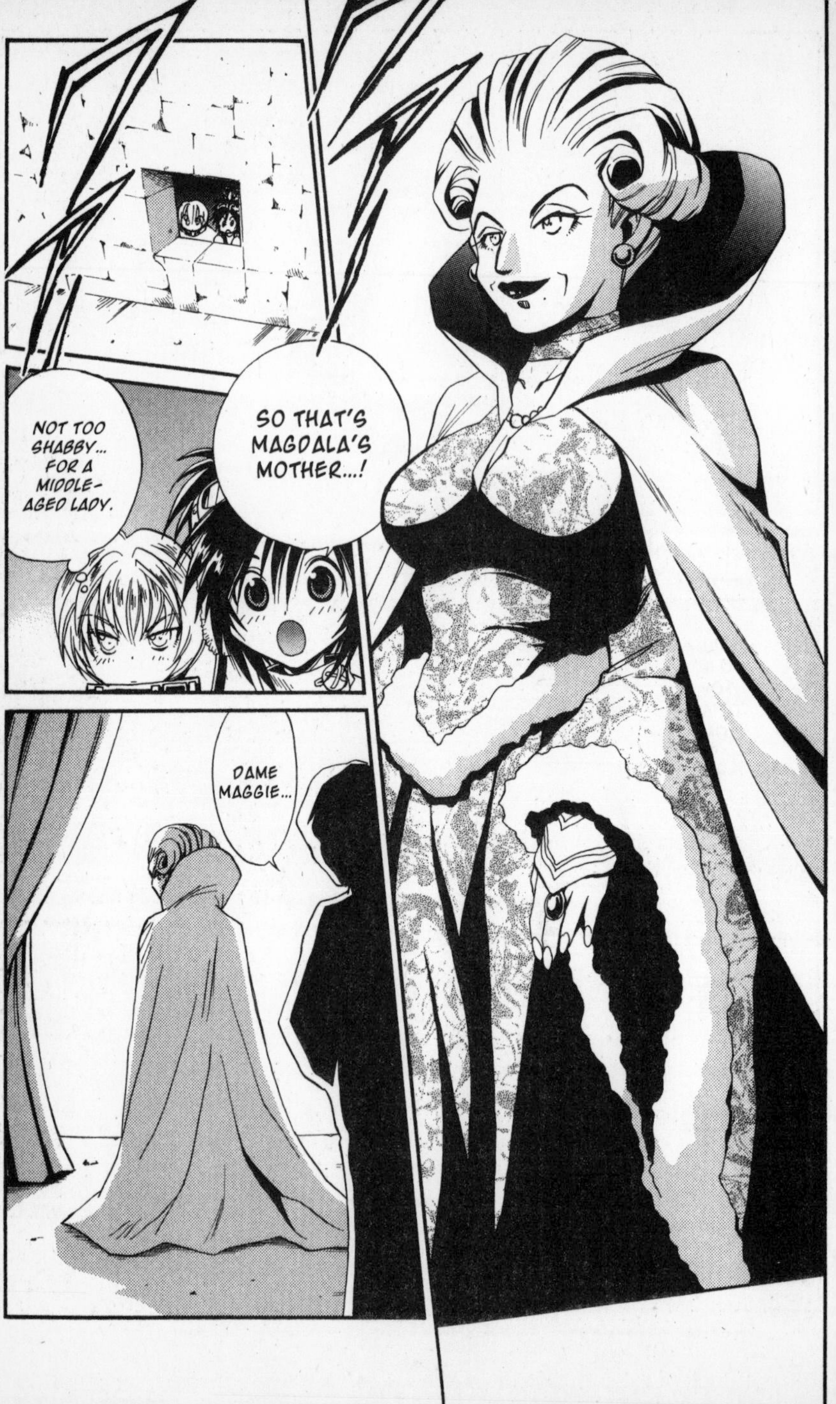
SO THAT'S MAGDALA'S MOTHER...!
NOT TOO SHABBY... FOR A MIDDLE-AGED LADY.
DAME MAGGIE...

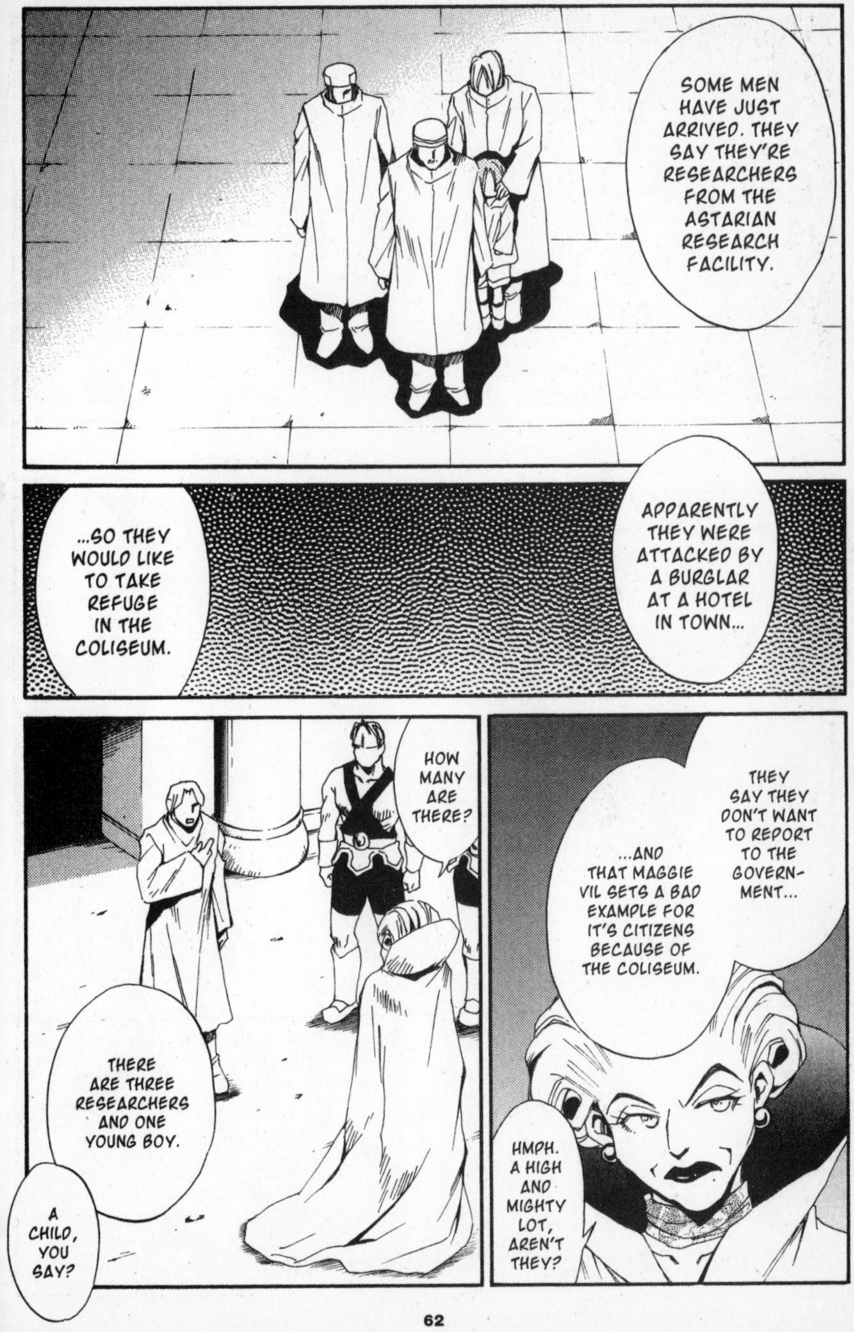
SOME MEN HAVE JUST ARRIVED. THEY SAY THEY'RE RESEARCHERS FROM THE ASTARIAN RESEARCH FACILITY.
APPARENTLY THEY WERE ATTACKED BY A BURGLAR AT A HOTEL IN TOWN...
...SO THEY WOULD LIKE TO TAKE REFUGE IN THE COLISEUM.
THEY SAY THEY DON'T WANT TO REPORT TO THE GOVERN-MENT...
...AND THAT MAGGIE VIL SETS A BAD EXAMPLE FOR IT'S CITIZENS BECAUSE OF THE COLISEUM.
HMPH. A HIGH AND MIGHTY LOT, AREN'T THEY?
HOW MANY ARE THERE?
THERE ARE THREE RESEARCHERS AND ONE YOUNG BOY.
A CHILD, YOU SAY?

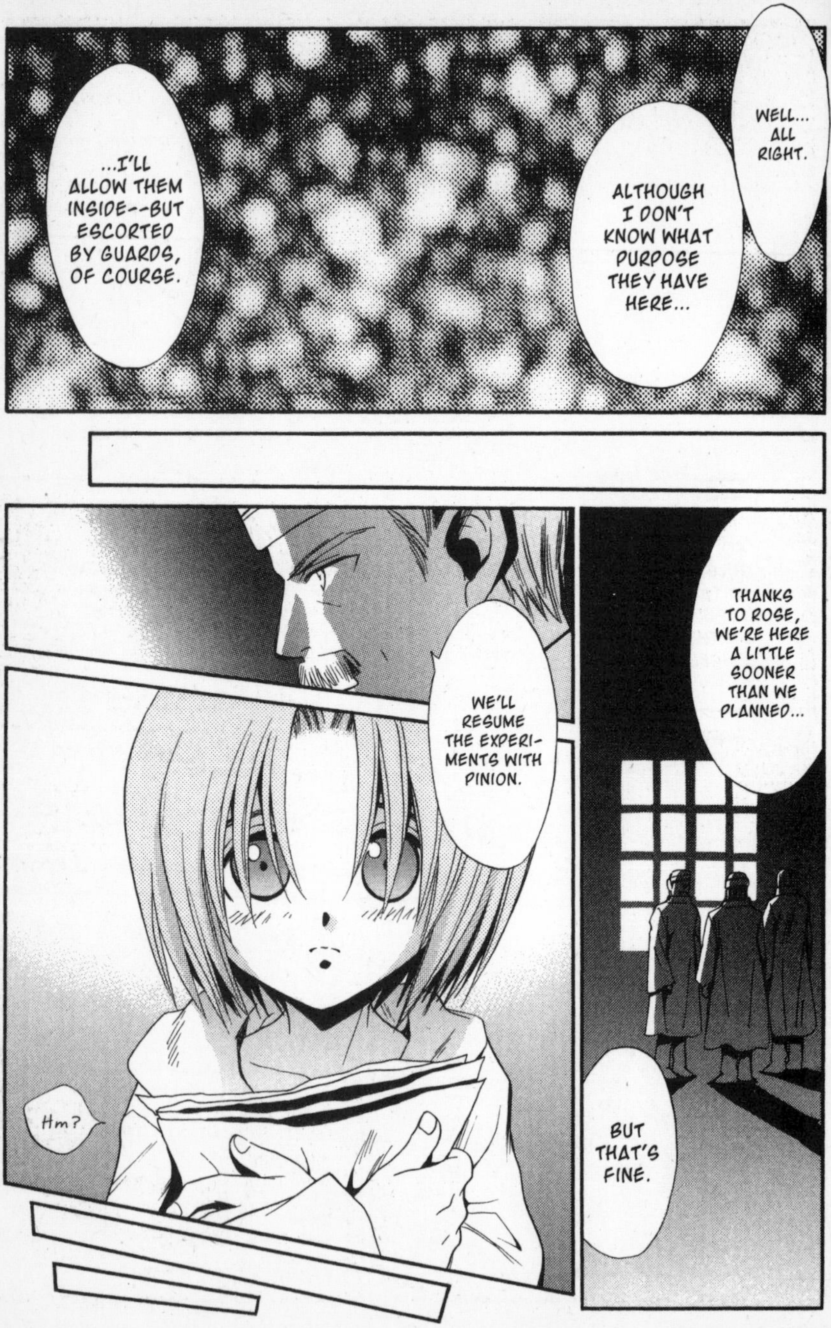
WELL... ALL RIGHT.
ALTHOUGH I DON'T KNOW WHAT PURPOSE THEY HAVE HERE...
...I'LL ALLOW THEM INSIDE--BUT ESCORTED BY GUARDS, OF COURSE.
THANKS TO ROSE, WE'RE HERE A LITTLE SOONER THAN WE PLANNED...
BUT THAT'S FINE.
WE'LL RESUME THE EXPERIMENTS WITH PINION.
Hm?

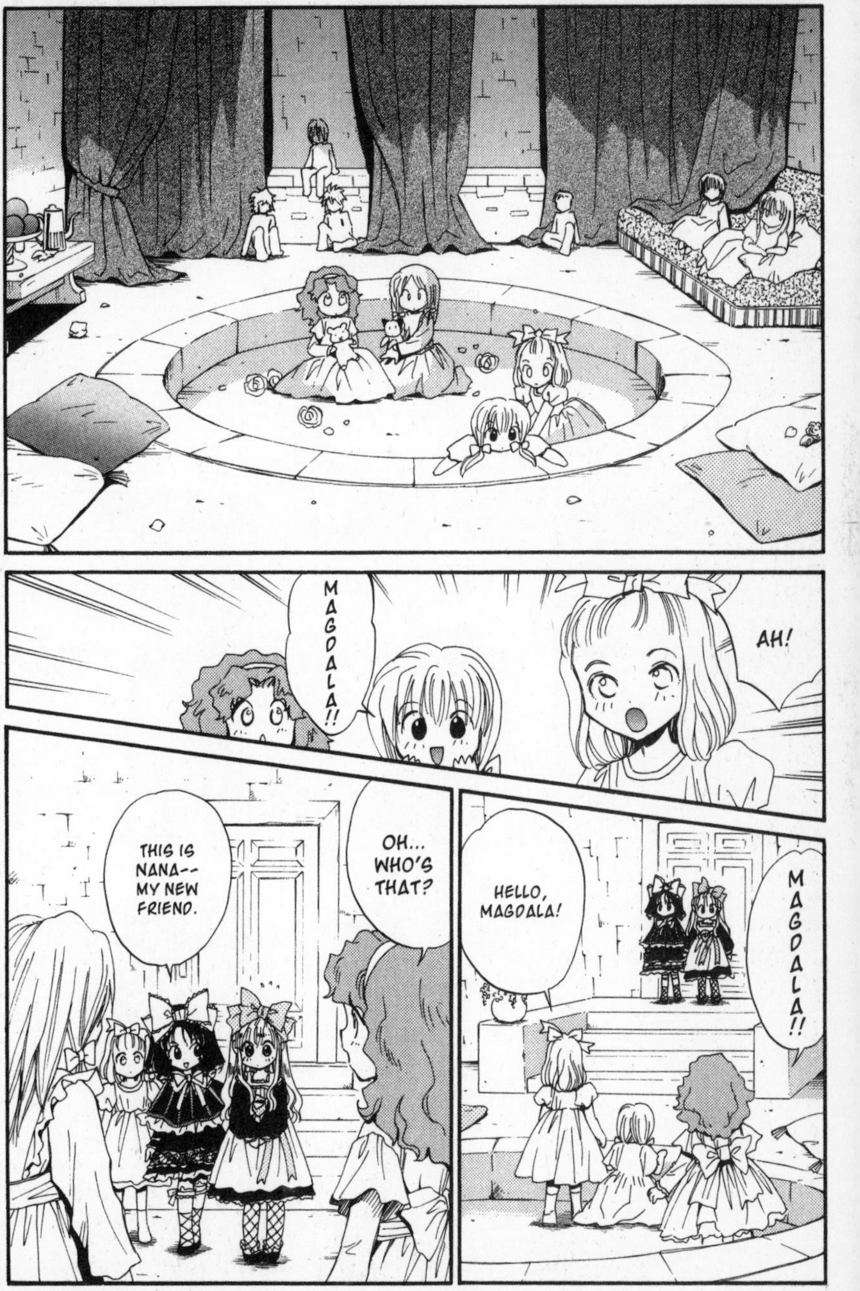
AH!
MAGDALA!!
MAGDALA!!
HELLO, MAGDALA!
OH... WHO'S THAT?
THIS IS NANA-- MY NEW FRIEND.

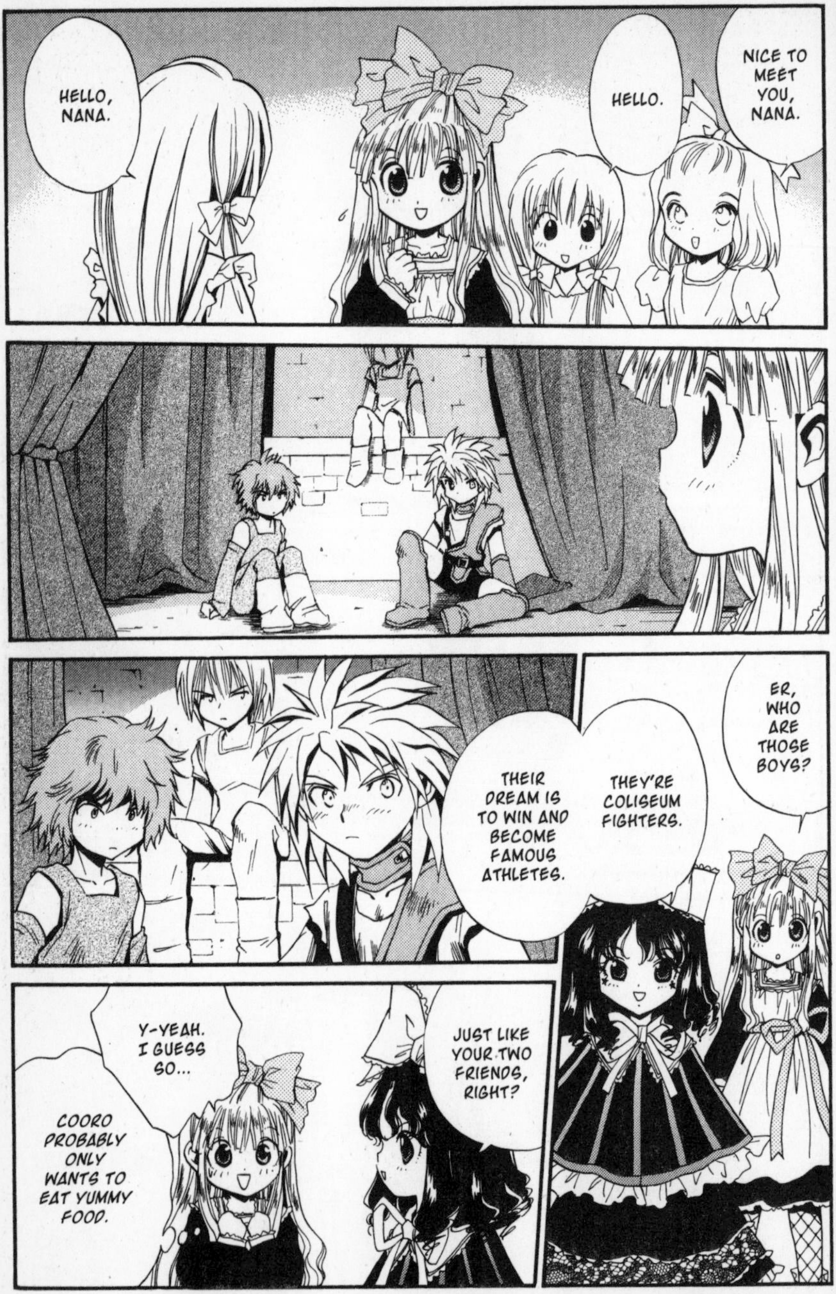
NICE TO MEET YOU, NANA.
HELLO.
HELLO, NANA.
ER, WHO ARE THOSE BOYS?
THEY'RE COLISEUM FIGHTERS.
THEIR DREAM IS TO WIN AND BECOME FAMOUS ATHLETES.
JUST LIKE YOUR TWO FRIENDS, RIGHT?
Y-YEAH. I GUESS SO...
COORO PROBABLY ONLY WANTS TO EAT YUMMY FOOD.

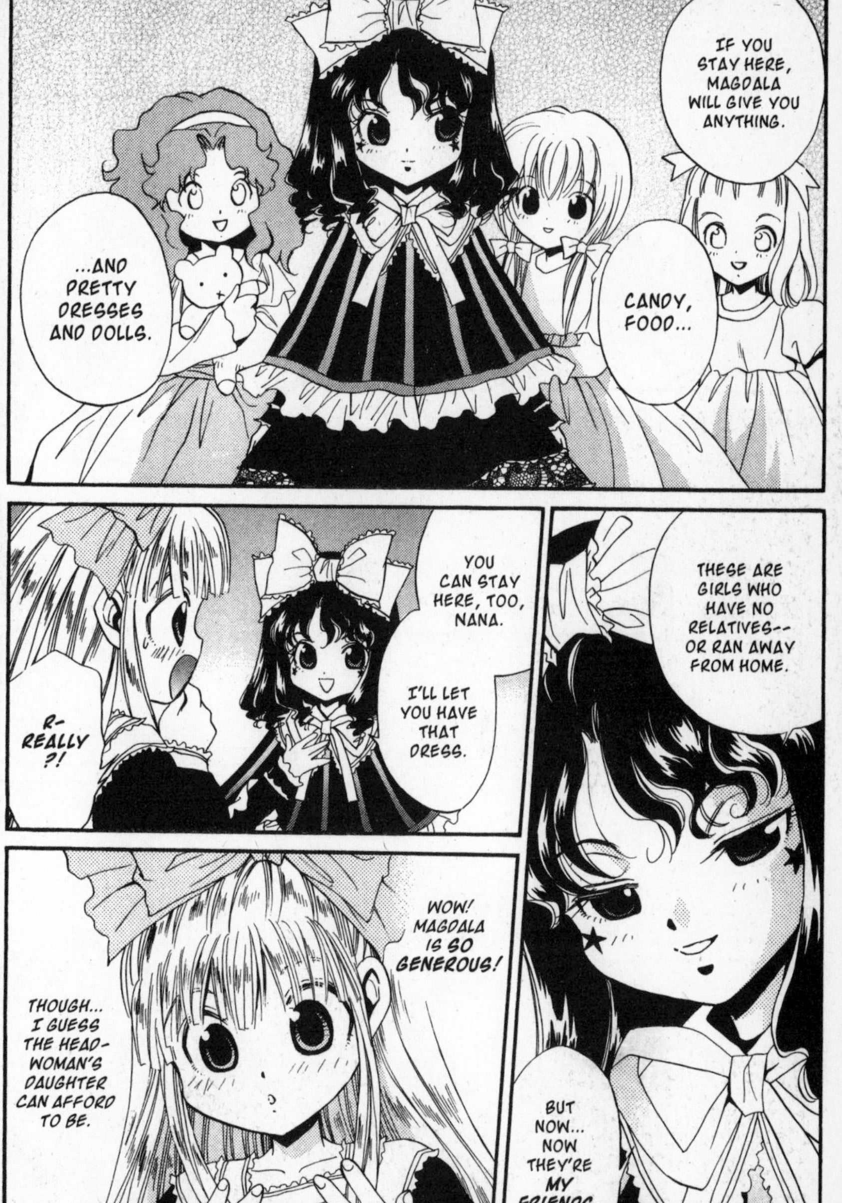
IF YOU STAY HERE, MAGDALA WILL GIVE YOU ANYTHING.
CANDY, FOOD...
...AND PRETTY DRESSES AND DOLLS.
THESE ARE GIRLS WHO HAVE NO RELATIVES-- OR RAN AWAY FROM HOME.
BUT NOW... NOW THEY'RE MY FRIENDS.
YOU CAN STAY HERE, TOO, NANA.
I'LL LET YOU HAVE THAT DRESS.
R-REALLY ?!
WOW! MAGDALA IS SO GENEROUS!
THOUGH... I GUESS THE HEAD-WOMAN'S DAUGHTER CAN AFFORD TO BE.

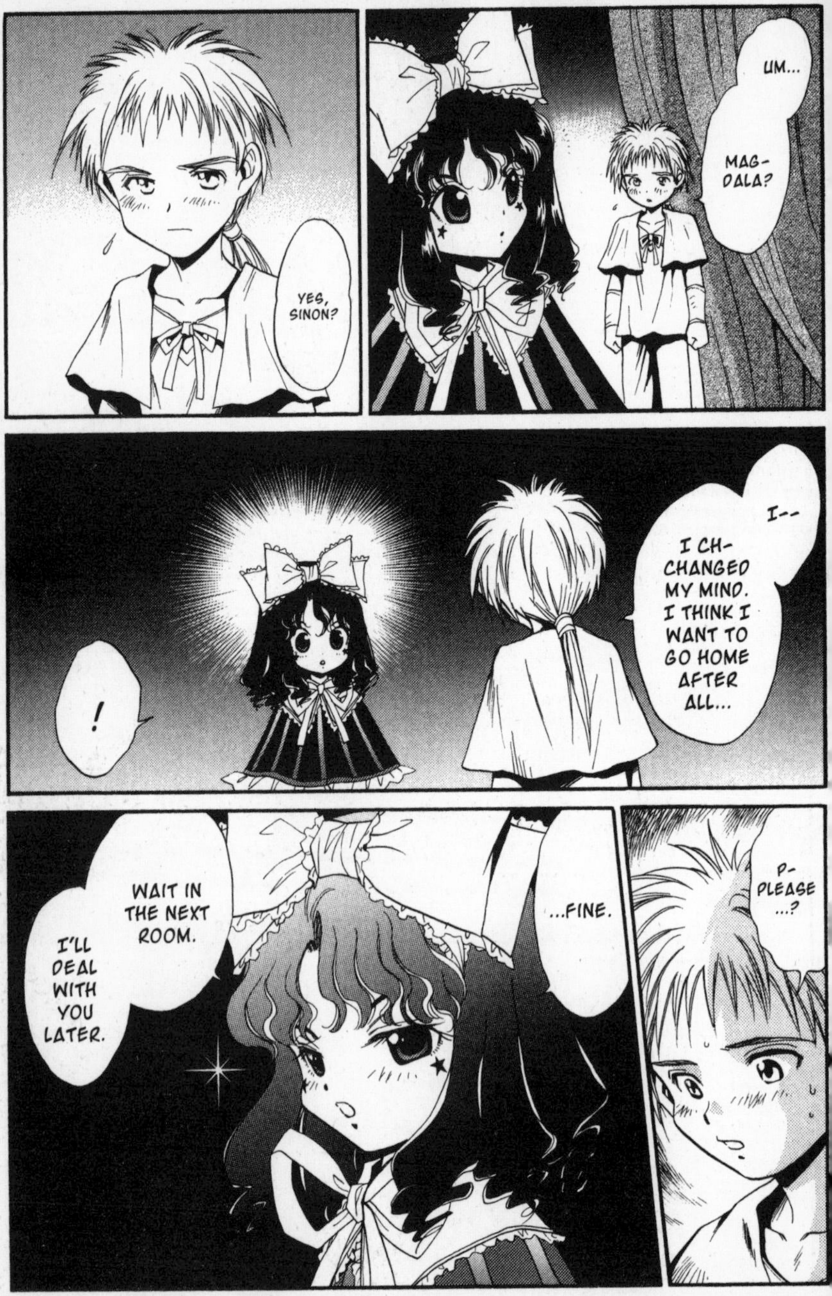
UM...
MAG-DALA?
YES, SINON?
I--
I CH-CHANGED MY MIND. I THINK I WANT TO GO HOME AFTER ALL...
!
P-PLEASE ...?
...FINE.
WAIT IN THE NEXT ROOM.
I'LL DEAL WITH YOU LATER.

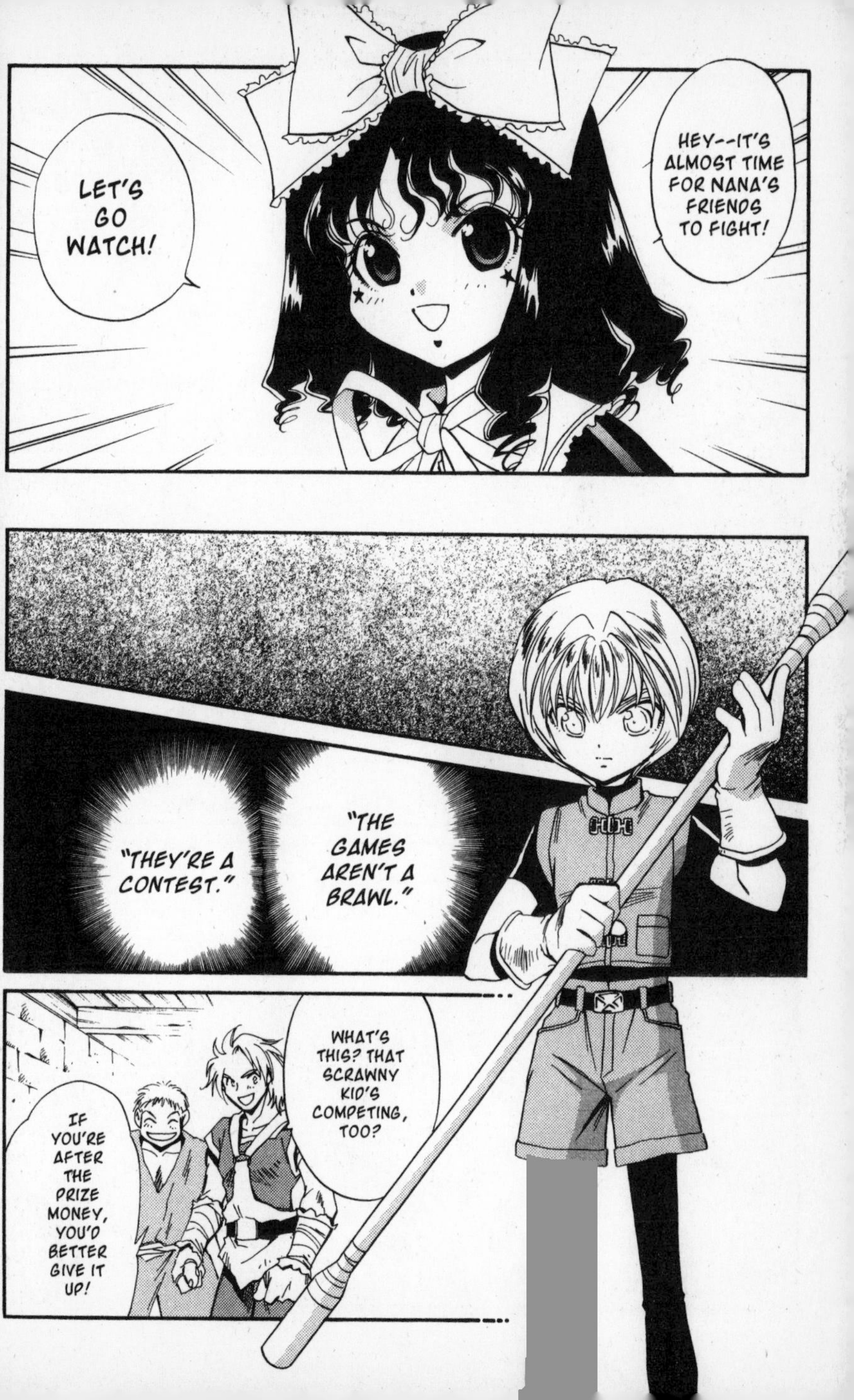
HEY--IT'S ALMOST TIME FOR NANA'S FRIENDS TO FIGHT!
LET'S GO WATCH!
"THE GAMES AREN'T A BRAWL."
"THEY'RE A CONTEST."
WHAT'S THIS? THAT SCRAWNY KID'S COMPETING, TOO?
IF YOU'RE AFTER THE PRIZE MONEY, YOU'D BETTER GIVE IT UP!

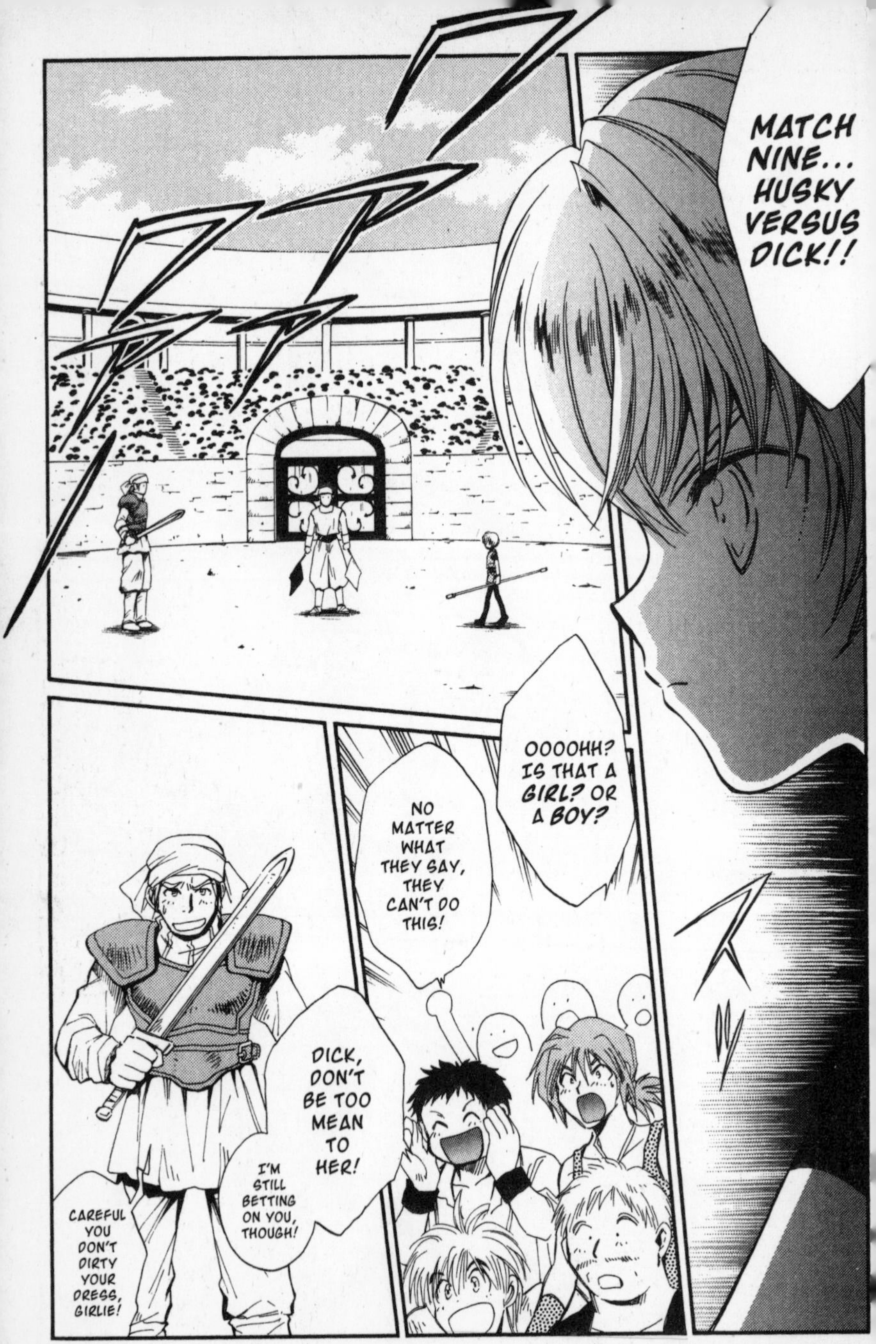
MATCH NINE... HUSKY VERSUS DICK!!
OOOOHH? IS THAT A GIRL? OR A BOY?
NO MATTER WHAT THEY SAY, THEY CAN'T DO THIS!
DICK, DON'T BE TOO MEAN TO HER!
I'M STILL BETTING ON YOU, THOUGH!
CAREFUL YOU DON'T DIRTY YOUR DRESS, GIRLIE!

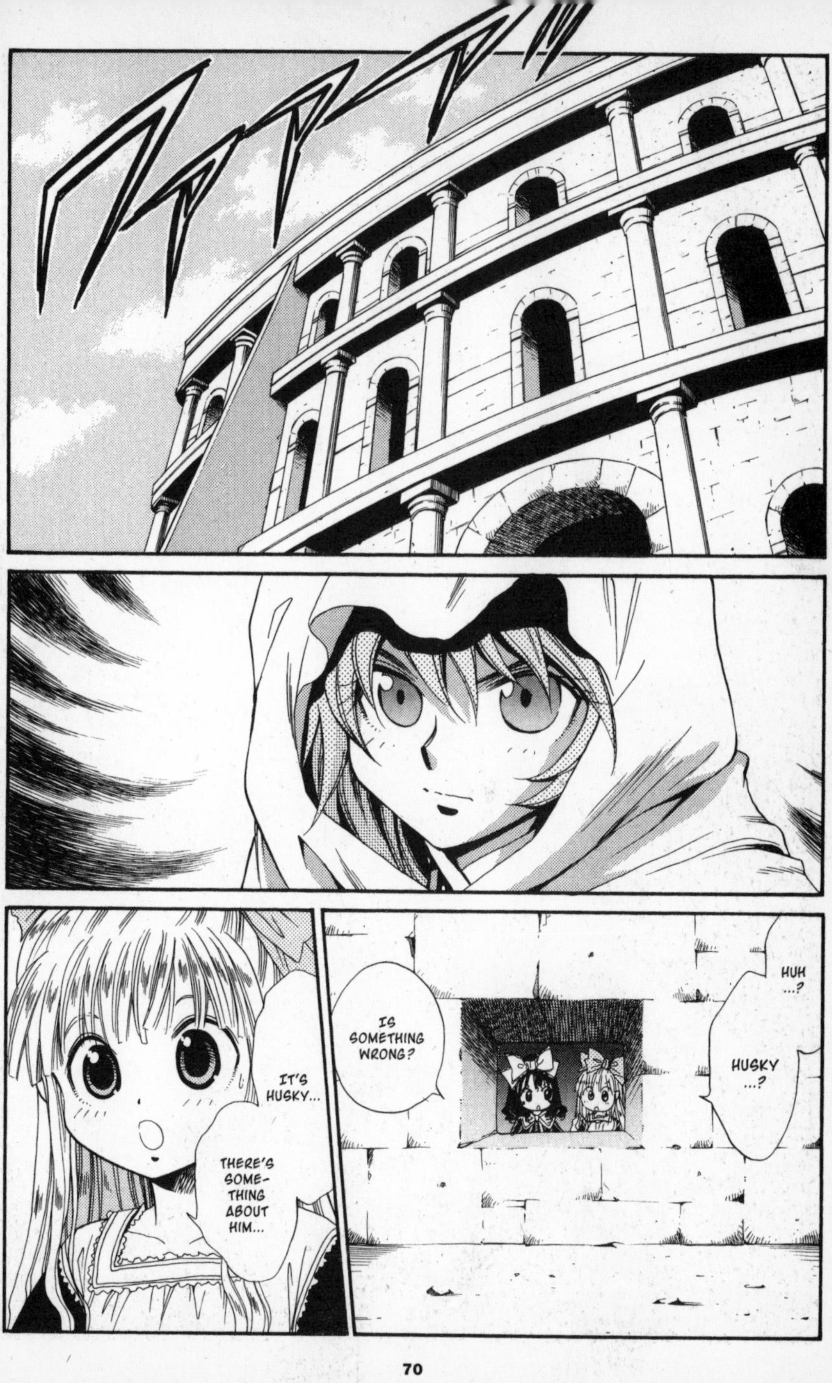
HUH ...?
IS SOMETHING WRONG?
HUSKY ...?
IT'S HUSKY...
THERE'S SOME-THING ABOUT HIM...

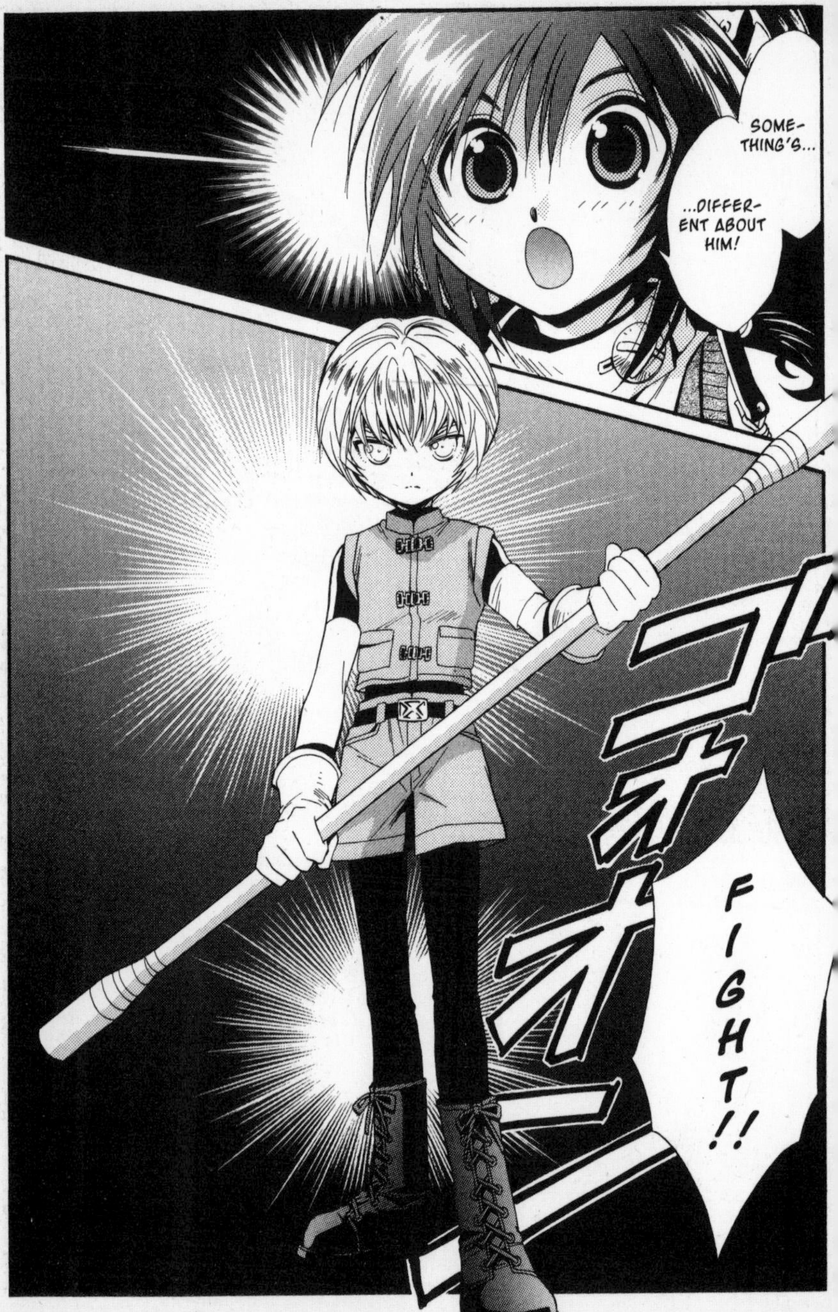
SOME-THING'S...
...DIFFER-ENT ABOUT HIM!
FIGHT!!

Princess feeling.

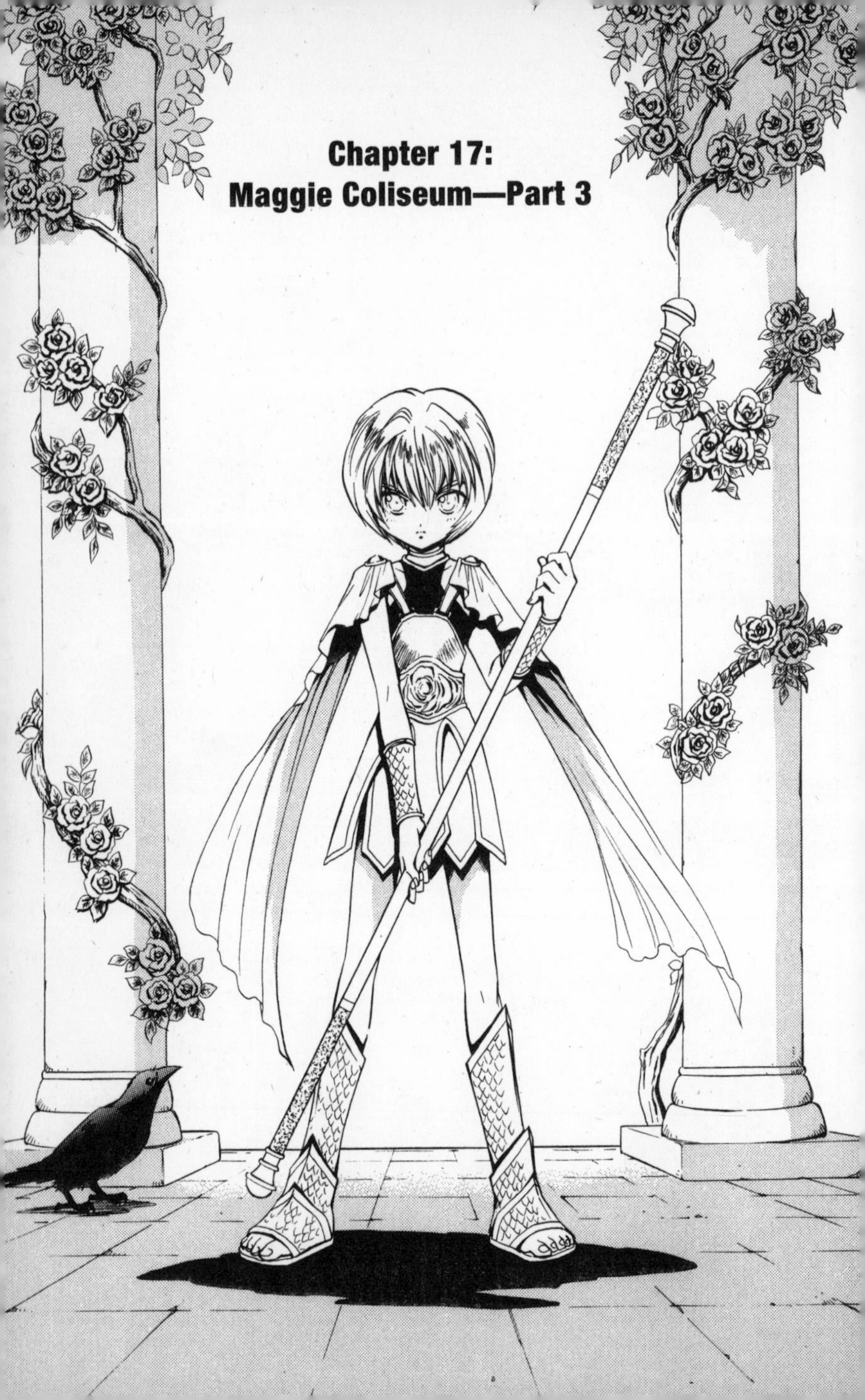
Chapter 17:
Maggie Coliseum—Part 3

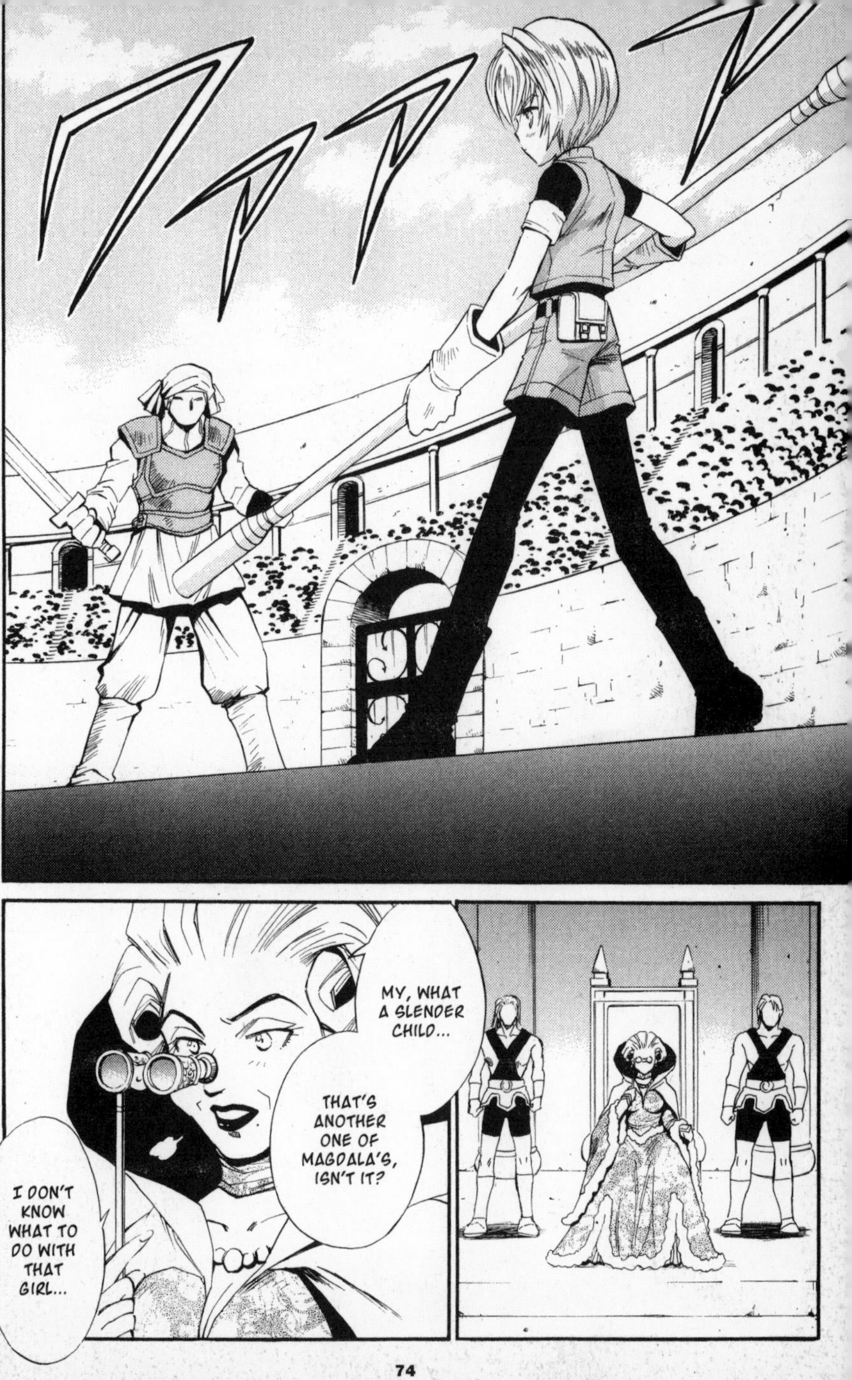
MY, WHAT A SLENDER CHILD...
THAT'S ANOTHER ONE OF MAGDALA'S, ISN'T IT?
I DON'T KNOW WHAT TO DO WITH THAT GIRL...

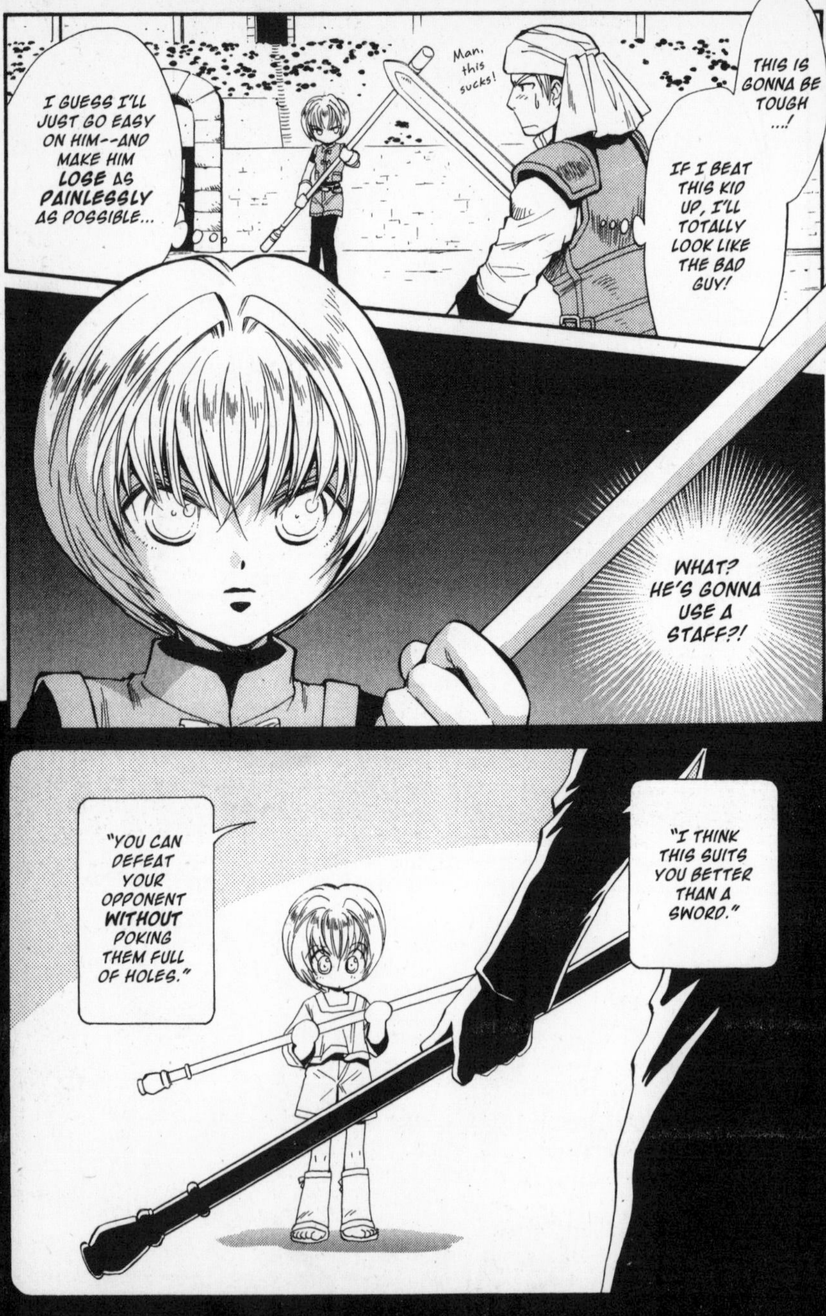
THIS IS GONNA BE TOUGH ...!
IF I BEAT THIS KID UP, I'LL TOTALLY LOOK LIKE THE BAD GUY!
Man, this sucks!
I GUESS I'LL JUST GO EASY ON HIM--AND MAKE HIM **LOSE** AS **PAINLESSLY** AS POSSIBLE...
WHAT? HE'S GONNA USE A STAFF?!
"I THINK THIS SUITS YOU BETTER THAN A SWORD."
"YOU CAN DEFEAT YOUR OPPONENT **WITHOUT** POKING THEM FULL OF HOLES."

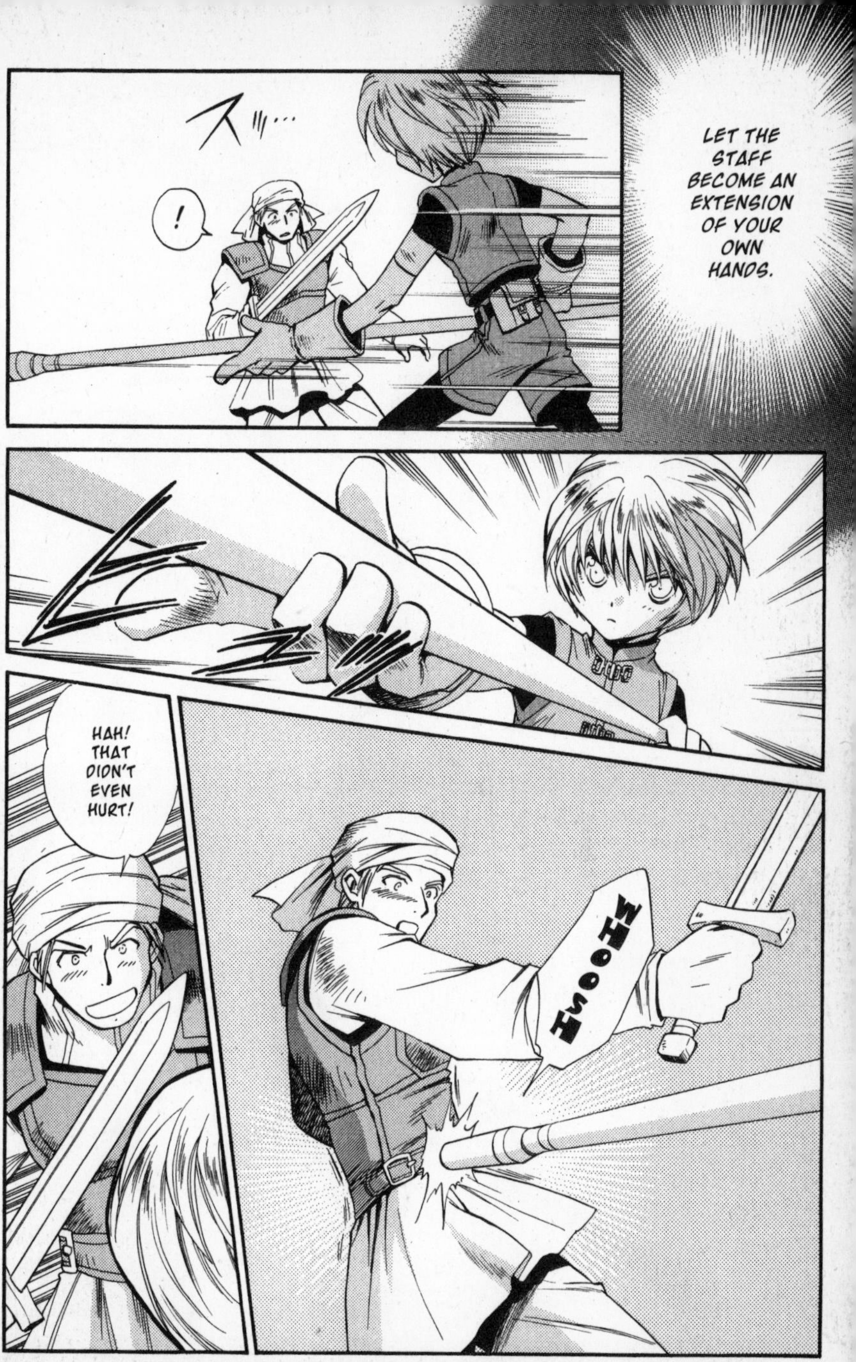
LET THE STAFF BECOME AN EXTENSION OF YOUR OWN HANDS.
スッ…
!
WHOOSH
HAH! THAT DIDN'T EVEN HURT!

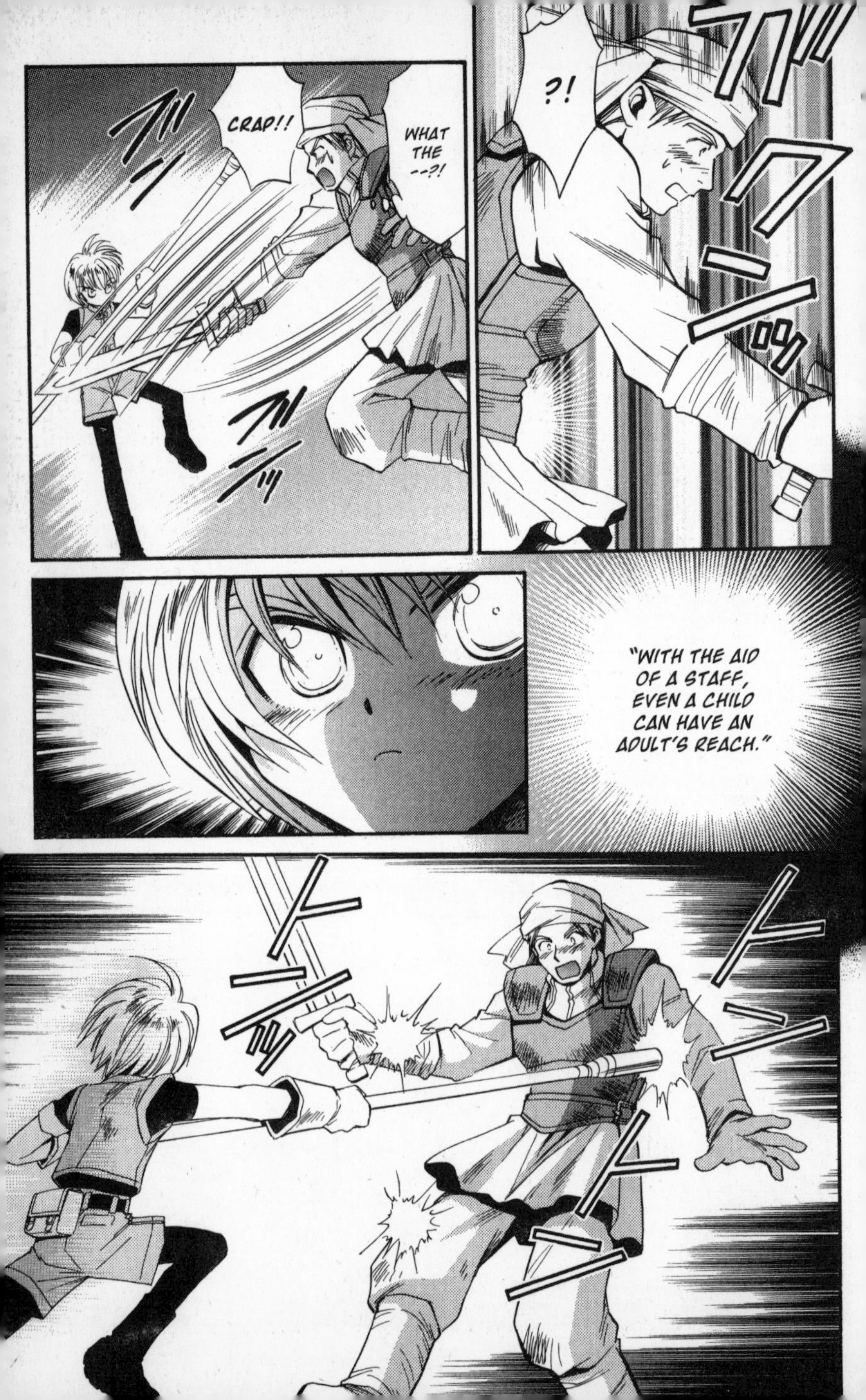
?!
WHAT THE --?!
CRAP!!
"WITH THE AID OF A STAFF, EVEN A CHILD CAN HAVE AN ADULT'S REACH."

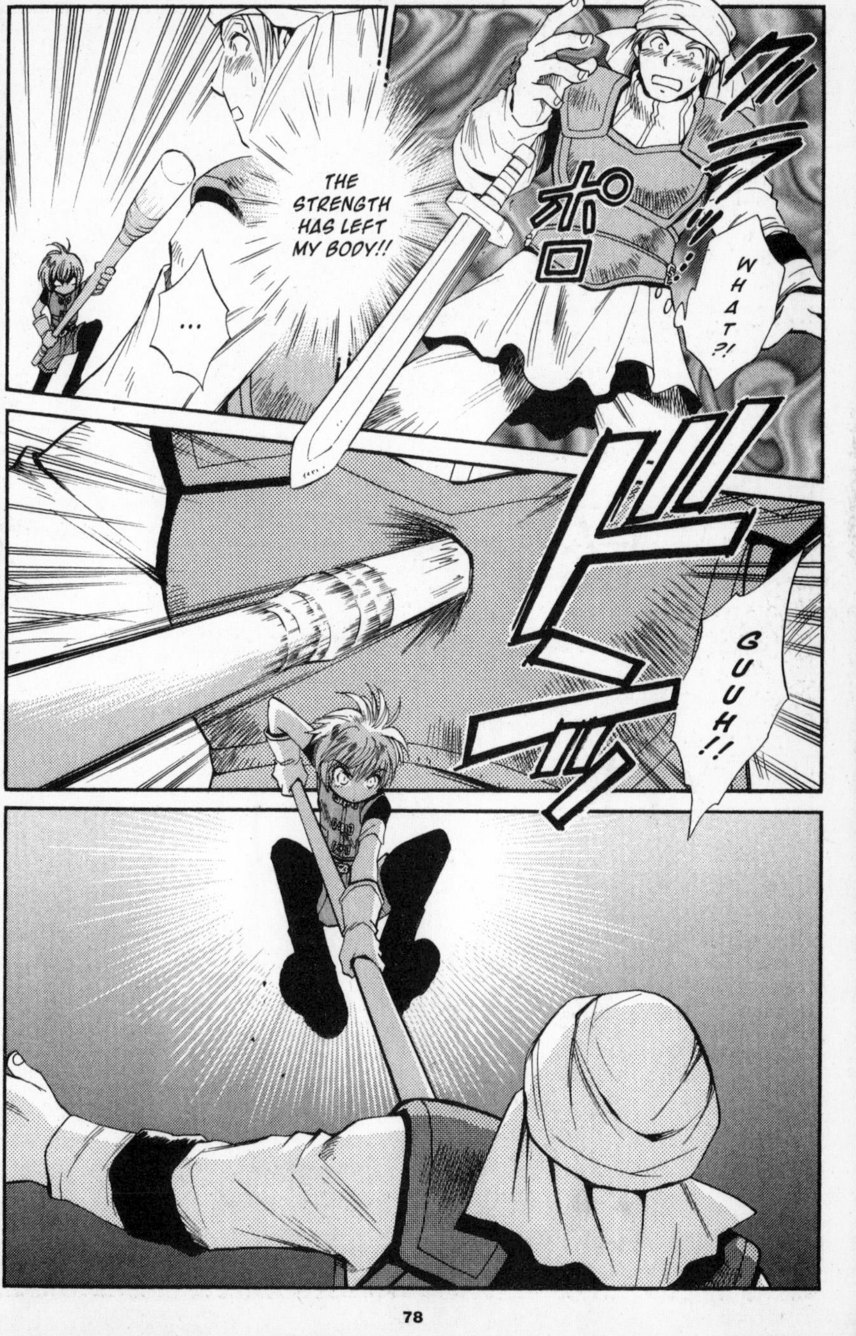
WHAT?!
ポロ
THE STRENGTH HAS LEFT MY BODY!!
...
GUUH!!

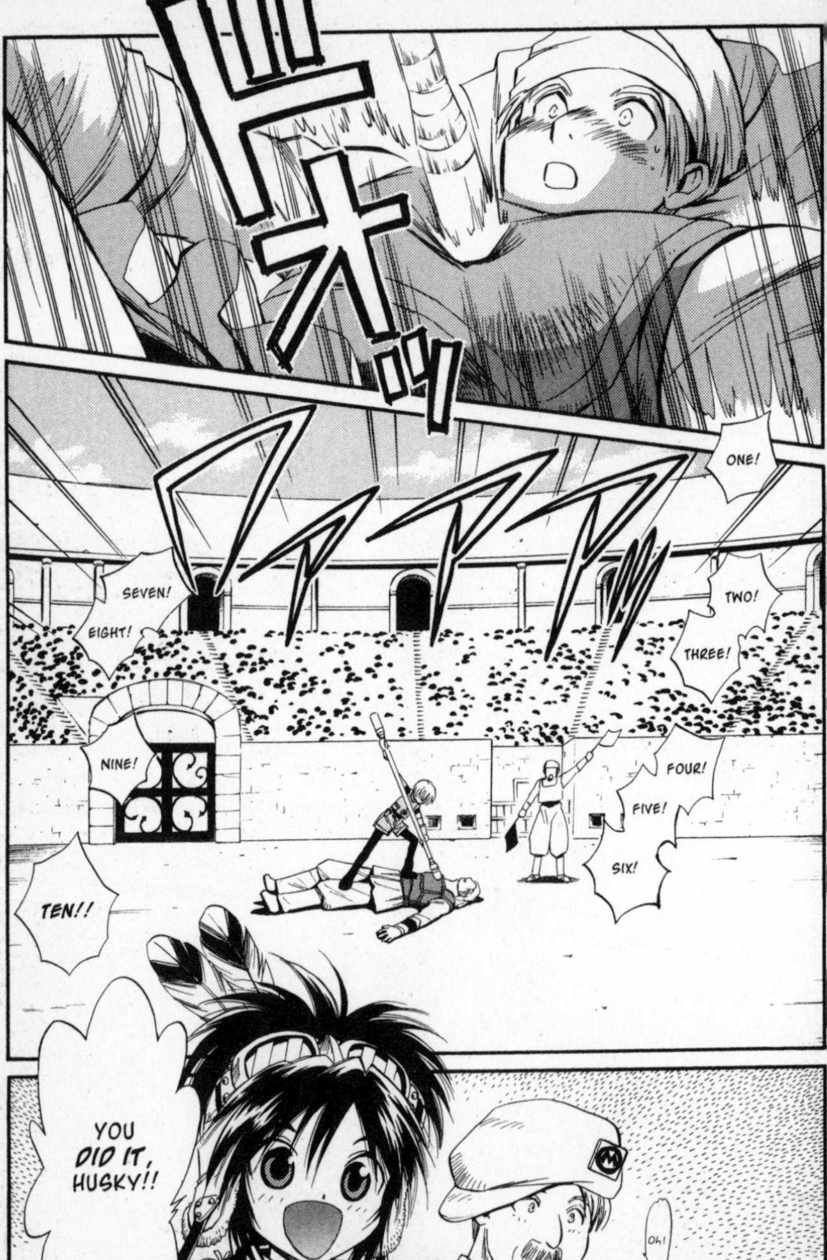
ドスッ
ワァァァ
ONE!
TWO!
THREE!
FOUR!
FIVE!
SIX!
SEVEN!
EIGHT!
NINE!
TEN!!
YOU DID IT, HUSKY!!
Oh!

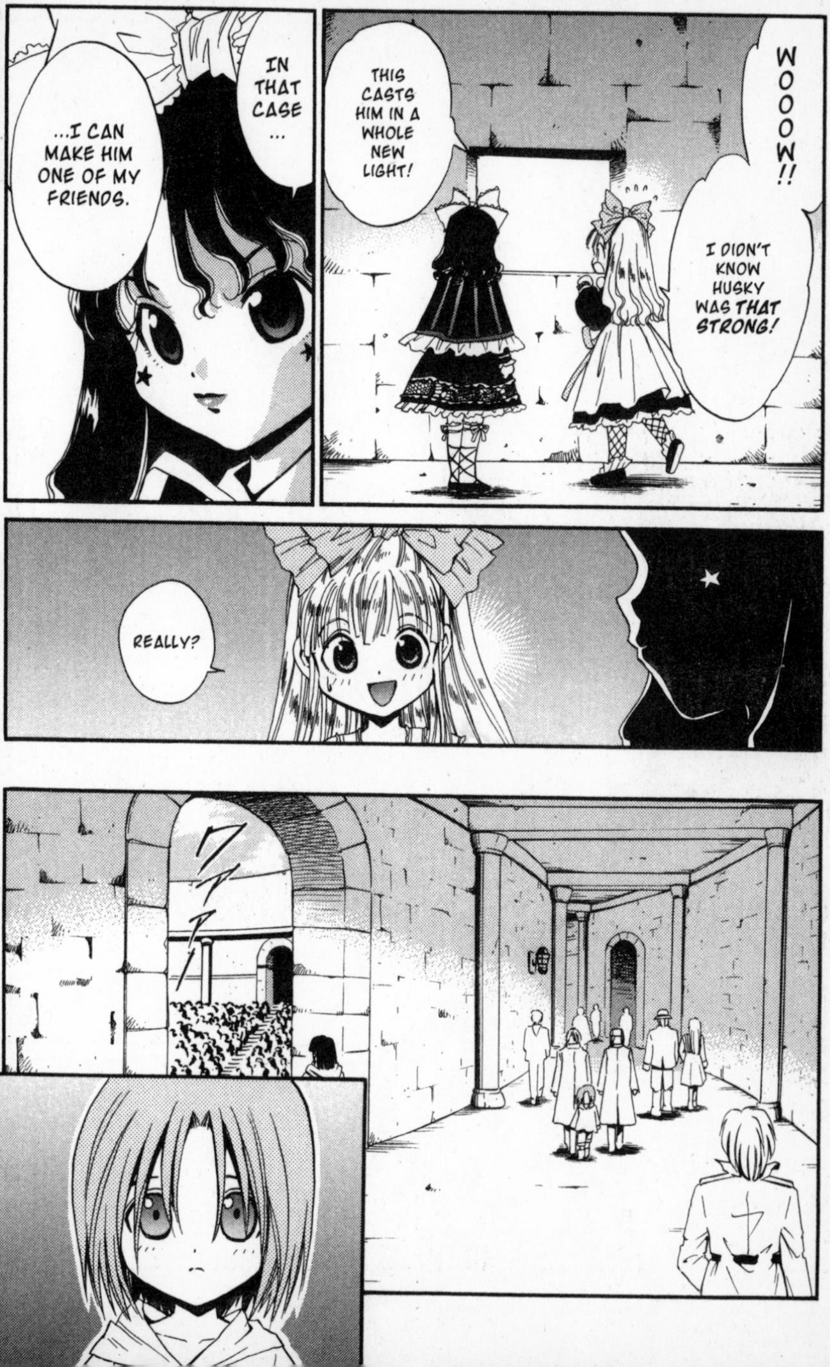
WOOOOW!!
I DIDN'T KNOW HUSKY WAS THAT STRONG!
THIS CASTS HIM IN A WHOLE NEW LIGHT!
IN THAT CASE ...
...I CAN MAKE HIM ONE OF MY FRIENDS.
REALLY?
ワァァ

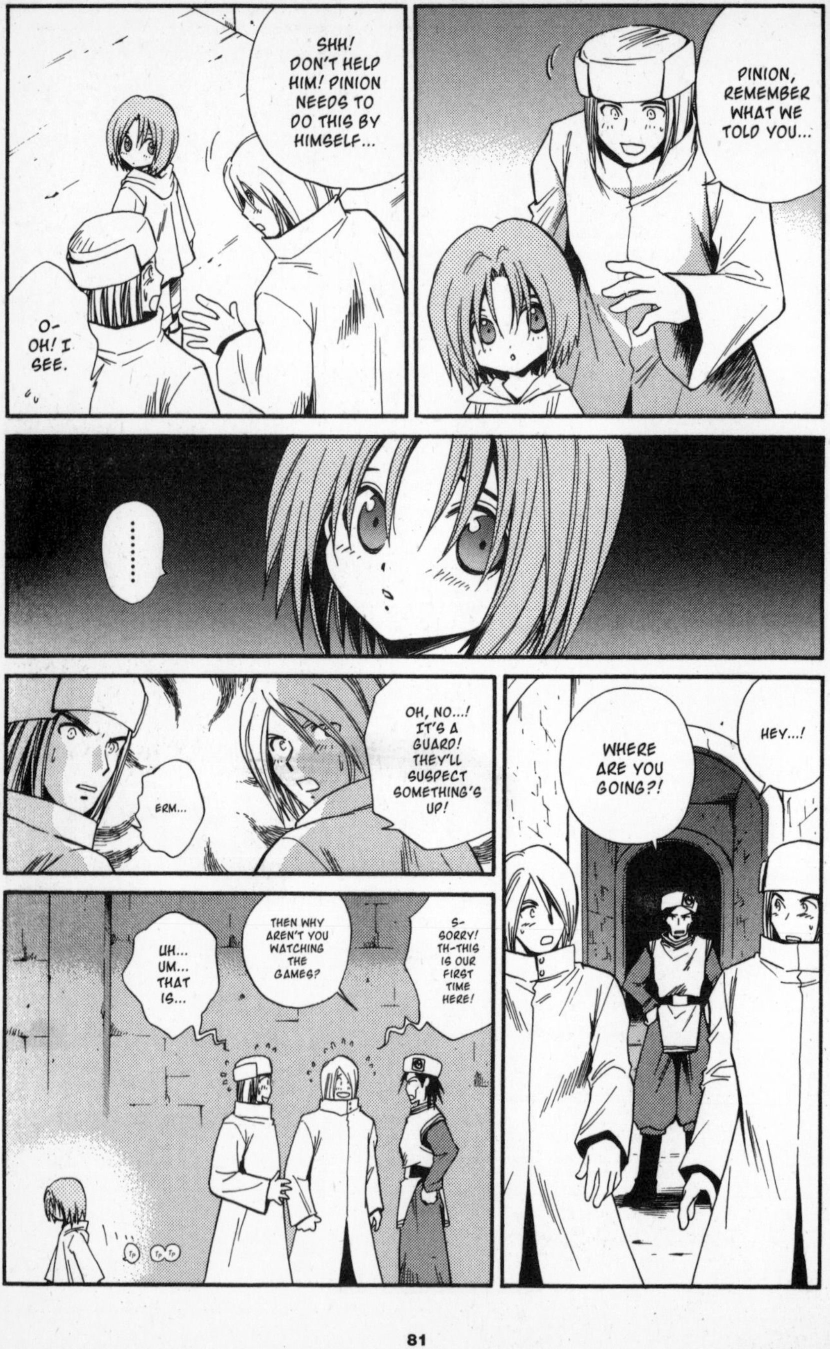
PINION, REMEMBER WHAT WE TOLD YOU...
SHH! DON'T HELP HIM! PINION NEEDS TO DO THIS BY HIMSELF...
O- OH! I SEE.
......
HEY...!
WHERE ARE YOU GOING?!
OH, NO...! IT'S A GUARD! THEY'LL SUSPECT SOMETHING'S UP!
ERM...
S- SORRY! TH-THIS IS OUR FIRST TIME HERE!
THEN WHY AREN'T YOU WATCHING THE GAMES?
UH... UM... THAT IS...

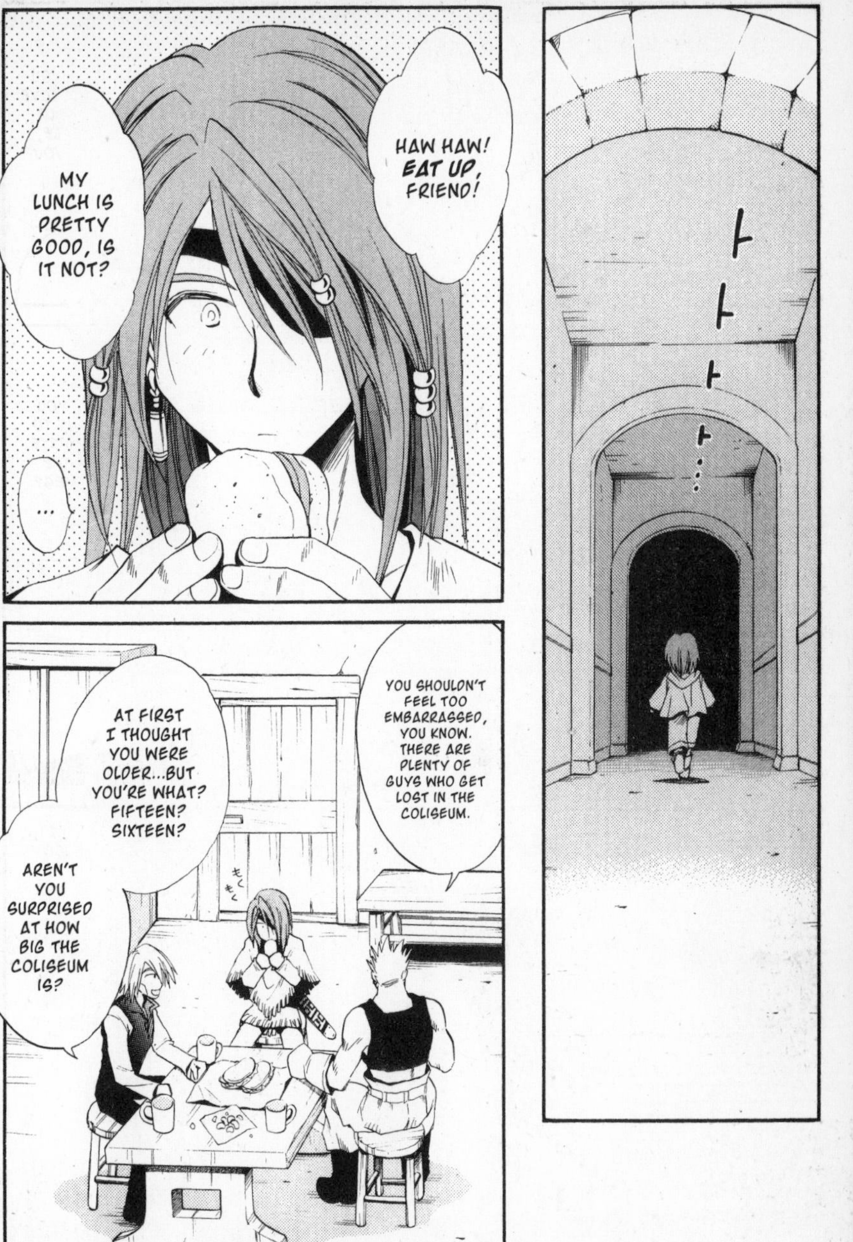
トトトト…
HAW HAW! EAT UP, FRIEND!
MY LUNCH IS PRETTY GOOD, IS IT NOT?
...
YOU SHOULDN'T FEEL TOO EMBARRASSED, YOU KNOW. THERE ARE PLENTY OF GUYS WHO GET LOST IN THE COLISEUM.
AT FIRST I THOUGHT YOU WERE OLDER...BUT YOU'RE WHAT? FIFTEEN? SIXTEEN?
もく もく
AREN'T YOU SURPRISED AT HOW BIG THE COLISEUM IS?

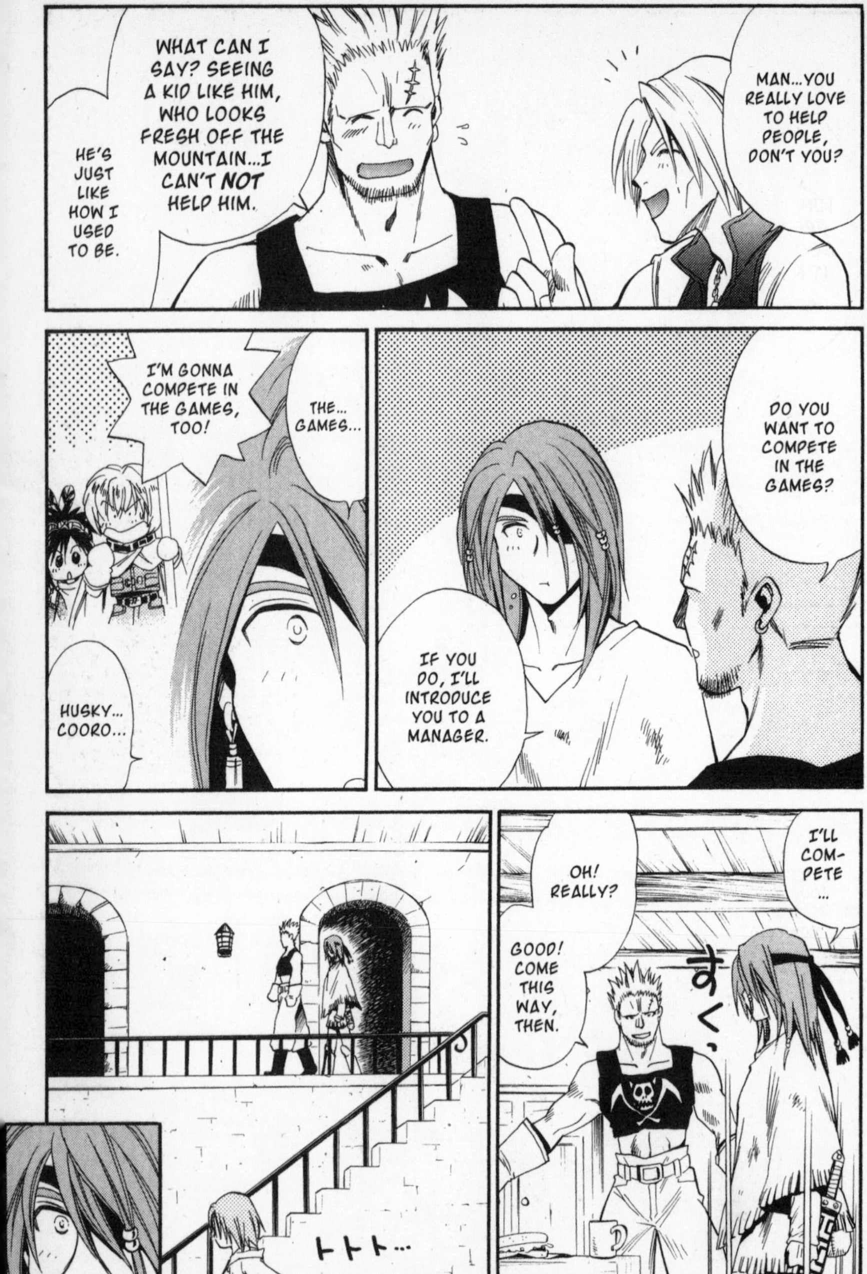
MAN...YOU REALLY LOVE TO HELP PEOPLE, DON'T YOU?
WHAT CAN I SAY? SEEING A KID LIKE HIM, WHO LOOKS FRESH OFF THE MOUNTAIN...I CAN'T **NOT** HELP HIM.
HE'S JUST LIKE HOW I USED TO BE.
DO YOU WANT TO COMPETE IN THE GAMES?
IF YOU DO, I'LL INTRODUCE YOU TO A MANAGER.
THE... GAMES...
I'M GONNA COMPETE IN THE GAMES, TOO!
HUSKY... COORO...
I'LL COM-PETE ...
OH! REALLY?
GOOD! COME THIS WAY, THEN.
すく、
トトト...

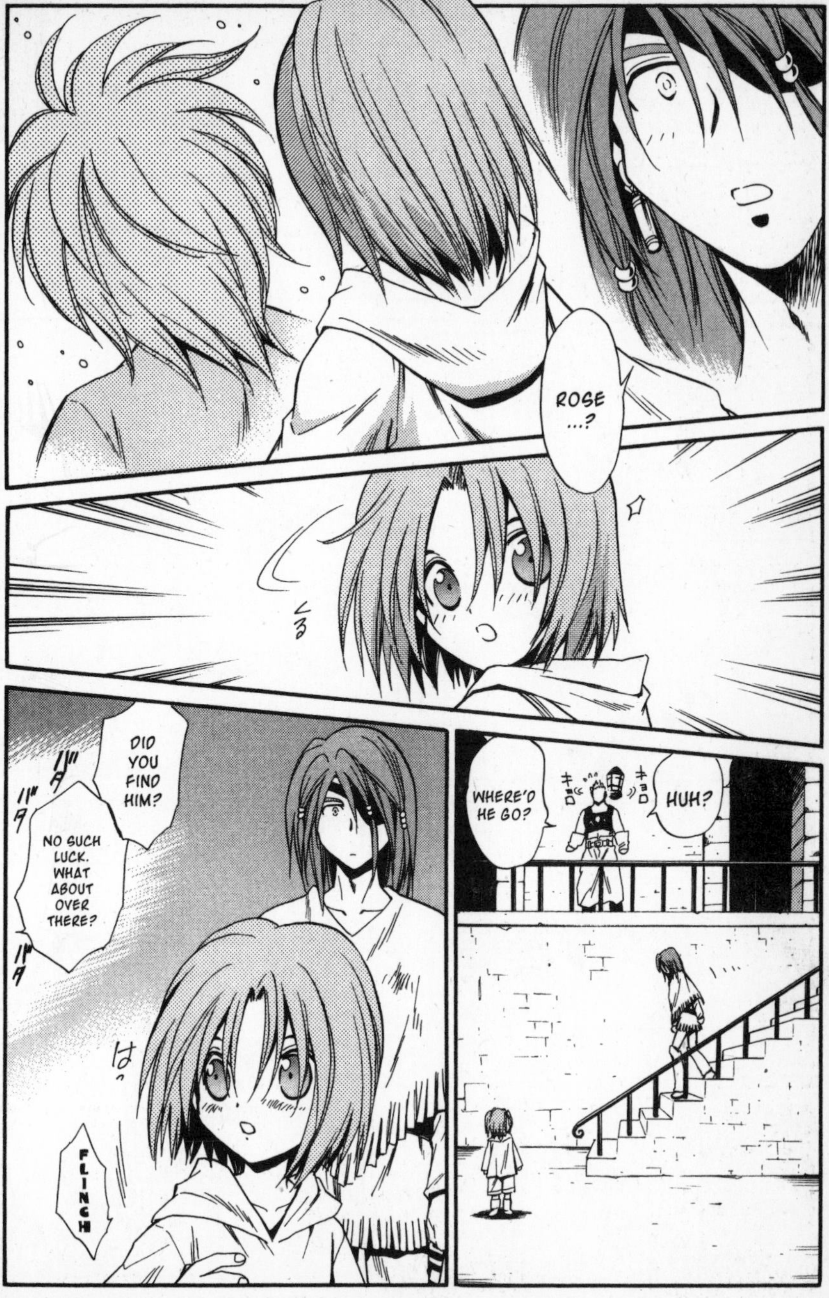
ROSE ...?
くる
HUH?
キョロ キョロ
WHERE'D HE GO?
DID YOU FIND HIM?
バタ バタ
NO SUCH LUCK. WHAT ABOUT OVER THERE?
バタ
はっ
FLINCH

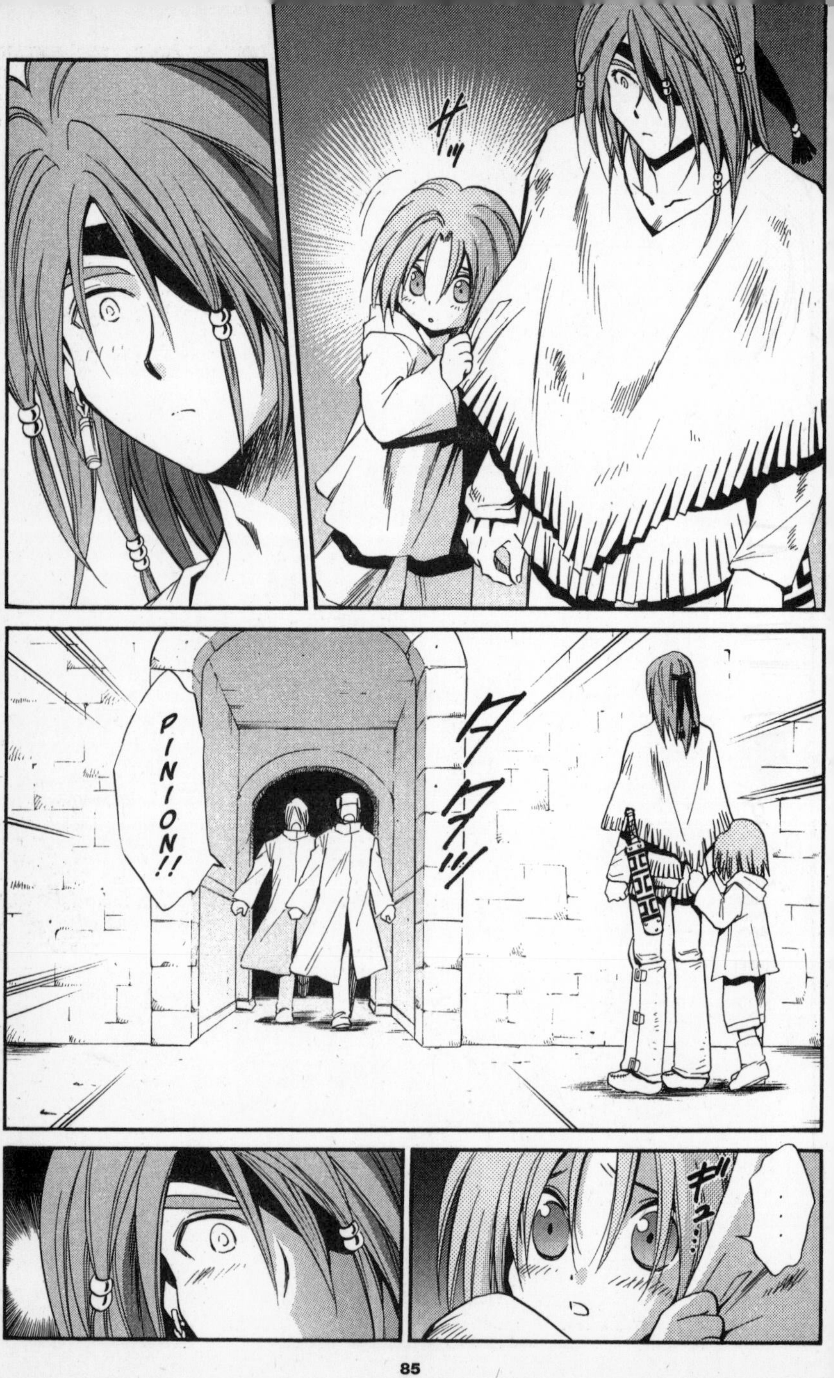
ザッ
タタッ
PINION!!
ギュ…
...

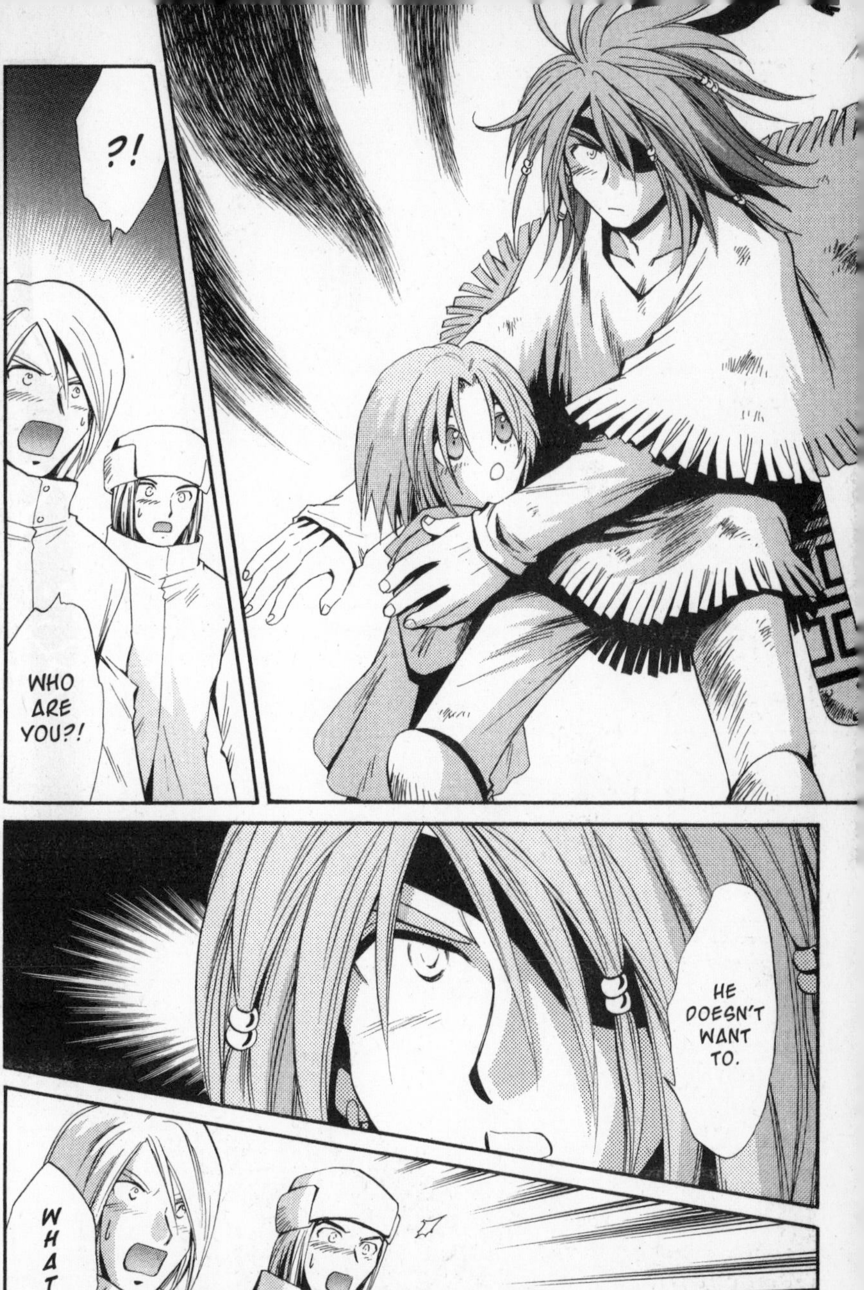
?!
WHO ARE YOU?!
HE DOESN'T WANT TO.
WHAT?!

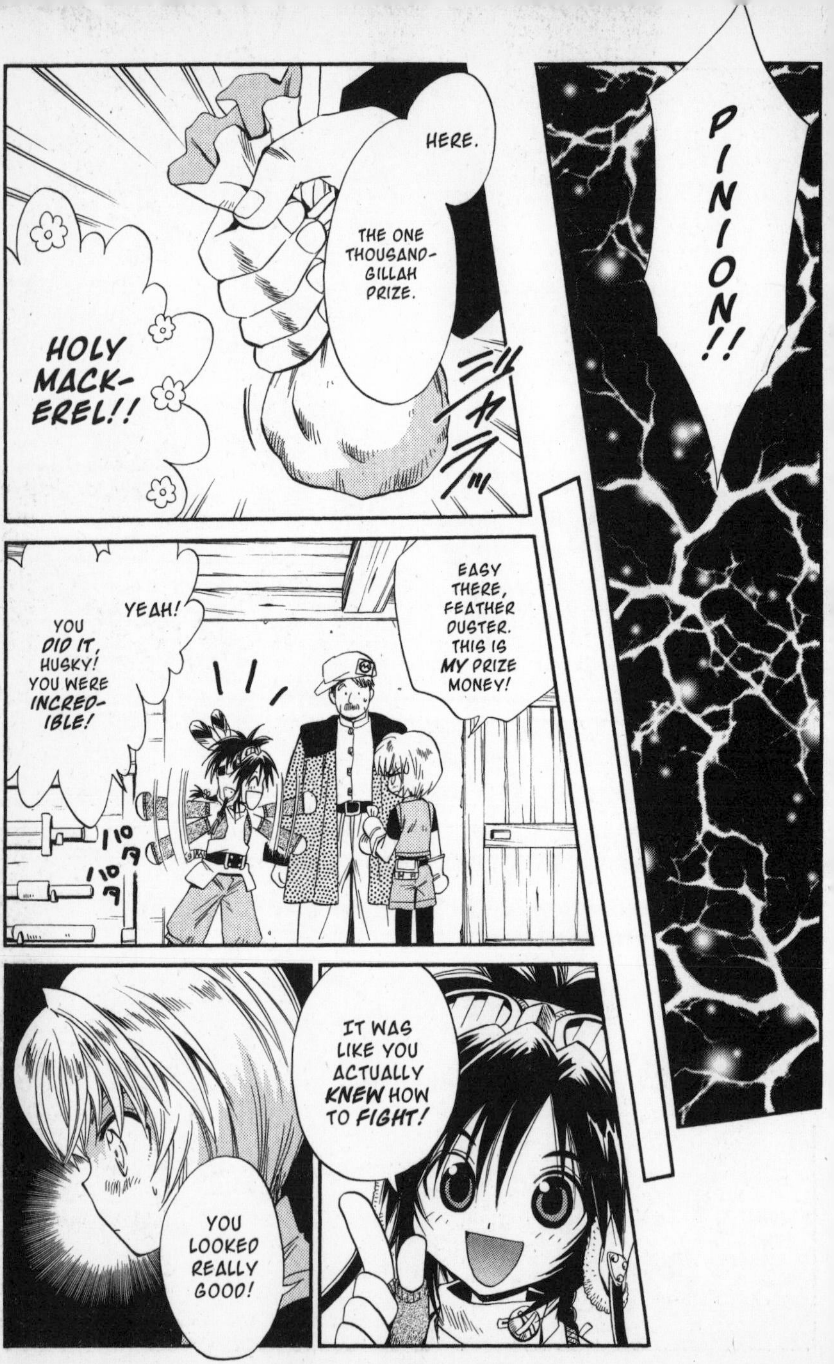
PINION!!
HERE.
THE ONE THOUSAND-GILLAH PRIZE.
HOLY MACKEREL!!
EASY THERE, FEATHER DUSTER. THIS IS MY PRIZE MONEY!
YEAH!
YOU DID IT, HUSKY! YOU WERE INCREDIBLE!
IT WAS LIKE YOU ACTUALLY KNEW HOW TO FIGHT!
YOU LOOKED REALLY GOOD!

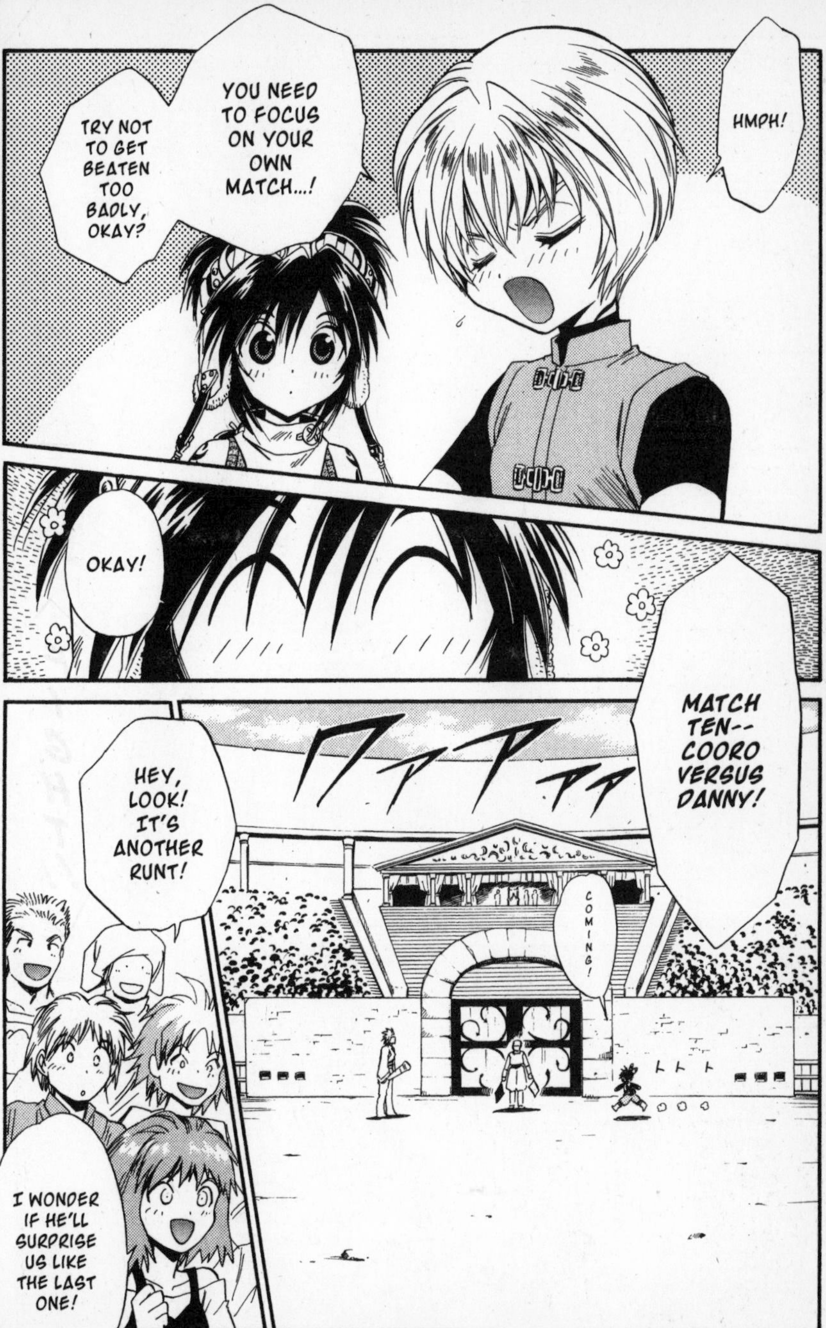
HMPH!
YOU NEED TO FOCUS ON YOUR OWN MATCH...!
TRY NOT TO GET BEATEN TOO BADLY, OKAY?
OKAY!
MATCH TEN--COORO VERSUS DANNY!
ワァァァァ
COMING!
トトト
HEY, LOOK! IT'S ANOTHER RUNT!
I WONDER IF HE'LL SURPRISE US LIKE THE LAST ONE!

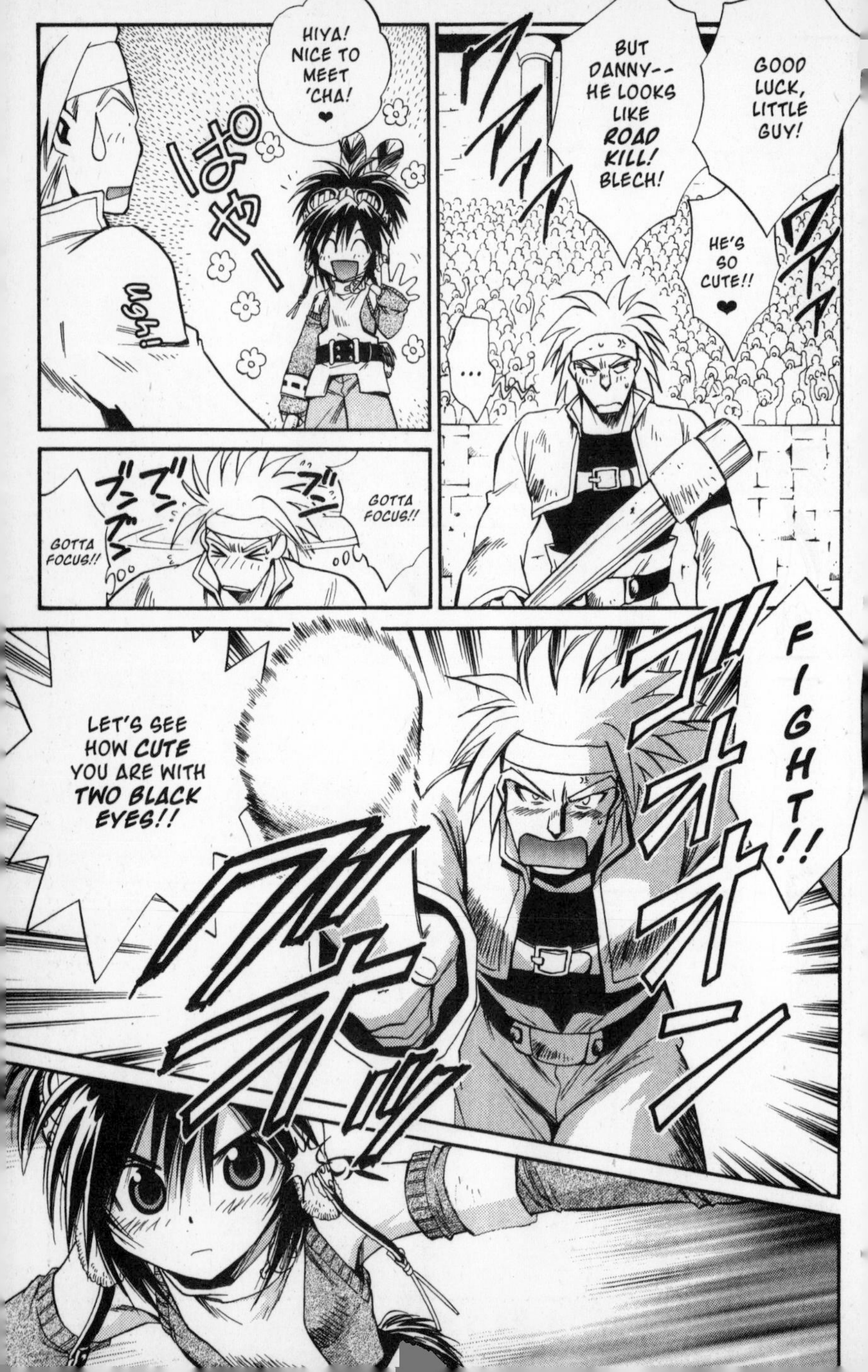
GOOD LUCK, LITTLE GUY!
BUT DANNY-- HE LOOKS LIKE ROAD KILL! BLECH!
HE'S SO CUTE!! ❤
...
HIYA! NICE TO MEET 'CHA! ❤
ぱやー
Ugh!
GOTTA FOCUS!!
GOTTA FOCUS!!
FIGHT!!
LET'S SEE HOW CUTE YOU ARE WITH TWO BLACK EYES!!

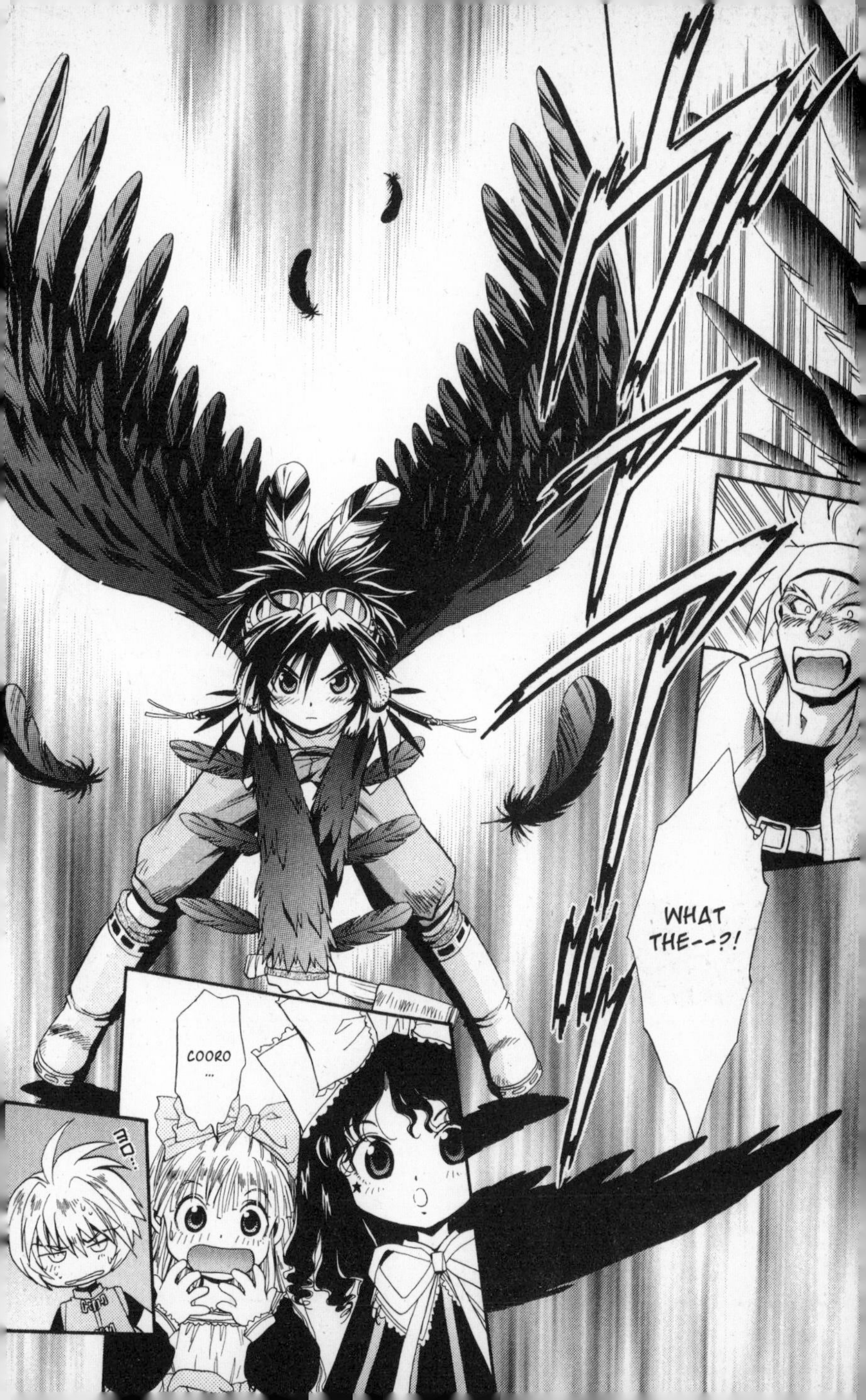
WHAT THE--?!
COORO ...
MO...

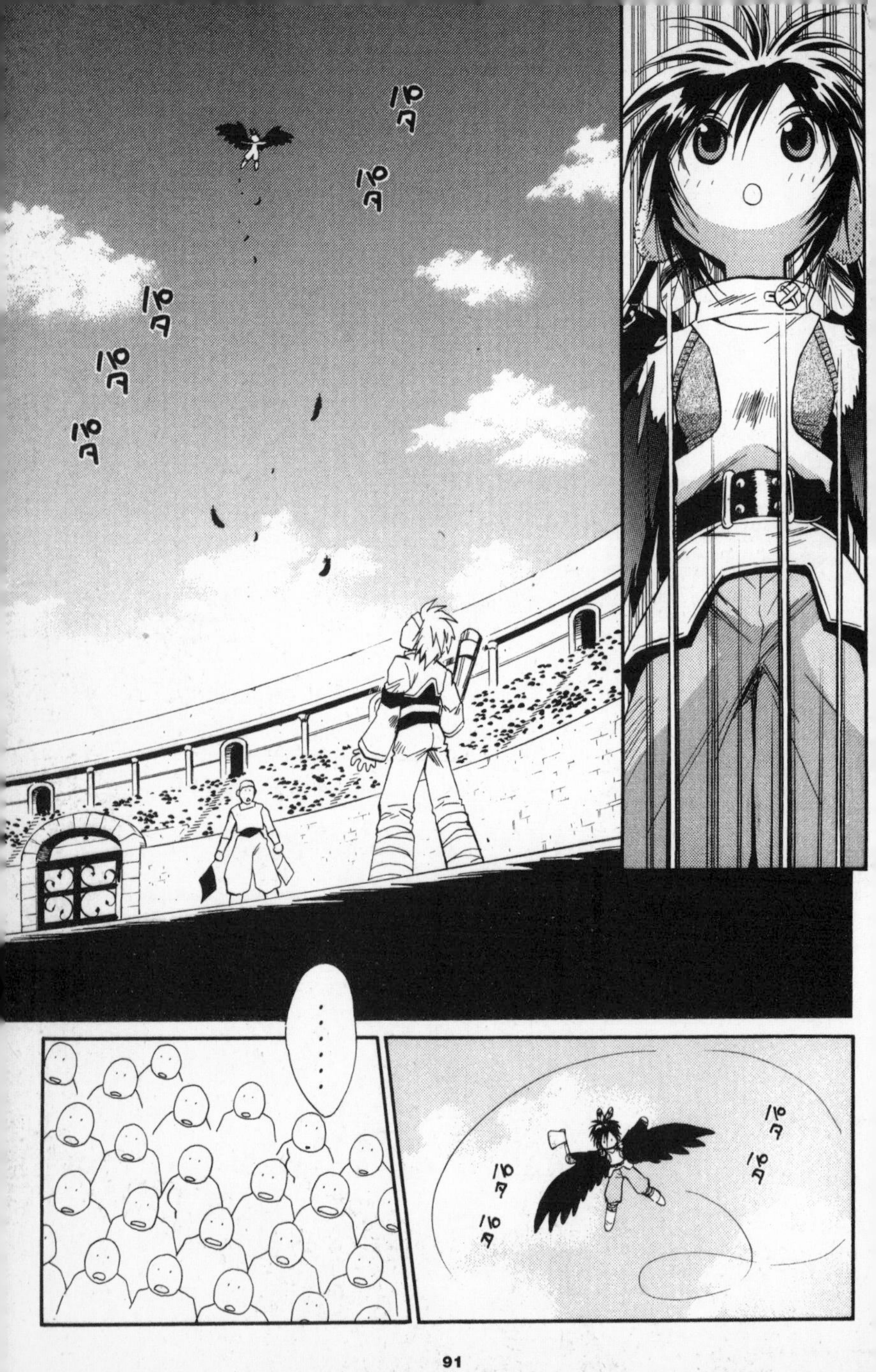
パタ
パタ
パタ
パタ
パタ
パタ
パタ
パタ
パタ
……

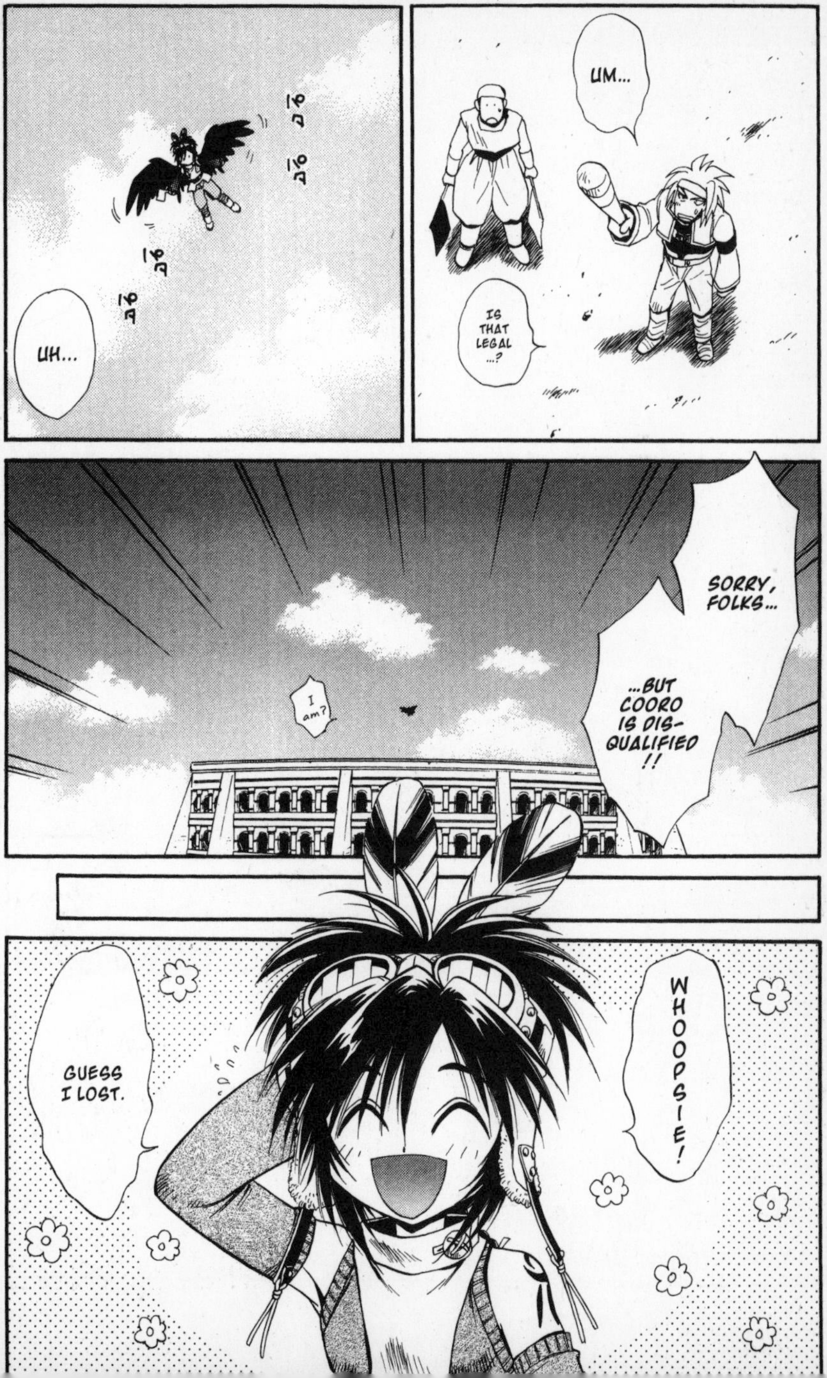
UM...
IS THAT LEGAL...?
UH...
SORRY, FOLKS...
...BUT COORO IS DIS-QUALIFIED!!
I am?
WHOOPSIE!
GUESS I LOST.

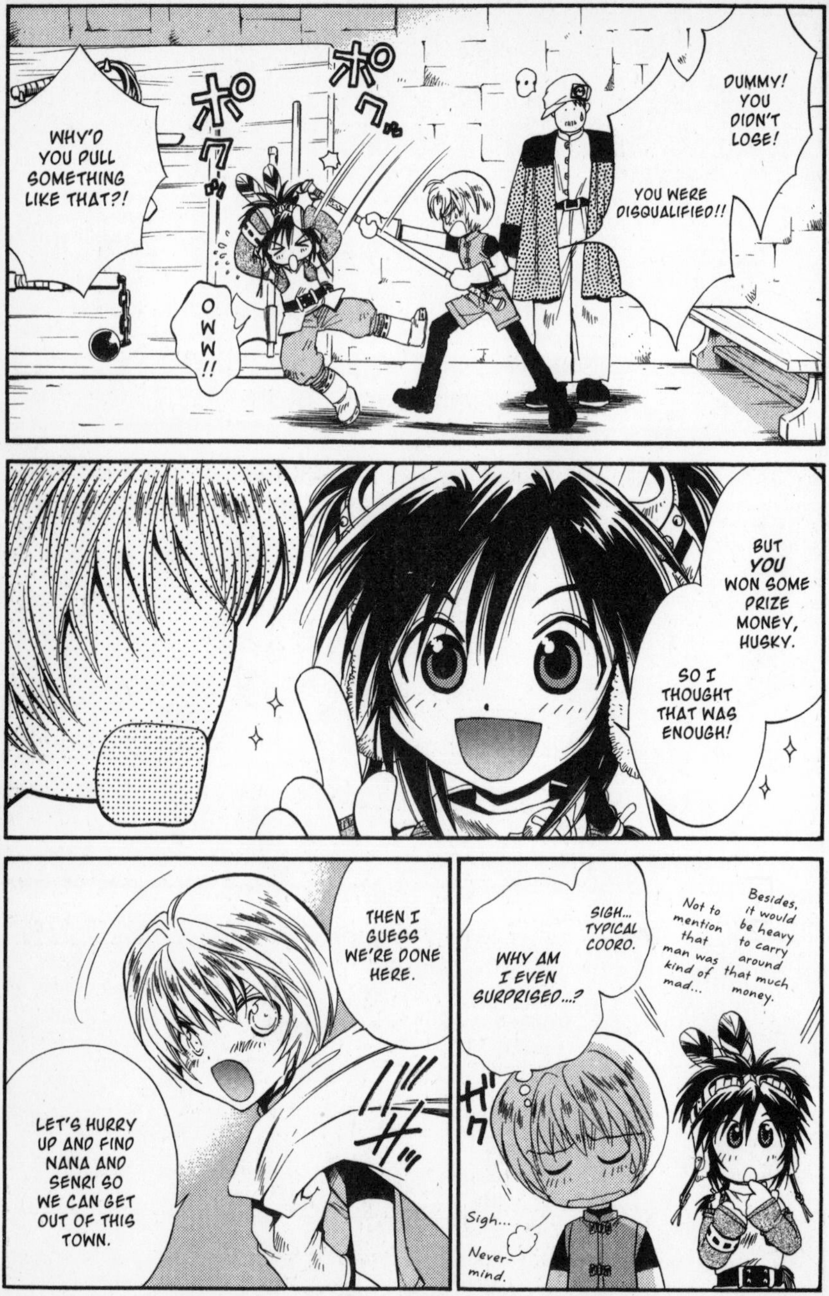
DUMMY! YOU DIDN'T LOSE!
YOU WERE DISQUALIFIED!!
ポク
ポク
WHY'D YOU PULL SOMETHING LIKE THAT?!
OWW!!
BUT *YOU* WON SOME PRIZE MONEY, HUSKY.
SO I THOUGHT THAT WAS ENOUGH!
Besides, it would be heavy to carry around that much money.
Not to mention that man was kind of mad...
SIGH... TYPICAL COORO.
WHY AM I EVEN SURPRISED...?
ギク
Sigh...
Never-mind.
THEN I GUESS WE'RE DONE HERE.
ガッ
LET'S HURRY UP AND FIND NANA AND SENRI SO WE CAN GET OUT OF THIS TOWN.

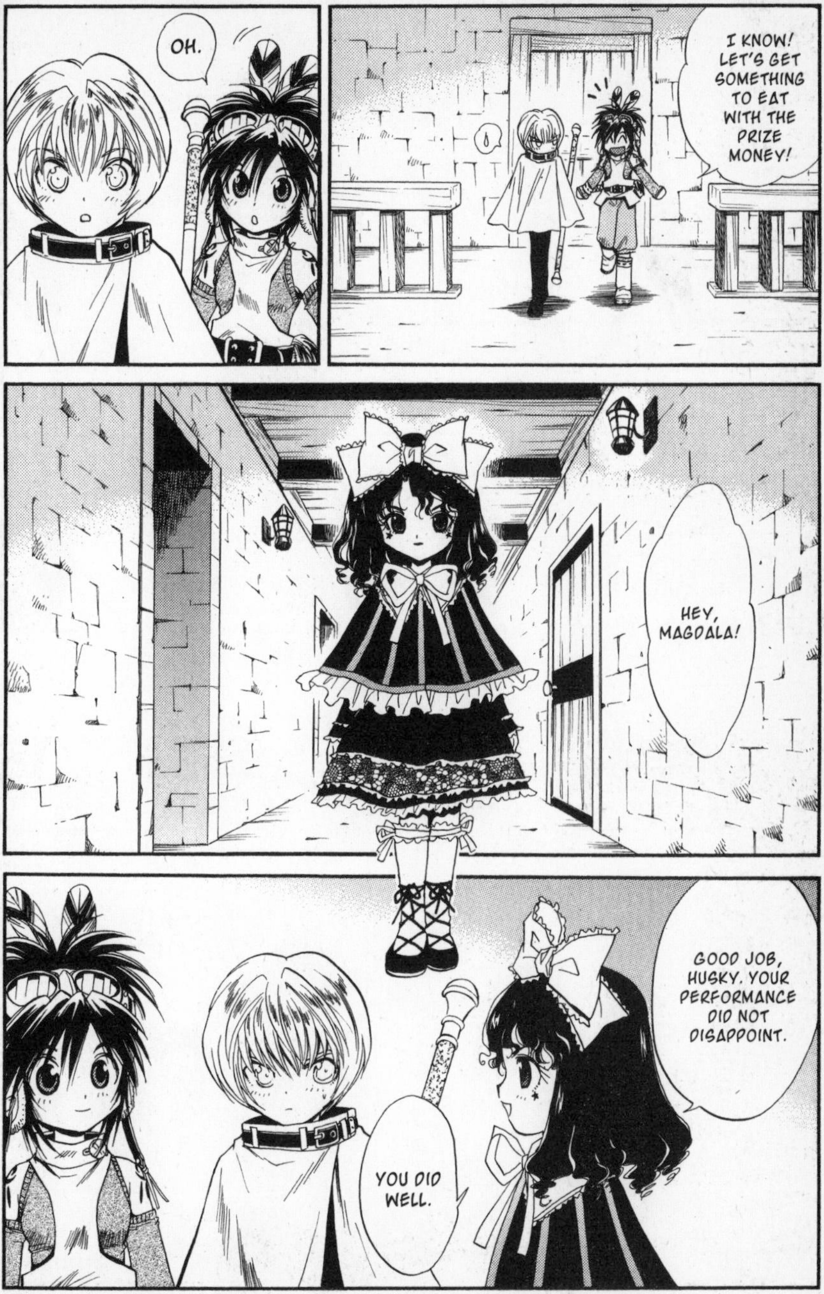
I KNOW! LET'S GET SOMETHING TO EAT WITH THE PRIZE MONEY!
OH.
HEY, MAGDALA!
GOOD JOB, HUSKY. YOUR PERFORMANCE DID NOT DISAPPOINT.
YOU DID WELL.

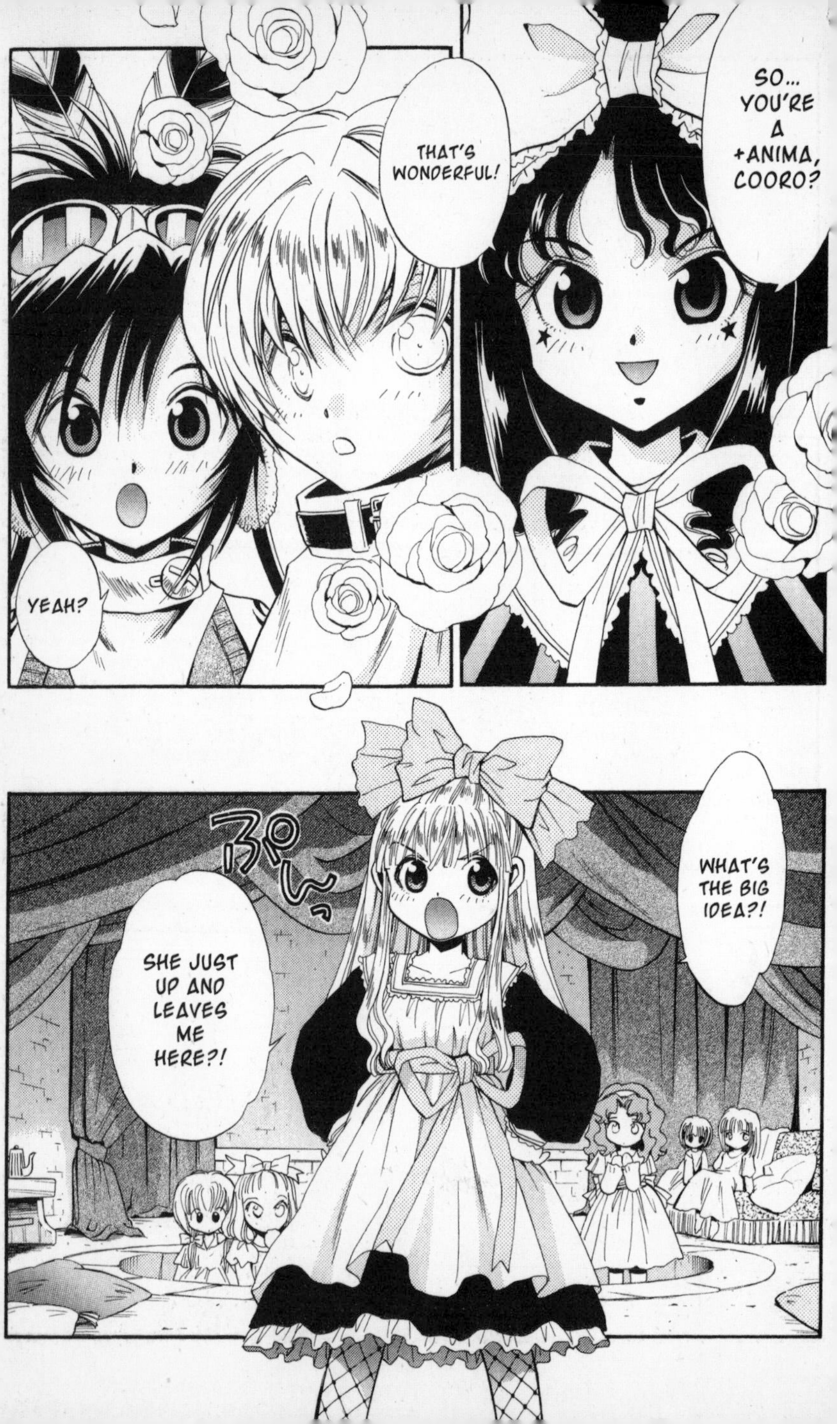
SO... YOU'RE A +ANIMA, COORO?
THAT'S WONDERFUL!
YEAH?
WHAT'S THE BIG IDEA?!
SHE JUST UP AND LEAVES ME HERE?!

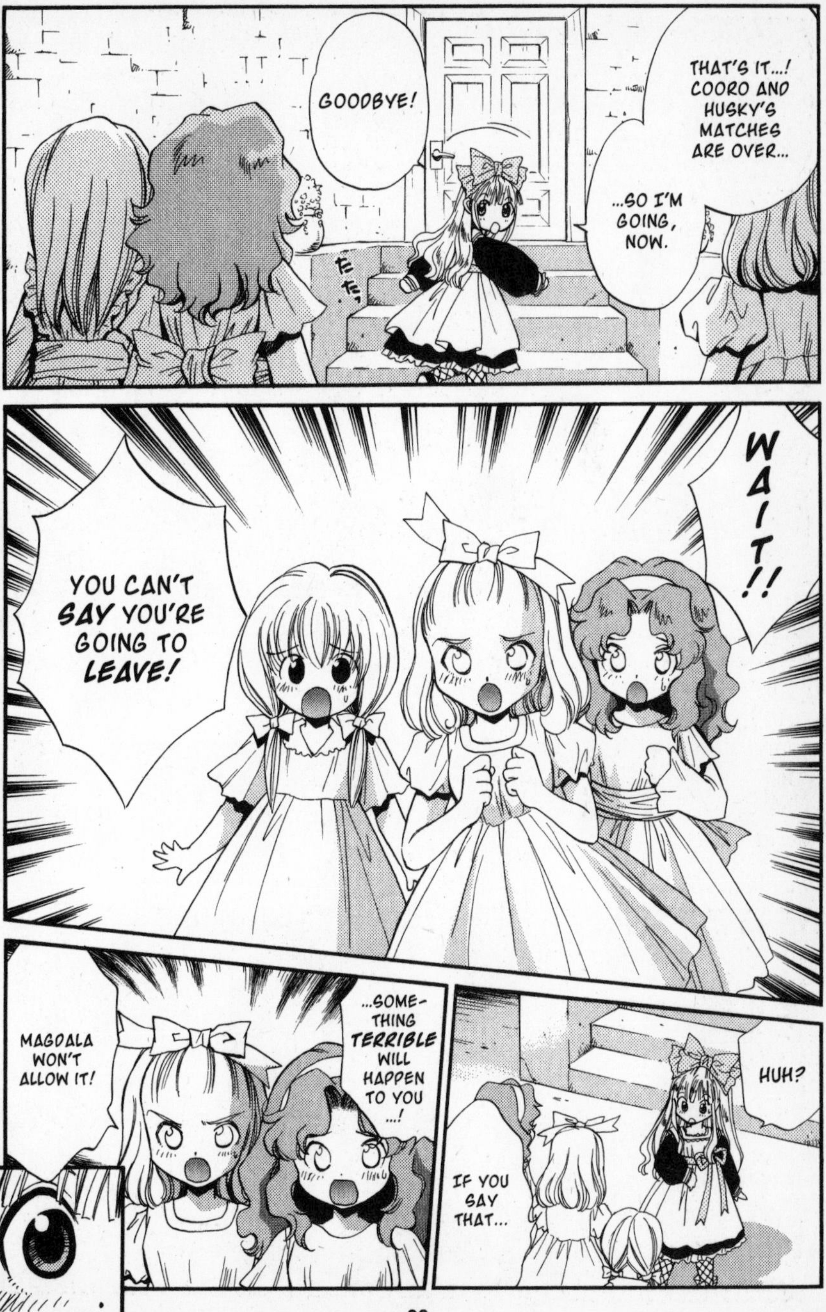
THAT'S IT...! COORO AND HUSKY'S MATCHES ARE OVER...
...SO I'M GOING, NOW.
GOODBYE!
たた
WAIT!!
YOU CAN'T *SAY* YOU'RE GOING TO *LEAVE!*
HUH?
IF YOU SAY THAT...
...SOMETHING *TERRIBLE* WILL HAPPEN TO YOU ...!
MAGDALA WON'T ALLOW IT!

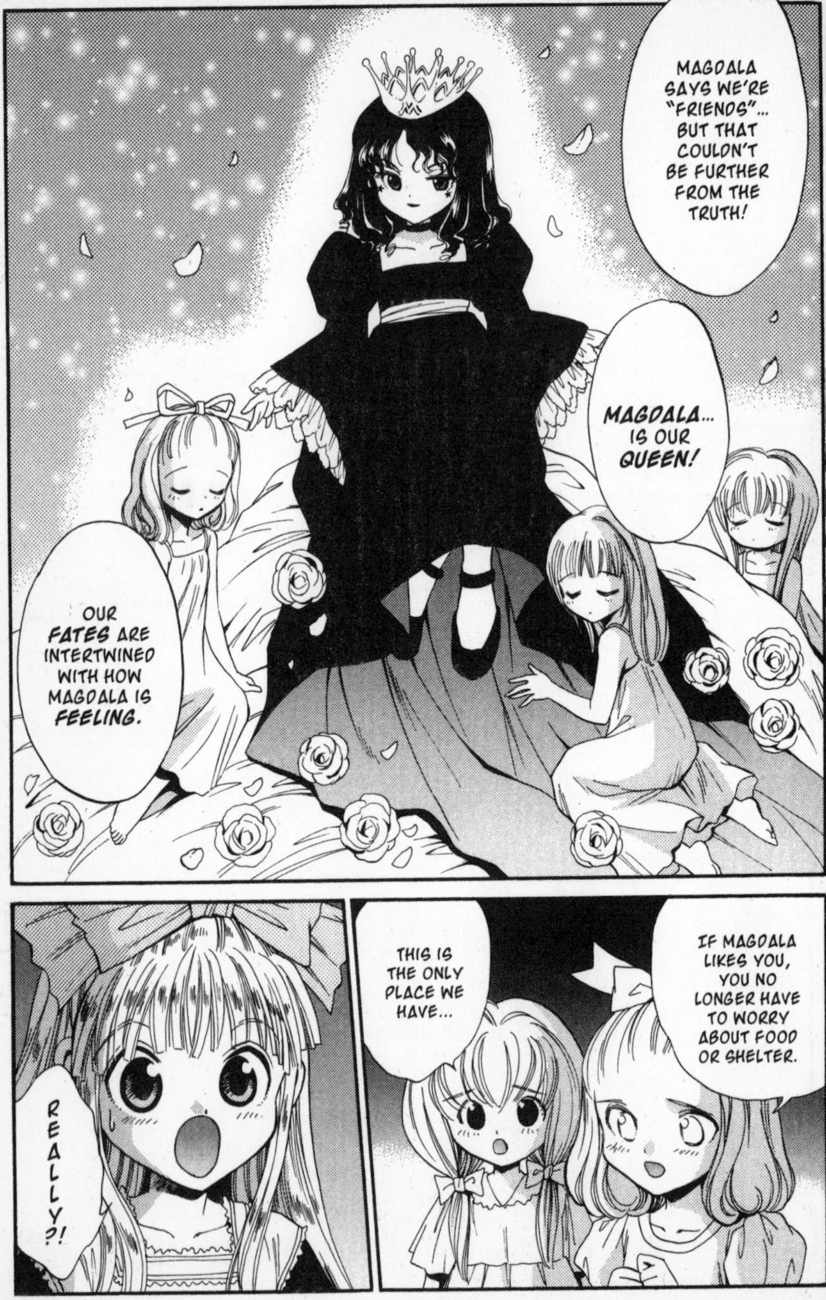
MAGDALA SAYS WE'RE "FRIENDS"... BUT THAT COULDN'T BE FURTHER FROM THE TRUTH!
MAGDALA... IS OUR QUEEN!
OUR FATES ARE INTERTWINED WITH HOW MAGDALA IS FEELING.
IF MAGDALA LIKES YOU, YOU NO LONGER HAVE TO WORRY ABOUT FOOD OR SHELTER.
THIS IS THE ONLY PLACE WE HAVE...
REALLY?!

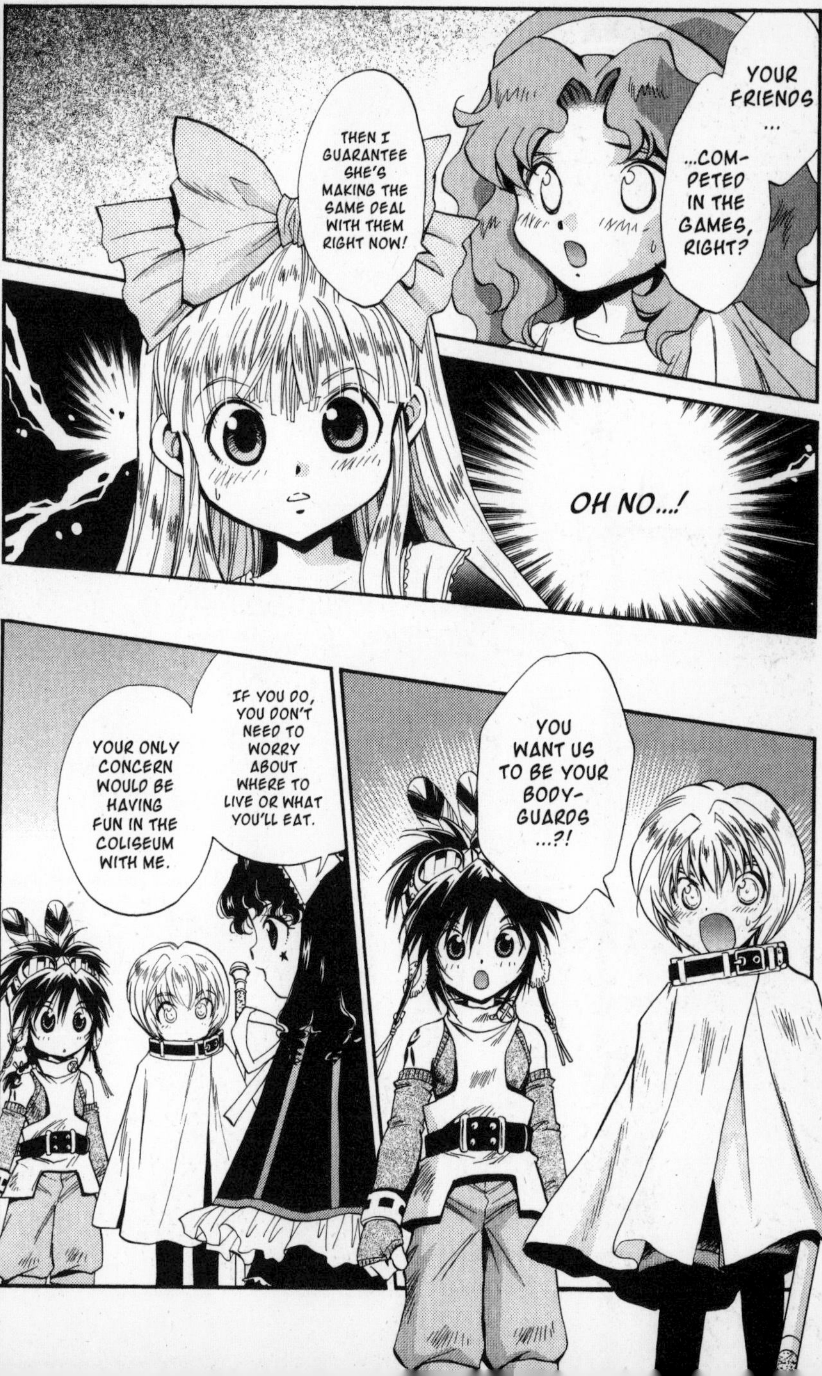
YOUR FRIENDS ... ...COMPETED IN THE GAMES, RIGHT?
THEN I GUARANTEE SHE'S MAKING THE SAME DEAL WITH THEM RIGHT NOW!
OH NO...!
YOU WANT US TO BE YOUR BODY-GUARDS ...?!
IF YOU DO, YOU DON'T NEED TO WORRY ABOUT WHERE TO LIVE OR WHAT YOU'LL EAT.
YOUR ONLY CONCERN WOULD BE HAVING FUN IN THE COLISEUM WITH ME.

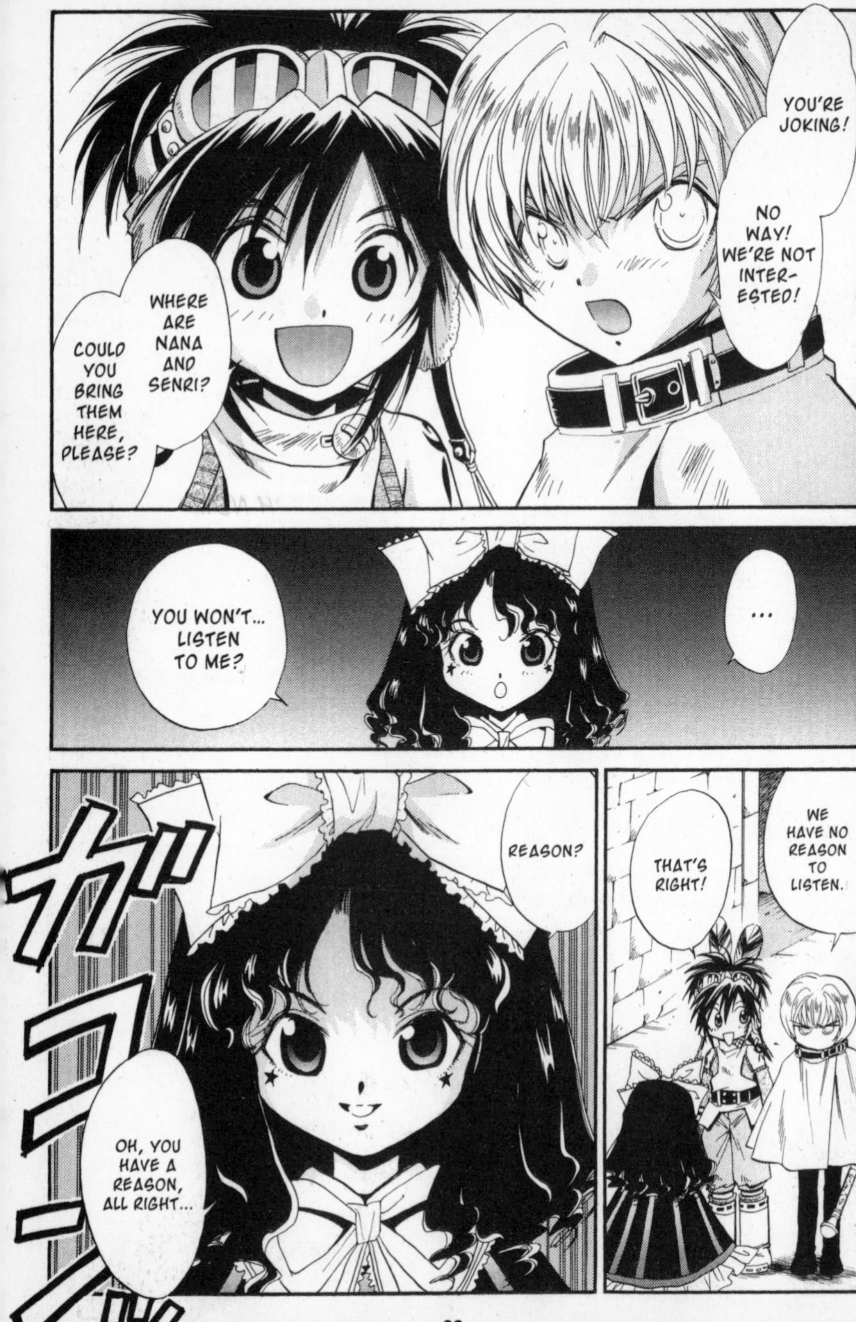
YOU'RE JOKING!
NO WAY! WE'RE NOT INTER-ESTED!
WHERE ARE NANA AND SENRI?
COULD YOU BRING THEM HERE, PLEASE?
...
YOU WON'T... LISTEN TO ME?
WE HAVE NO REASON TO LISTEN.
THAT'S RIGHT!
REASON?
OH, YOU HAVE A REASON, ALL RIGHT...

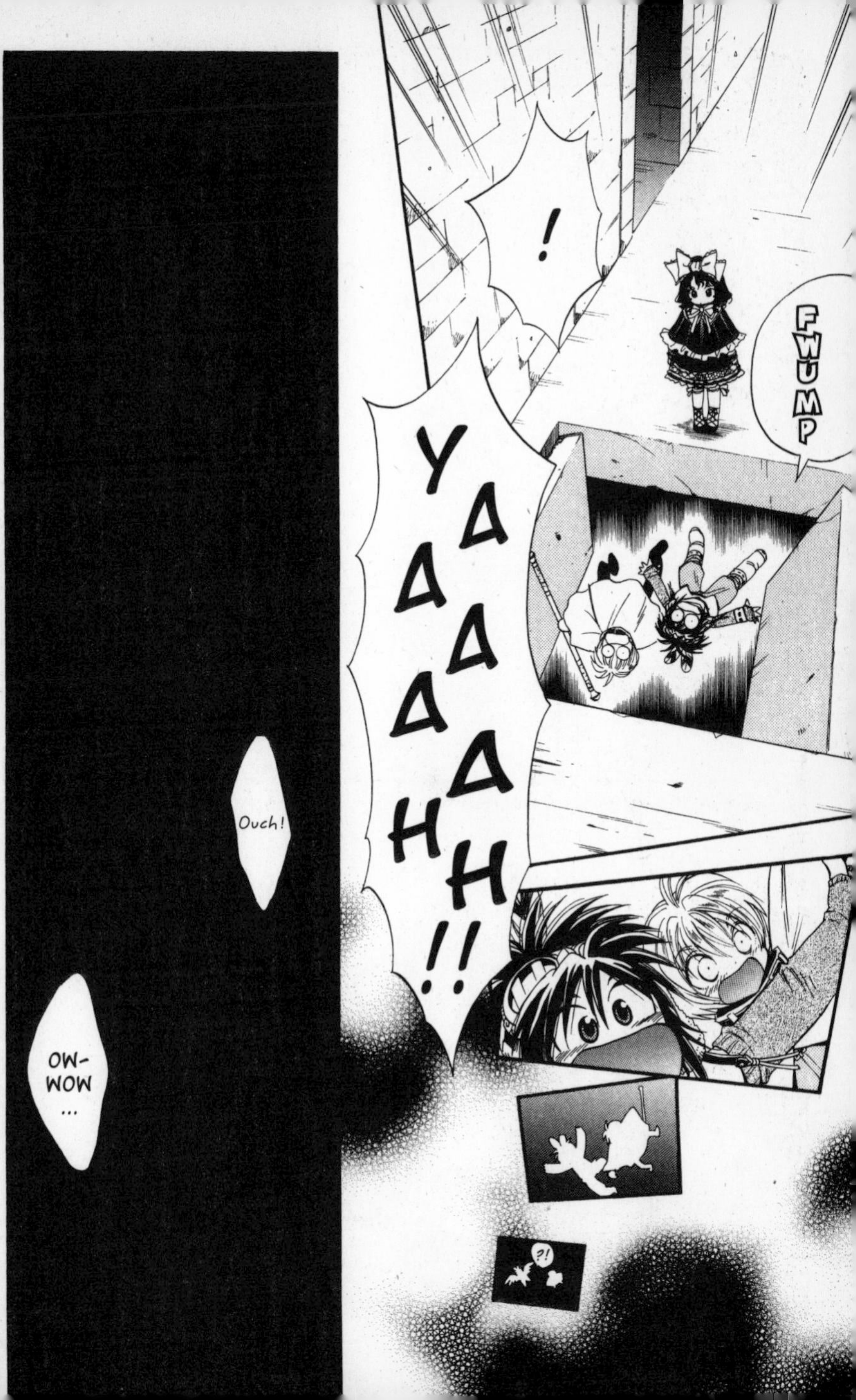

FWUMP
!
YAAAAAAH!!
?!
Ouch!
OW-WOW ...

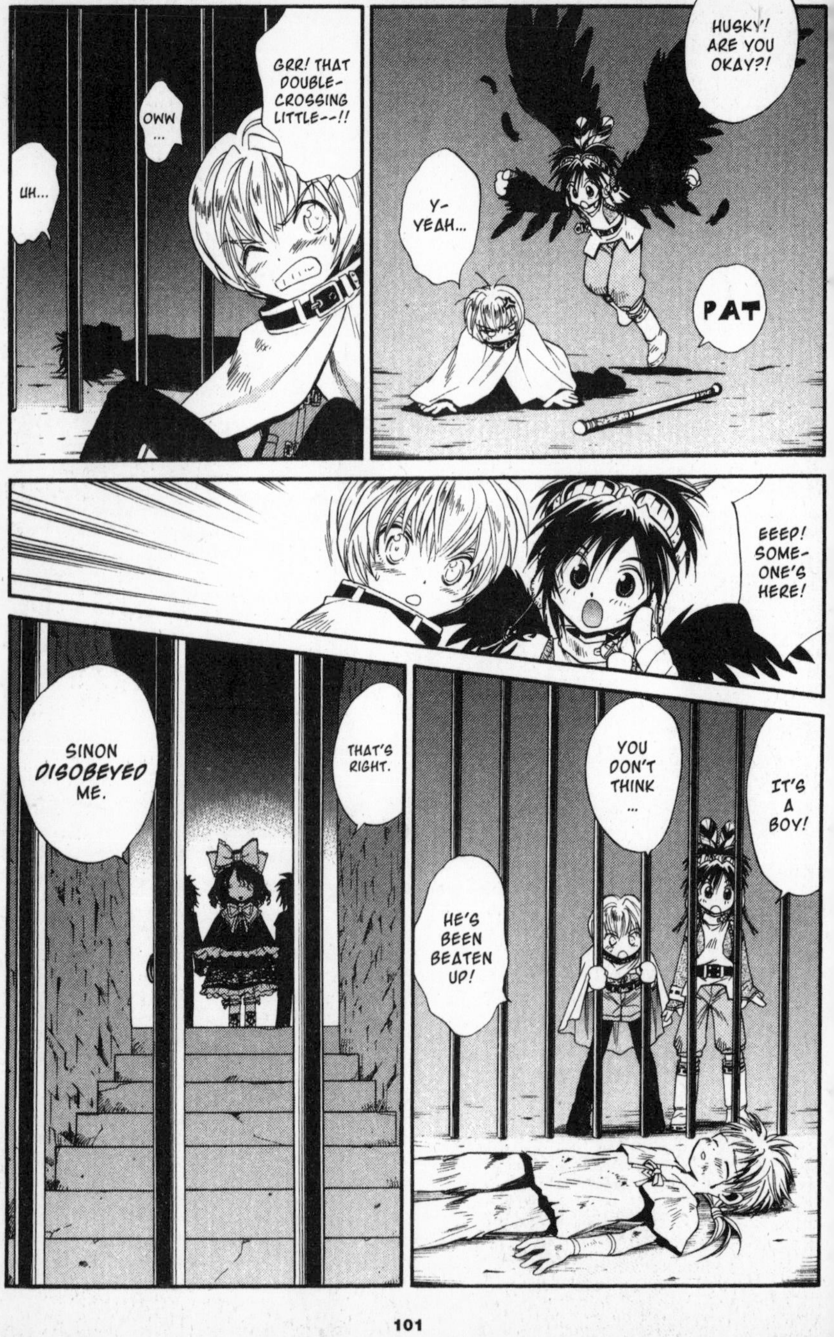
HUSKY! ARE YOU OKAY?!
Y-YEAH...
PAT
GRR! THAT DOUBLE-CROSSING LITTLE--!!
OWW ...
UH...
EEEP! SOME-ONE'S HERE!
IT'S A BOY!
YOU DON'T THINK ...
HE'S BEEN BEATEN UP!
THAT'S RIGHT.
SINON *DISOBEYED* ME.

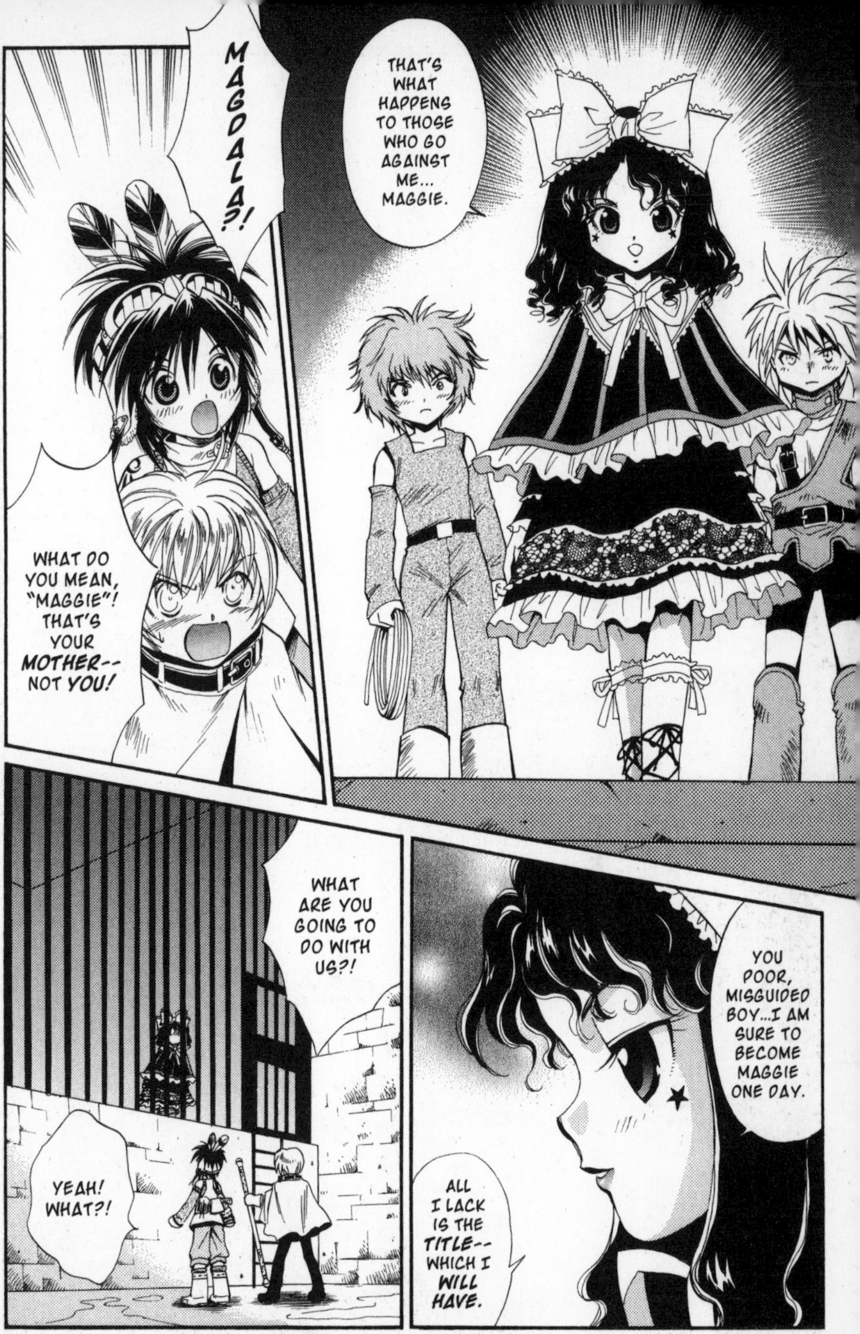
THAT'S WHAT HAPPENS TO THOSE WHO GO AGAINST ME... MAGGIE.
MAGDALA?!
WHAT DO YOU MEAN, "MAGGIE"! THAT'S YOUR MOTHER--NOT YOU!
YOU POOR, MISGUIDED BOY...I AM SURE TO BECOME MAGGIE ONE DAY.
ALL I LACK IS THE TITLE--WHICH I WILL HAVE.
WHAT ARE YOU GOING TO DO WITH US?!
YEAH! WHAT?!

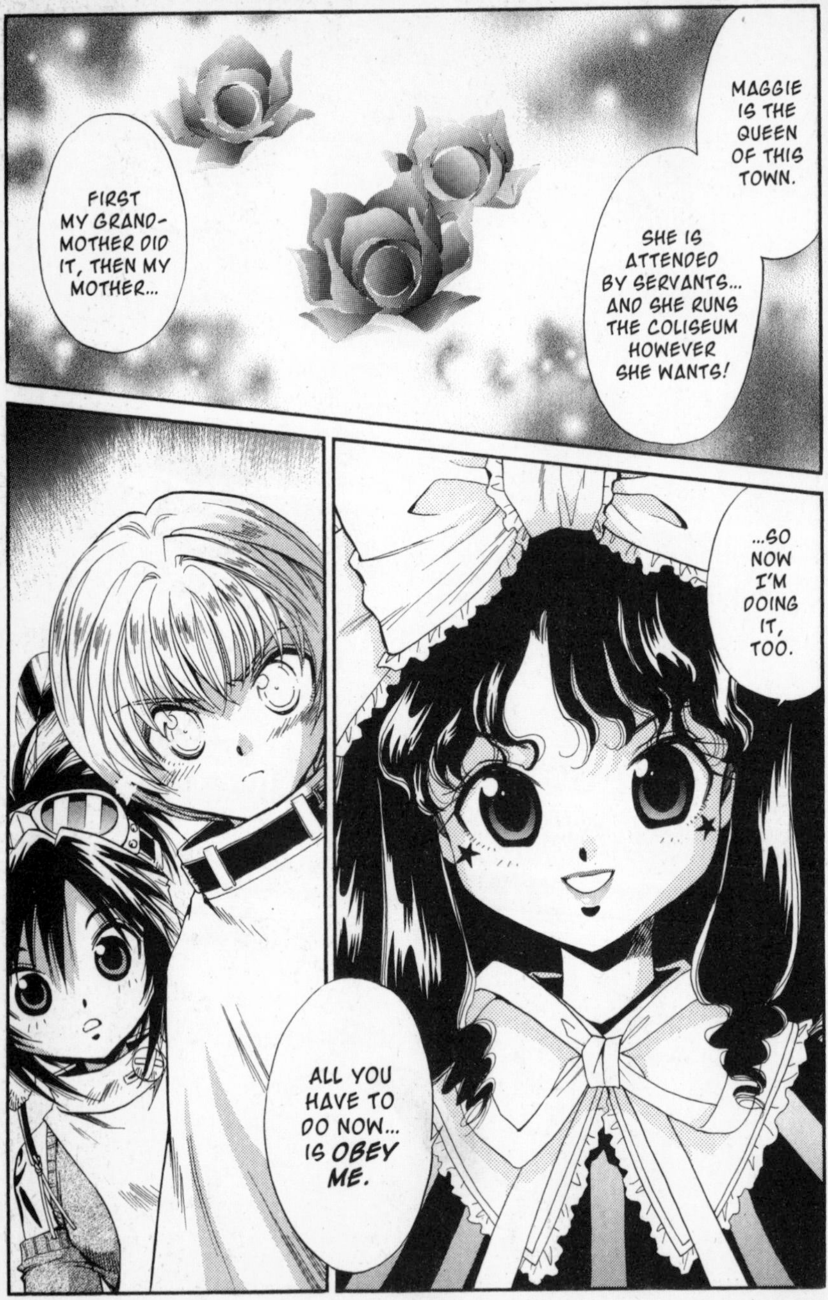
MAGGIE IS THE QUEEN OF THIS TOWN.
SHE IS ATTENDED BY SERVANTS... AND SHE RUNS THE COLISEUM HOWEVER SHE WANTS!
FIRST MY GRAND-MOTHER DID IT, THEN MY MOTHER...
...SO NOW I'M DOING IT, TOO.
ALL YOU HAVE TO DO NOW... IS *OBEY ME.*

The birth of Husky bank?!

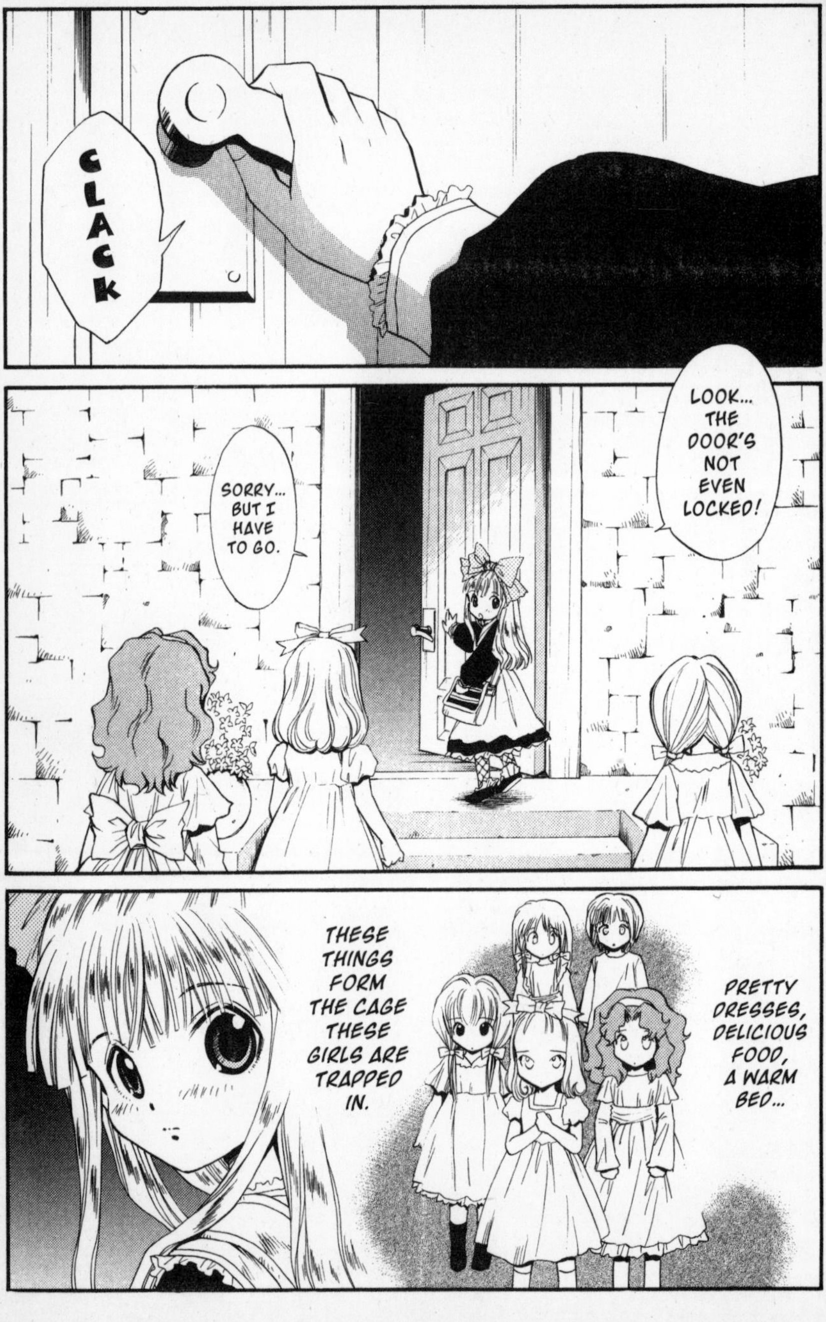
CLACK
LOOK... THE DOOR'S NOT EVEN LOCKED!
SORRY... BUT I HAVE TO GO.
PRETTY DRESSES, DELICIOUS FOOD, A WARM BED...
THESE THINGS FORM THE CAGE THESE GIRLS ARE TRAPPED IN.

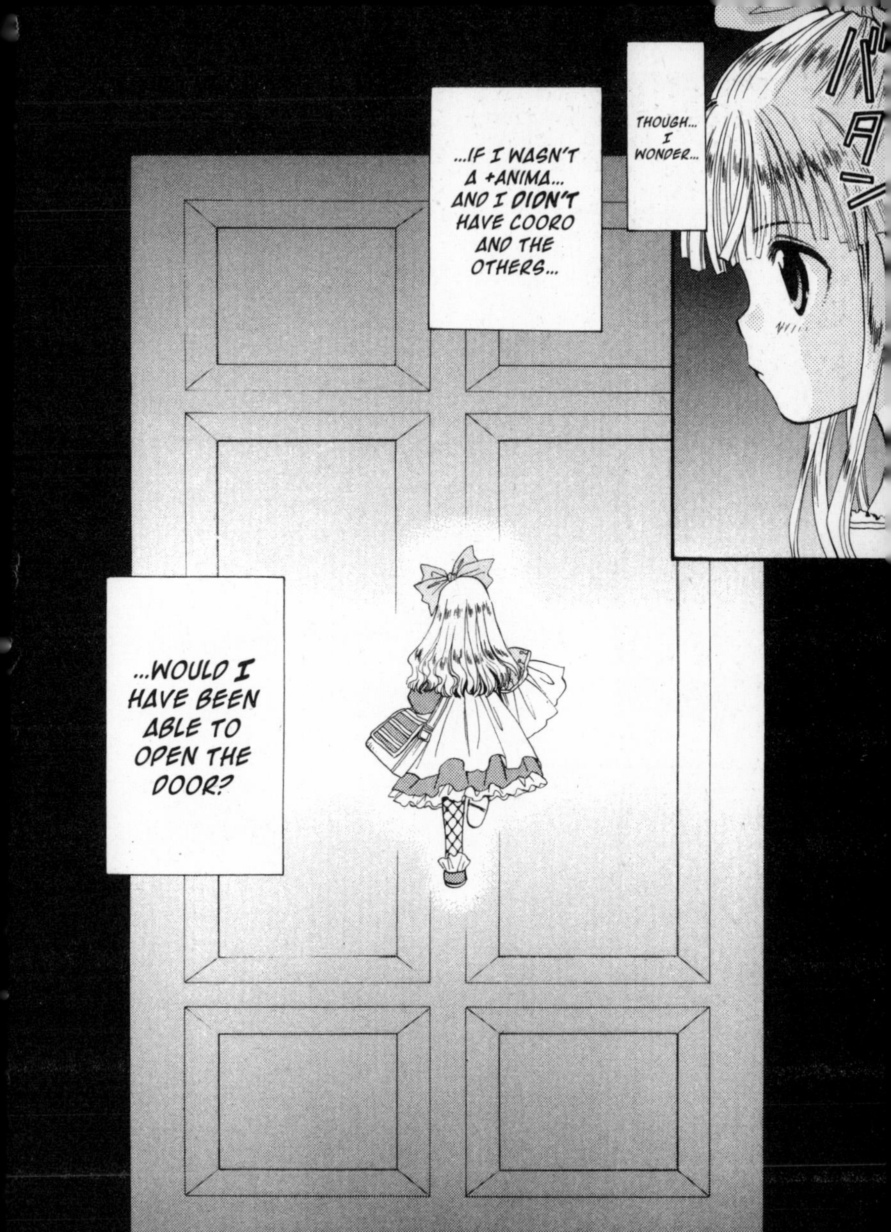
THOUGH... I WONDER...
...IF I WASN'T A +ANIMA... AND I DIDN'T HAVE COORO AND THE OTHERS...
...WOULD I HAVE BEEN ABLE TO OPEN THE DOOR?

Chapter 18: Maggie Coliseum—Part 4

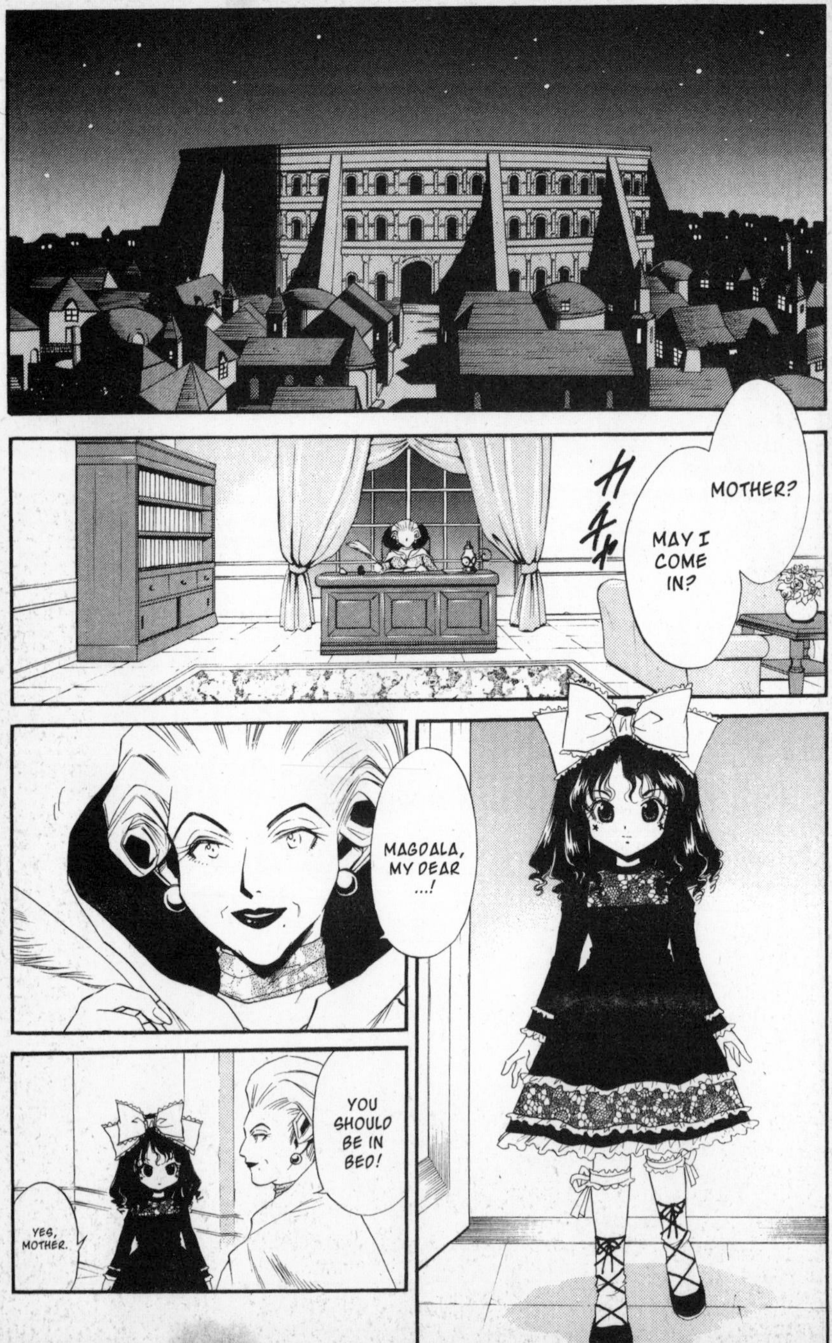
ガチャ
MOTHER? MAY I COME IN?
MAGDALA, MY DEAR ...!
YOU SHOULD BE IN BED!
YES, MOTHER.

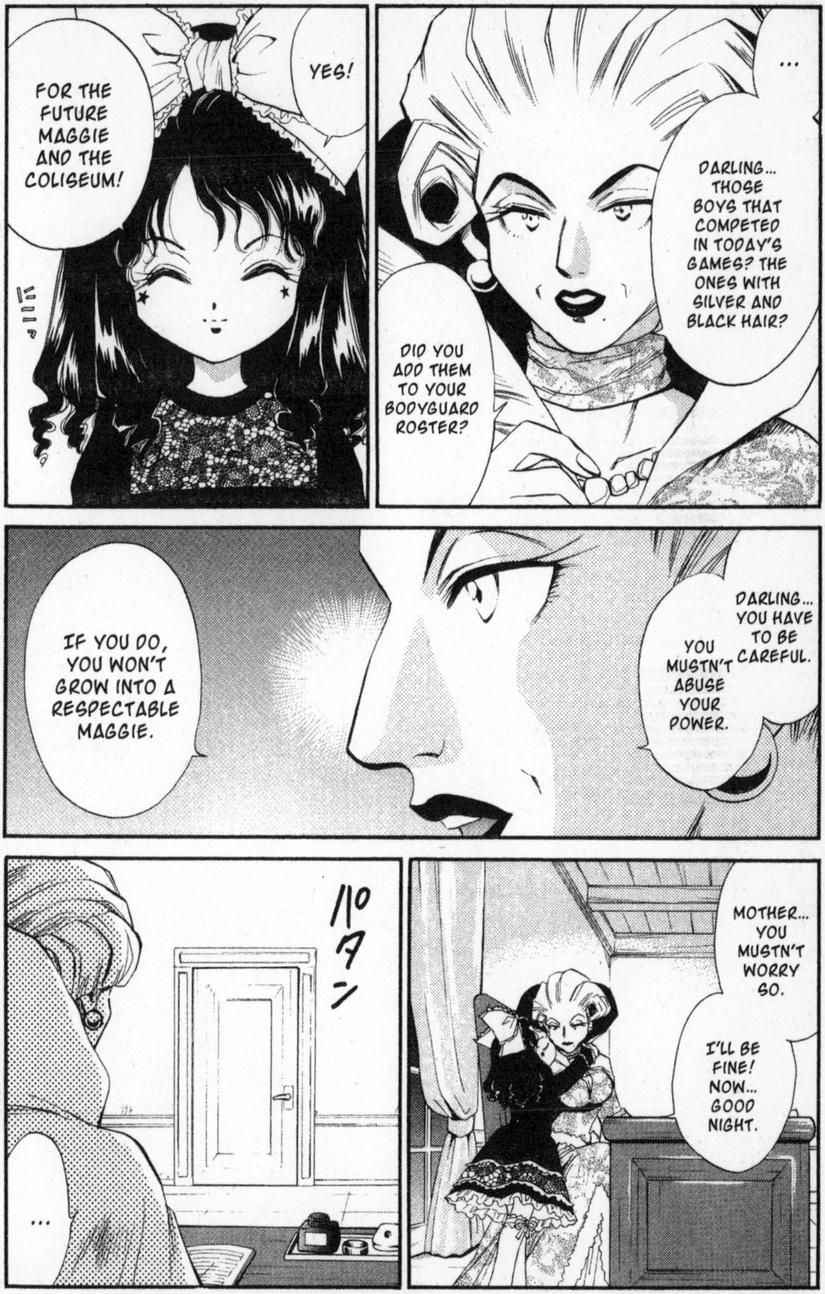
...
DARLING... THOSE BOYS THAT COMPETED IN TODAY'S GAMES? THE ONES WITH SILVER AND BLACK HAIR?
DID YOU ADD THEM TO YOUR BODYGUARD ROSTER?
YES!
FOR THE FUTURE MAGGIE AND THE COLISEUM!
DARLING... YOU HAVE TO BE CAREFUL.
YOU MUSTN'T ABUSE YOUR POWER.
IF YOU DO, YOU WON'T GROW INTO A RESPECTABLE MAGGIE.
MOTHER... YOU MUSTN'T WORRY SO.
I'LL BE FINE! NOW... GOOD NIGHT.
パタン
...

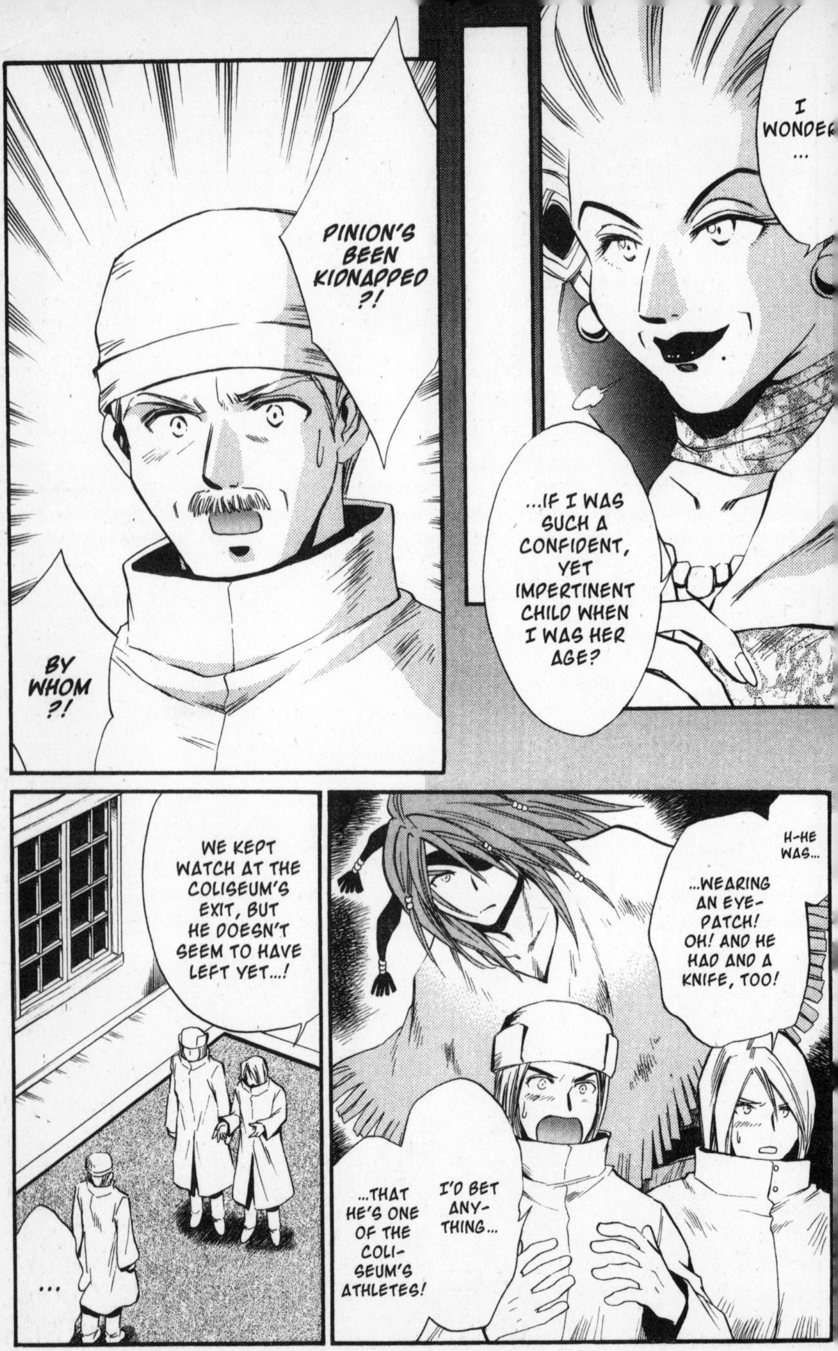
I WONDER...
...IF I WAS SUCH A CONFIDENT, YET IMPERTINENT CHILD WHEN I WAS HER AGE?
PINION'S BEEN KIDNAPPED?!
BY WHOM?!
H-HE WAS...
...WEARING AN EYE-PATCH! OH! AND HE HAD AND A KNIFE, TOO!
I'D BET ANY-THING...
...THAT HE'S ONE OF THE COLI-SEUM'S ATHLETES!
WE KEPT WATCH AT THE COLISEUM'S EXIT, BUT HE DOESN'T SEEM TO HAVE LEFT YET...!
...

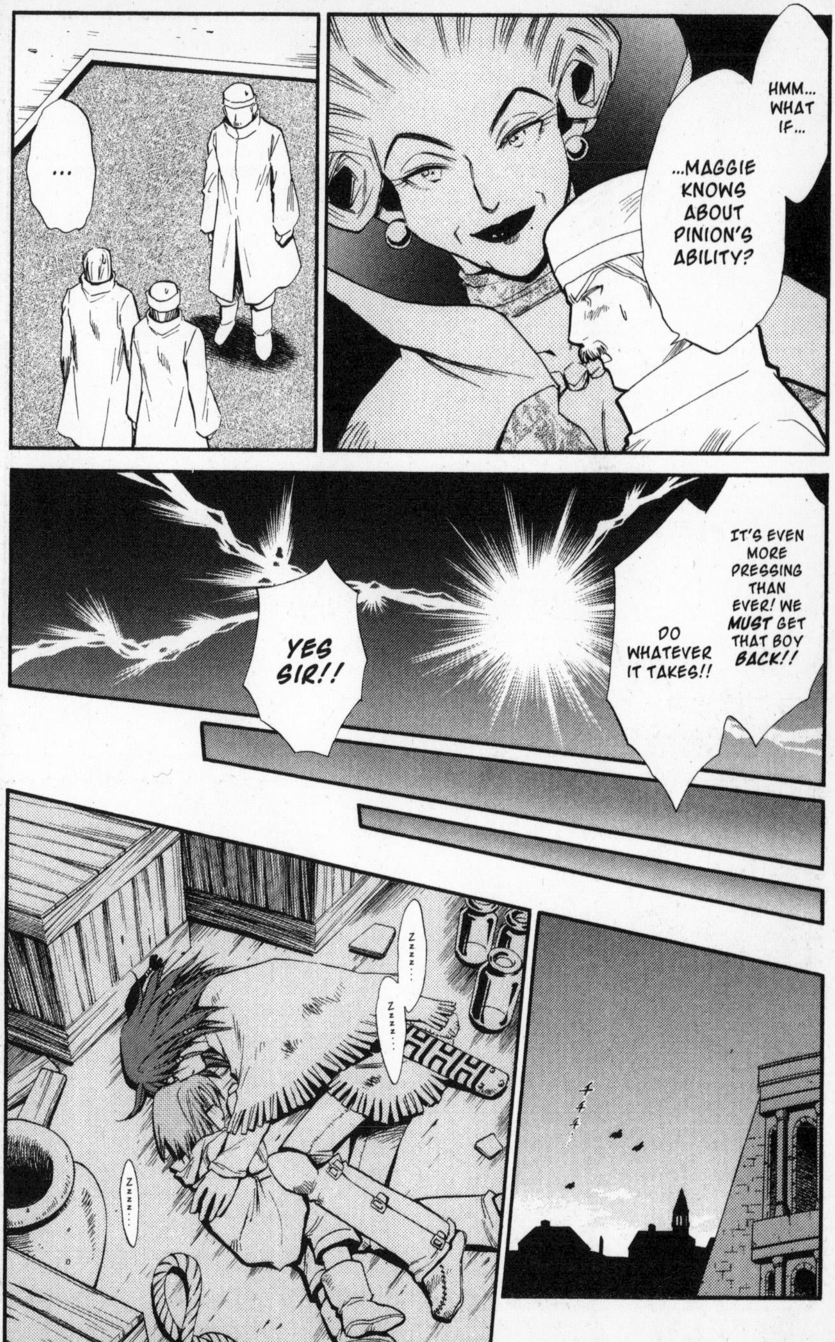
HMM... WHAT IF...
...MAGGIE KNOWS ABOUT PINION'S ABILITY?
...
IT'S EVEN MORE PRESSING THAN EVER! WE **MUST** GET THAT BOY **BACK!!**
DO WHATEVER IT TAKES!!
YES SIR!!
Zzzz...
Zzzz...
Zzzz...

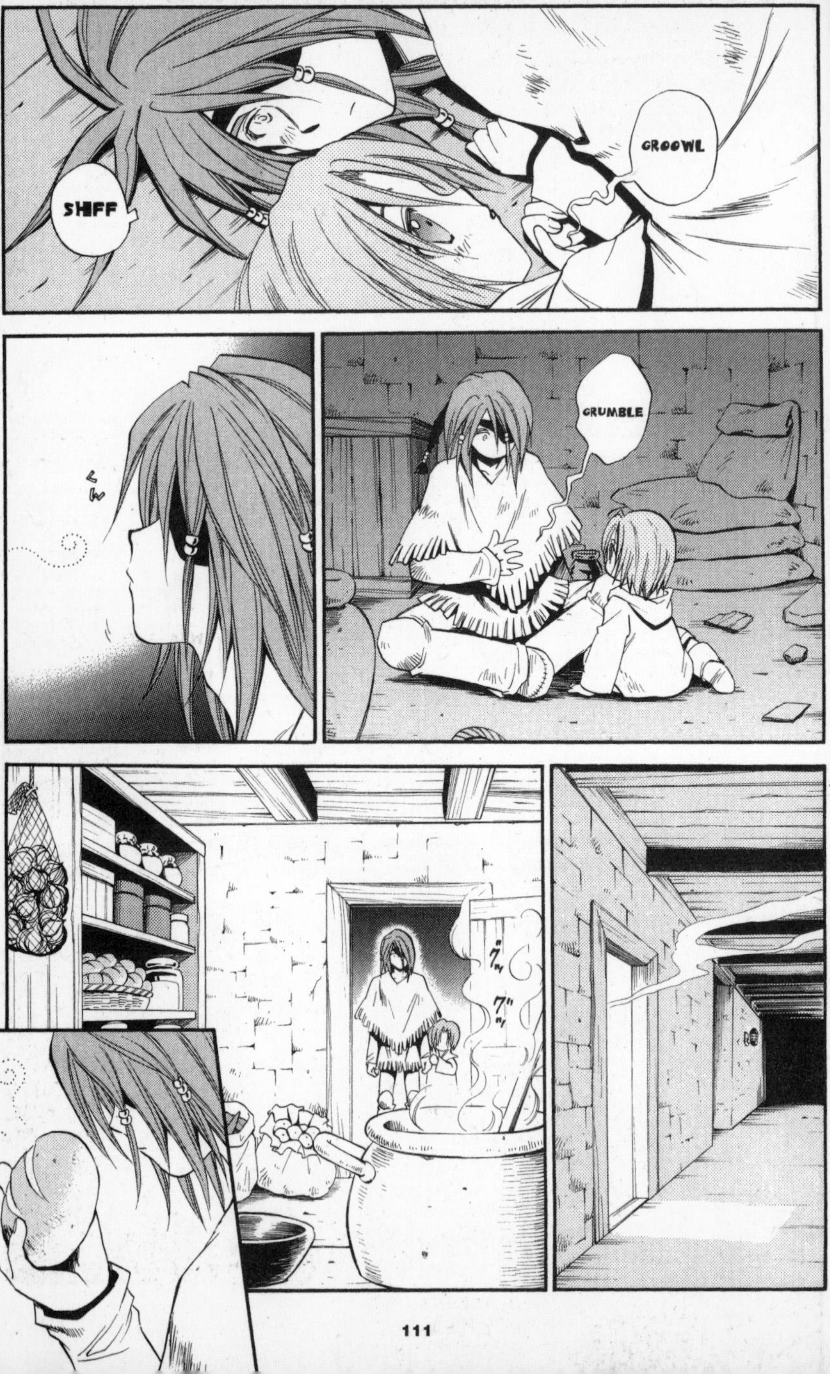
GROOWL
SHIFF
GRUMBLE

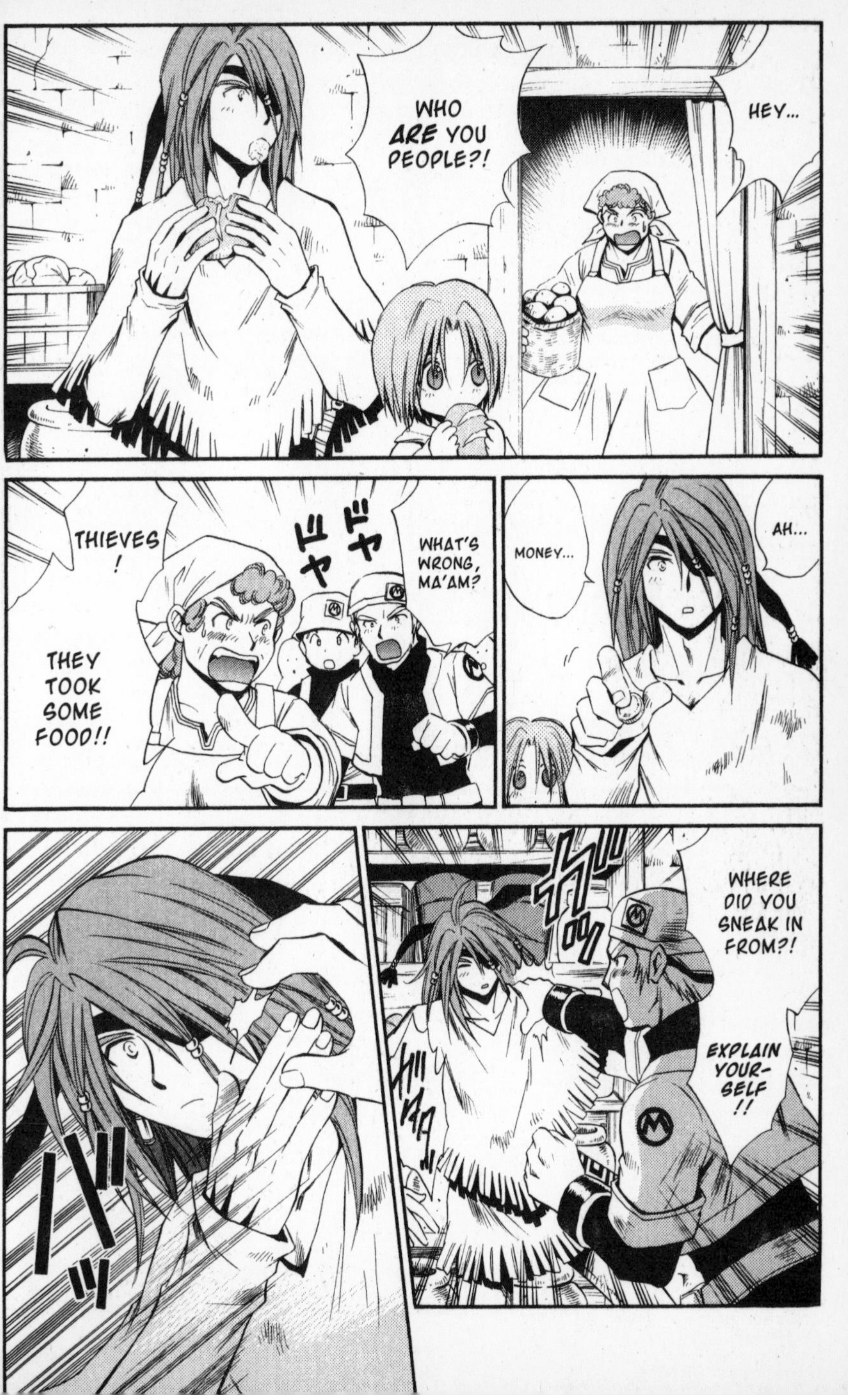
HEY...
WHO **ARE** YOU PEOPLE?!
AH...
MONEY...
WHAT'S WRONG, MA'AM?
ドヤドヤ
THIEVES!
THEY TOOK SOME FOOD!!
WHERE DID YOU SNEAK IN FROM?!
EXPLAIN YOURSELF!!

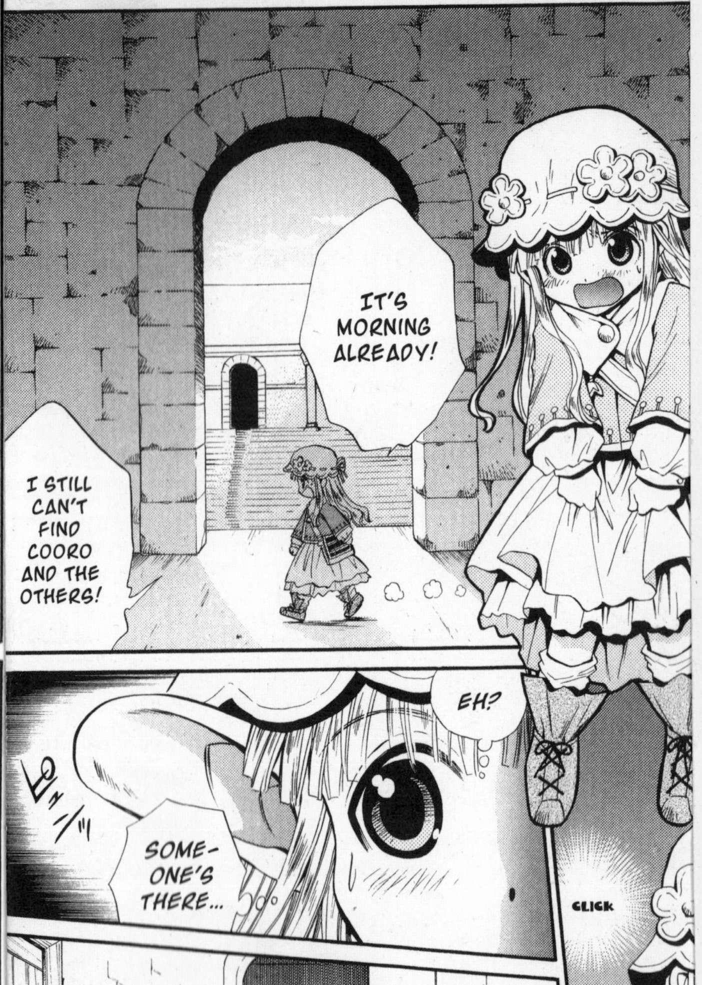

IT'S MORNING ALREADY!
I STILL CAN'T FIND COORO AND THE OTHERS!
EH?
SOME-ONE'S THERE...
CLICK
CLICK

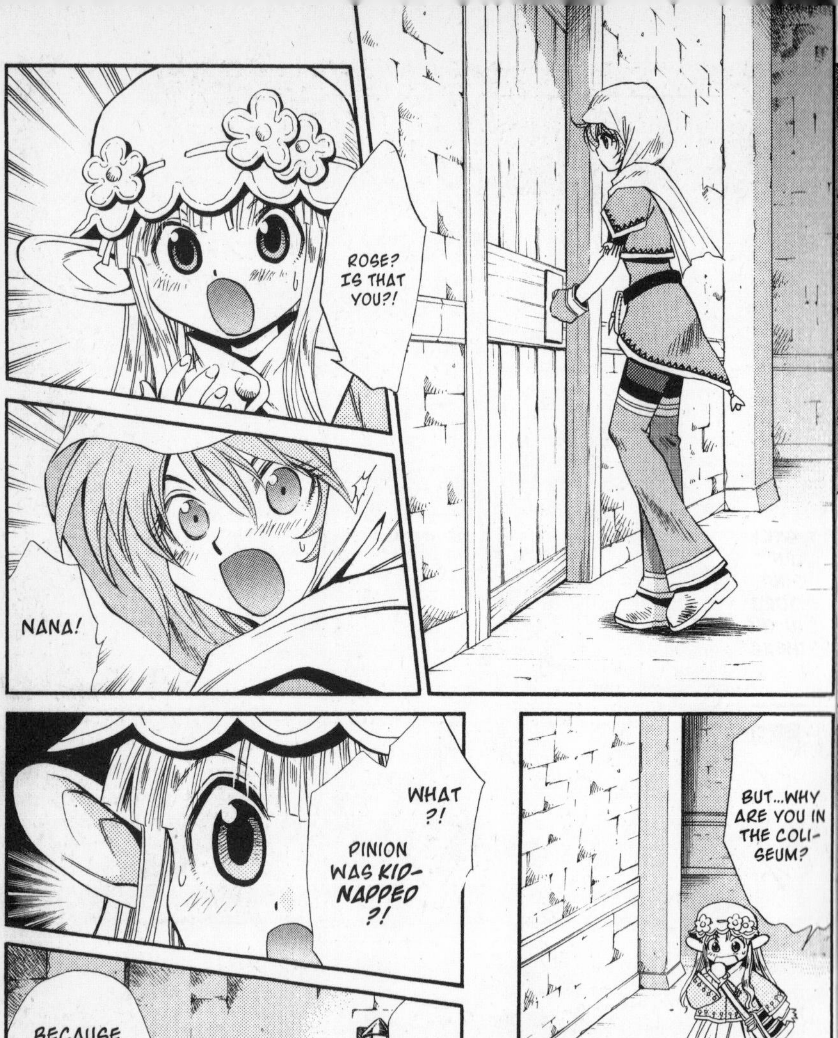

ROSE? IS THAT YOU?!
NANA!
BUT...WHY ARE YOU IN THE COLI-SEUM?
AH...W-WELL...IT'S ABOUT MY BROTHER ...
WHAT ?!
PINION WAS KID-NAPPED ?!
BUT... WHY?
BECAUSE PINION HAS A RATHER **UNUSUAL** ABILITY...

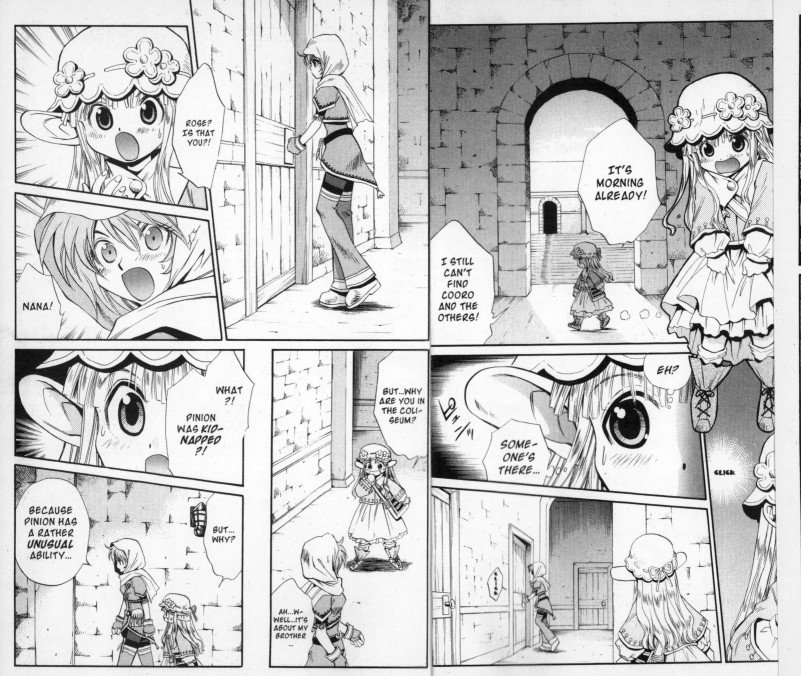

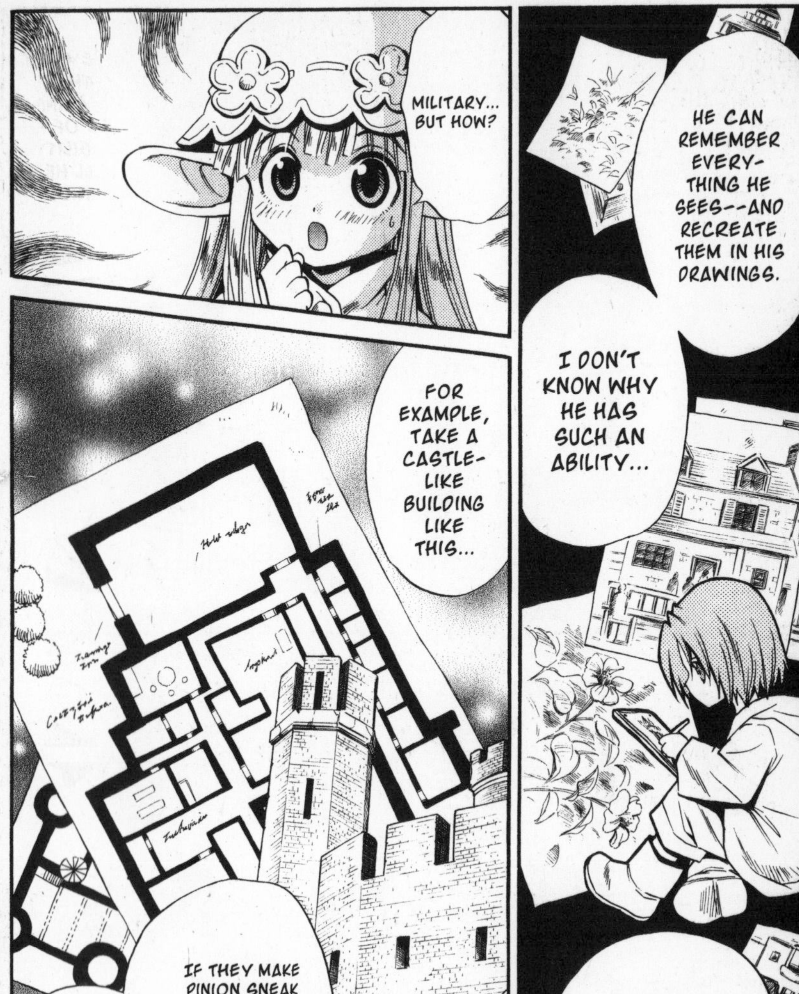
HE CAN REMEMBER EVERYTHING HE SEES--AND RECREATE THEM IN HIS DRAWINGS.
I DON'T KNOW WHY HE HAS SUCH AN ABILITY...
ASTARIAN RESEARCHERS ARE TRYING TO USE IT FOR MILITARY PURPOSES...!
MILITARY... BUT HOW?
FOR EXAMPLE, TAKE A CASTLE-LIKE BUILDING LIKE THIS...
IF THEY MAKE PINION SNEAK IN AND DRAW A MAP, THEN THEY WOULD HAVE A GREAT ADVANTAGE IN CAPTURING IT.
FROM A SIMPLE BLUEPRINT DRAWN BY PINION, YOU CAN FIGURE OUT HOW MANY SOLDIERS THERE ARE AND HOW STRONG--OR WEAK--THE CASTLE IS.

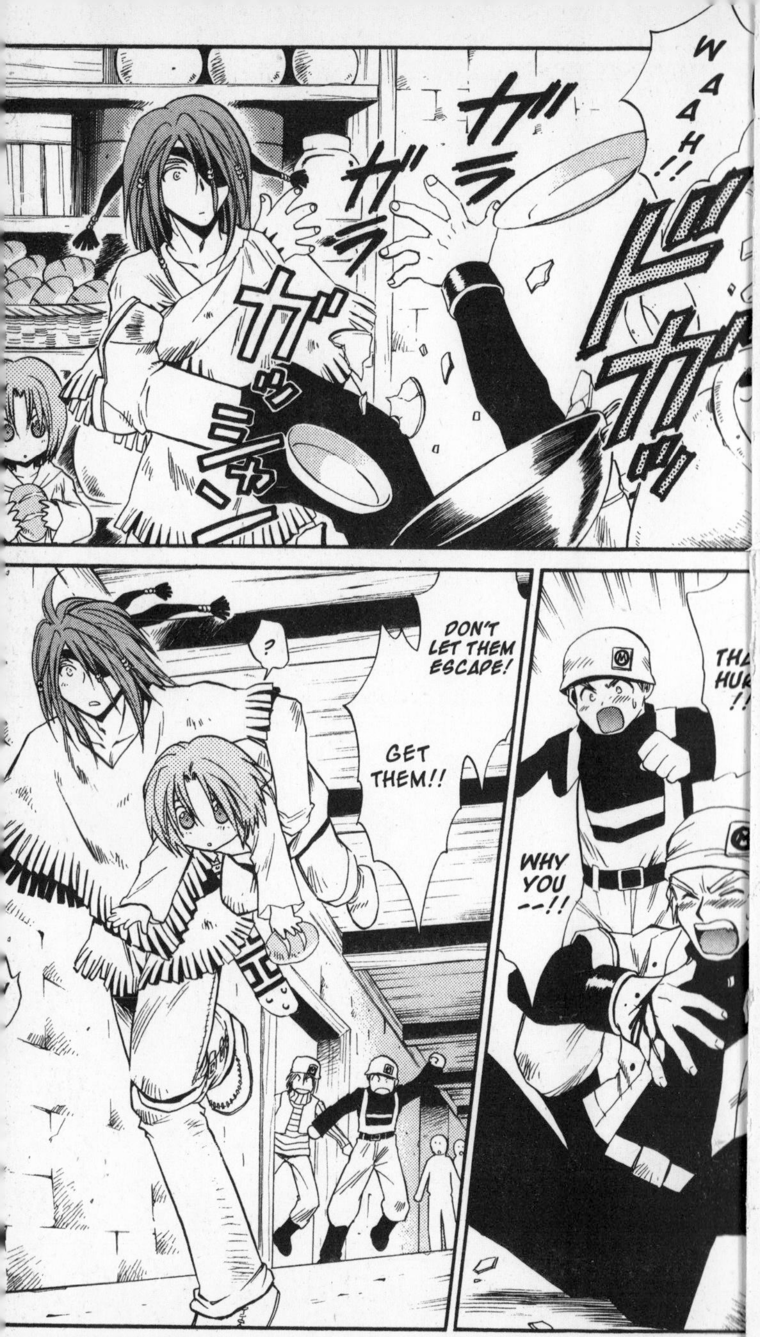
WAAAH!!
WHY YOU--!!
DON'T LET THEM ESCAPE!
GET THEM!!
?

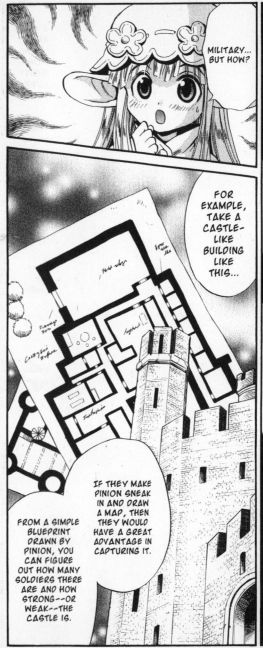

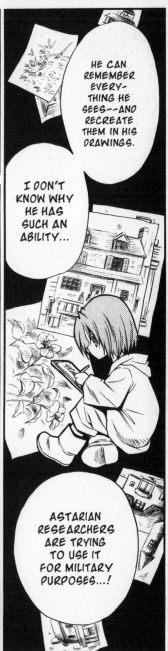

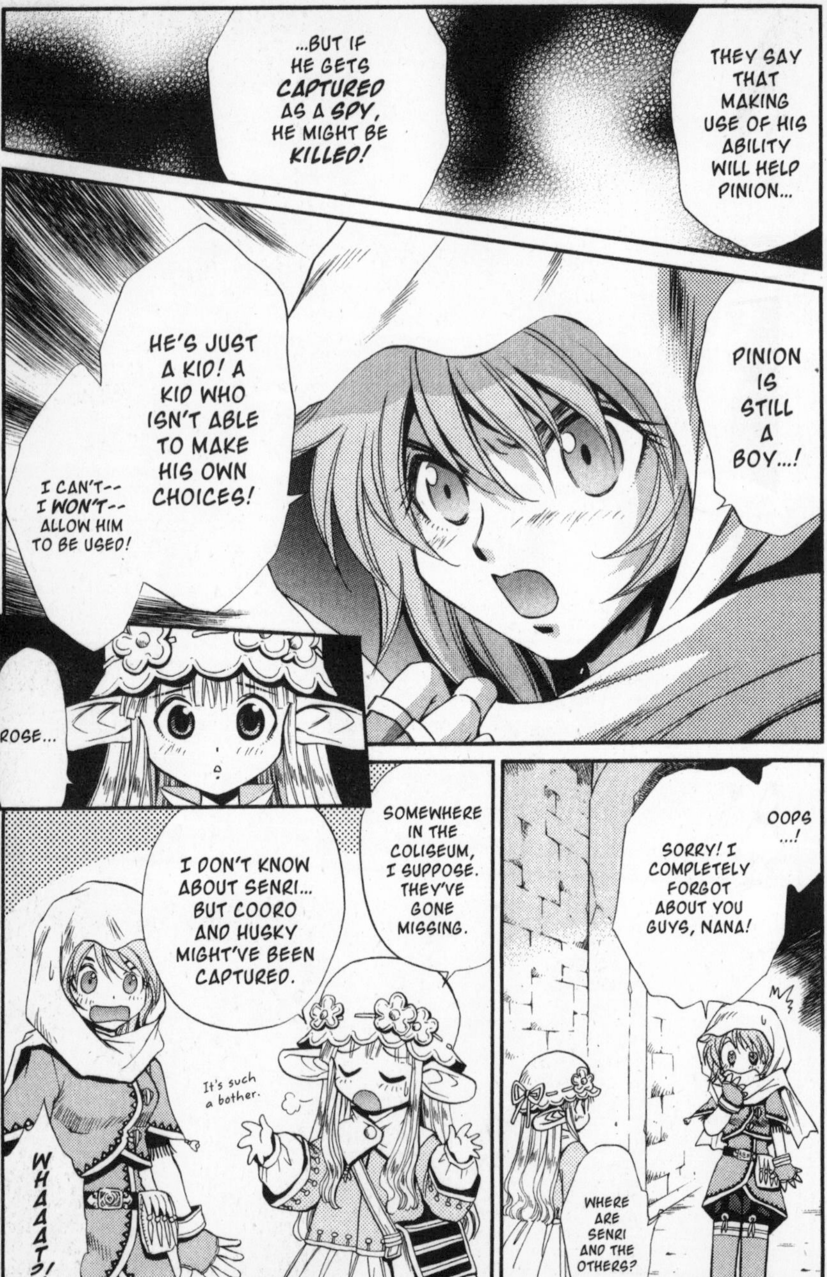
THEY SAY THAT MAKING USE OF HIS ABILITY WILL HELP PINION...
...BUT IF HE GETS CAPTURED AS A SPY, HE MIGHT BE KILLED!
PINION IS STILL A BOY...!
HE'S JUST A KID! A KID WHO ISN'T ABLE TO MAKE HIS OWN CHOICES!
I CAN'T-- I WON'T-- ALLOW HIM TO BE USED!
ROSE...
OOPS...!
SORRY! I COMPLETELY FORGOT ABOUT YOU GUYS, NANA!
WHERE ARE SENRI AND THE OTHERS?
SOMEWHERE IN THE COLISEUM, I SUPPOSE. THEY'VE GONE MISSING.
I DON'T KNOW ABOUT SENRI... BUT COORO AND HUSKY MIGHT'VE BEEN CAPTURED.
It's such a bother.
WHAAAT?!

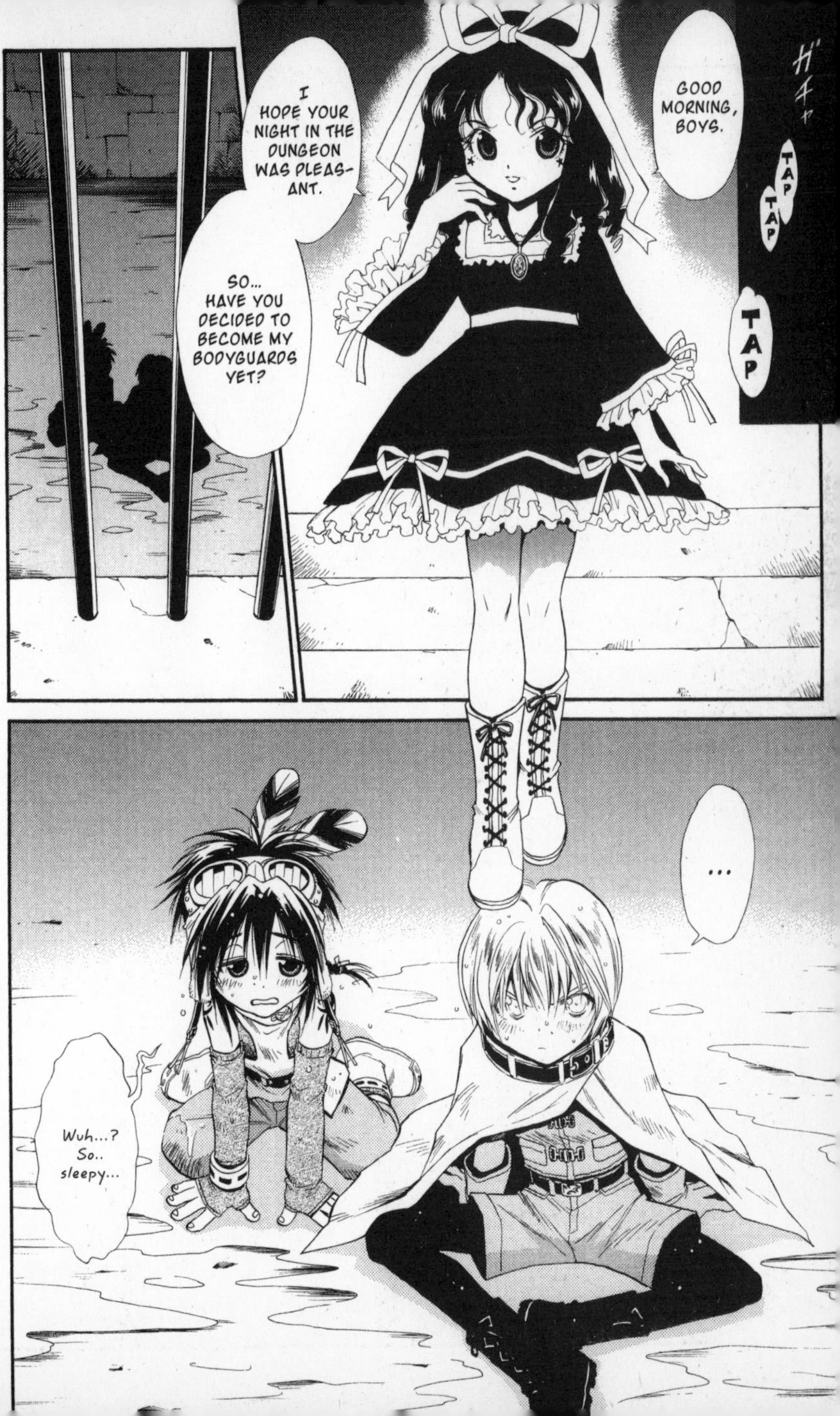
ガチャ
GOOD MORNING, BOYS.
TAP
TAP
TAP
TAP
I HOPE YOUR NIGHT IN THE DUNGEON WAS PLEAS-ANT.
SO... HAVE YOU DECIDED TO BECOME MY BODYGUARDS YET?
...
Wuh...? So.. sleepy...

Using a low voice.

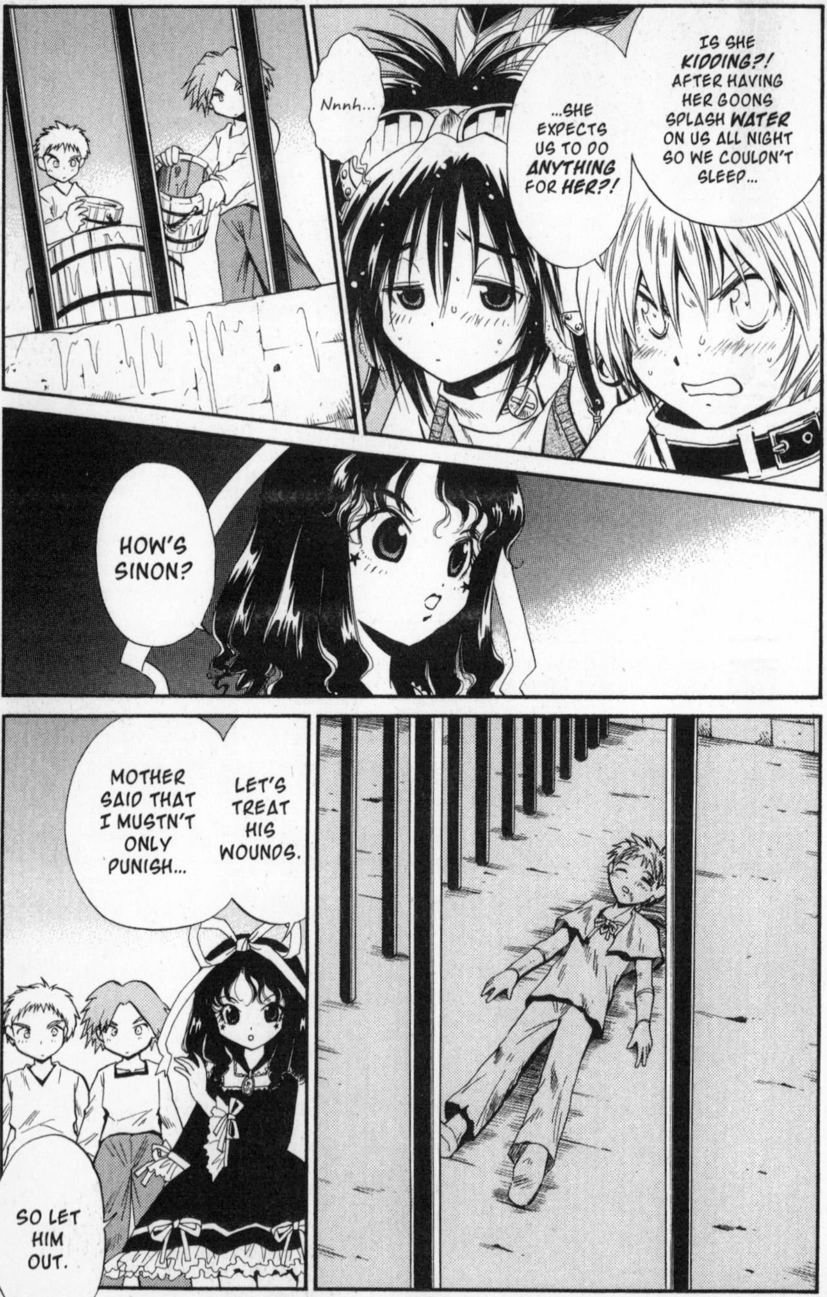
IS SHE KIDDING?! AFTER HAVING HER GOONS SPLASH WATER ON US ALL NIGHT SO WE COULDN'T SLEEP...
...SHE EXPECTS US TO DO ANYTHING FOR HER?!
Nnnh...
HOW'S SINON?
MOTHER SAID THAT I MUSTN'T ONLY PUNISH... LET'S TREAT HIS WOUNDS.
SO LET HIM OUT.

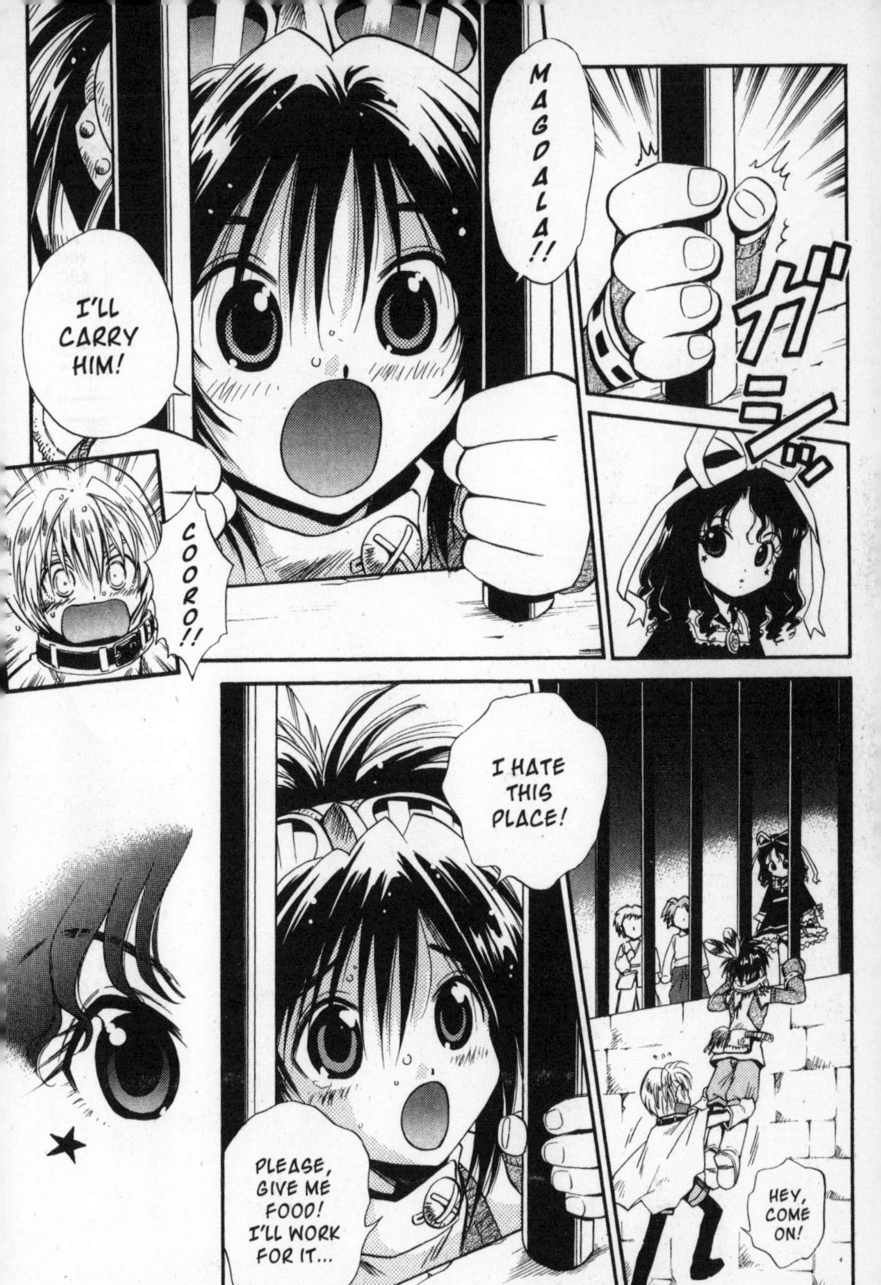
ガシッ
MAGDALA!!
I'LL CARRY HIM!
COORO!!
HEY, COME ON!
I HATE THIS PLACE!
PLEASE, GIVE ME FOOD! I'LL WORK FOR IT...

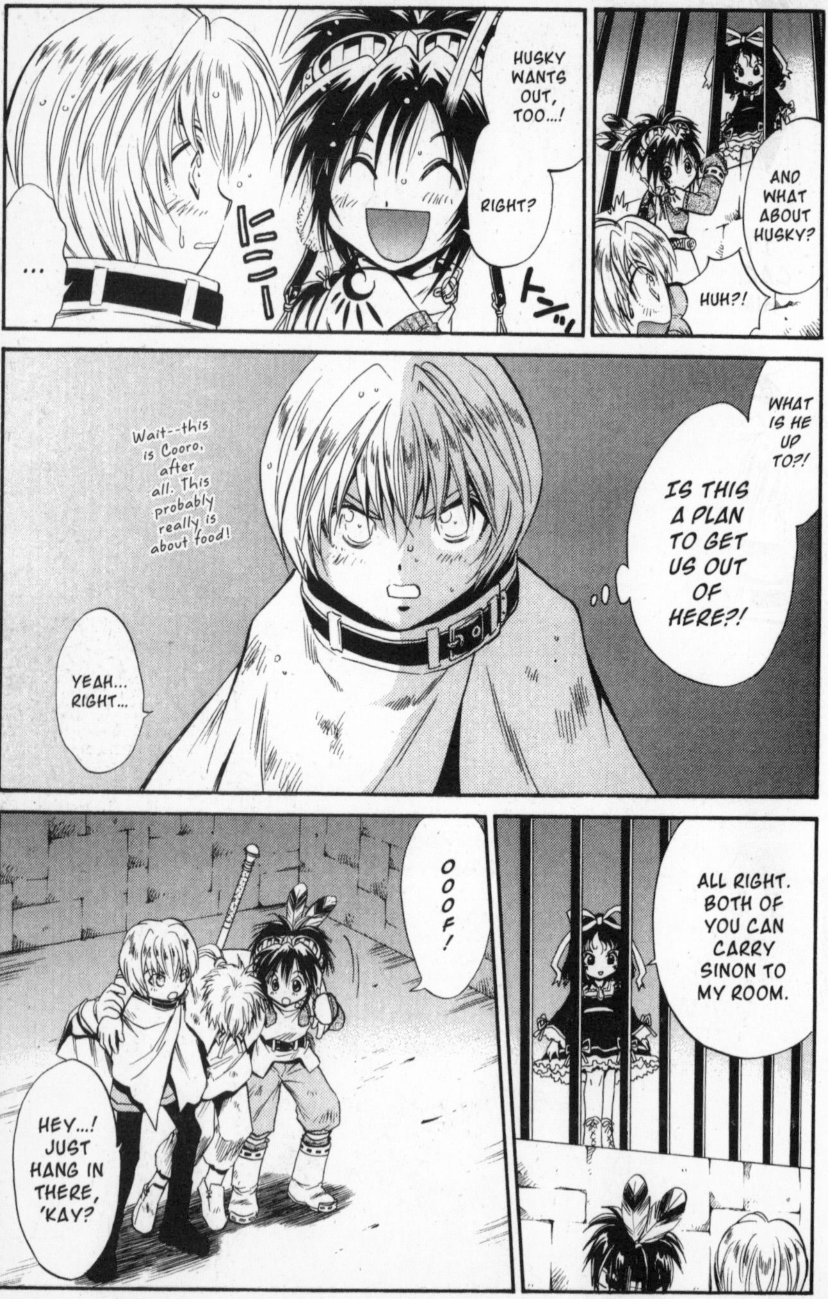
AND WHAT ABOUT HUSKY?
HUH?!
HUSKY WANTS OUT, TOO...!
RIGHT?
...
WHAT IS HE UP TO?!
IS THIS A PLAN TO GET US OUT OF HERE?!
Wait--this is Cooro, after all. This probably really is about food!
YEAH... RIGHT...
ALL RIGHT. BOTH OF YOU CAN CARRY SINON TO MY ROOM.
OOOF!
HEY...! JUST HANG IN THERE, 'KAY?

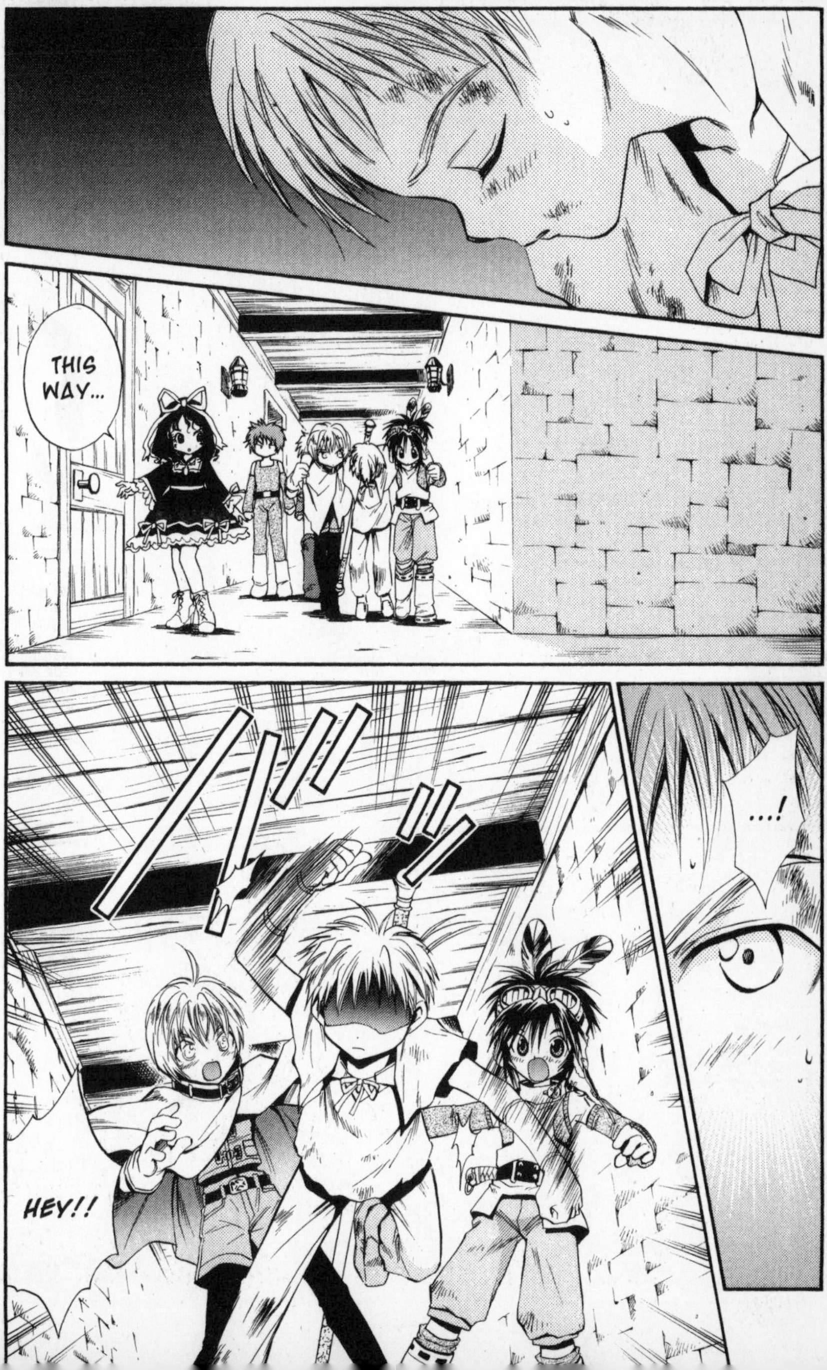
THIS WAY...
...!
HEY!!

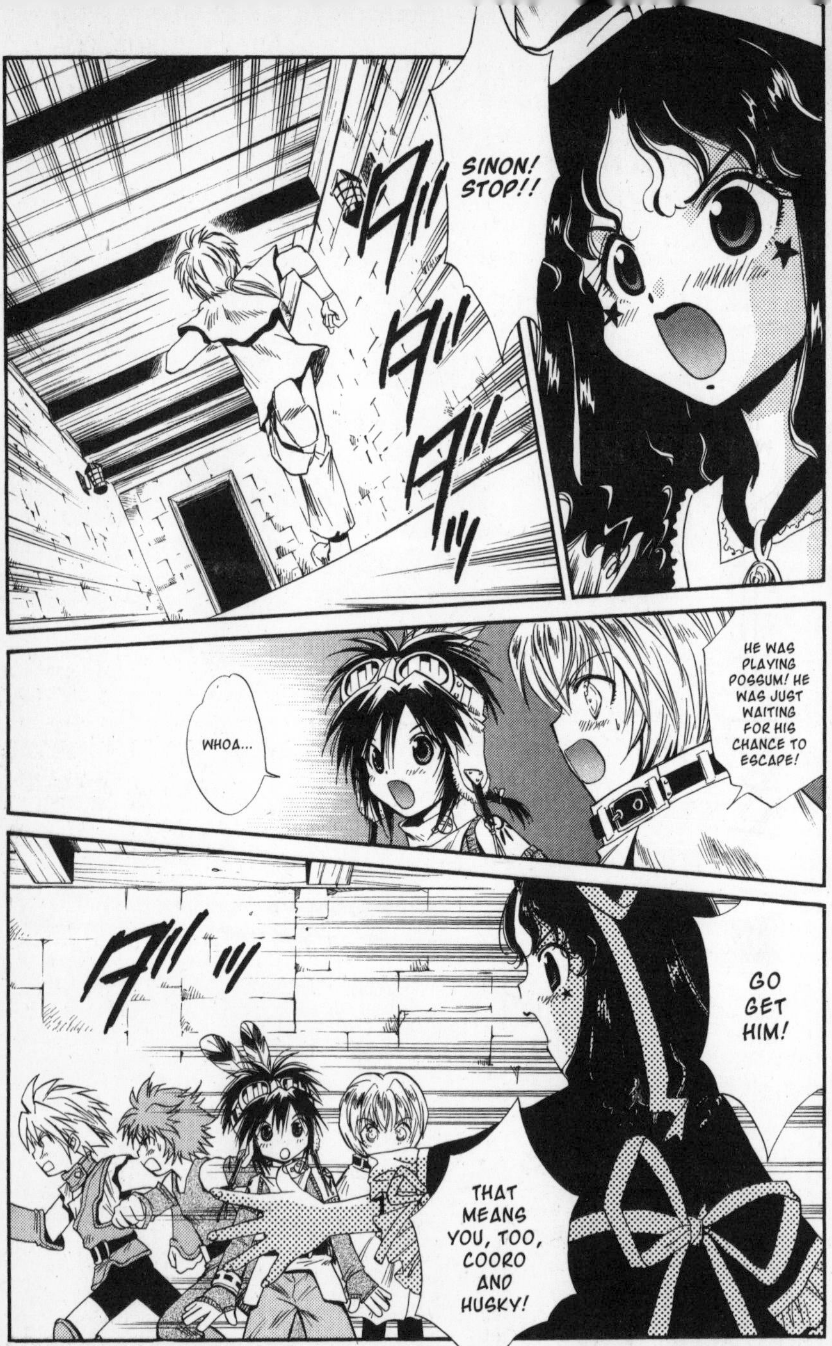
SINON! STOP!!
HE WAS PLAYING POSSUM! HE WAS JUST WAITING FOR HIS CHANCE TO ESCAPE!
WHOA...
GO GET HIM!
THAT MEANS YOU, TOO, COORO AND HUSKY!

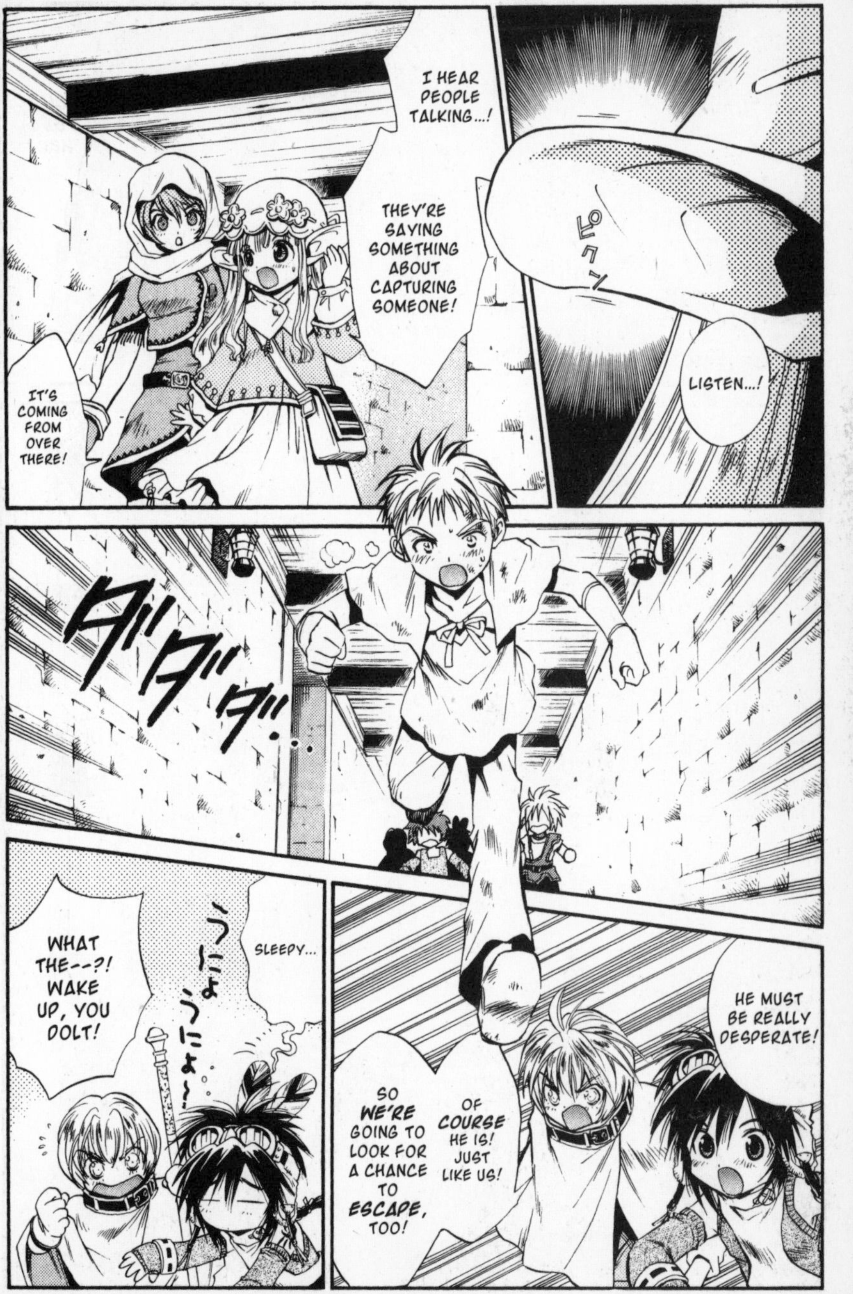
ピクン
LISTEN...!
I HEAR PEOPLE TALKING...!
THEY'RE SAYING SOMETHING ABOUT CAPTURING SOMEONE!
IT'S COMING FROM OVER THERE!
ダダダ...
HE MUST BE REALLY DESPERATE!
OF COURSE HE IS! JUST LIKE US!
SO WE'RE GOING TO LOOK FOR A CHANCE TO ESCAPE, TOO!
SLEEPY...
うにょうにょ~
WHAT THE--?! WAKE UP, YOU DOLT!

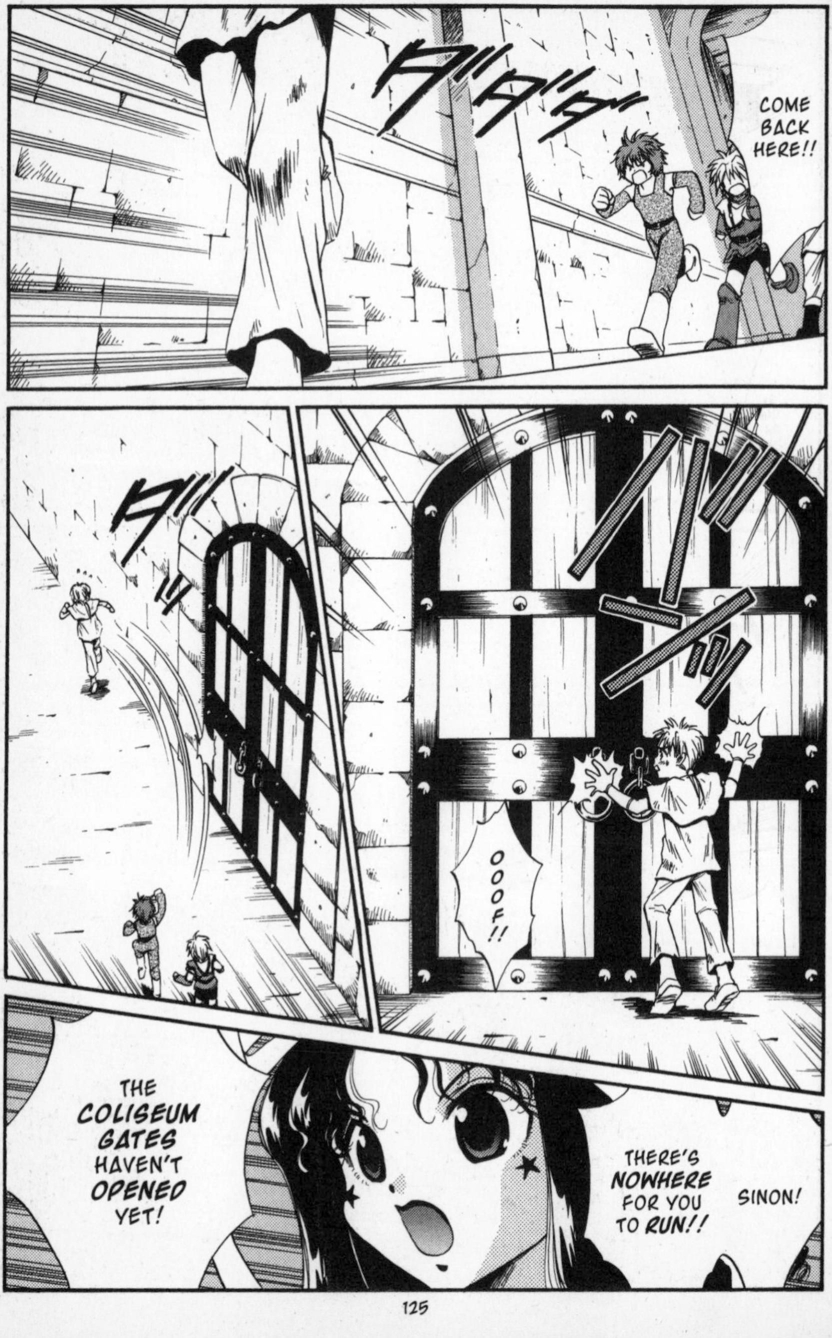
COME BACK HERE!!
OOOF!!
SINON!
THERE'S NOWHERE FOR YOU TO RUN!!
THE COLISEUM GATES HAVEN'T OPENED YET!

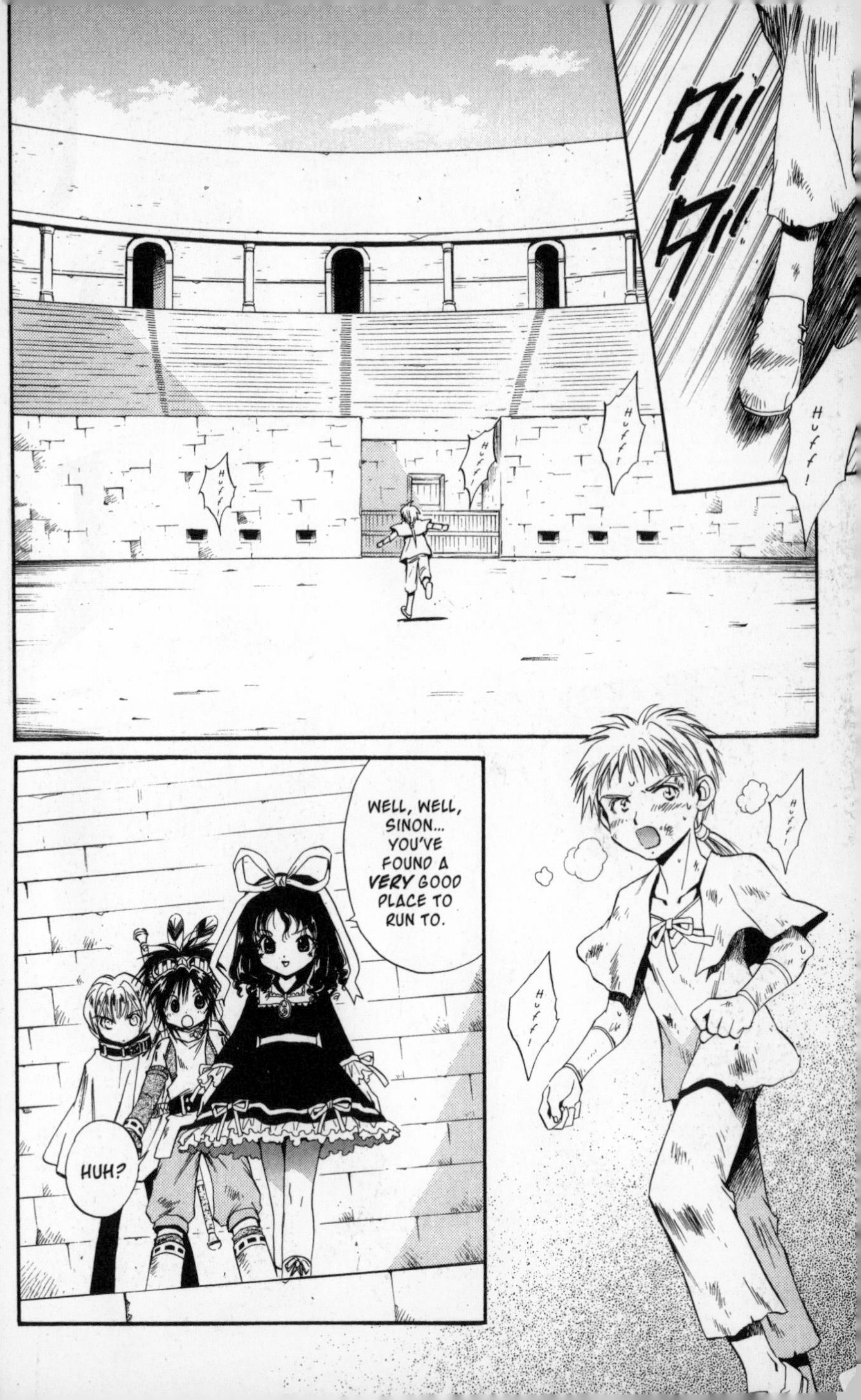

ダッ
ダッ
Huff!
Huff!
Huff!
Huff!
Huff!
Huff!
WELL, WELL, SINON... YOU'VE FOUND A ***VERY*** GOOD PLACE TO RUN TO.
HUH?

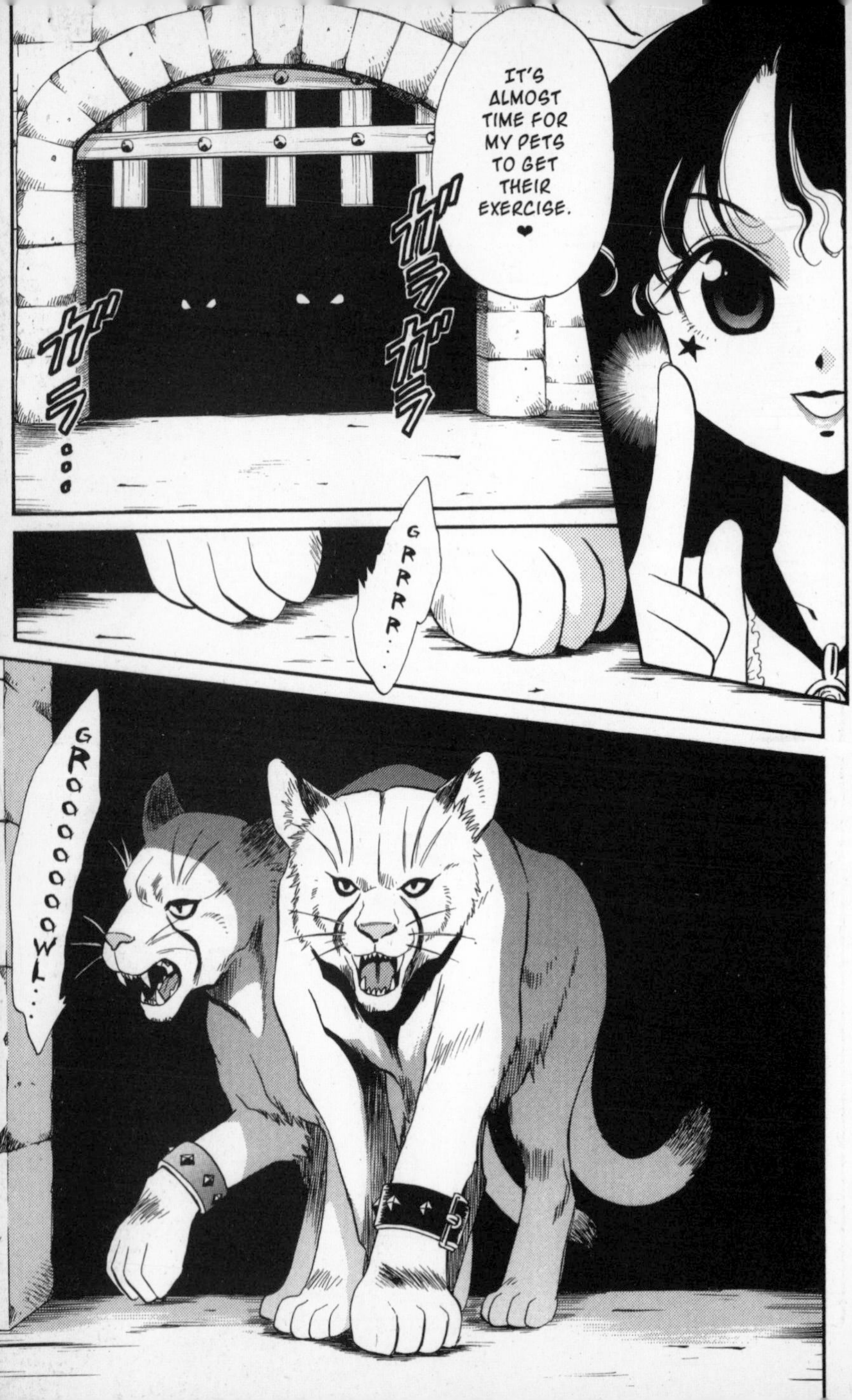
IT'S ALMOST TIME FOR MY PETS TO GET THEIR EXERCISE. ❤
ガラガラ
ガラ…
GRRRR…
GROOOOOOOWL…

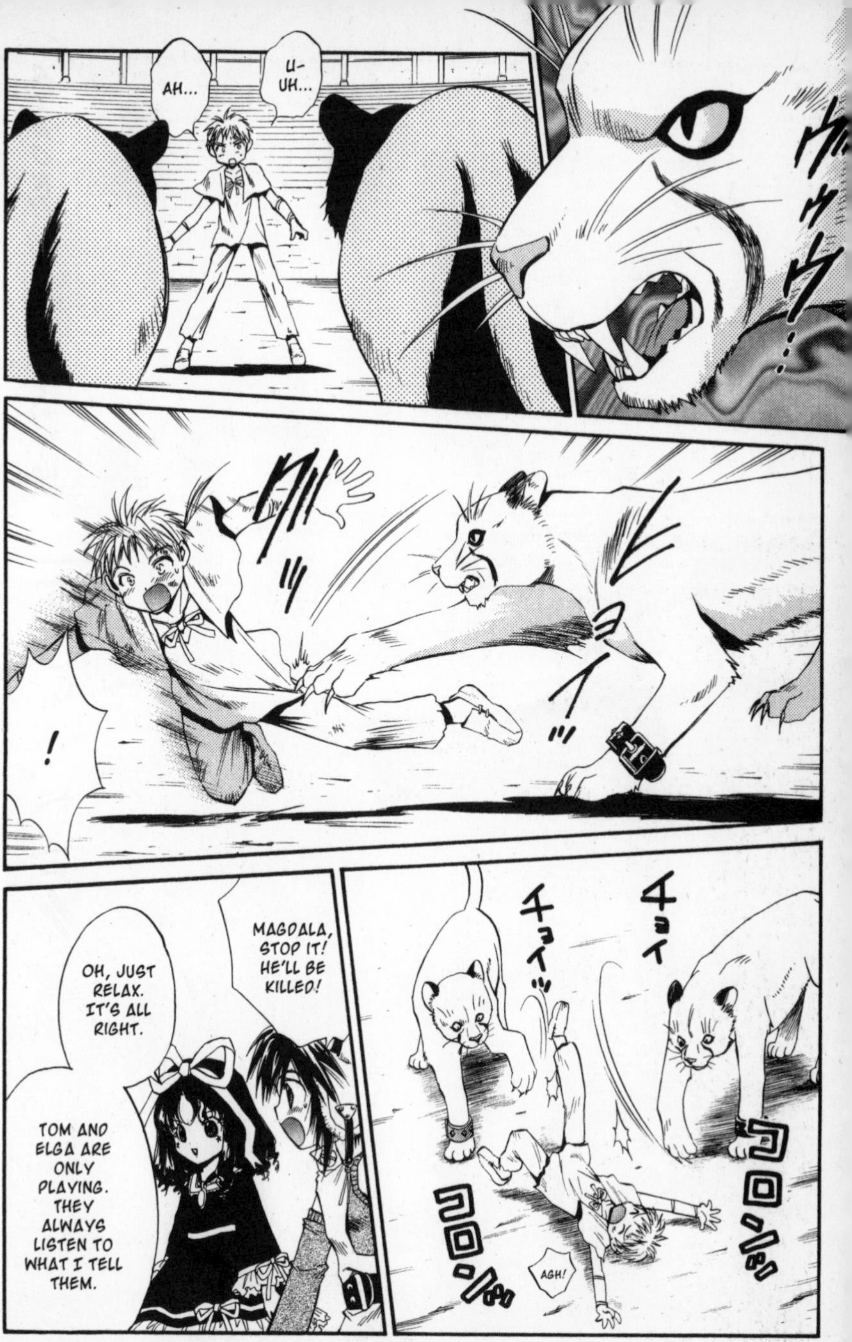
ヴゥゥゥ……
U-UH...
AH...
ヒョイッ
!
チョイチョイッ
AGH!
MAGDALA, STOP IT! HE'LL BE KILLED!
OH, JUST RELAX. IT'S ALL RIGHT.
TOM AND ELGA ARE ONLY PLAYING. THEY ALWAYS LISTEN TO WHAT I TELL THEM.

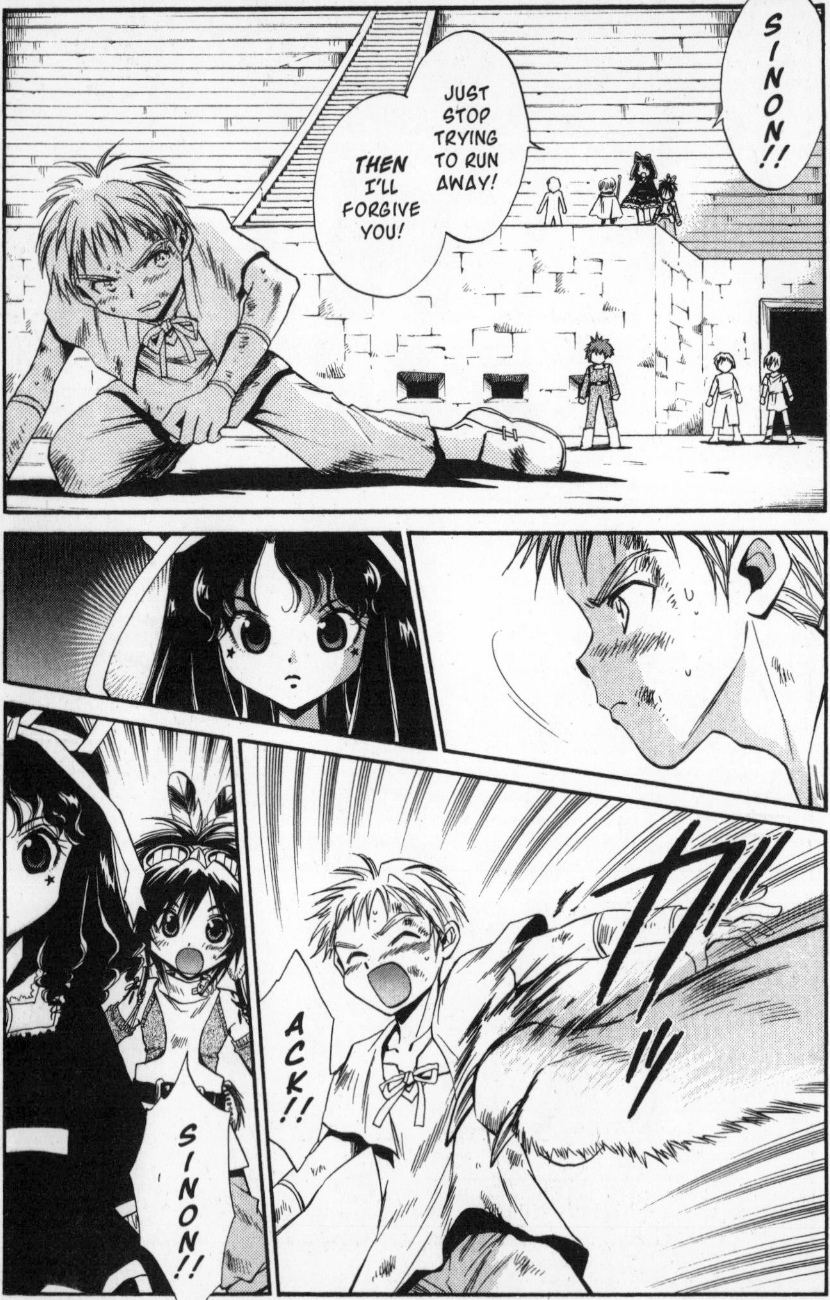
SINON!!
JUST STOP TRYING TO RUN AWAY! THEN I'LL FORGIVE YOU!
ACK!!
SINON!!

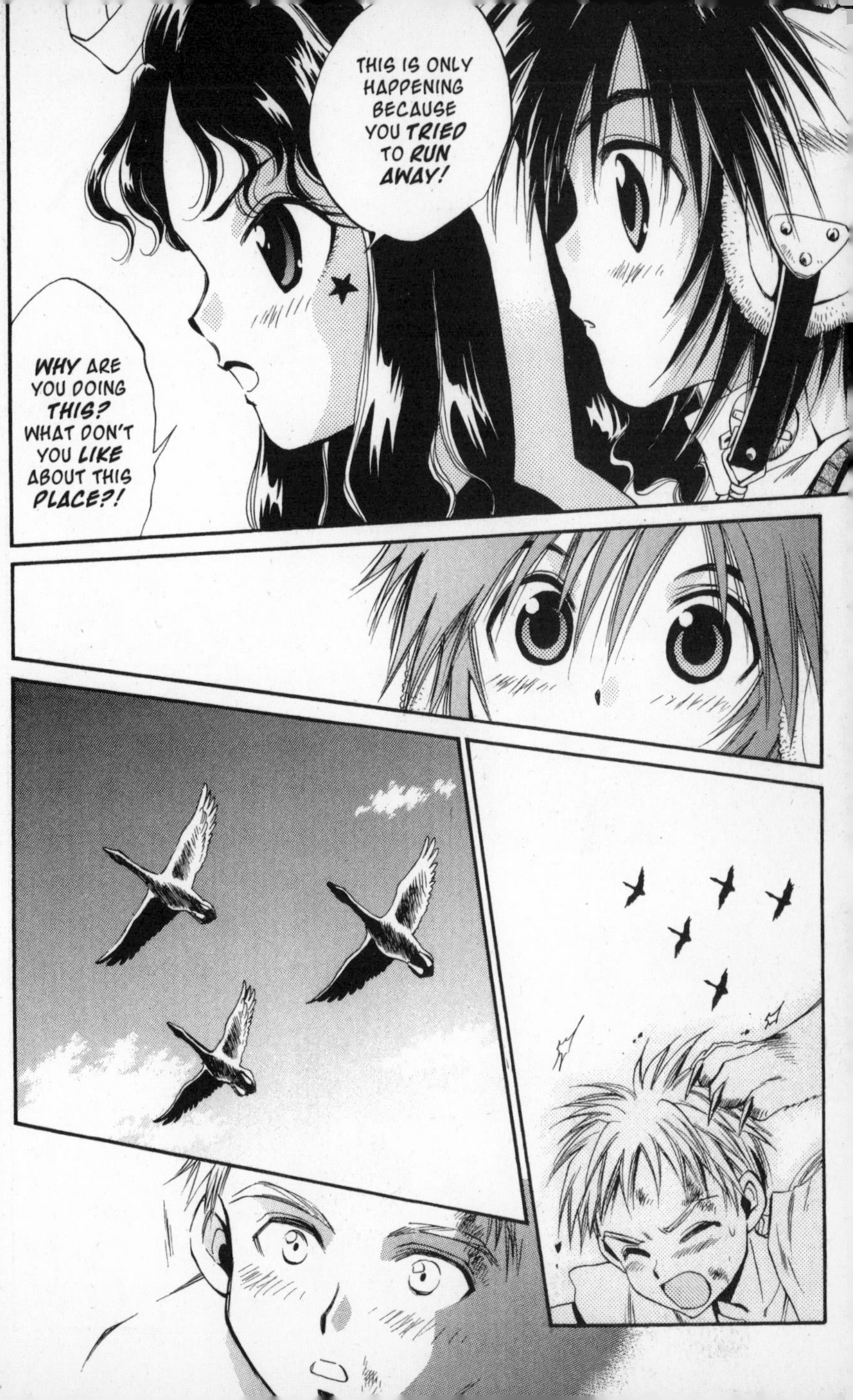
THIS IS ONLY HAPPENING BECAUSE YOU TRIED TO RUN AWAY!
WHY ARE YOU DOING THIS? WHAT DON'T YOU LIKE ABOUT THIS PLACE?!

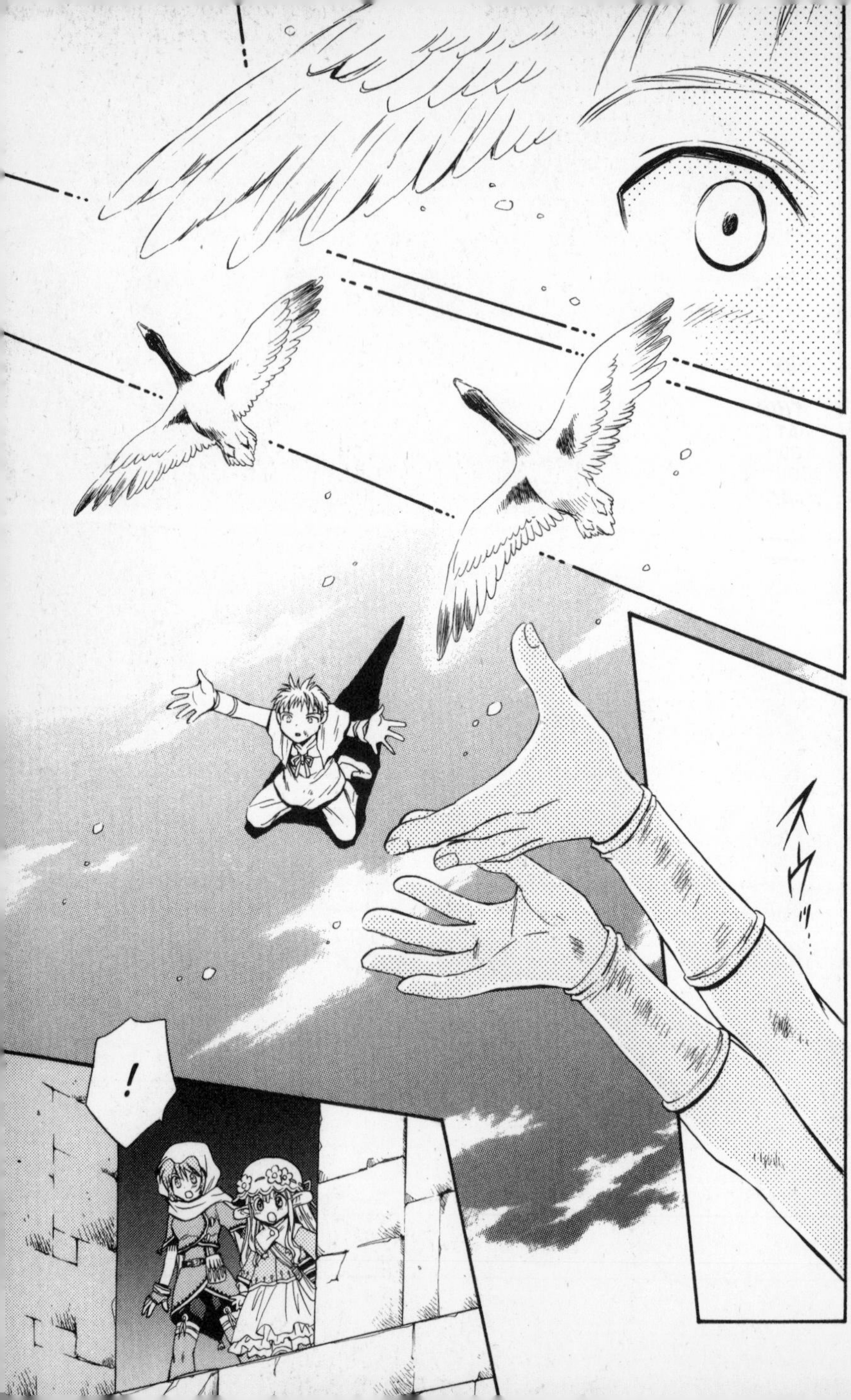
スゥッ…
!

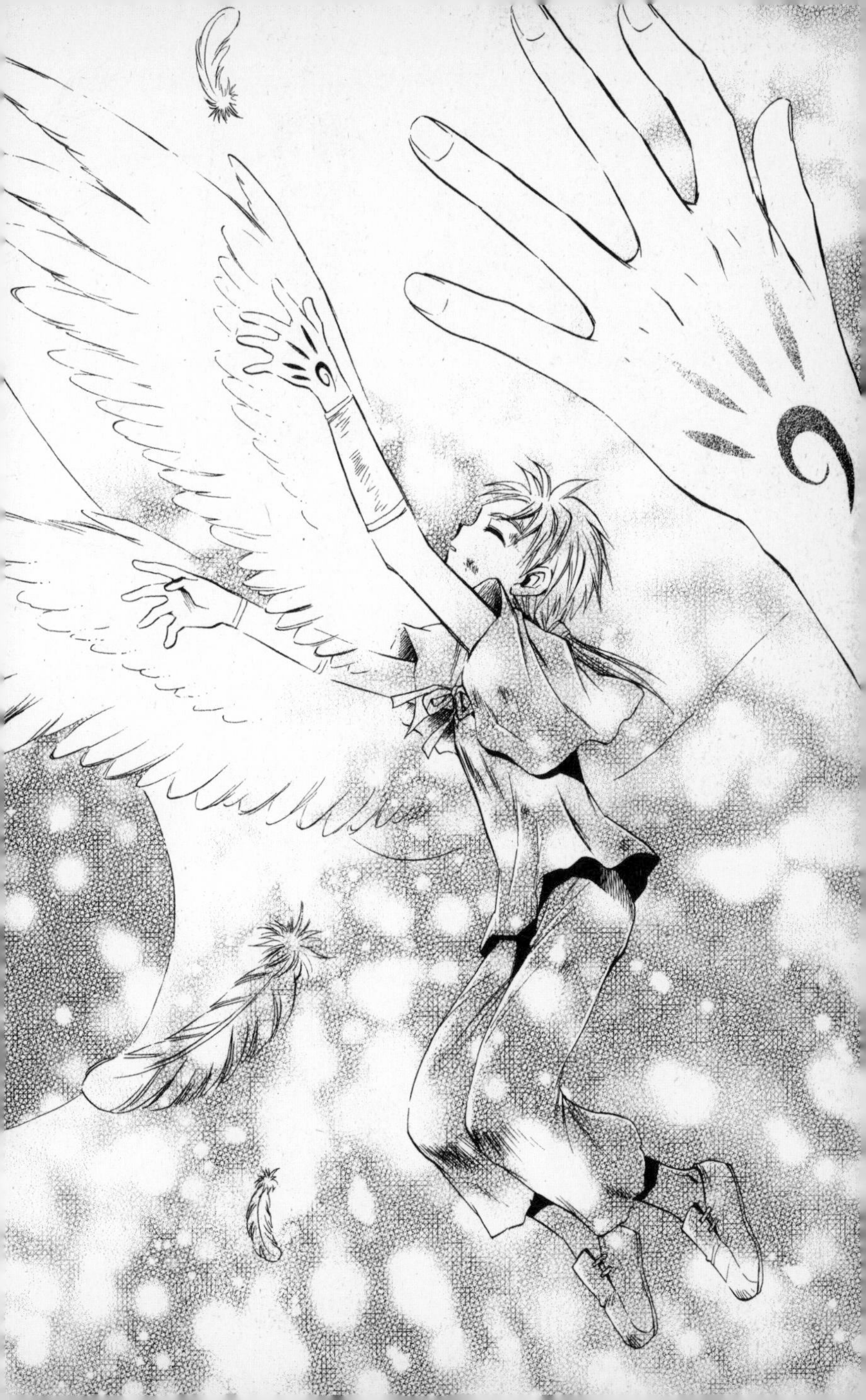

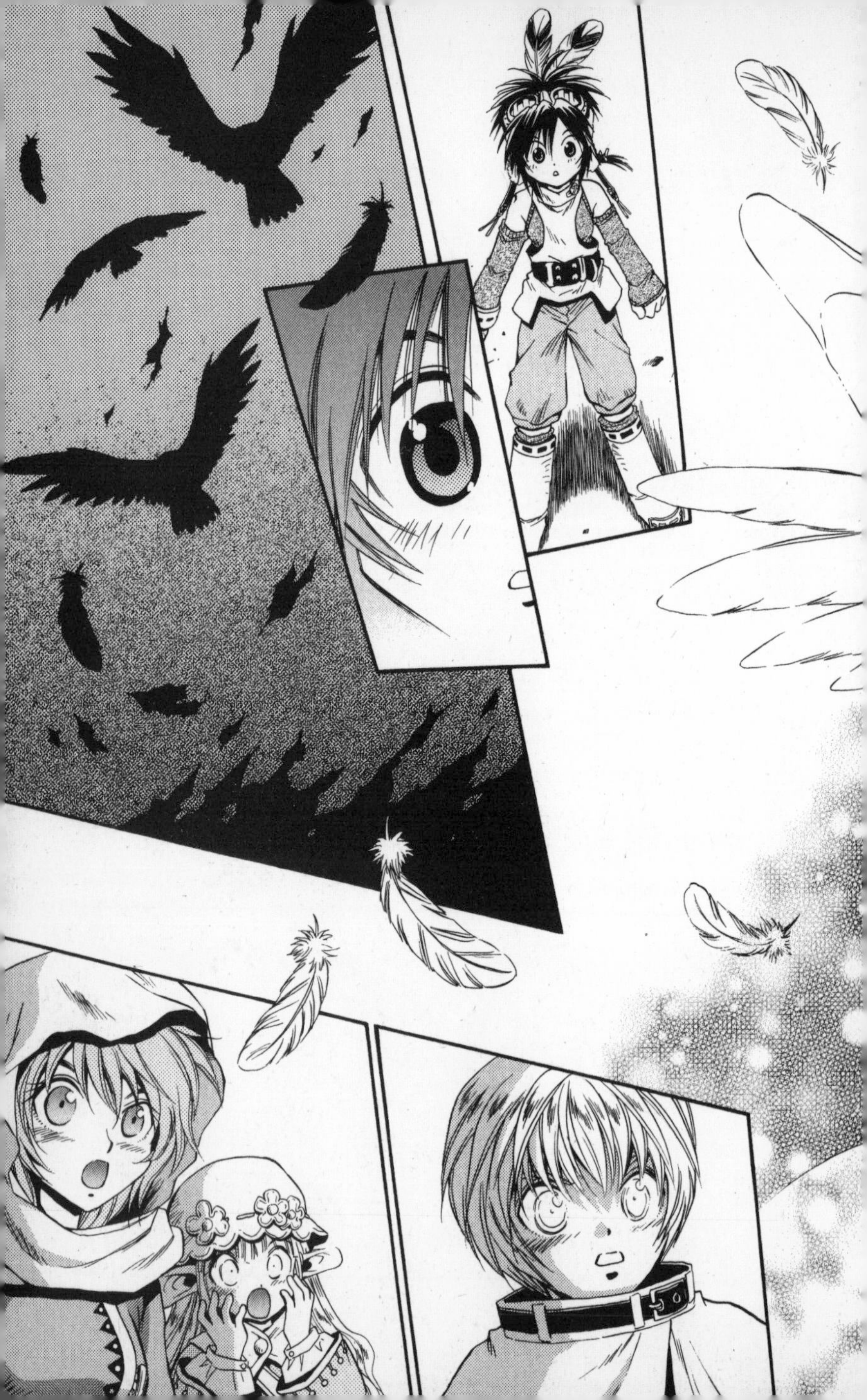

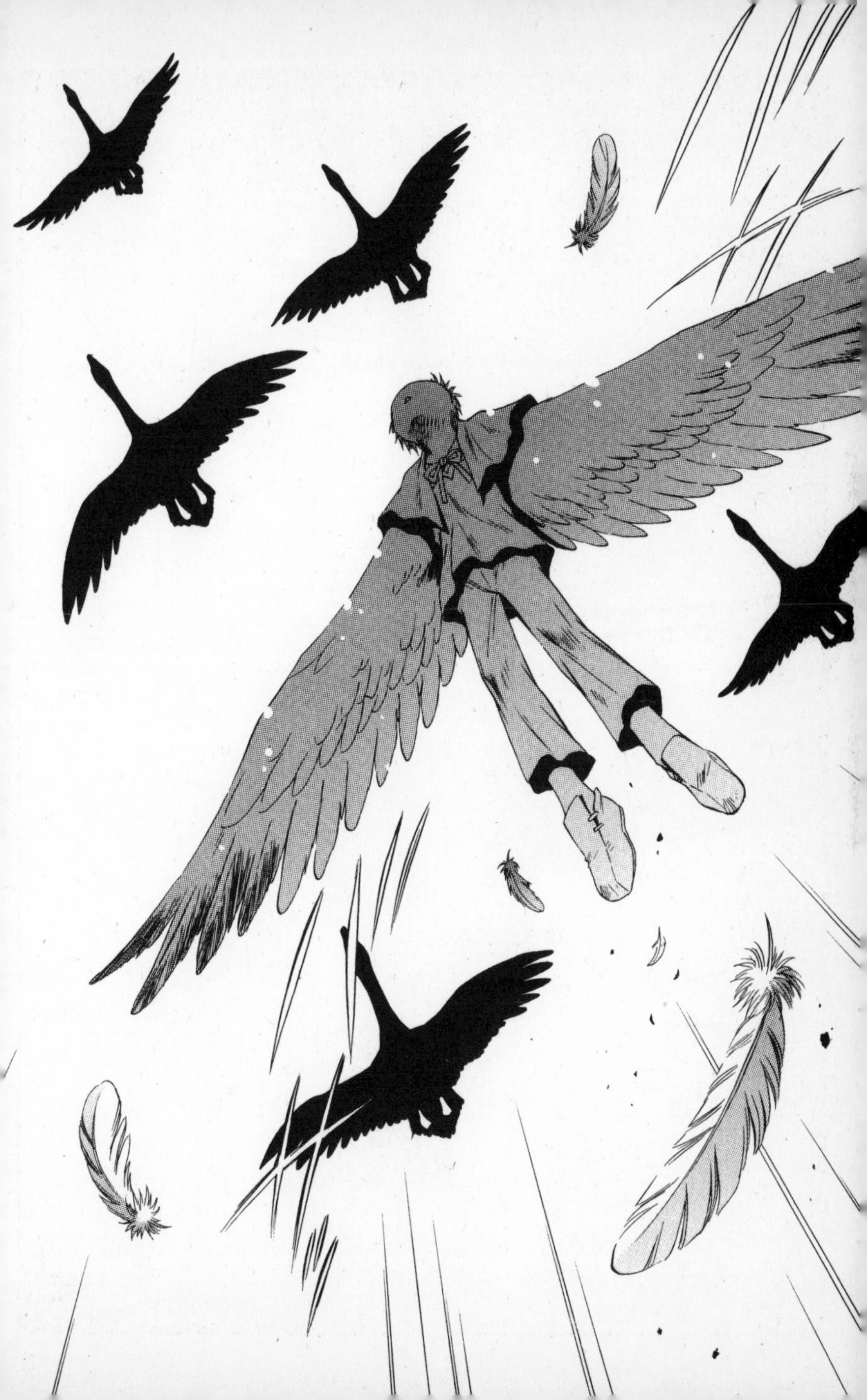

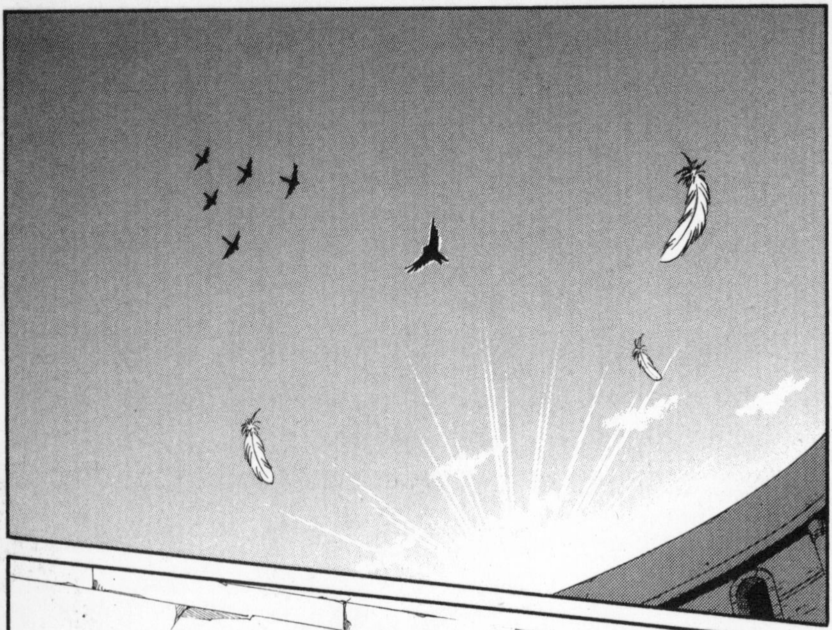
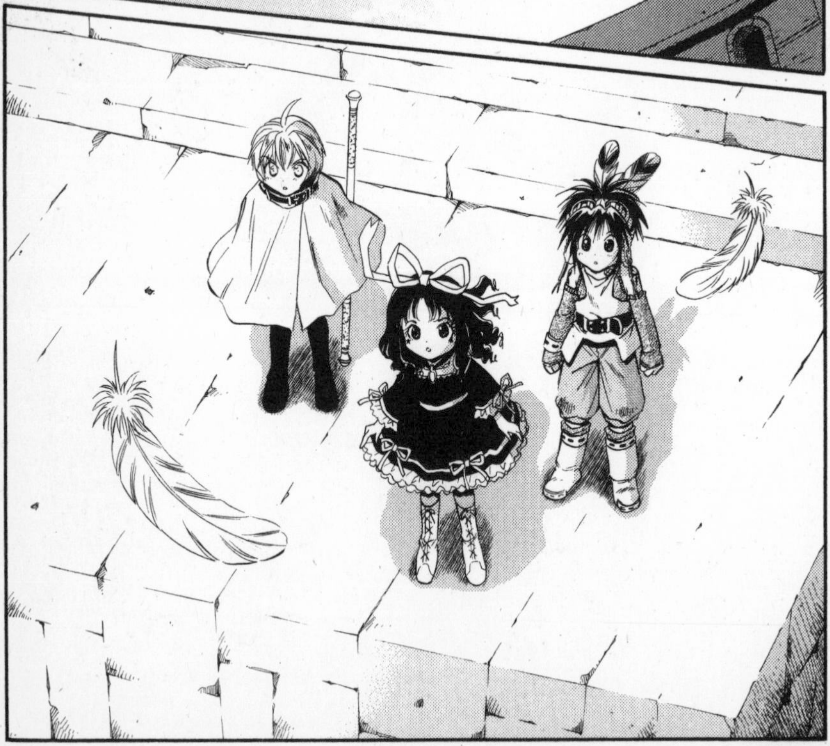

Good friend.

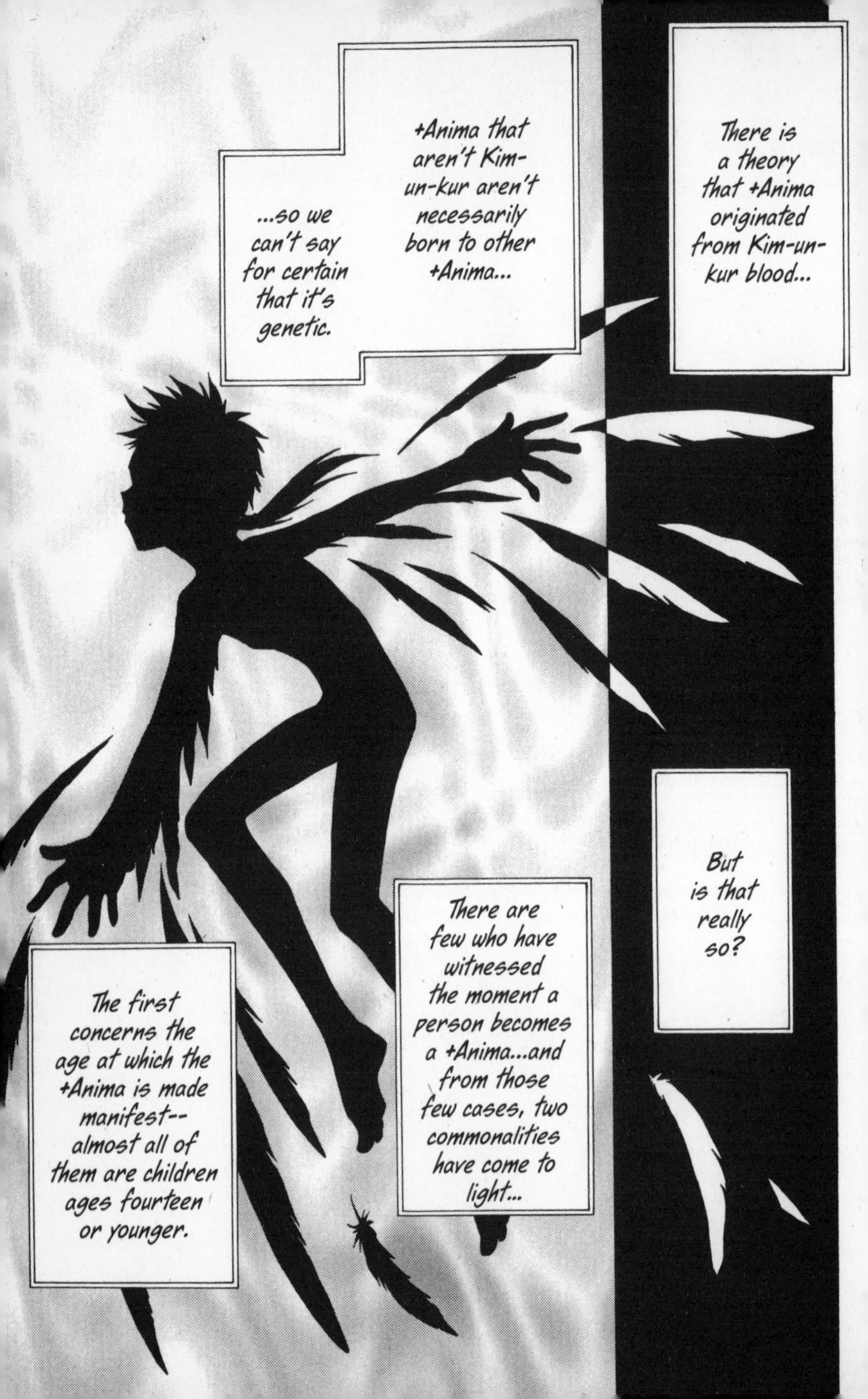
There is a theory that +Anima originated from Kim-un-kur blood...
+Anima that aren't Kim-un-kur aren't necessarily born to other +Anima...
...so we can't say for certain that it's genetic.
But is that really so?
There are few who have witnessed the moment a person becomes a +Anima...and from those few cases, two commonalities have come to light...
The first concerns the age at which the +Anima is made manifest--almost all of them are children ages fourteen or younger.

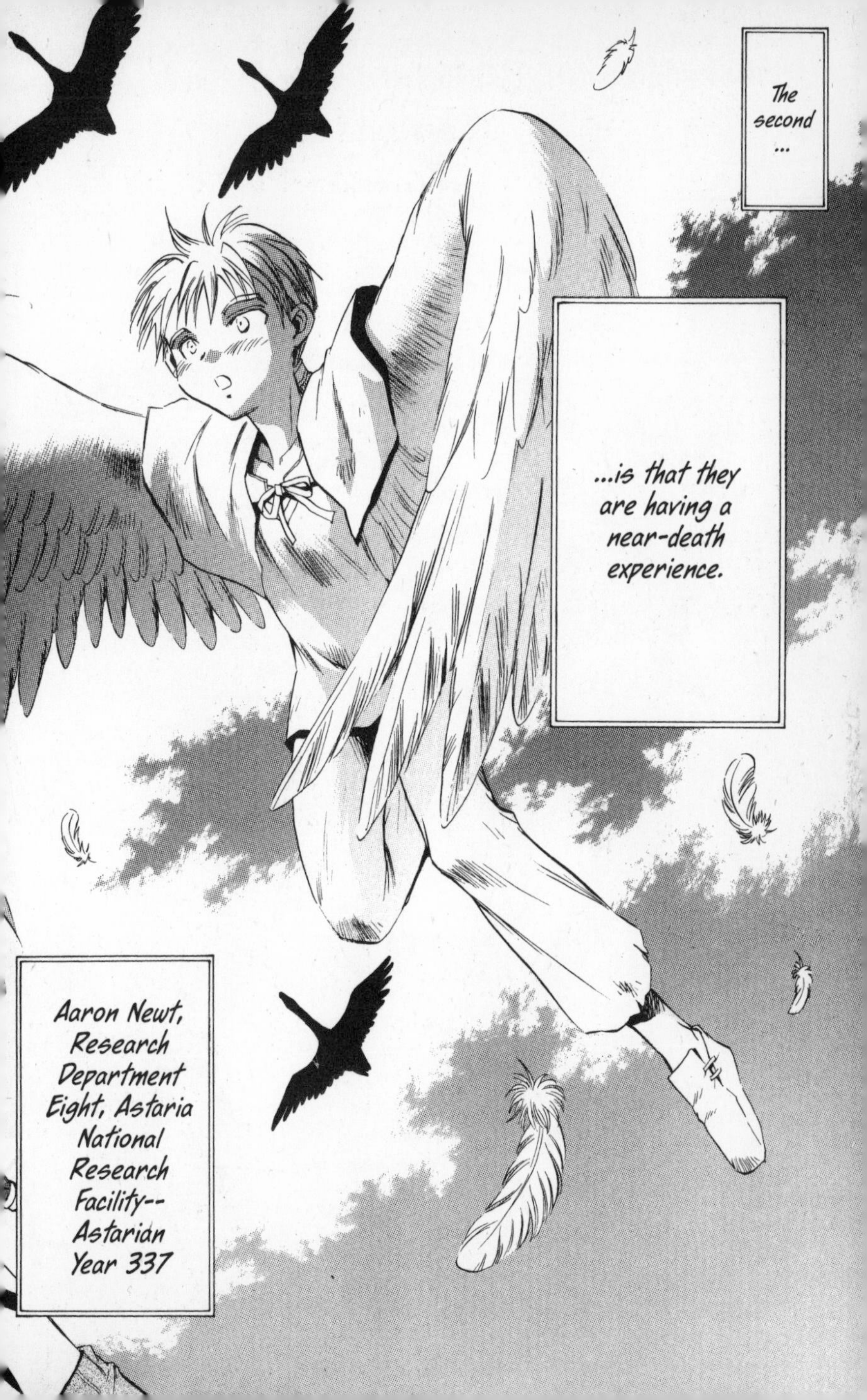
The second ...
...is that they are having a near-death experience.
Aaron Newt, Research Department Eight, Astaria National Research Facility-- Astarian Year 337

Chapter 19:
Maggie Coliseum—Part 5

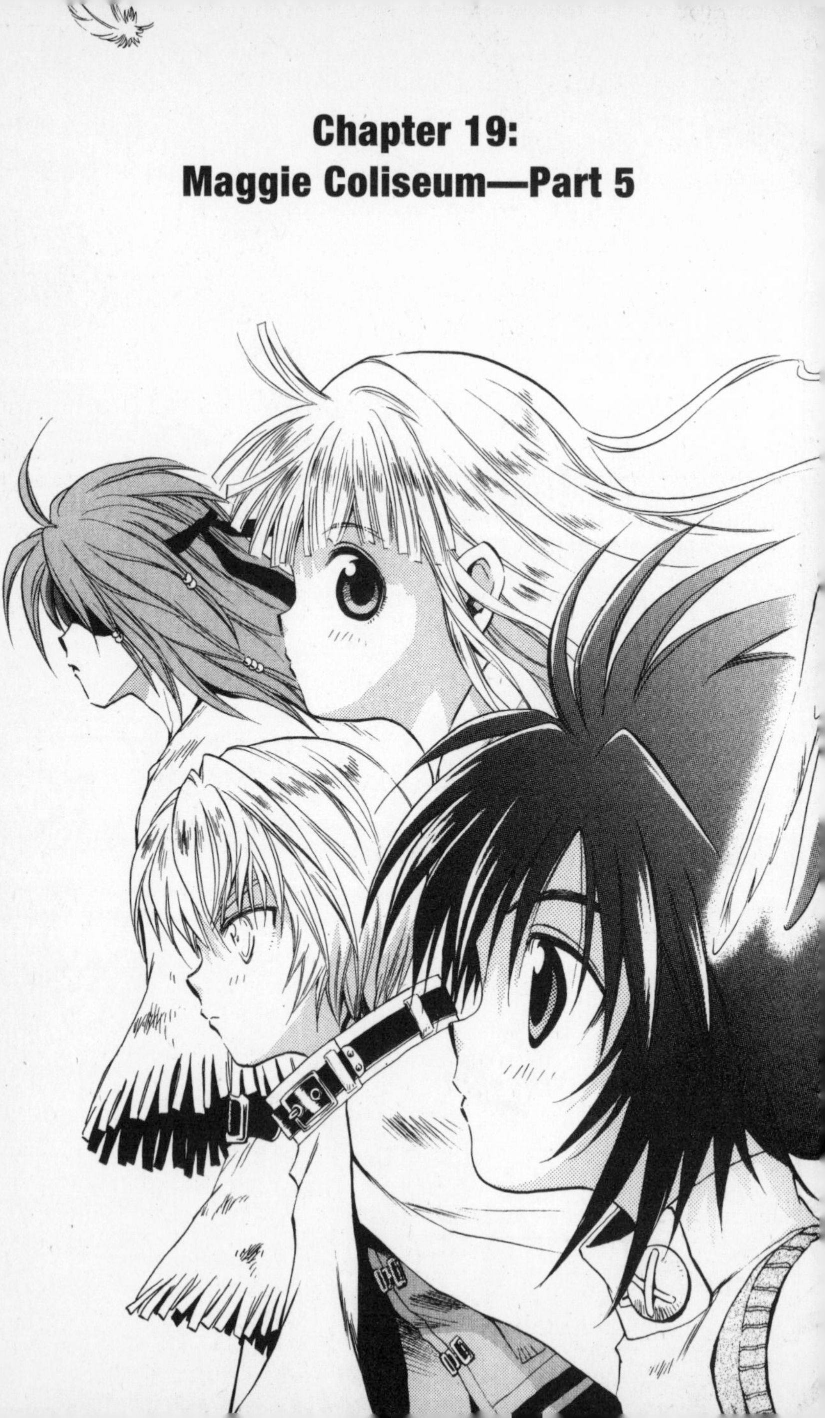

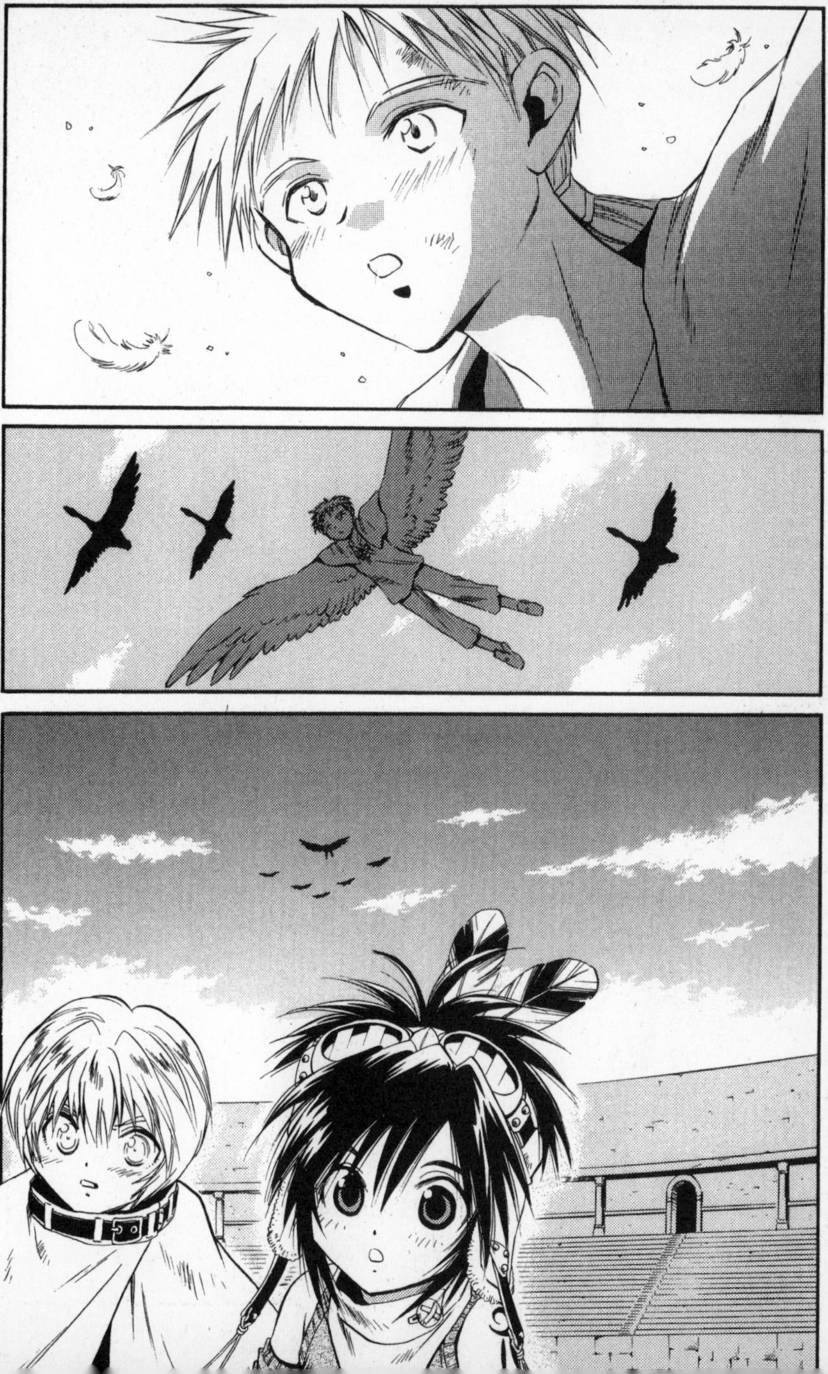

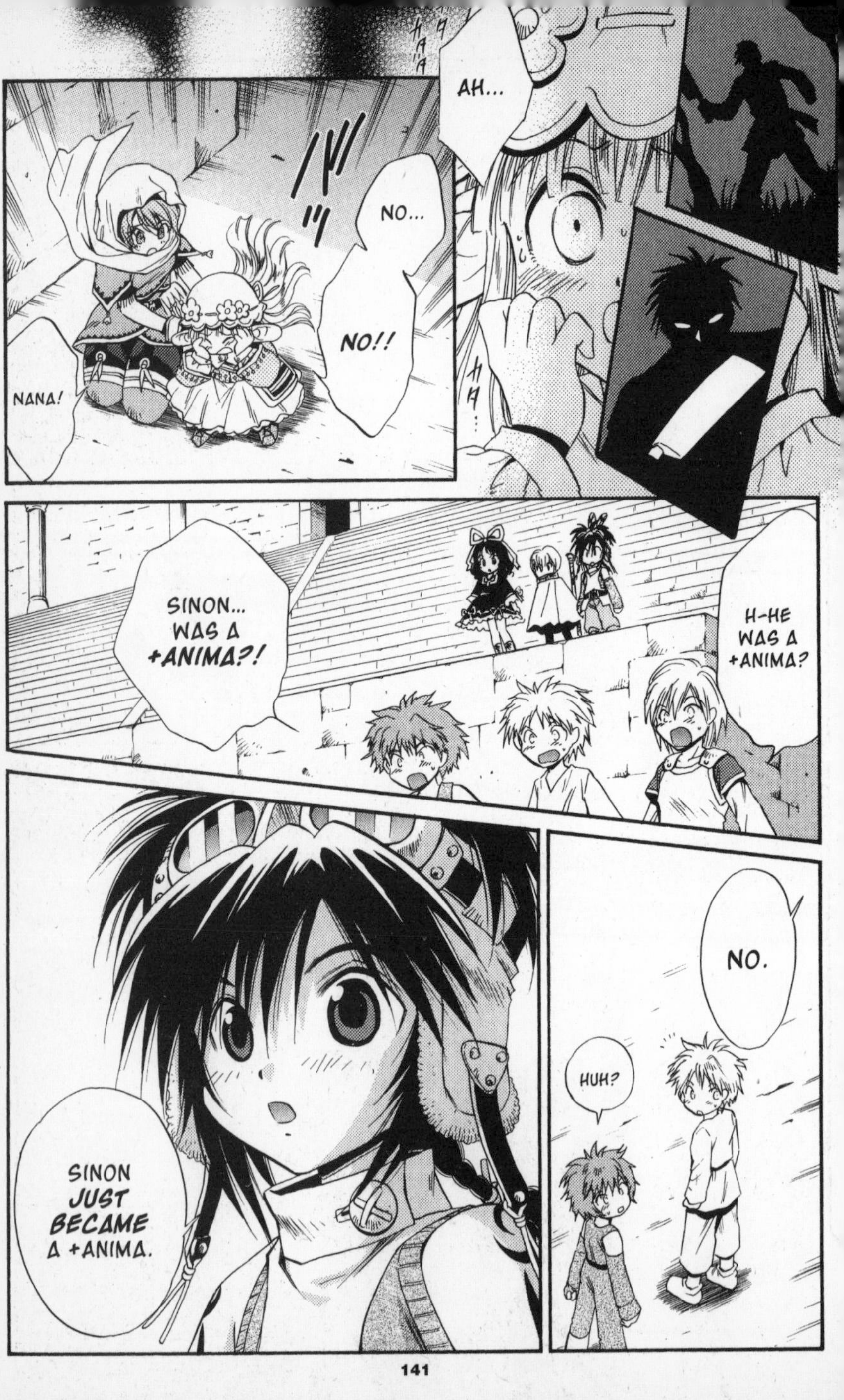
AH...
NO...
NO!!
NANA!
H-HE WAS A +ANIMA?
SINON... WAS A +ANIMA?!
NO.
HUH?
SINON JUST BECAME A +ANIMA.

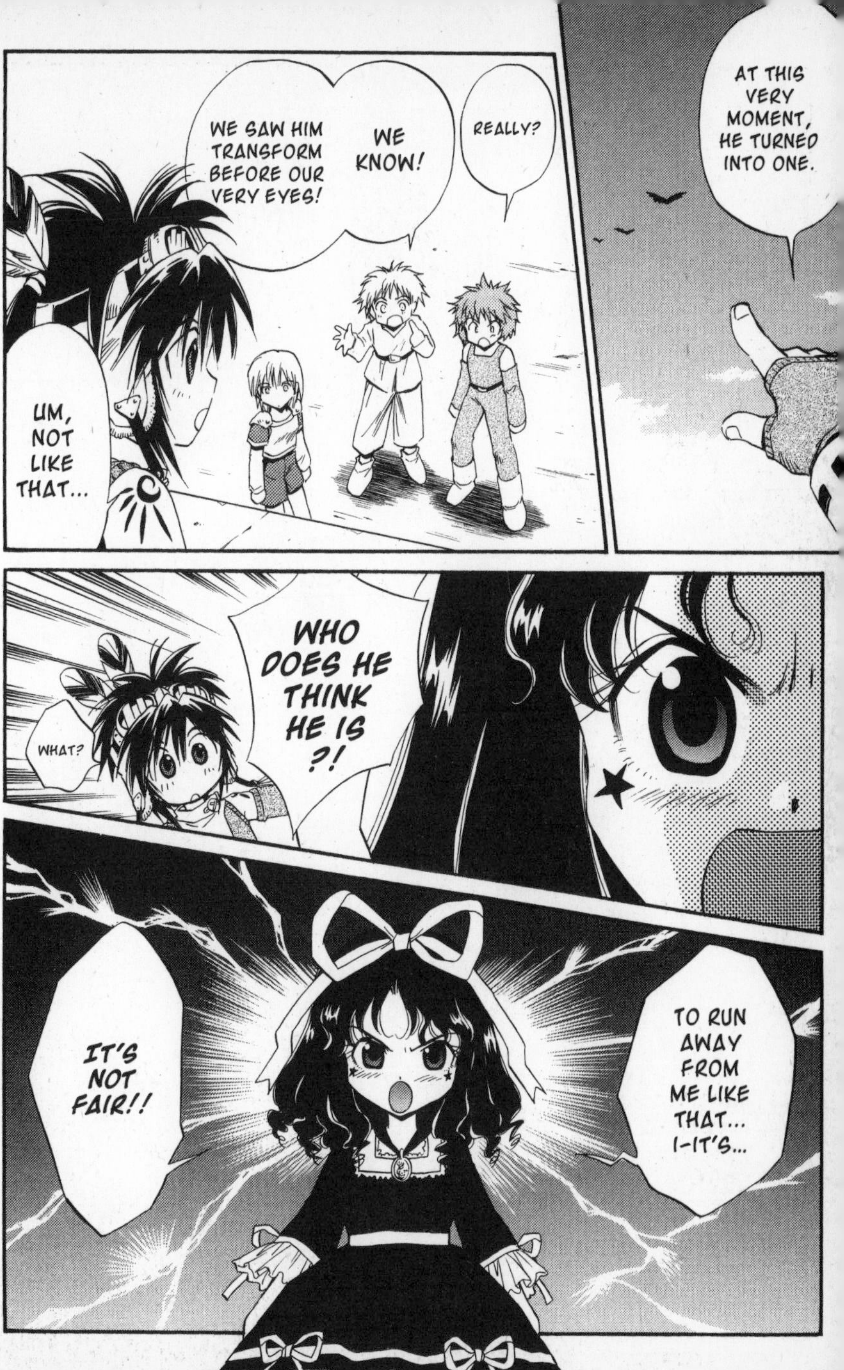
AT THIS VERY MOMENT, HE TURNED INTO ONE.
REALLY?
WE KNOW!
WE SAW HIM TRANSFORM BEFORE OUR VERY EYES!
UM, NOT LIKE THAT...
WHO DOES HE THINK HE IS ?!
WHAT?
TO RUN AWAY FROM ME LIKE THAT... I-IT'S...
IT'S NOT FAIR!!

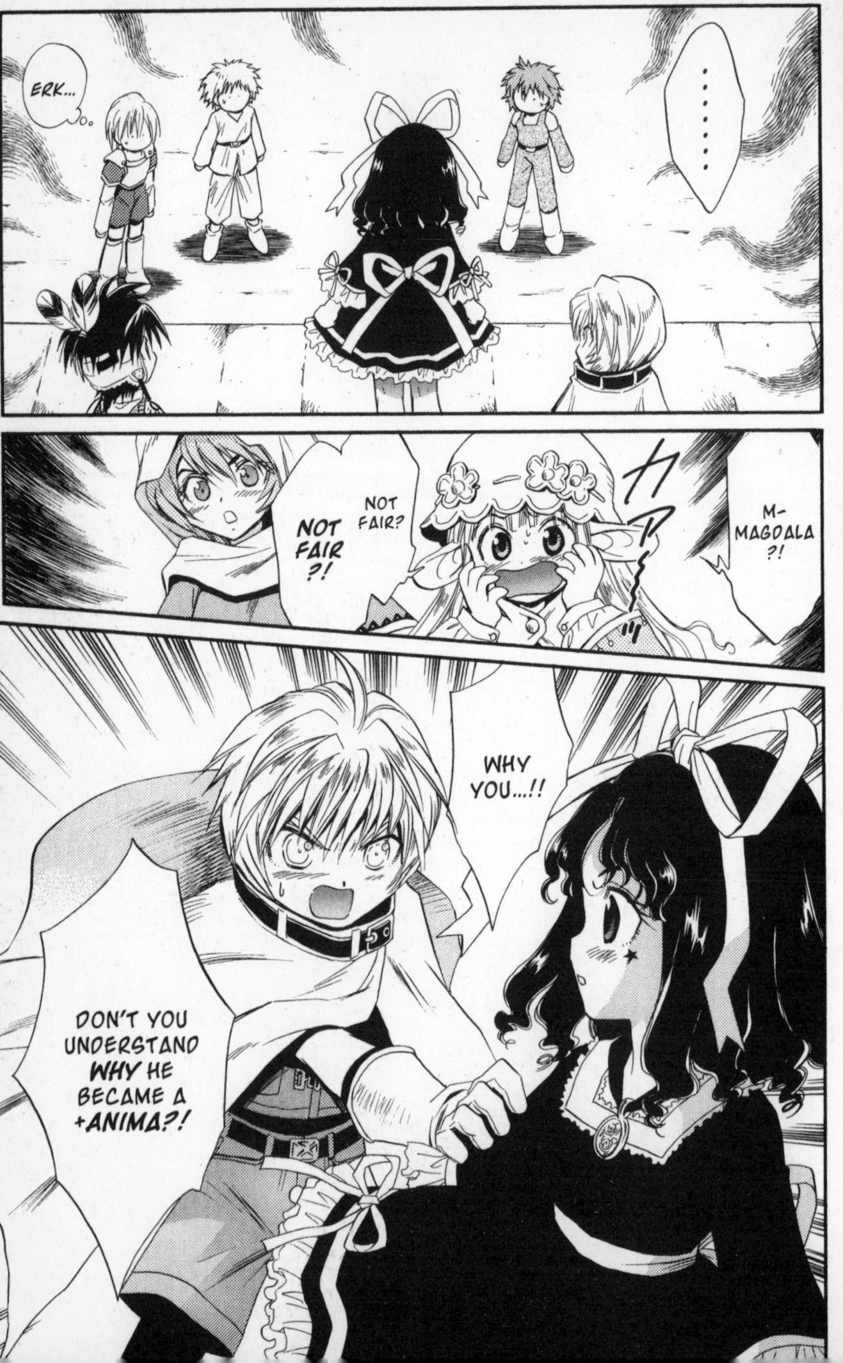

......
ERK...
M-MAGDALA?!
NOT FAIR?
NOT FAIR?!
WHY YOU...!!
DON'T YOU UNDERSTAND WHY HE BECAME A +ANIMA?!

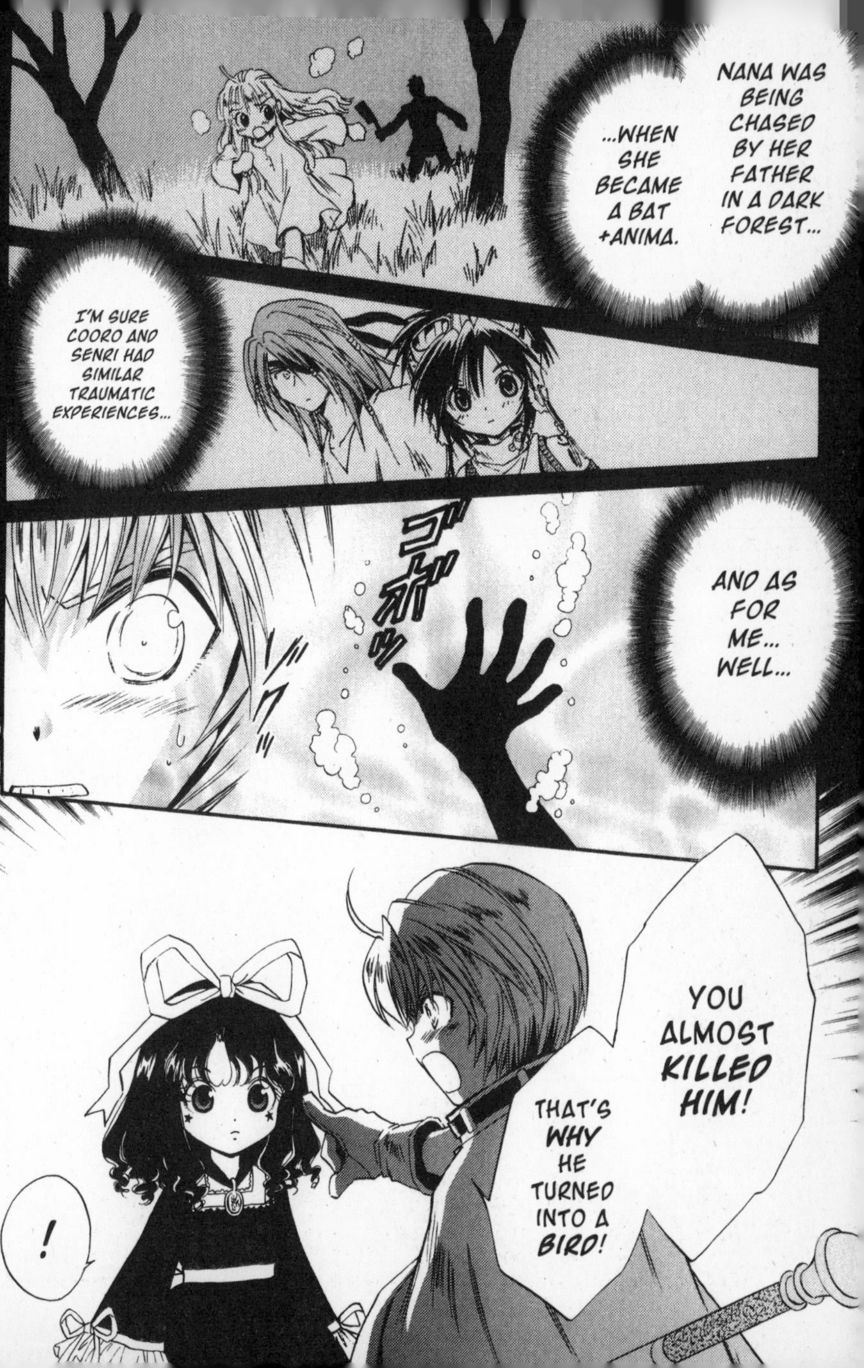
NANA WAS BEING CHASED BY HER FATHER IN A DARK FOREST...
...WHEN SHE BECAME A BAT +ANIMA.
I'M SURE COORO AND SENRI HAD SIMILAR TRAUMATIC EXPERIENCES...
AND AS FOR ME... WELL...
YOU ALMOST KILLED HIM!
THAT'S WHY HE TURNED INTO A BIRD!
!

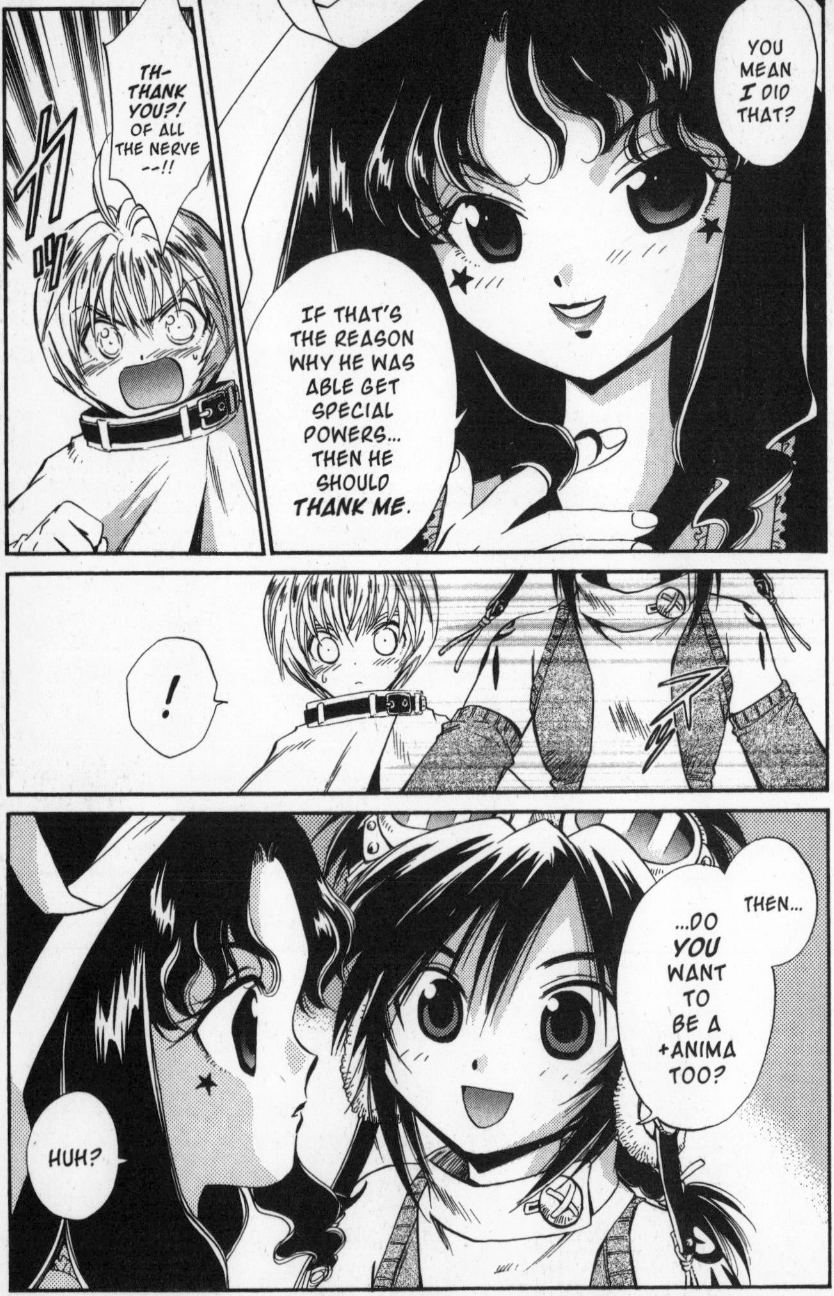
YOU MEAN I DID THAT?
IF THAT'S THE REASON WHY HE WAS ABLE GET SPECIAL POWERS... THEN HE SHOULD THANK ME.
TH-THANK YOU?! OF ALL THE NERVE --!!
!
THEN...
...DO YOU WANT TO BE A +ANIMA TOO?
HUH?

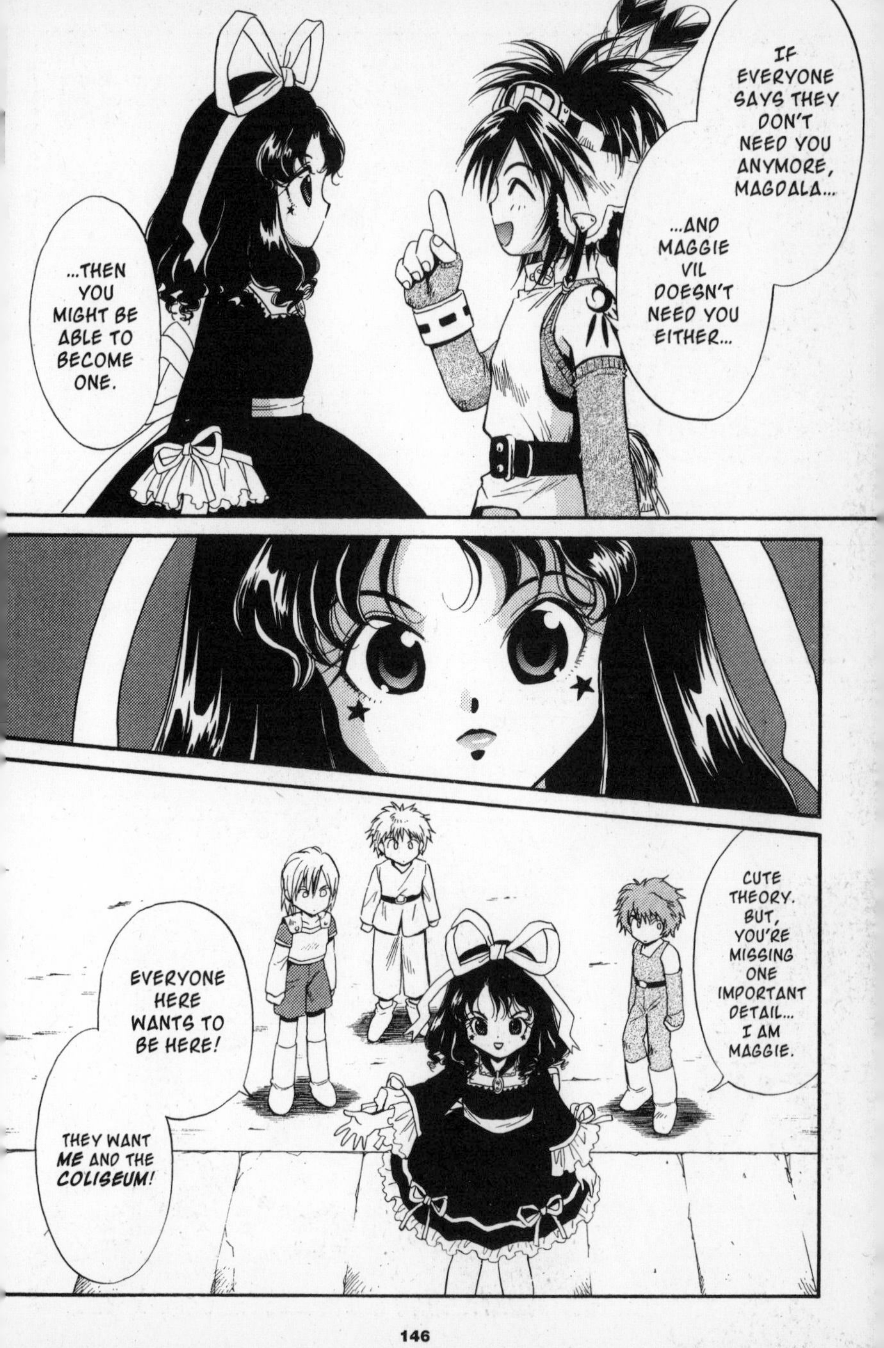
IF EVERYONE SAYS THEY DON'T NEED YOU ANYMORE, MAGDALA...
...AND MAGGIE VIL DOESN'T NEED YOU EITHER...
...THEN YOU MIGHT BE ABLE TO BECOME ONE.
CUTE THEORY. BUT, YOU'RE MISSING ONE IMPORTANT DETAIL... I AM MAGGIE.
EVERYONE HERE WANTS TO BE HERE!
THEY WANT *ME* AND THE *COLISEUM!*

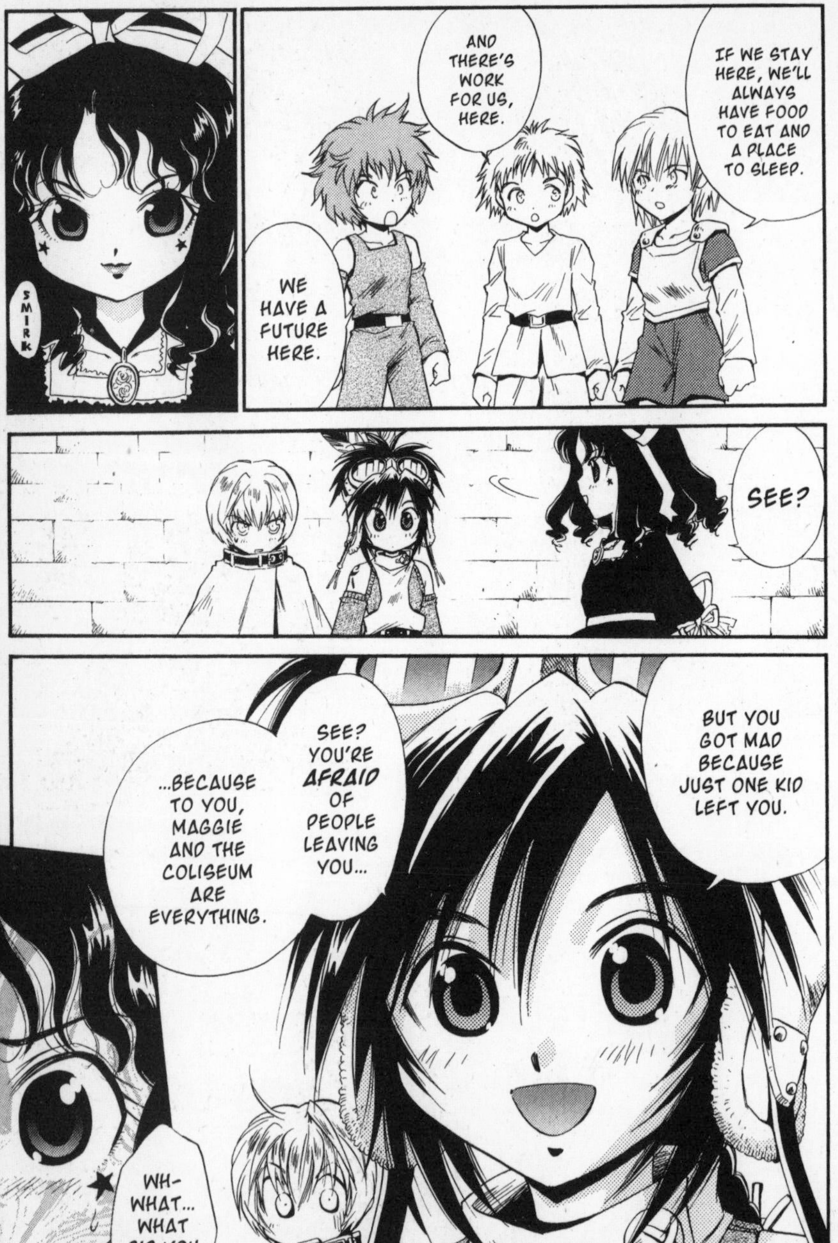
IF WE STAY HERE, WE'LL ALWAYS HAVE FOOD TO EAT AND A PLACE TO SLEEP.
AND THERE'S WORK FOR US, HERE.
WE HAVE A FUTURE HERE.
SMIRK
SEE?
BUT YOU GOT MAD BECAUSE JUST ONE KID LEFT YOU.
SEE? YOU'RE AFRAID OF PEOPLE LEAVING YOU...
...BECAUSE TO YOU, MAGGIE AND THE COLISEUM ARE EVERYTHING.
WH- WHAT... WHAT DID YOU SAY?

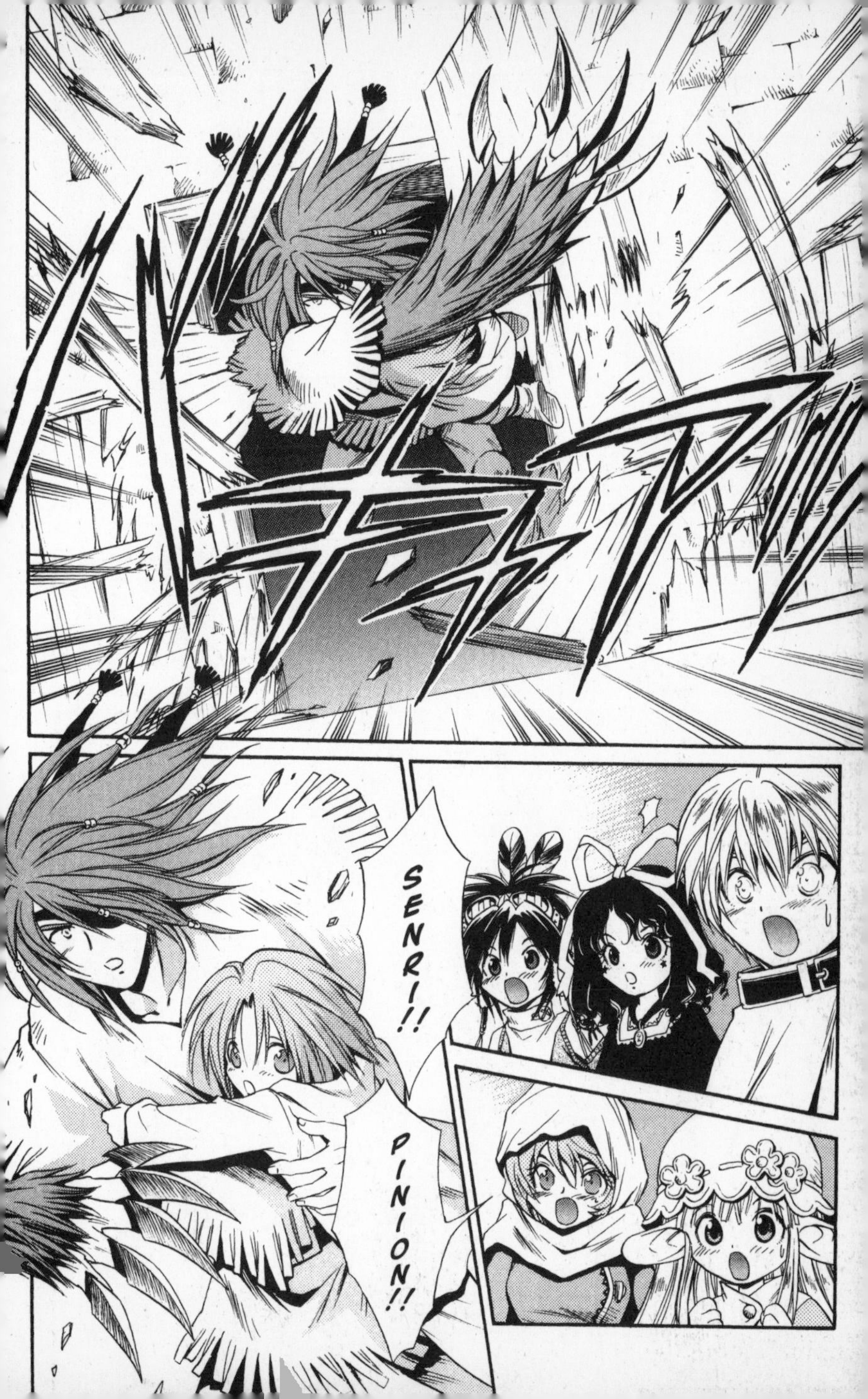
SENRI!!
PINION!!

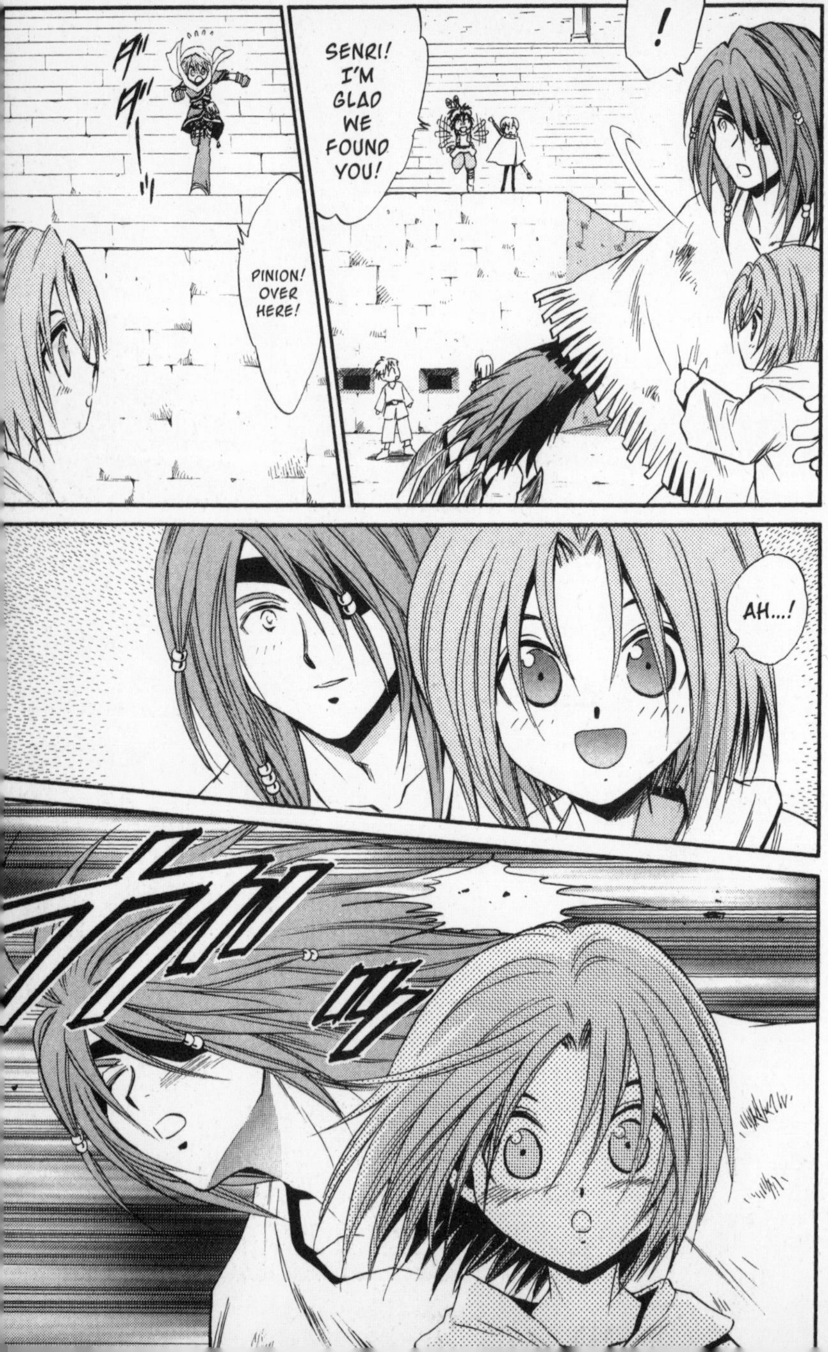
!
SENRI! I'M GLAD WE FOUND YOU!
PINION! OVER HERE!
AH...!

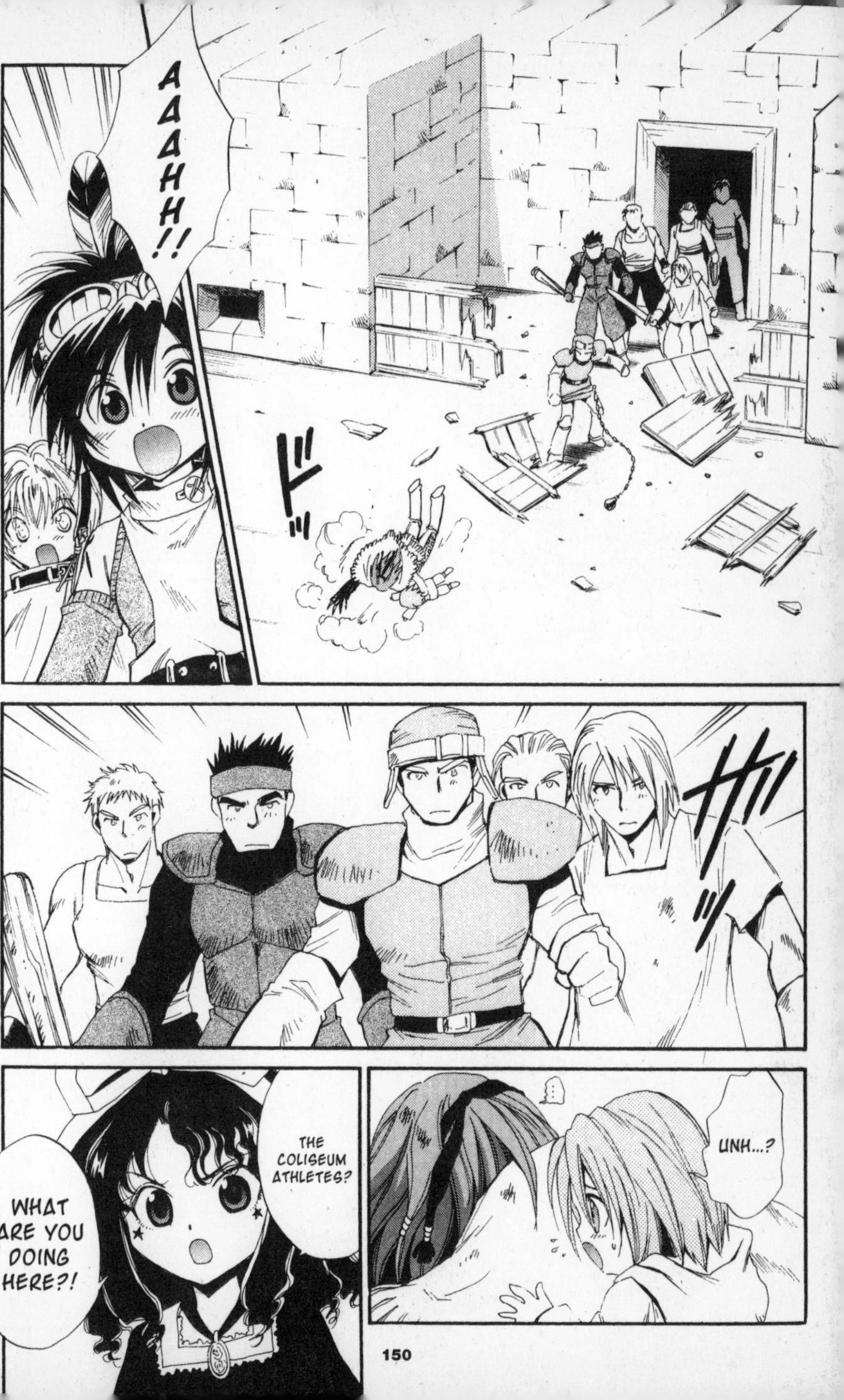
AAAHH!!
ザッ
...
UNH...?
THE COLISEUM ATHLETES?
WHAT ARE YOU DOING HERE?!

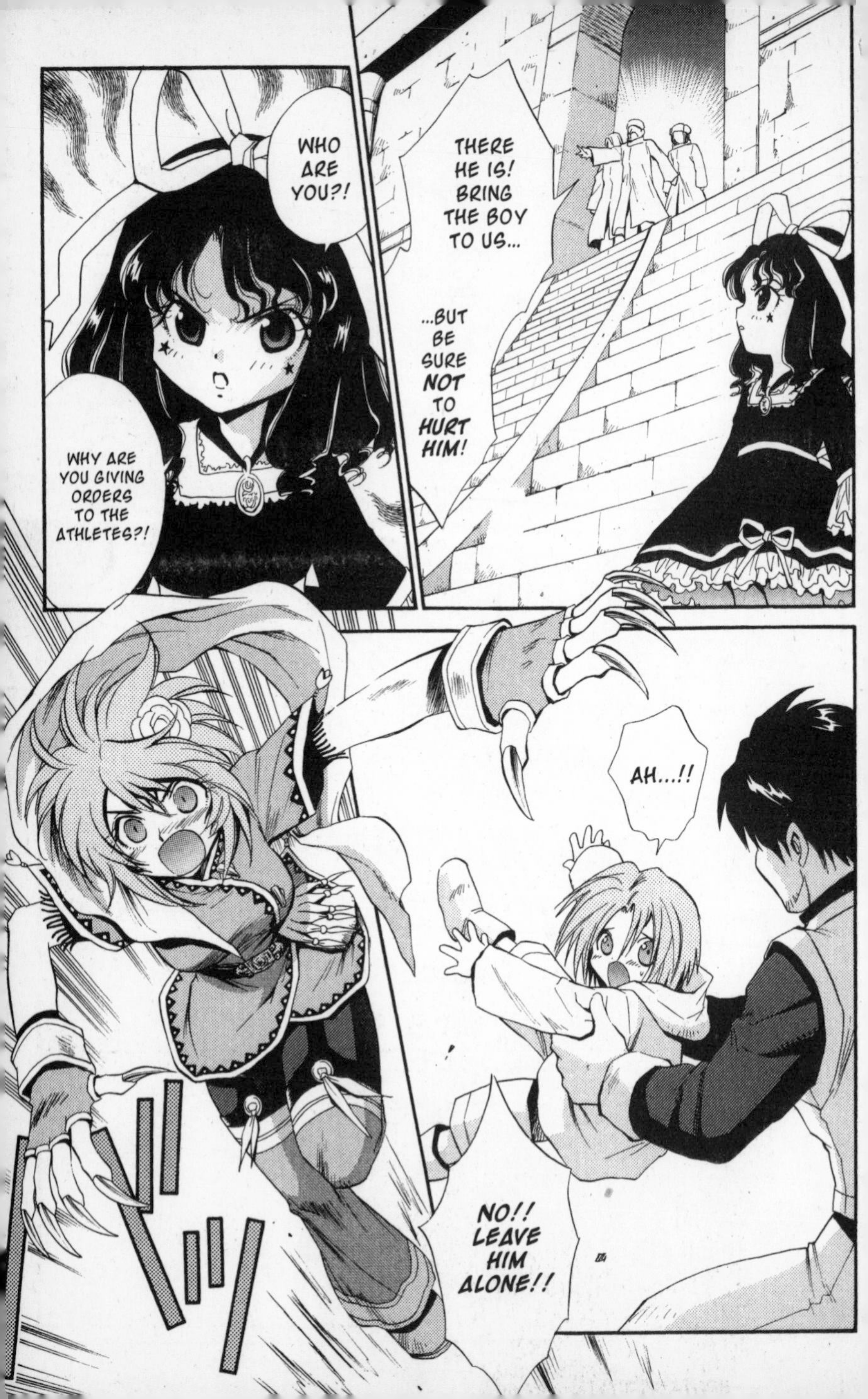
THERE HE IS! BRING THE BOY TO US...
...BUT BE SURE NOT TO HURT HIM!
WHO ARE YOU?!
WHY ARE YOU GIVING ORDERS TO THE ATHLETES?!
AH...!!
NO!! LEAVE HIM ALONE!!

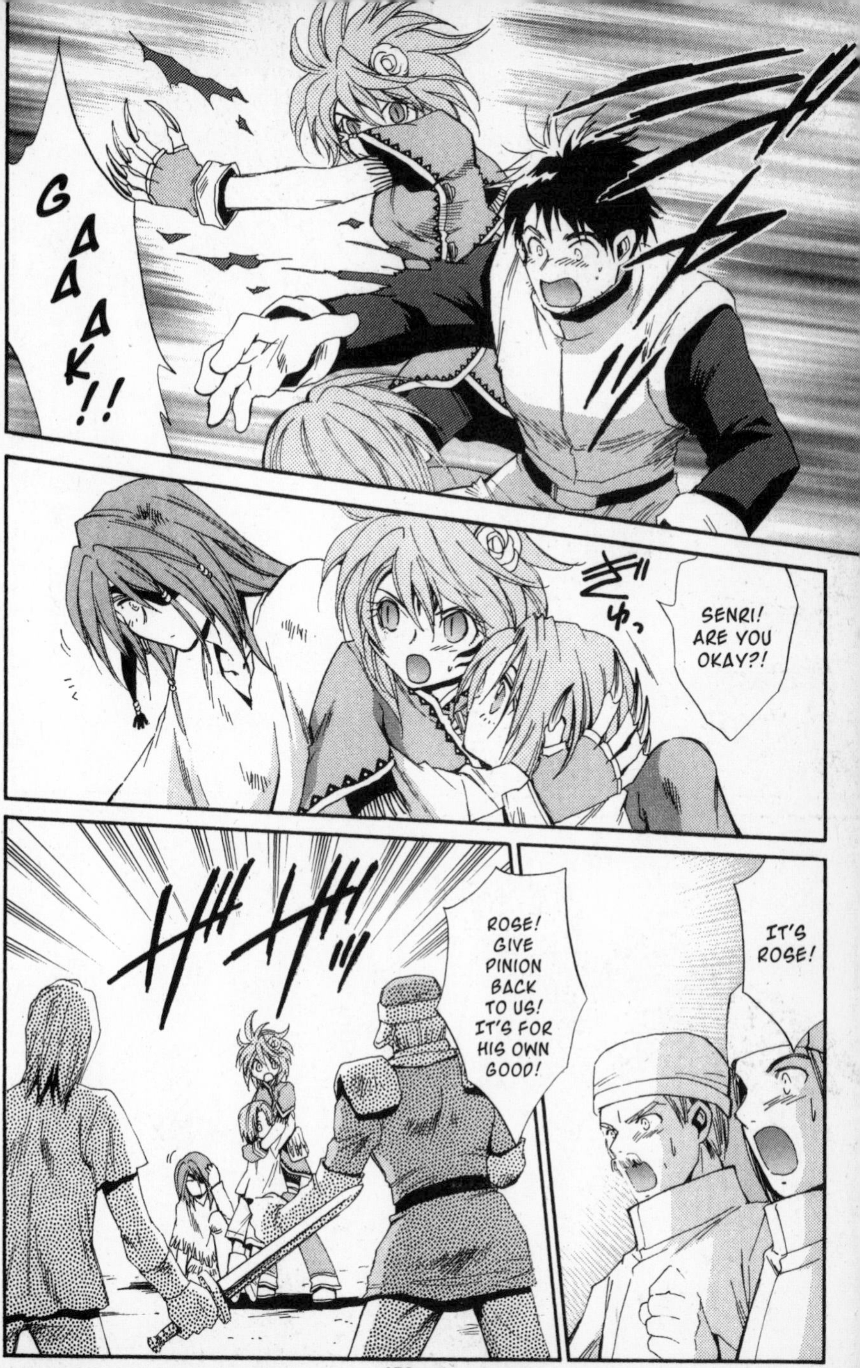
GAAAK!!
SENRI! ARE YOU OKAY?!
IT'S ROSE!
ROSE! GIVE PINION BACK TO US! IT'S FOR HIS OWN GOOD!

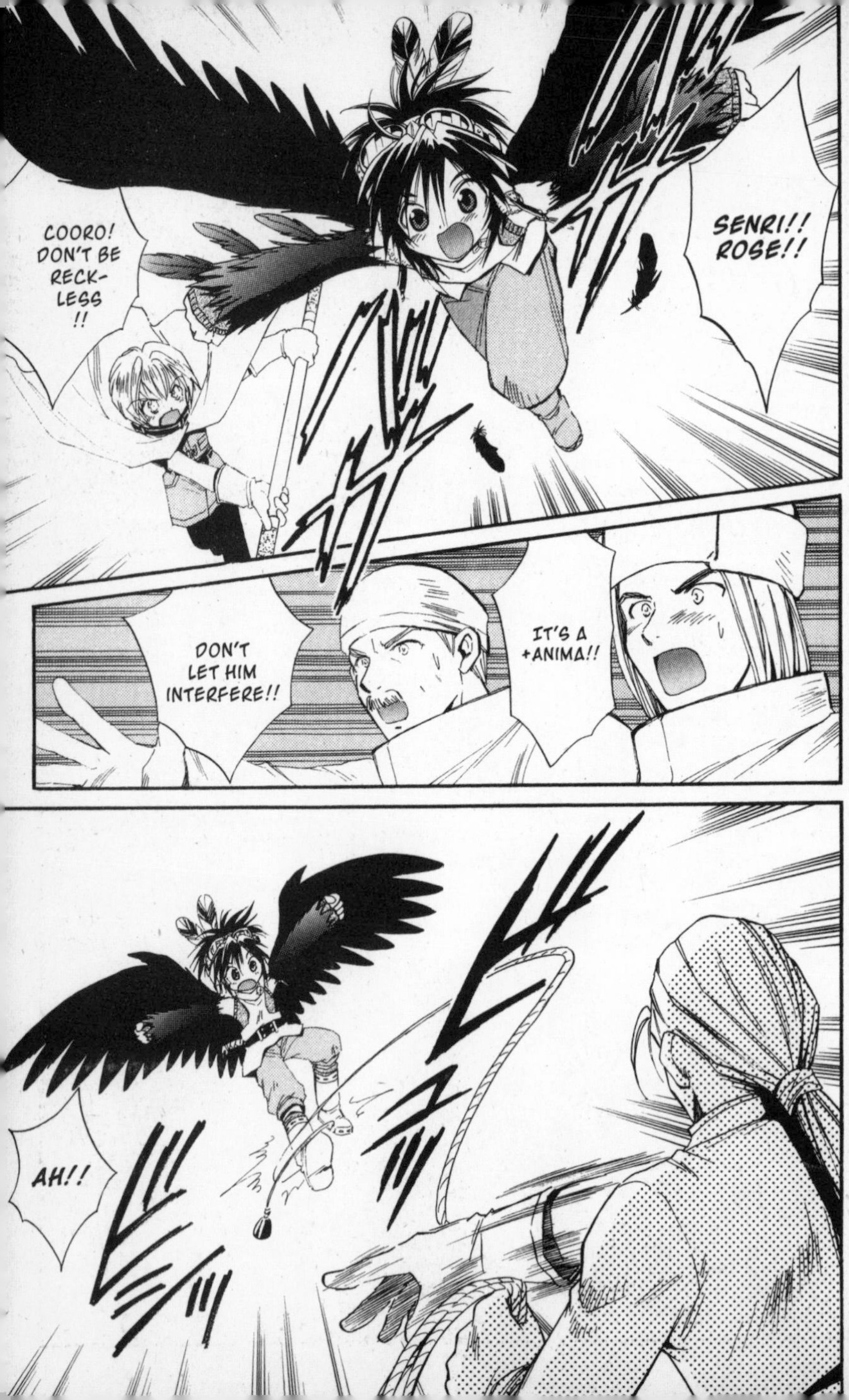
SENRI!! ROSE!!
COORO! DON'T BE RECK-LESS !!
IT'S A +ANIMA!!
DON'T LET HIM INTERFERE!!
AH!!

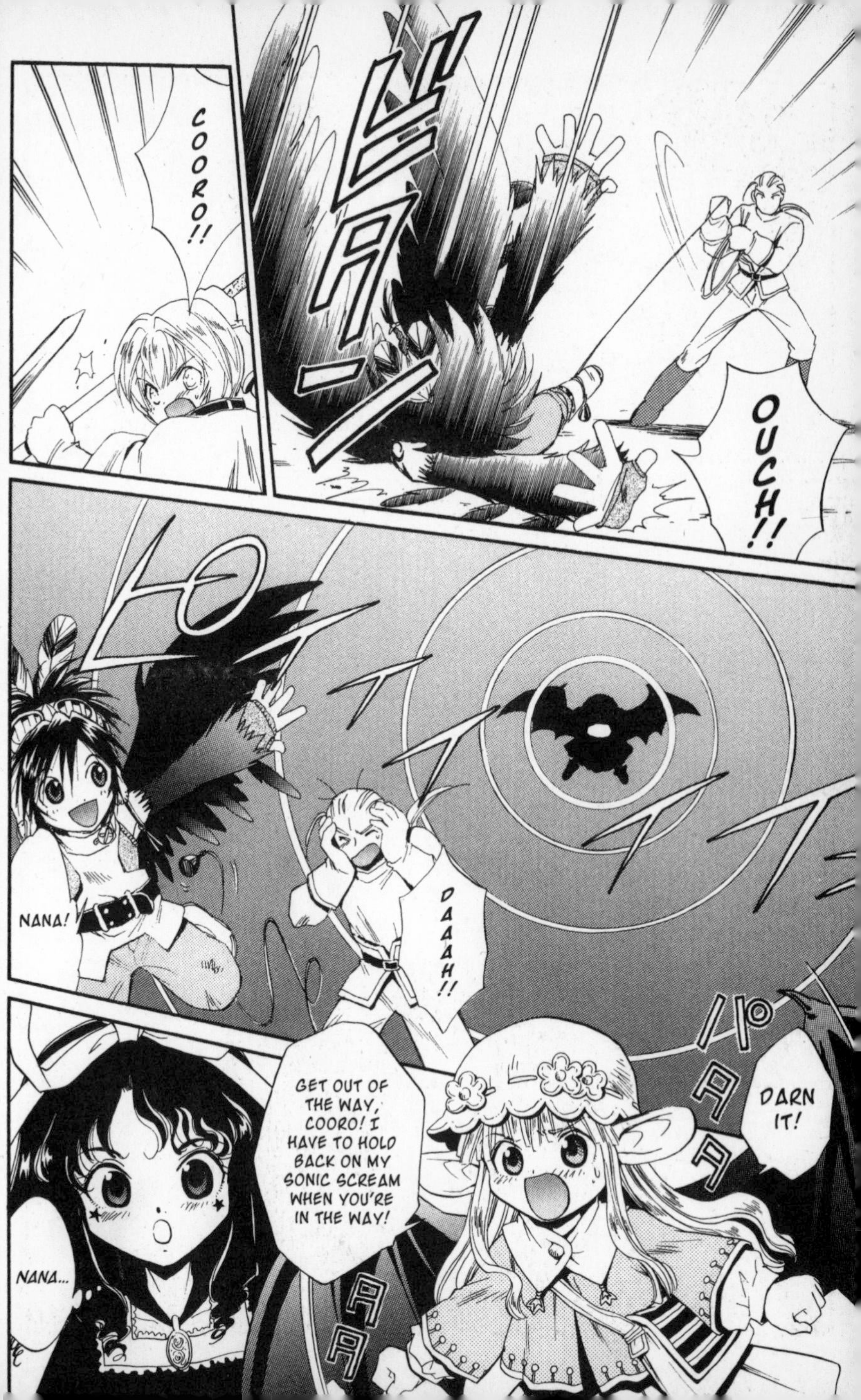
OUCH!!
COORO!!
DAAAAH!!
NANA!
DARN IT!
GET OUT OF THE WAY, COORO! I HAVE TO HOLD BACK ON MY SONIC SCREAM WHEN YOU'RE IN THE WAY!
NANA...

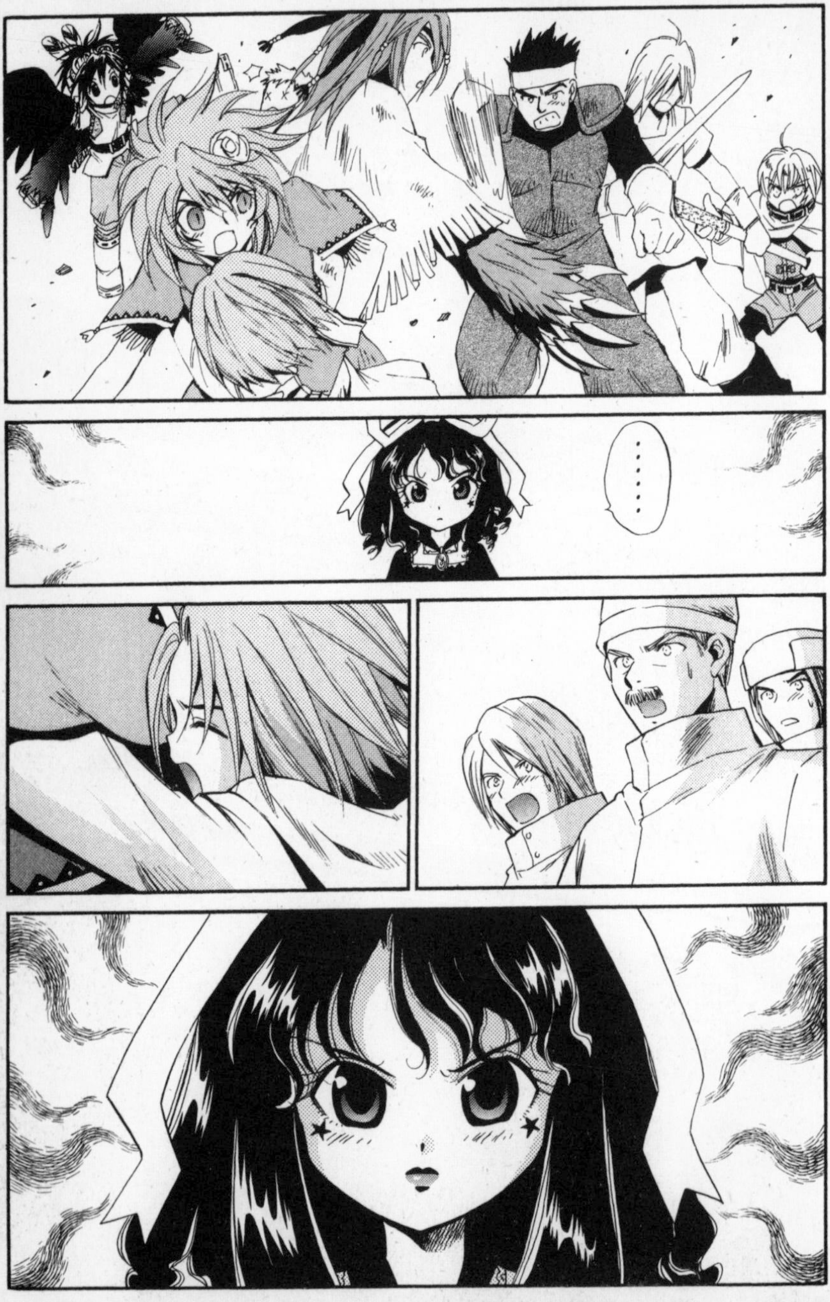
……

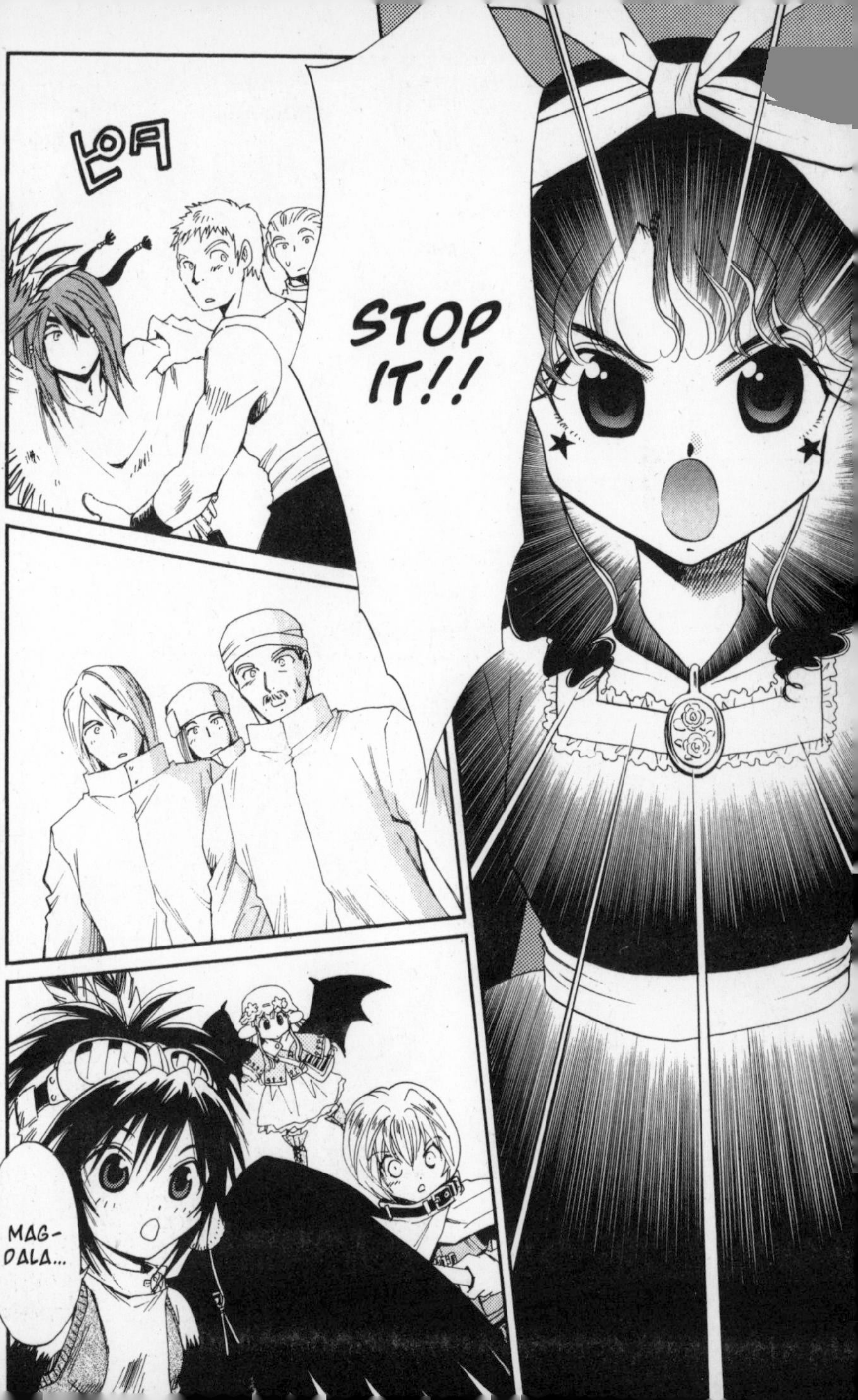
STOP IT!!
MAG-DALA...

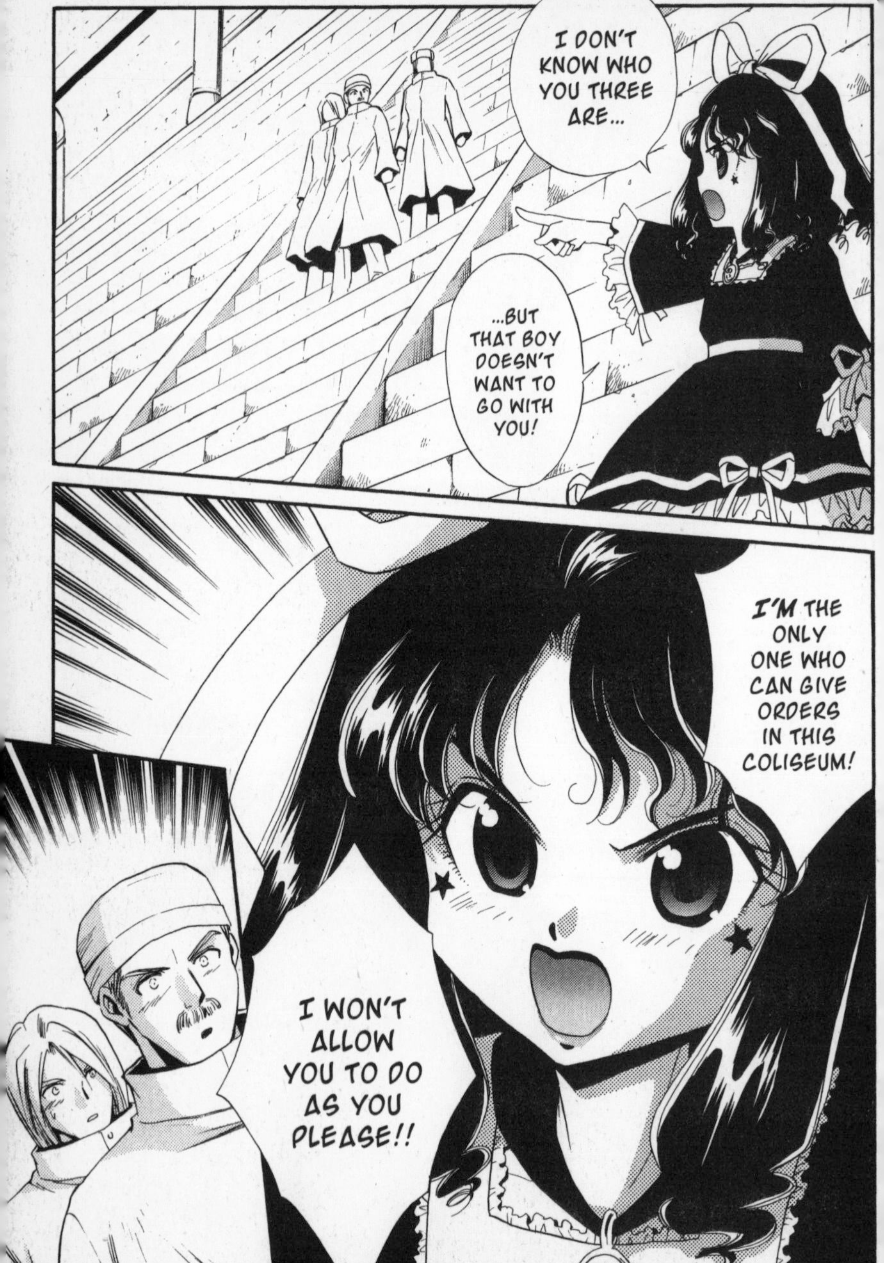
I DON'T KNOW WHO YOU THREE ARE...
...BUT THAT BOY DOESN'T WANT TO GO WITH YOU!
I'M THE ONLY ONE WHO CAN GIVE ORDERS IN THIS COLISEUM!
I WON'T ALLOW YOU TO DO AS YOU PLEASE!!

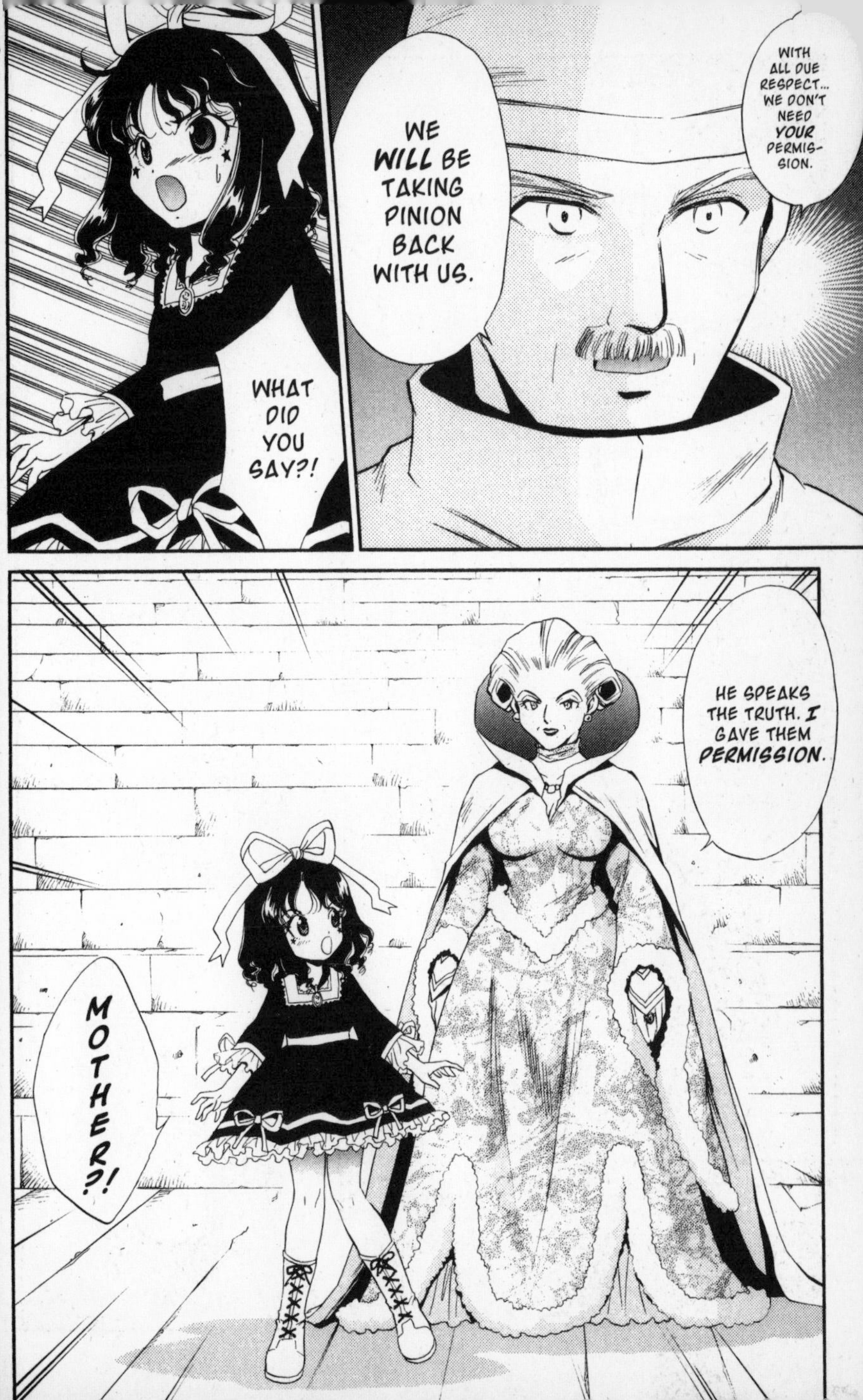
WITH ALL DUE RESPECT... WE DON'T NEED YOUR PERMISSION.
WE WILL BE TAKING PINION BACK WITH US.
WHAT DID YOU SAY?!
HE SPEAKS THE TRUTH. I GAVE THEM PERMISSION.
MOTHER?!

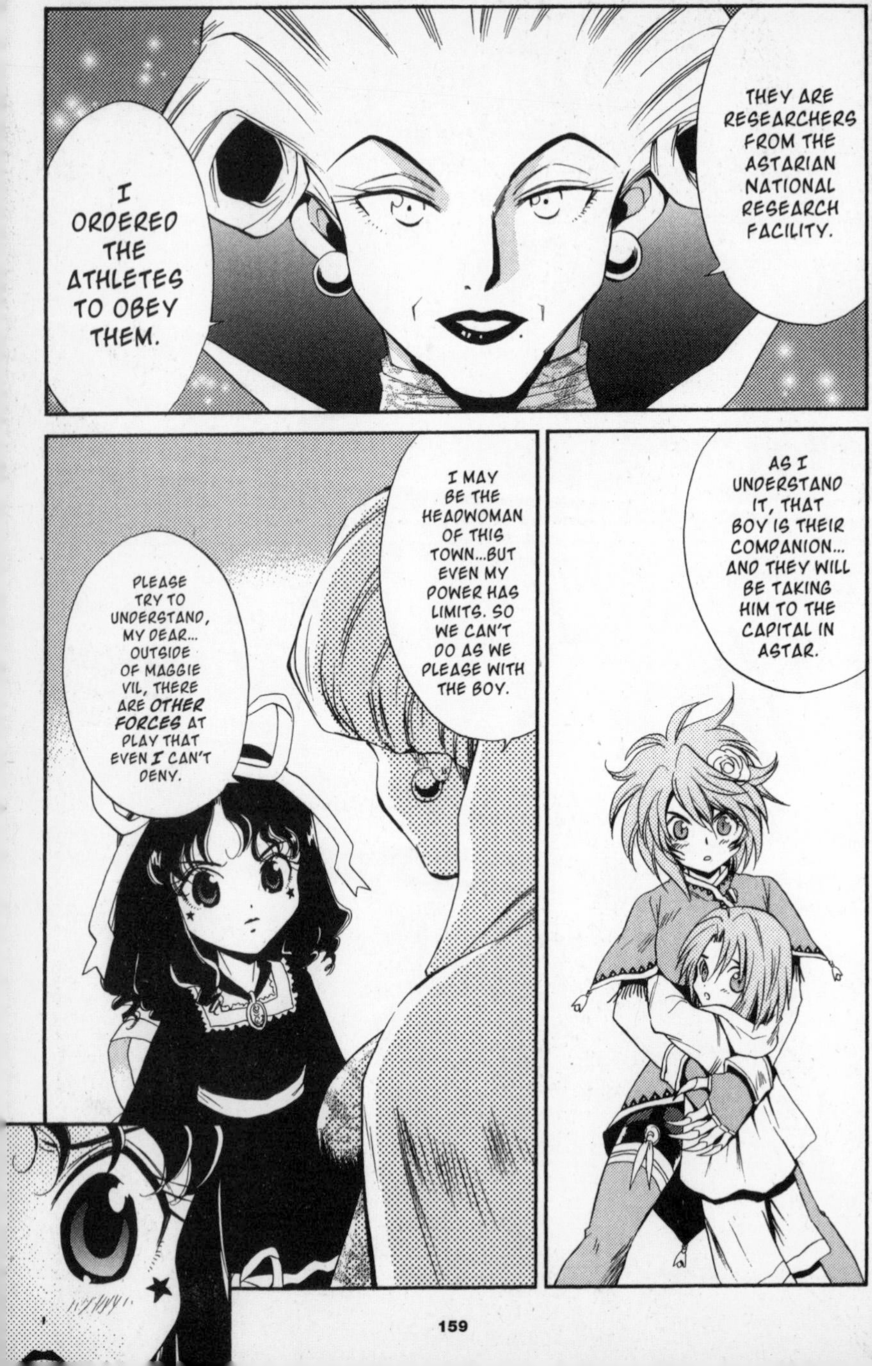
THEY ARE RESEARCHERS FROM THE ASTARIAN NATIONAL RESEARCH FACILITY.
I ORDERED THE ATHLETES TO OBEY THEM.
AS I UNDERSTAND IT, THAT BOY IS THEIR COMPANION... AND THEY WILL BE TAKING HIM TO THE CAPITAL IN ASTAR.
I MAY BE THE HEADWOMAN OF THIS TOWN...BUT EVEN MY POWER HAS LIMITS. SO WE CAN'T DO AS WE PLEASE WITH THE BOY.
PLEASE TRY TO UNDERSTAND, MY DEAR... OUTSIDE OF MAGGIE VIL, THERE ARE OTHER FORCES AT PLAY THAT EVEN I CAN'T DENY.

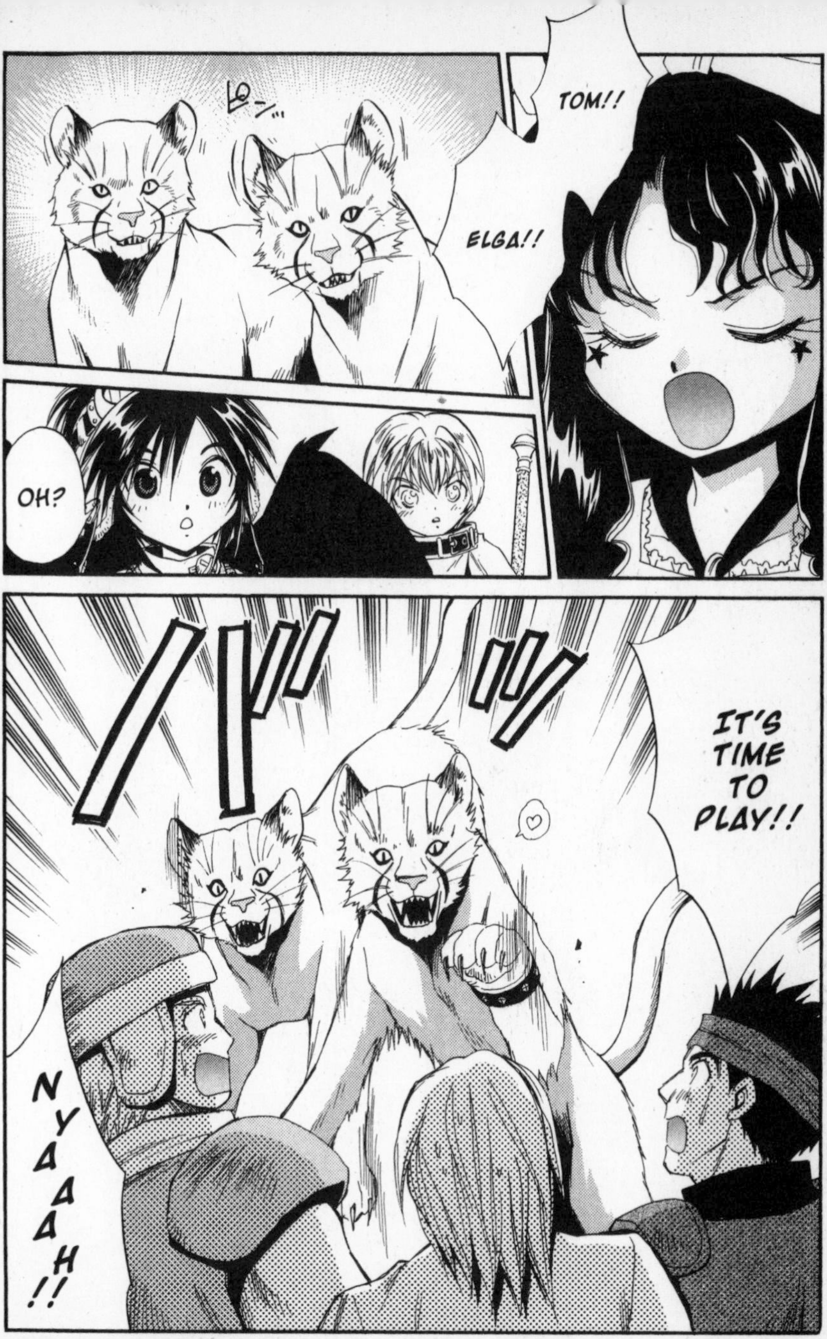
TOM!!
ELGA!!
OH?
IT'S TIME TO PLAY!!
NYAAAH!!

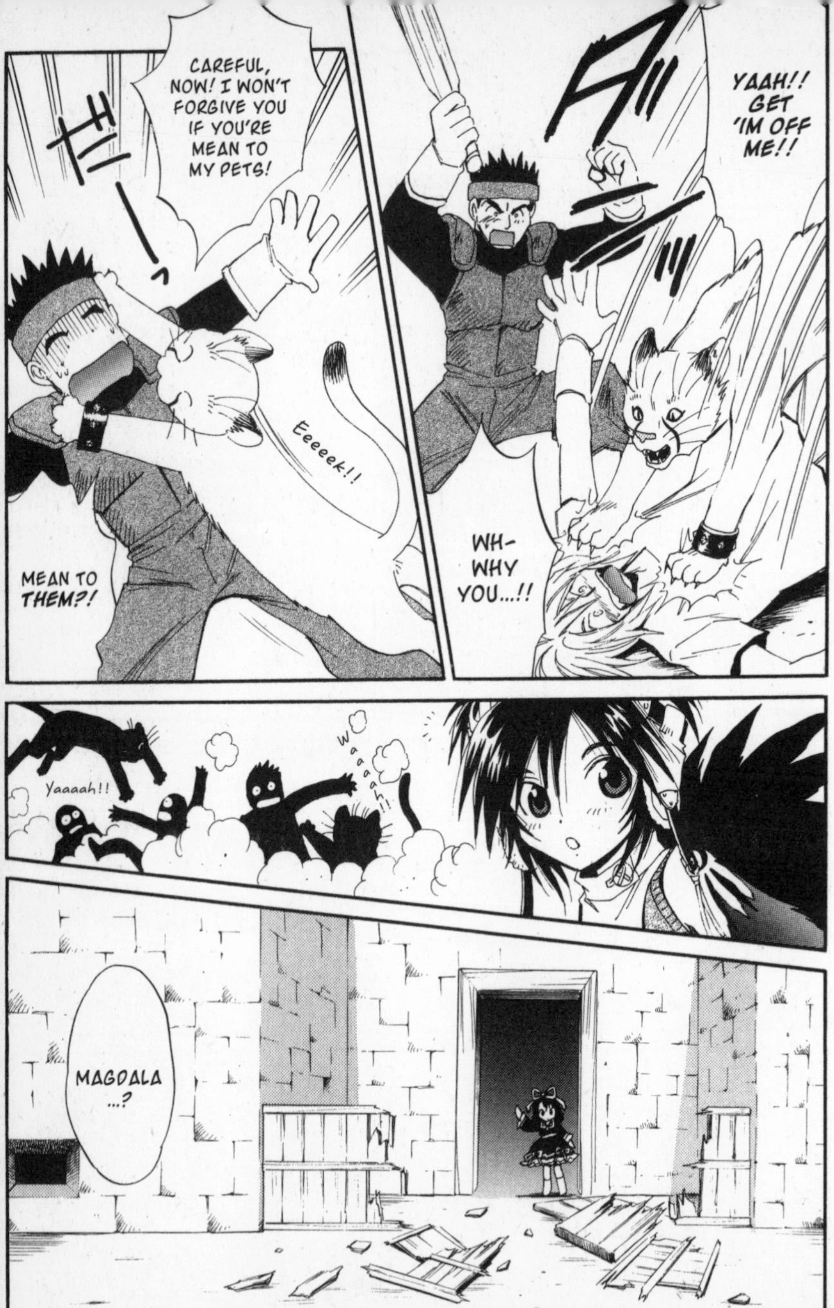
YAAH!! GET 'IM OFF ME!!
WH-WHY YOU...!!
CAREFUL, NOW! I WON'T FORGIVE YOU IF YOU'RE MEAN TO MY PETS!
Eeeeek!!
MEAN TO THEM?!
Waaaah!!
Yaaaah!!
MAGDALA ...?

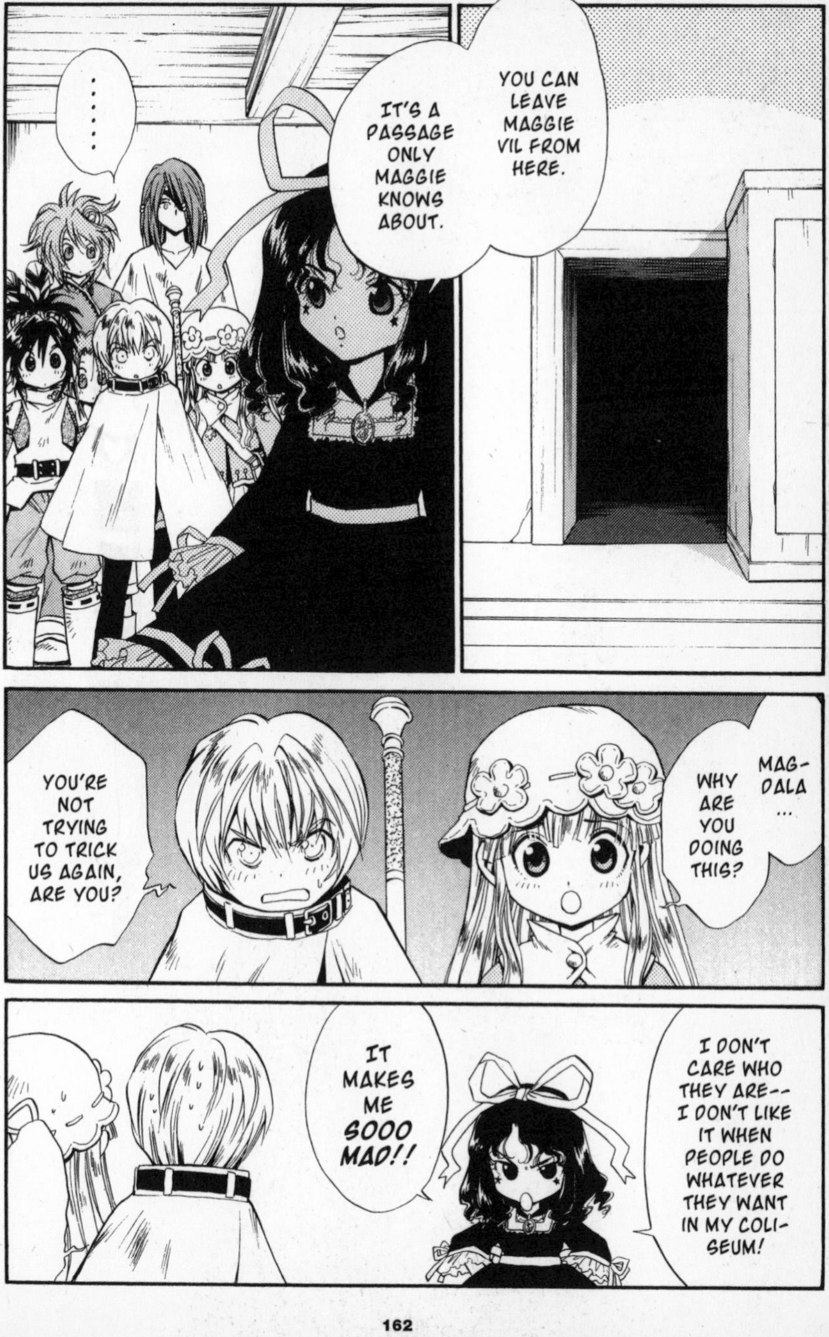
YOU CAN LEAVE MAGGIE VIL FROM HERE.
IT'S A PASSAGE ONLY MAGGIE KNOWS ABOUT.
......
MAG-DALA...
WHY ARE YOU DOING THIS?
YOU'RE NOT TRYING TO TRICK US AGAIN, ARE YOU?
I DON'T CARE WHO THEY ARE-- I DON'T LIKE IT WHEN PEOPLE DO WHATEVER THEY WANT IN MY COLI-SEUM!
IT MAKES ME *SOOO* MAD!!

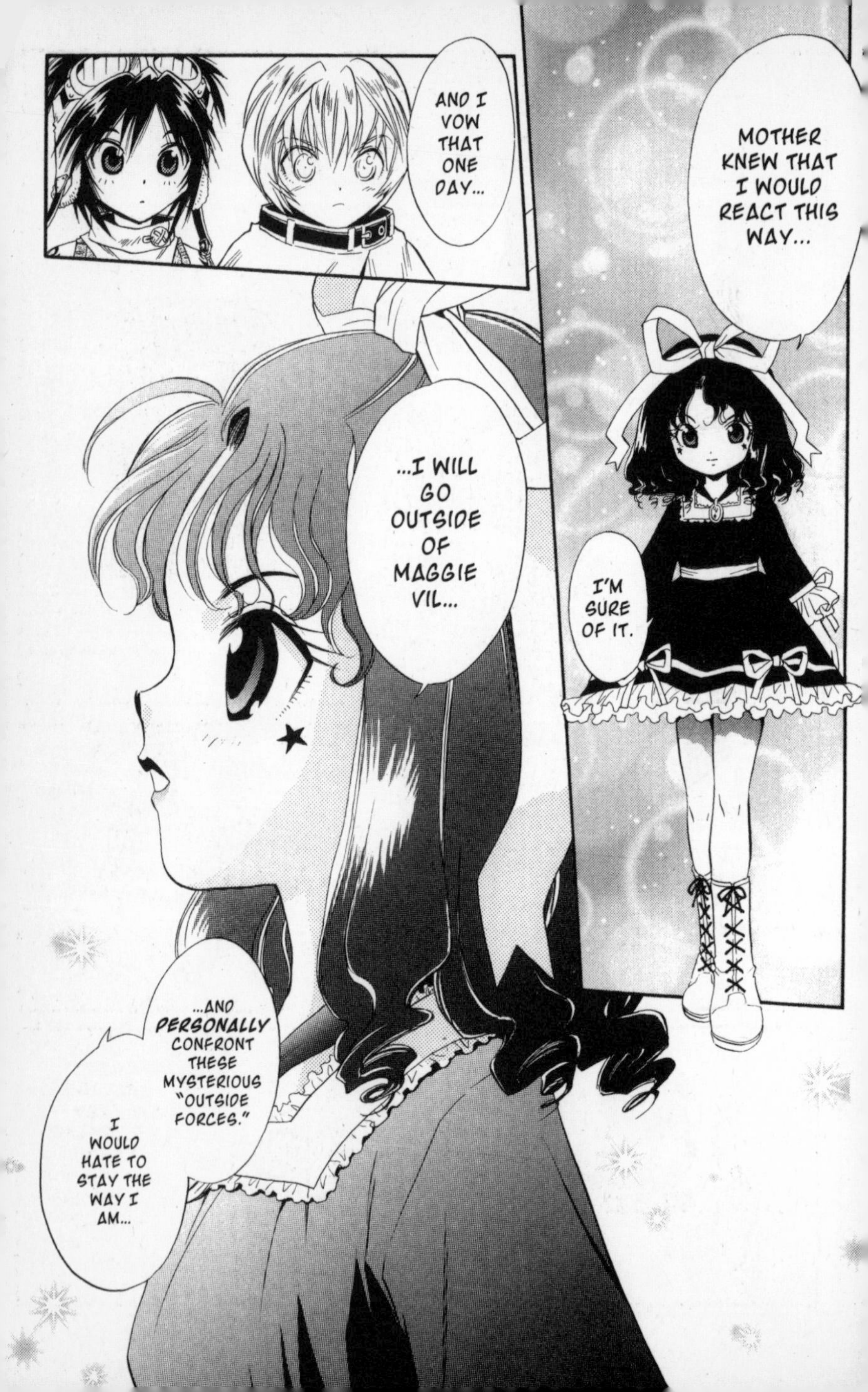
MOTHER KNEW THAT I WOULD REACT THIS WAY...
I'M SURE OF IT.
AND I VOW THAT ONE DAY...
...I WILL GO OUTSIDE OF MAGGIE VIL...
...AND **PERSONALLY** CONFRONT THESE MYSTERIOUS "OUTSIDE FORCES."
I WOULD HATE TO STAY THE WAY I AM...

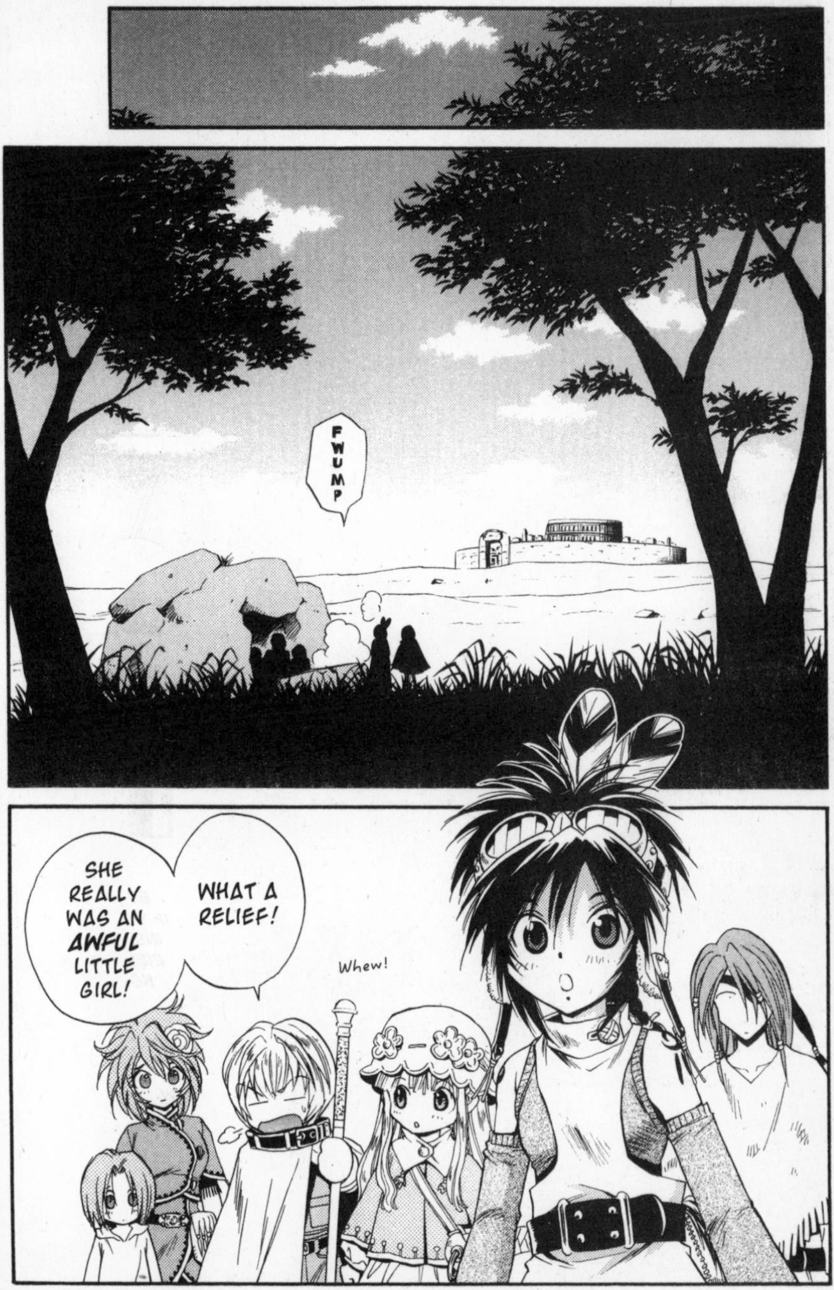
FWUMP
WHAT A RELIEF!
SHE REALLY WAS AN **AWFUL** LITTLE GIRL!
Whew!

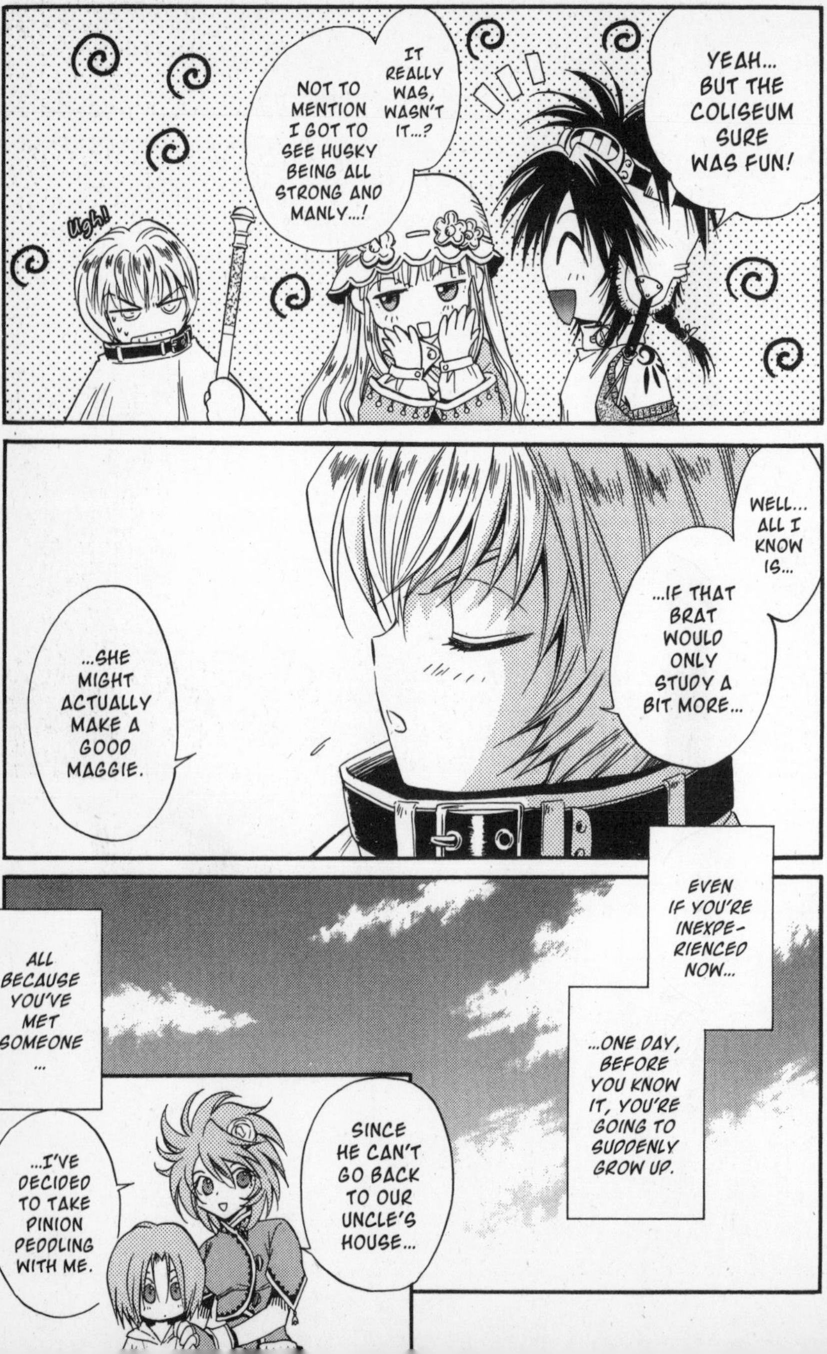
YEAH... BUT THE COLISEUM SURE WAS FUN!
IT REALLY WAS, WASN'T IT...?
NOT TO MENTION I GOT TO SEE HUSKY BEING ALL STRONG AND MANLY...!
Ugh!
WELL... ALL I KNOW IS...
...IF THAT BRAT WOULD ONLY STUDY A BIT MORE...
...SHE MIGHT ACTUALLY MAKE A GOOD MAGGIE.
EVEN IF YOU'RE INEXPE-RIENCED NOW...
...ONE DAY, BEFORE YOU KNOW IT, YOU'RE GOING TO SUDDENLY GROW UP.
ALL BECAUSE YOU'VE MET SOMEONE...
SINCE HE CAN'T GO BACK TO OUR UNCLE'S HOUSE...
...I'VE DECIDED TO TAKE PINION PEDDLING WITH ME.

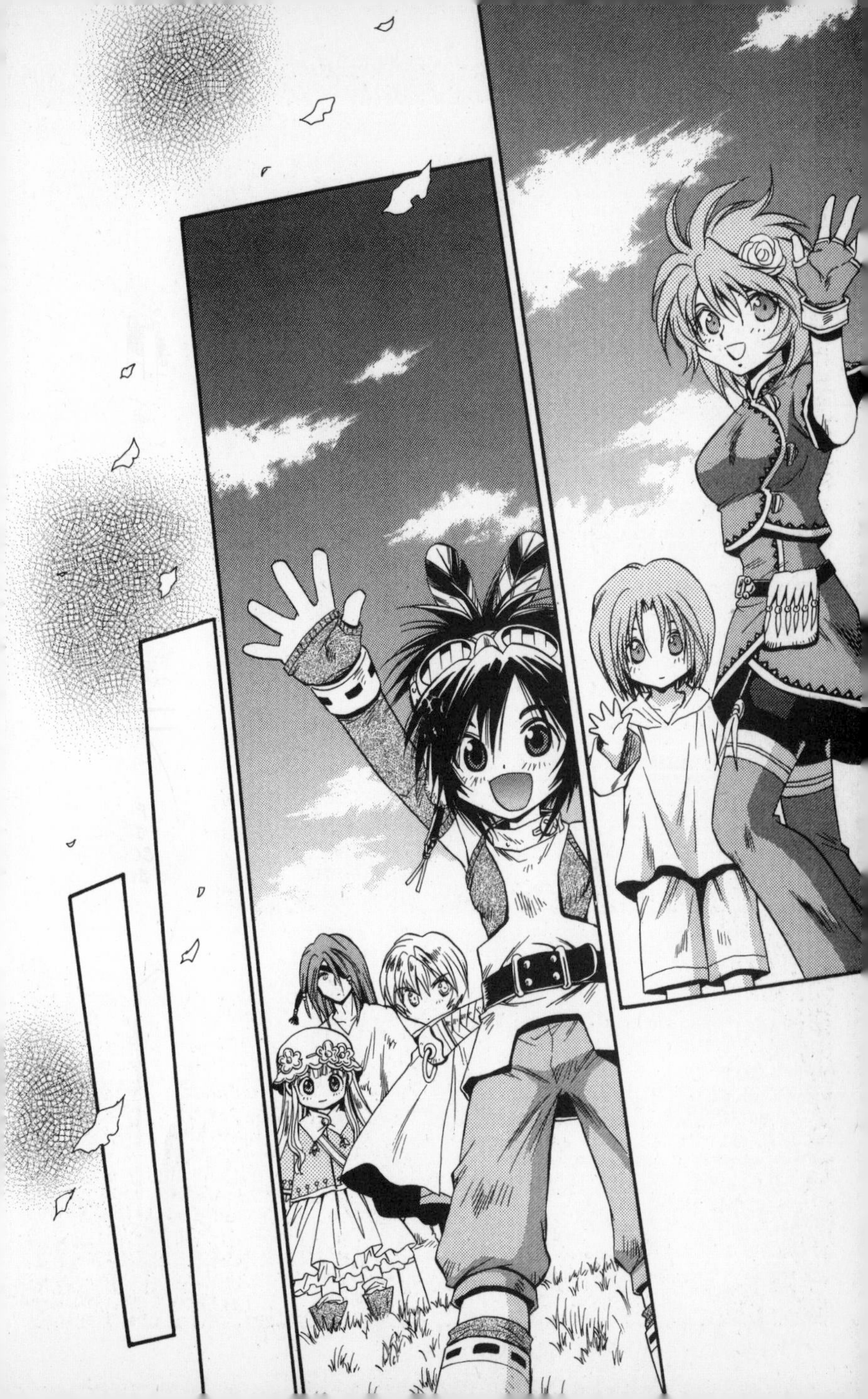

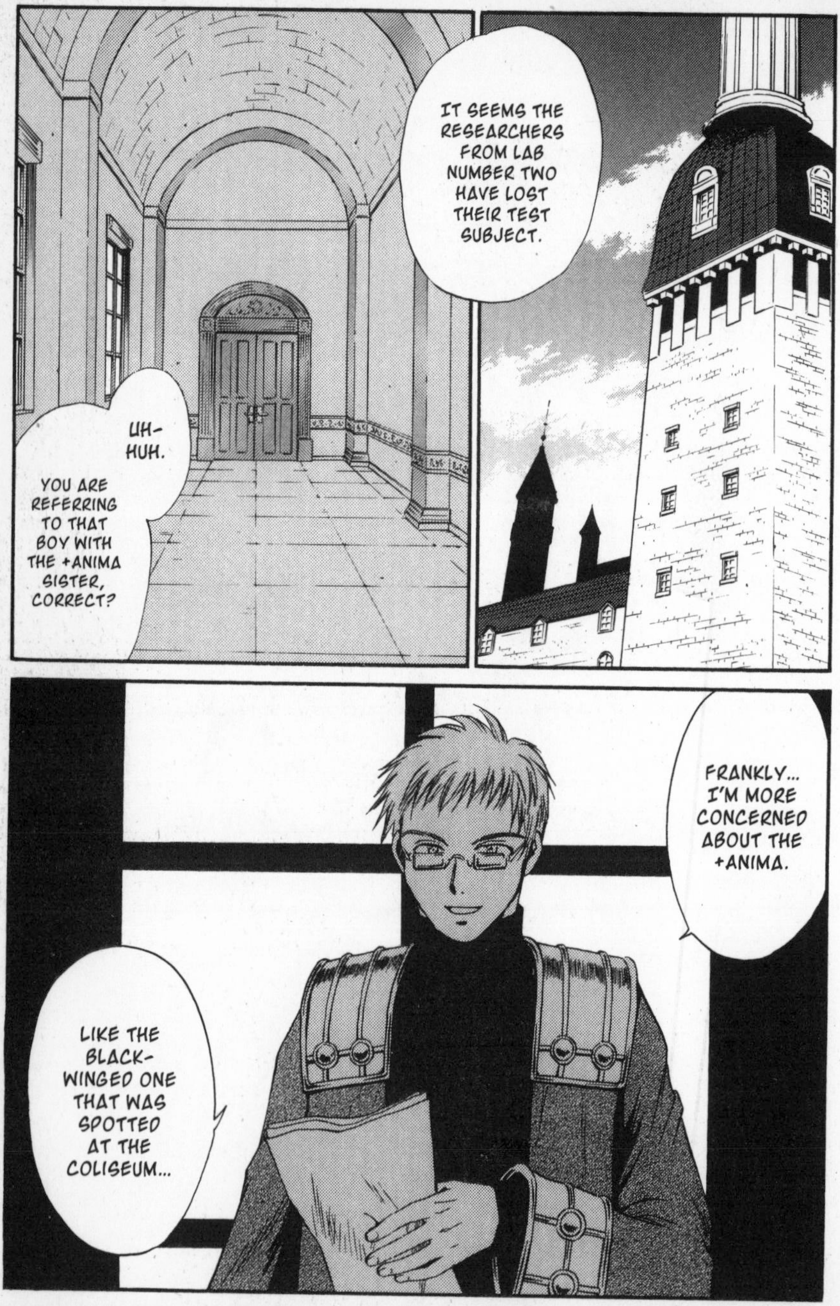
IT SEEMS THE RESEARCHERS FROM LAB NUMBER TWO HAVE LOST THEIR TEST SUBJECT.
UH-HUH.
YOU ARE REFERRING TO THAT BOY WITH THE +ANIMA SISTER, CORRECT?
FRANKLY... I'M MORE CONCERNED ABOUT THE +ANIMA.
LIKE THE BLACK-WINGED ONE THAT WAS SPOTTED AT THE COLISEUM...

Peaceful place.

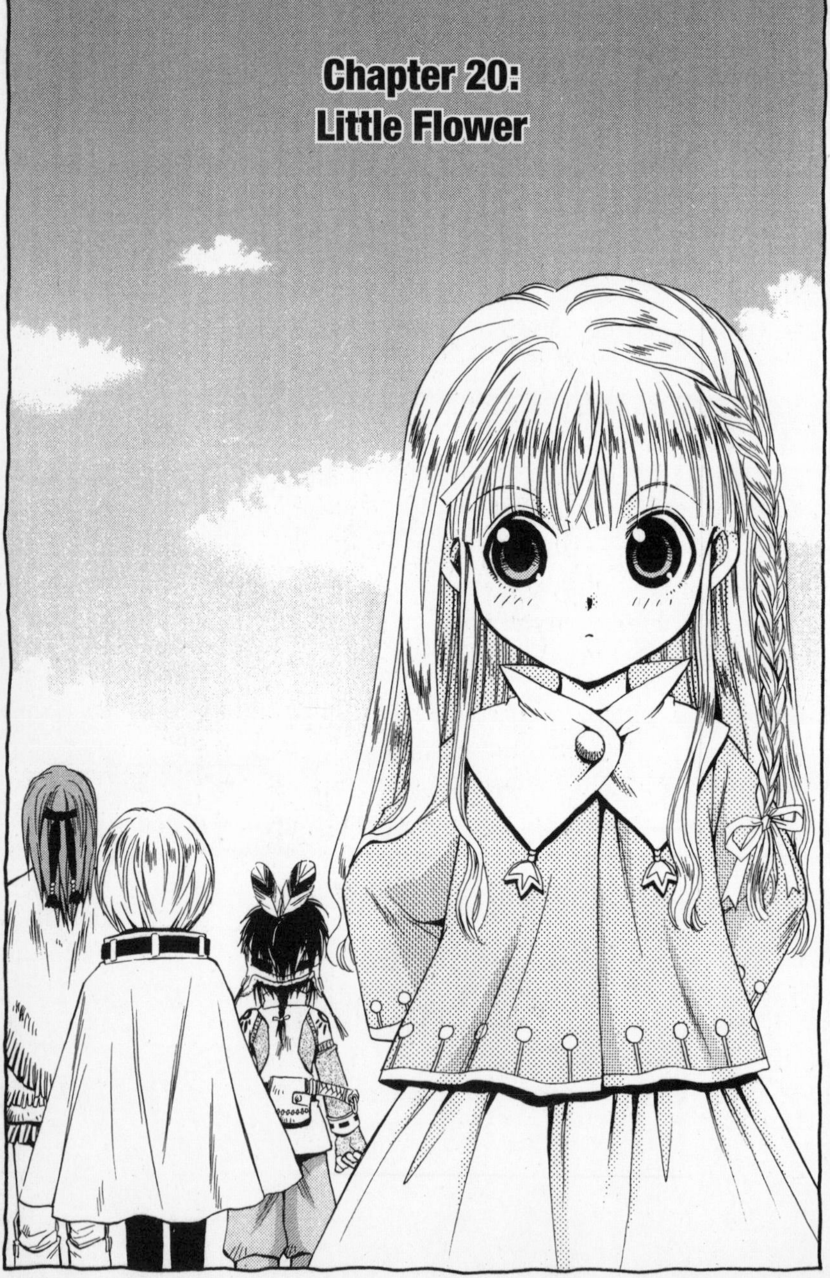
Chapter 20:
Little Flower

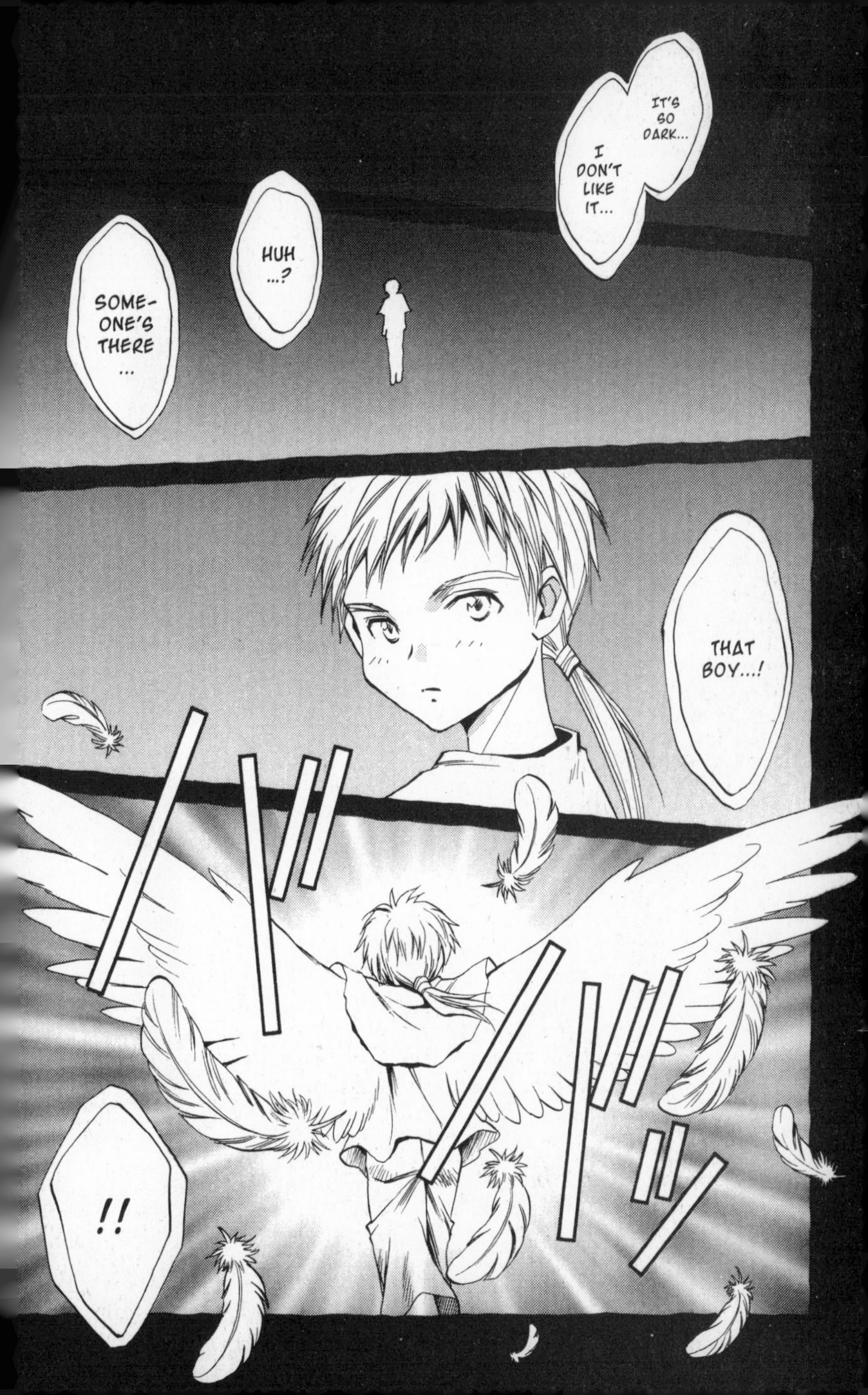
IT'S SO DARK...
I DON'T LIKE IT...
HUH ...?
SOME-ONE'S THERE ...
THAT BOY...!
!!

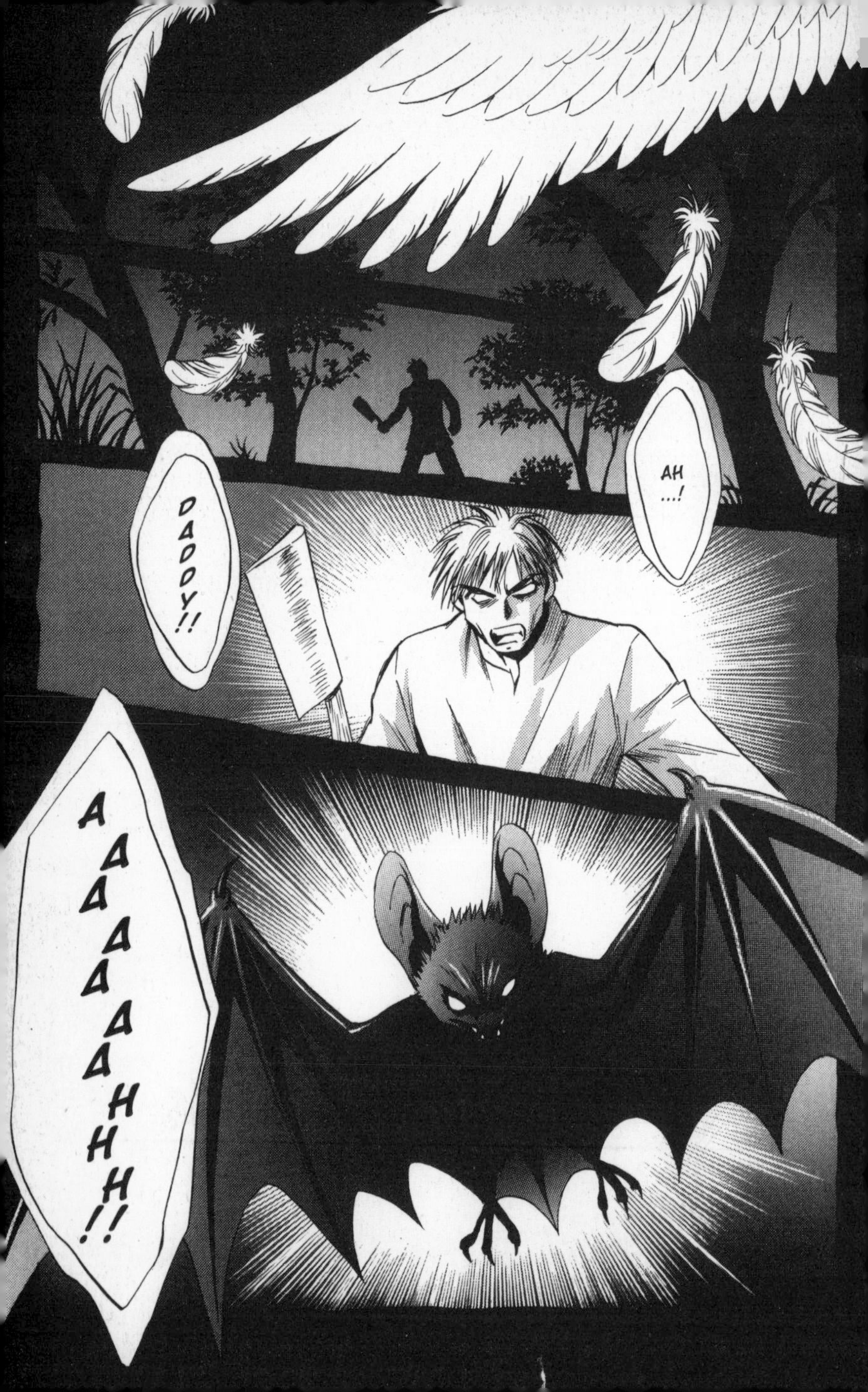
AH ...!
DADDY!!
AAAAAAAAHHHH!!

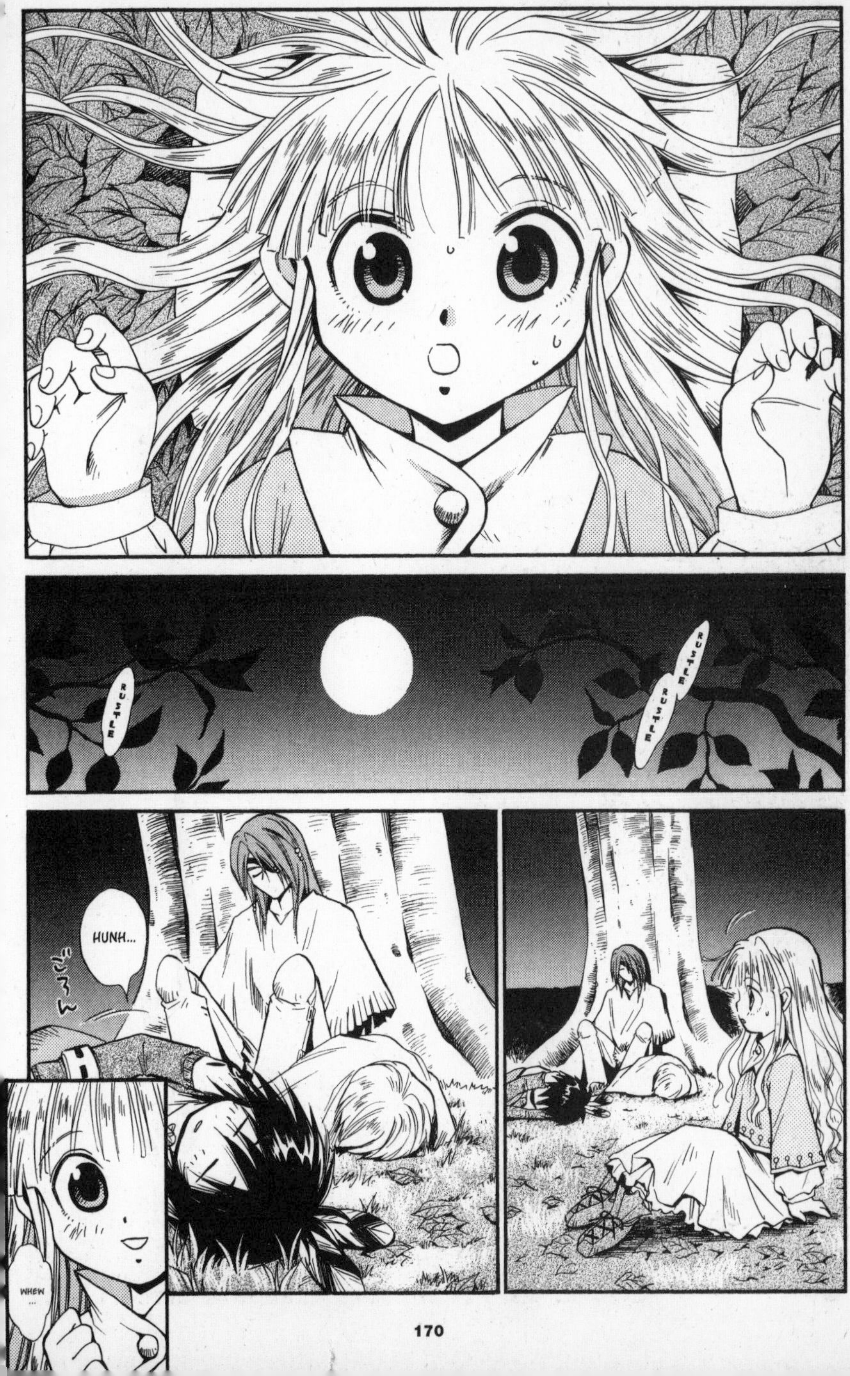
RUSTLE
RUSTLE
RUSTLE
HUNH...
WHEW ...

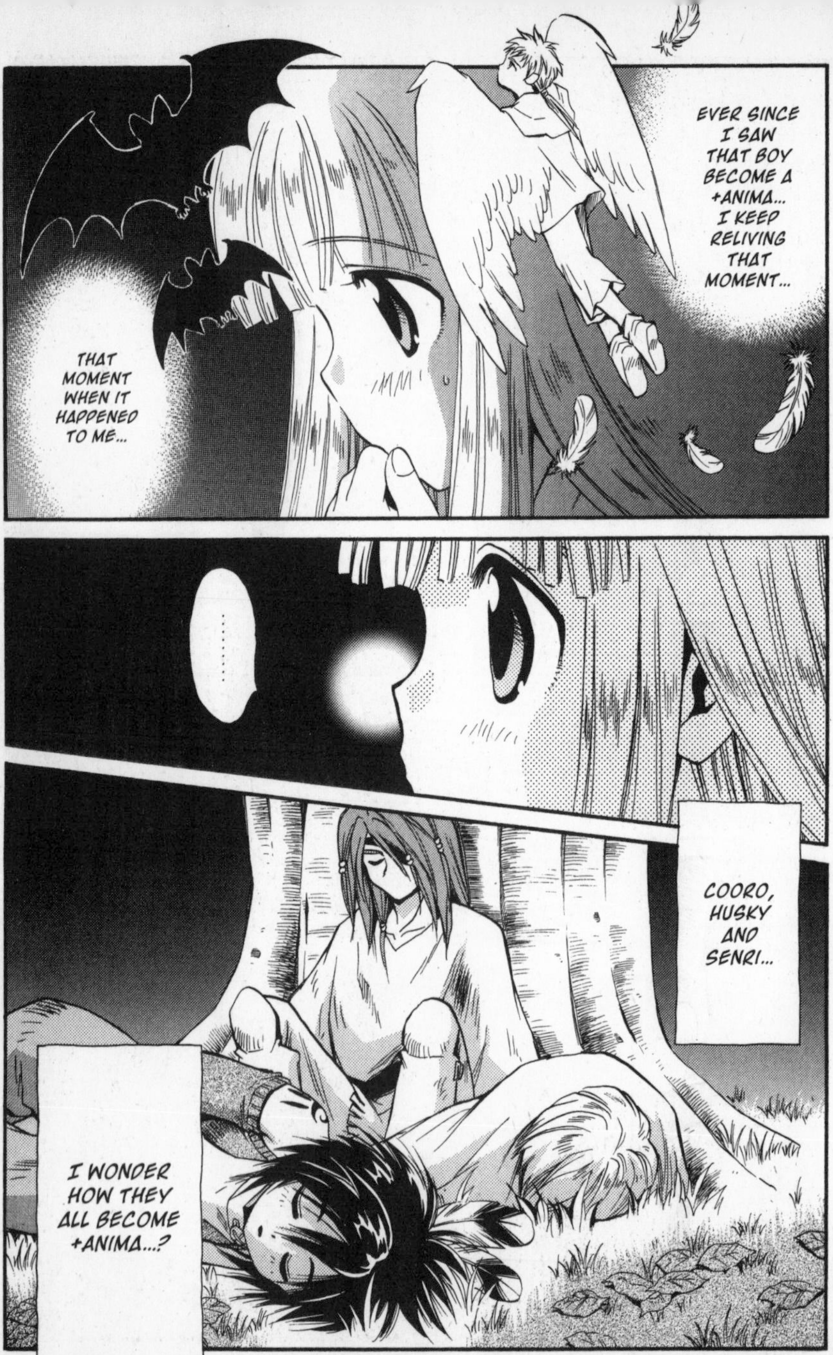
EVER SINCE I SAW THAT BOY BECOME A +ANIMA... I KEEP RELIVING THAT MOMENT...
THAT MOMENT WHEN IT HAPPENED TO ME...
......
COORO, HUSKY AND SENRI...
I WONDER HOW THEY ALL BECOME +ANIMA...?

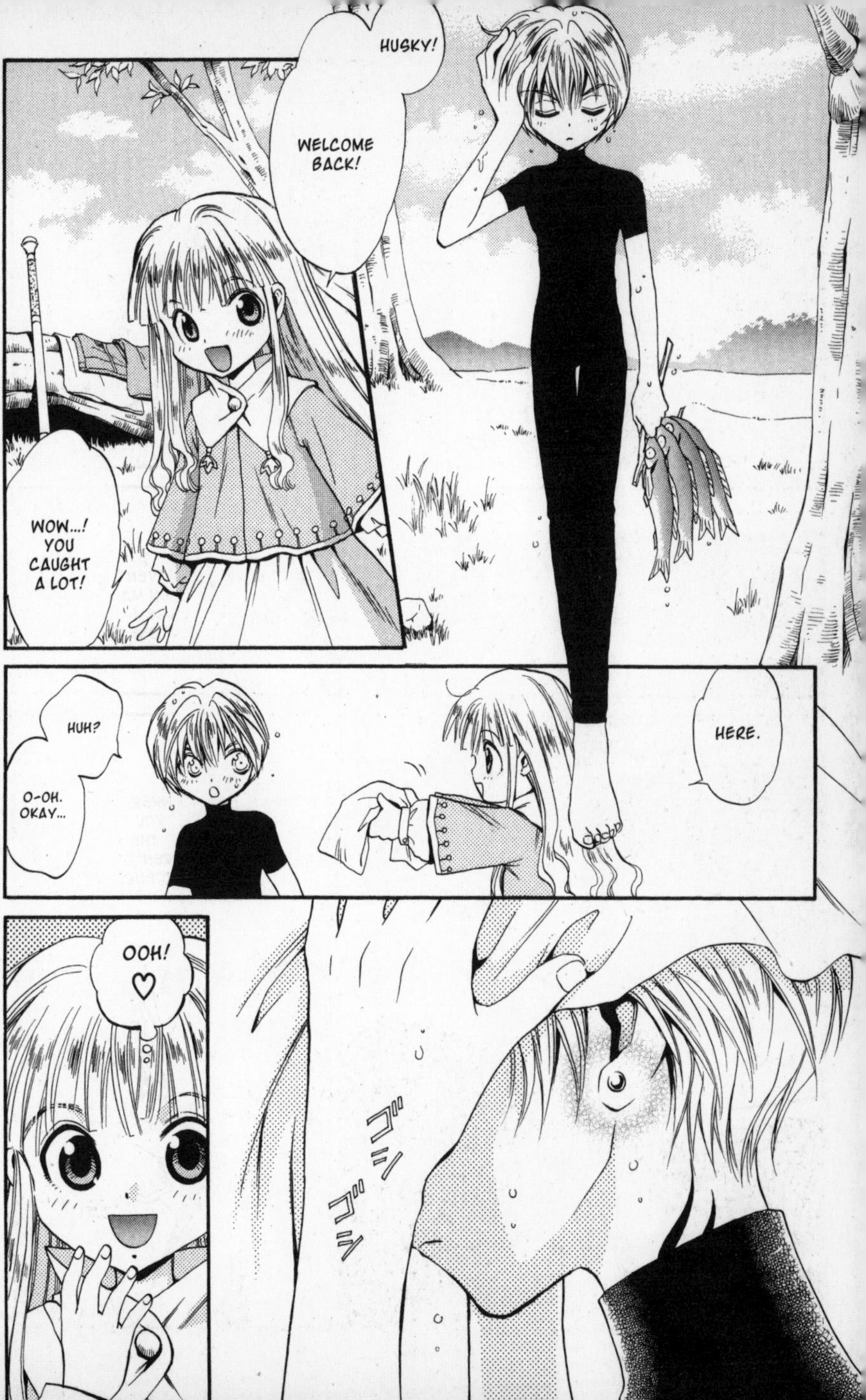

HUSKY!
WELCOME BACK!
WOW...! YOU CAUGHT A LOT!
HERE.
HUH?
O-OH. OKAY...
ゴシ ゴシ
OOH! ♡

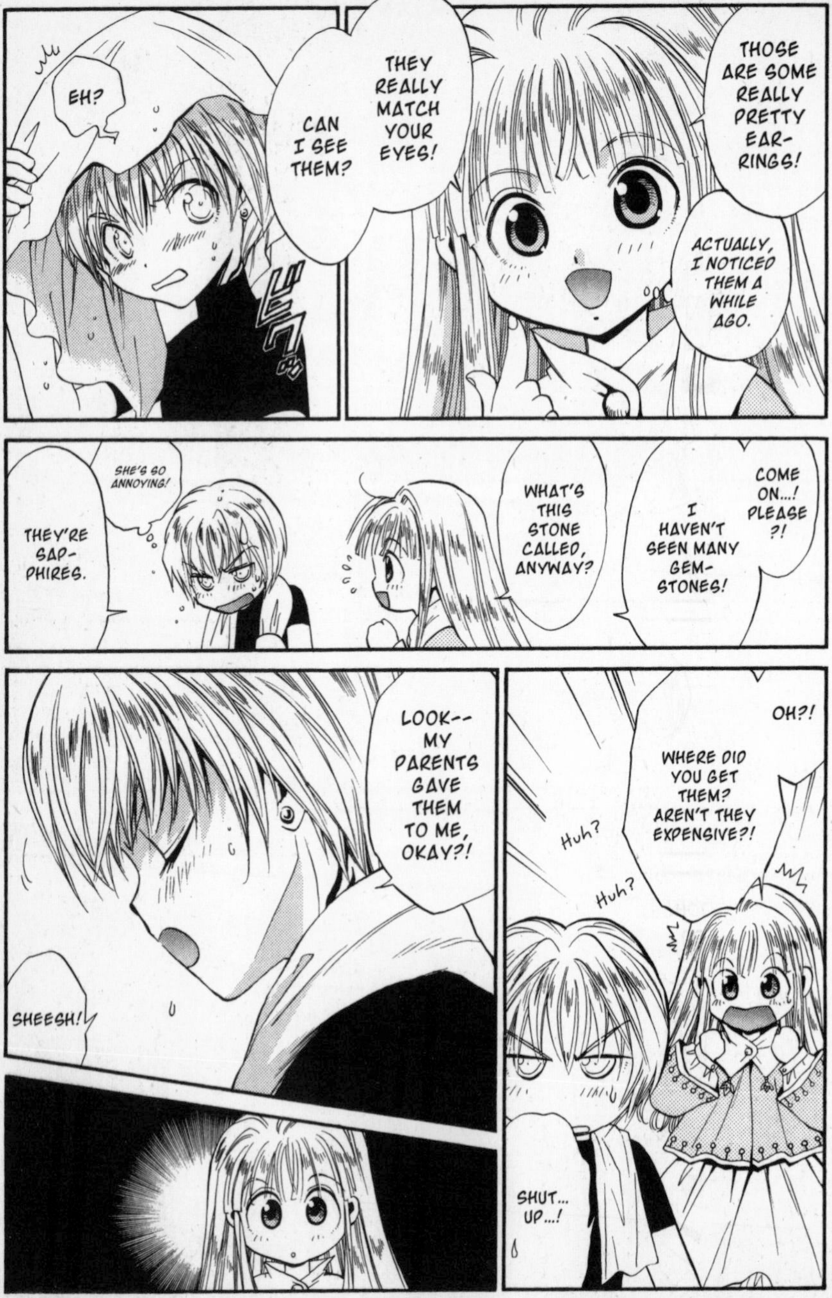
THOSE ARE SOME REALLY PRETTY EAR-RINGS!
ACTUALLY, I NOTICED THEM A WHILE AGO.
THEY REALLY MATCH YOUR EYES!
CAN I SEE THEM?
EH?
COME ON...! PLEASE?!
I HAVEN'T SEEN MANY GEM-STONES!
WHAT'S THIS STONE CALLED, ANYWAY?
SHE'S SO ANNOYING!
THEY'RE SAP-PHIRES.
OH?!
WHERE DID YOU GET THEM? AREN'T THEY EXPENSIVE?!
Huh?
Huh?
SHUT... UP...!
LOOK-- MY PARENTS GAVE THEM TO ME, OKAY?!
SHEESH!

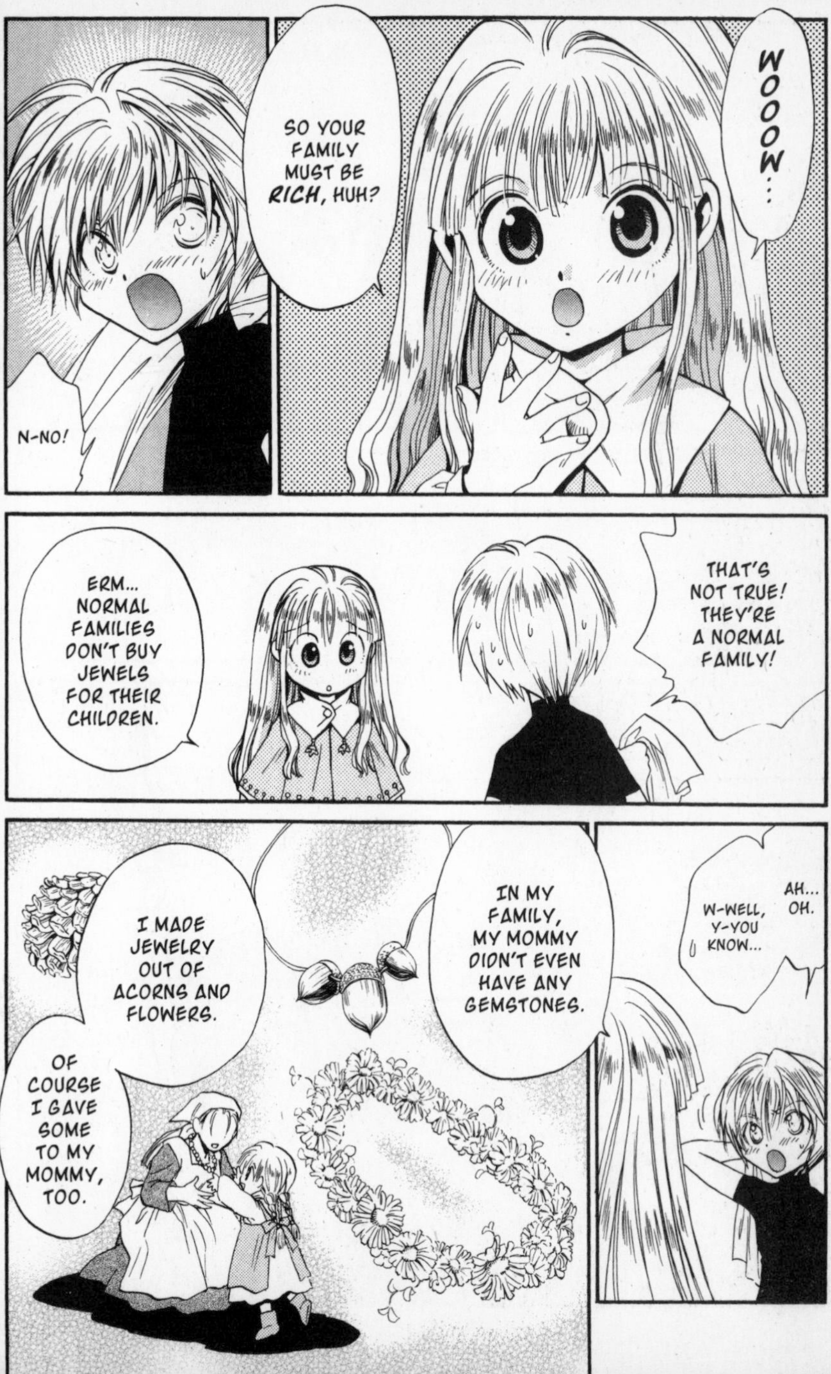
WOOOOW...
SO YOUR FAMILY MUST BE RICH, HUH?
N-NO!
THAT'S NOT TRUE! THEY'RE A NORMAL FAMILY!
ERM... NORMAL FAMILIES DON'T BUY JEWELS FOR THEIR CHILDREN.
AH... OH.
W-WELL, Y-YOU KNOW...
IN MY FAMILY, MY MOMMY DIDN'T EVEN HAVE ANY GEMSTONES.
I MADE JEWELRY OUT OF ACORNS AND FLOWERS.
OF COURSE I GAVE SOME TO MY MOMMY, TOO.

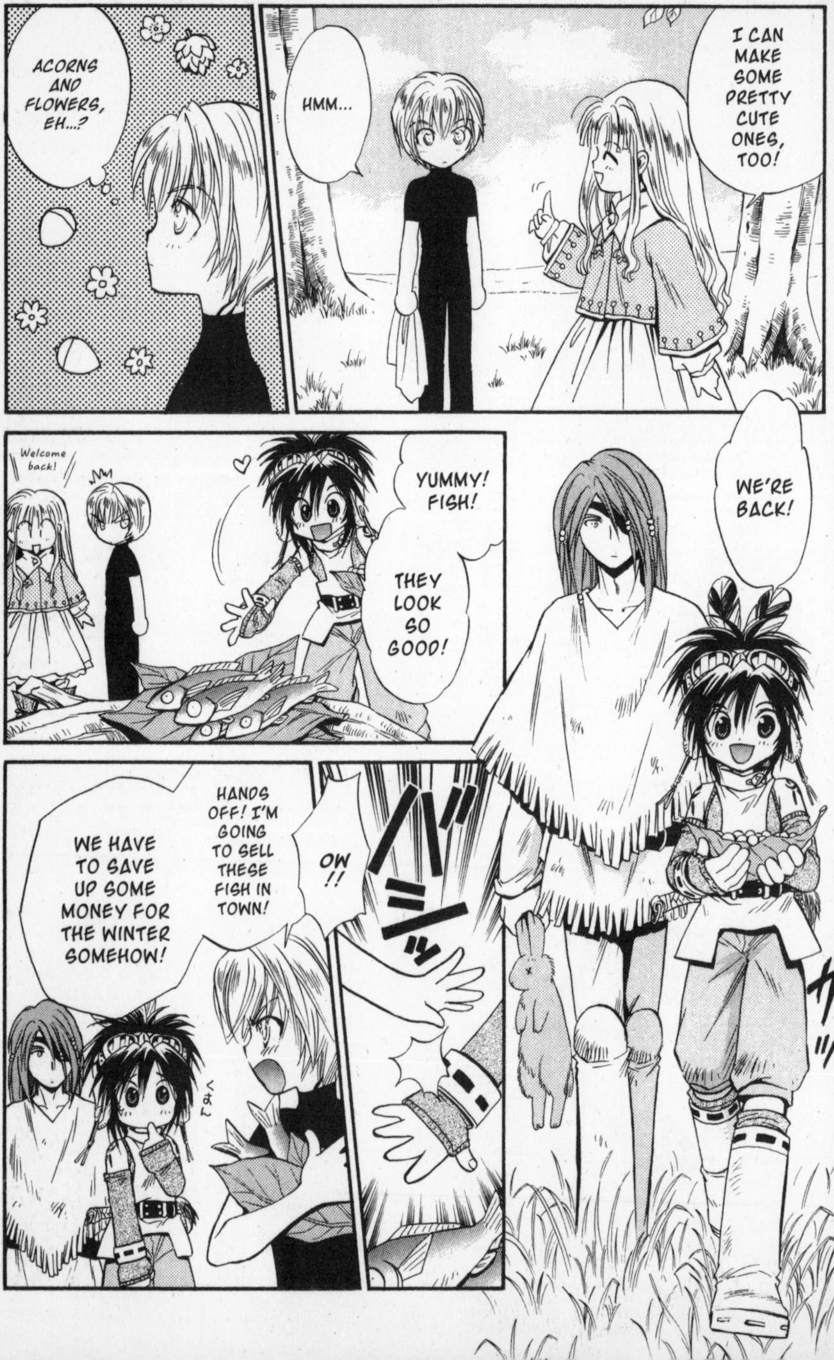
I CAN MAKE SOME PRETTY CUTE ONES, TOO!
HMM...
ACORNS AND FLOWERS, EH...?
WE'RE BACK!
YUMMY! FISH!
THEY LOOK SO GOOD!
Welcome back!
HANDS OFF! I'M GOING TO SELL THESE FISH IN TOWN!
OW !!
WE HAVE TO SAVE UP SOME MONEY FOR THE WINTER SOMEHOW!

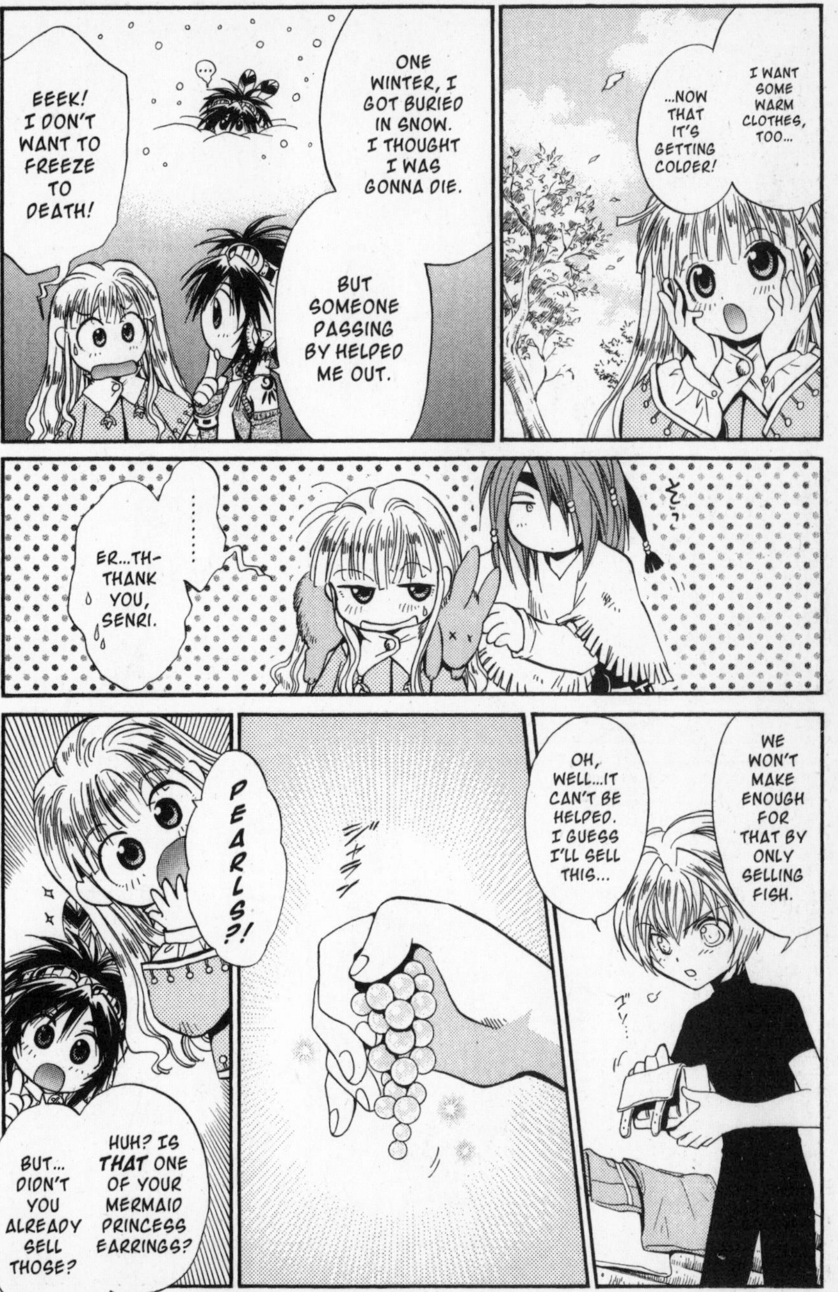
I WANT SOME WARM CLOTHES, TOO...
...NOW THAT IT'S GETTING COLDER!
ONE WINTER, I GOT BURIED IN SNOW. I THOUGHT I WAS GONNA DIE.
BUT SOMEONE PASSING BY HELPED ME OUT.
EEEK! I DON'T WANT TO FREEZE TO DEATH!
......
ER...TH-THANK YOU, SENRI.
WE WON'T MAKE ENOUGH FOR THAT BY ONLY SELLING FISH.
OH, WELL...IT CAN'T BE HELPED. I GUESS I'LL SELL THIS...
PEARLS?!
HUH? IS *THAT* ONE OF YOUR MERMAID PRINCESS EARRINGS?
BUT... DIDN'T YOU ALREADY SELL THOSE?

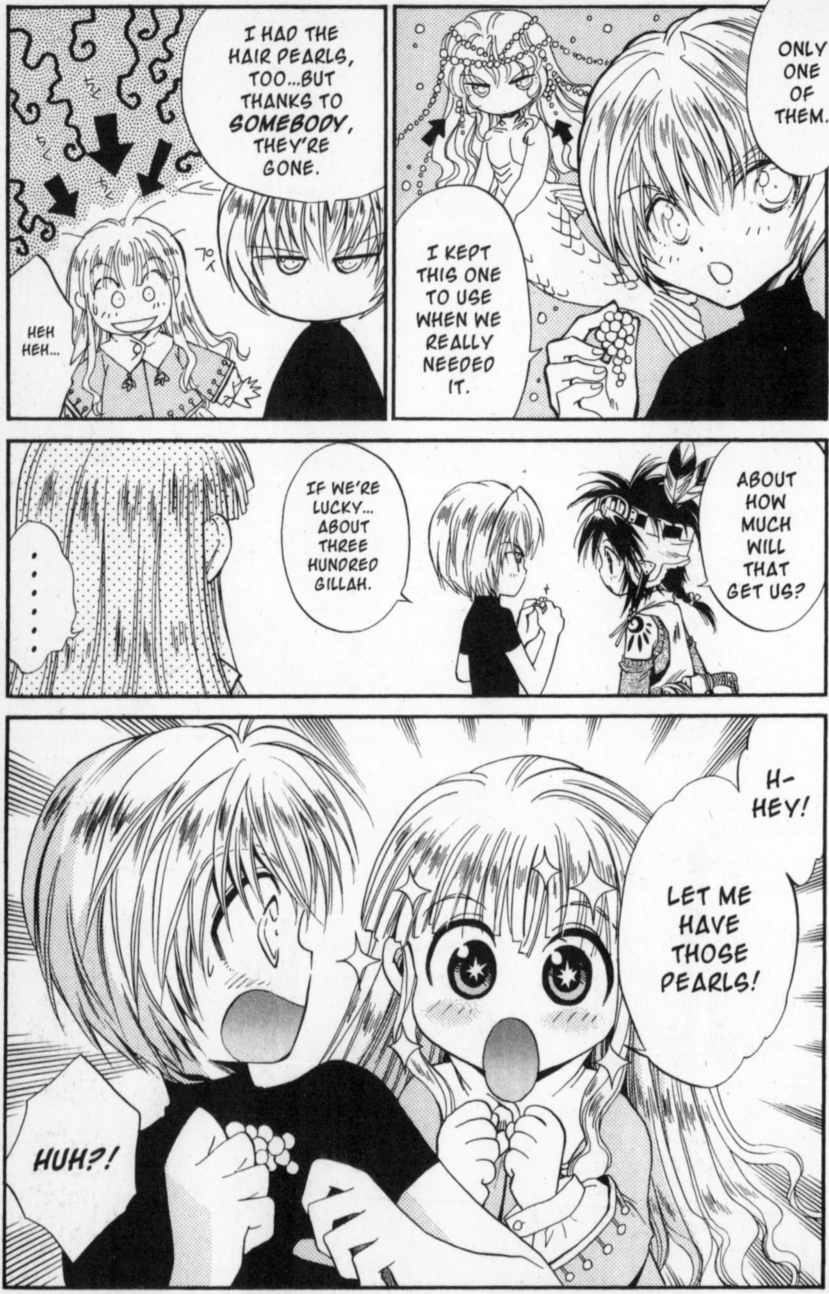
ONLY ONE OF THEM.
I KEPT THIS ONE TO USE WHEN WE REALLY NEEDED IT.
I HAD THE HAIR PEARLS, TOO...BUT THANKS TO SOMEBODY, THEY'RE GONE.
HEH HEH...
ABOUT HOW MUCH WILL THAT GET US?
IF WE'RE LUCKY... ABOUT THREE HUNDRED GILLAH.
......
H-HEY!
LET ME HAVE THOSE PEARLS!
HUH?!

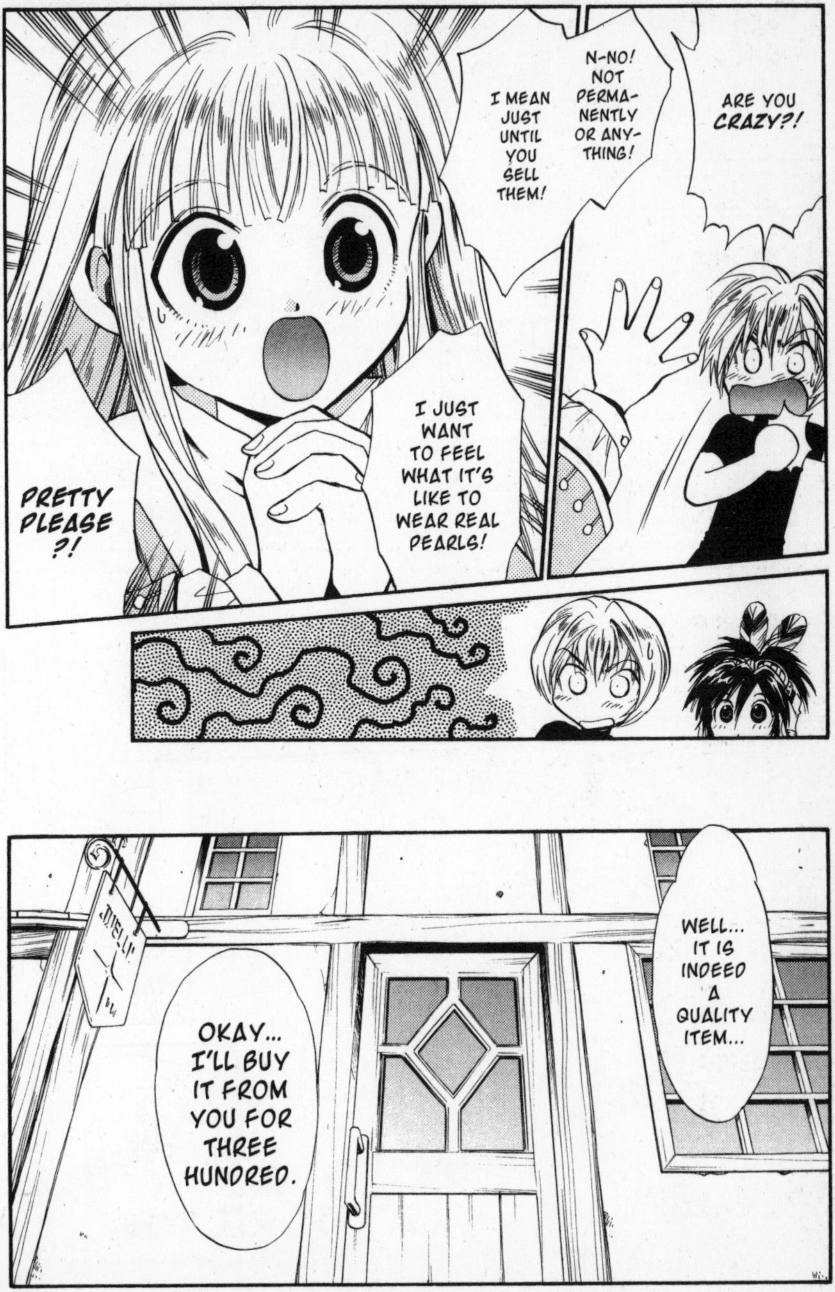

ARE YOU CRAZY?!
N-NO! NOT PERMA-NENTLY OR ANY-THING!
I MEAN JUST UNTIL YOU SELL THEM!
I JUST WANT TO FEEL WHAT IT'S LIKE TO WEAR REAL PEARLS!
PRETTY PLEASE ?!
WELL... IT IS INDEED A QUALITY ITEM...
OKAY... I'LL BUY IT FROM YOU FOR THREE HUNDRED.

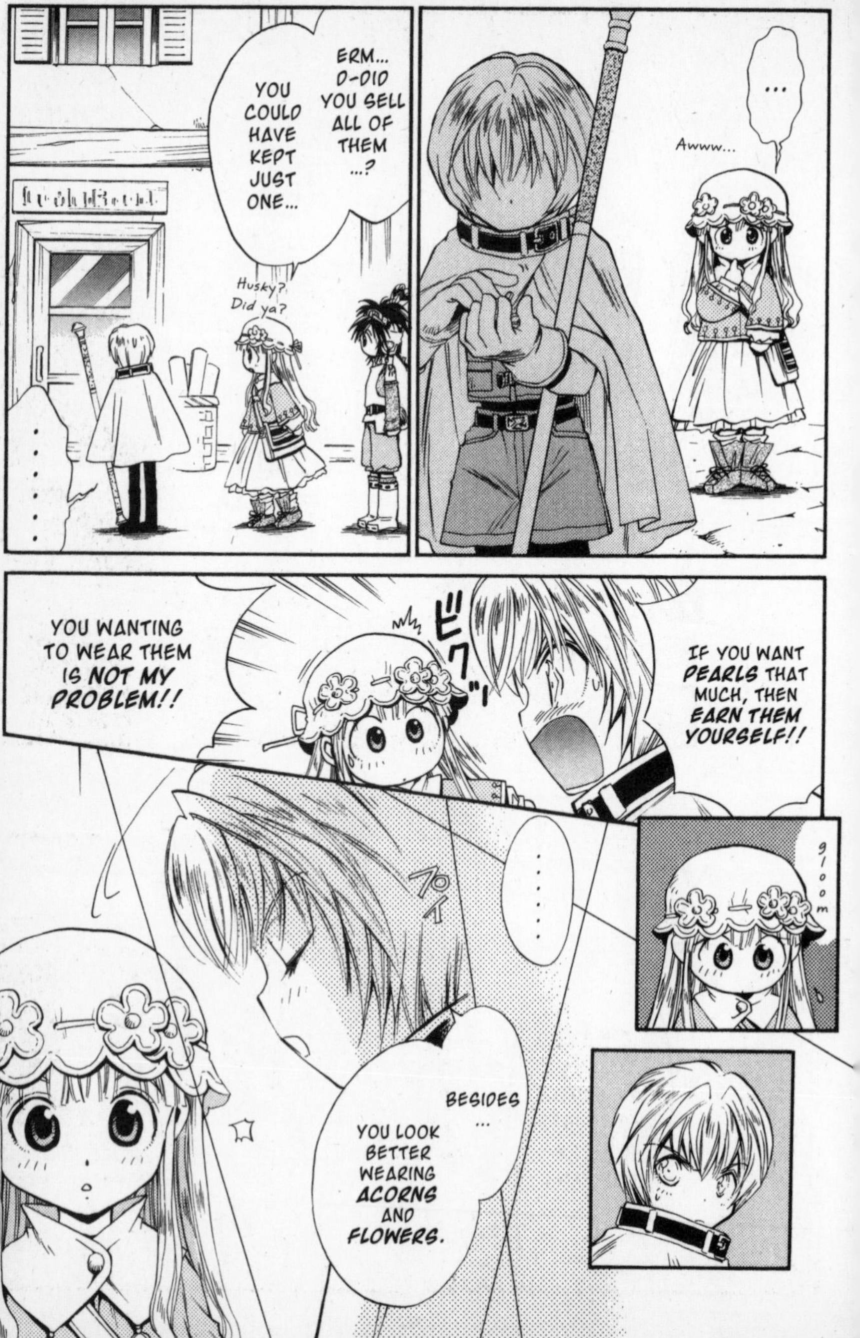
...
Awww...
ERM... D-DID YOU SELL ALL OF THEM ...?
YOU COULD HAVE KEPT JUST ONE...
Husky? Did ya?
IF YOU WANT PEARLS THAT MUCH, THEN EARN THEM YOURSELF!!
YOU WANTING TO WEAR THEM IS NOT MY PROBLEM!!
gloom
......
BESIDES ...
YOU LOOK BETTER WEARING ACORNS AND FLOWERS.

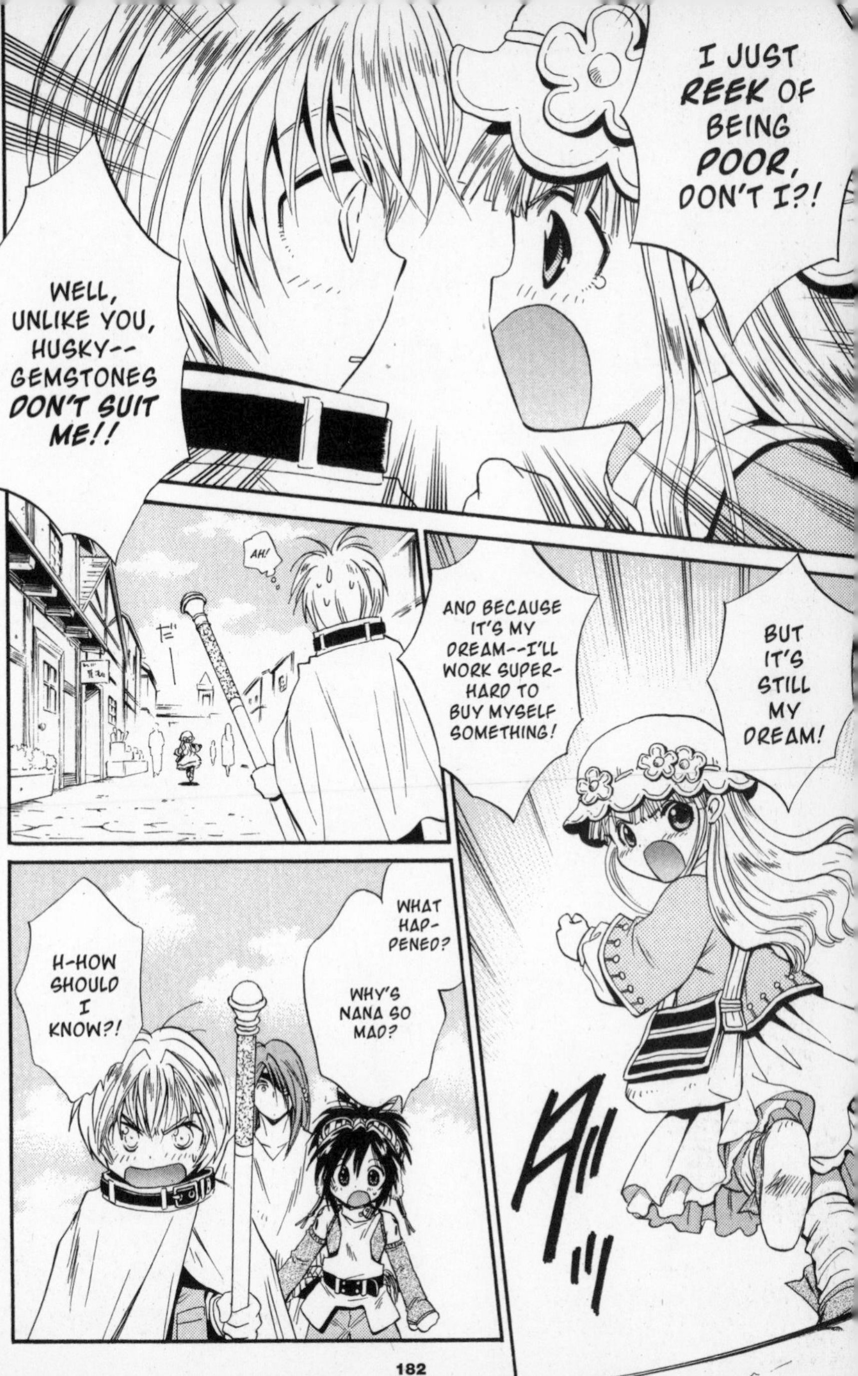
I JUST REEK OF BEING POOR, DON'T I?!
WELL, UNLIKE YOU, HUSKY--GEMSTONES DON'T SUIT ME!!
BUT IT'S STILL MY DREAM!
AND BECAUSE IT'S MY DREAM--I'LL WORK SUPER-HARD TO BUY MYSELF SOMETHING!
ダッ
AH!
だー
WHAT HAP-PENED?
WHY'S NANA SO MAD?
H-HOW SHOULD I KNOW?!

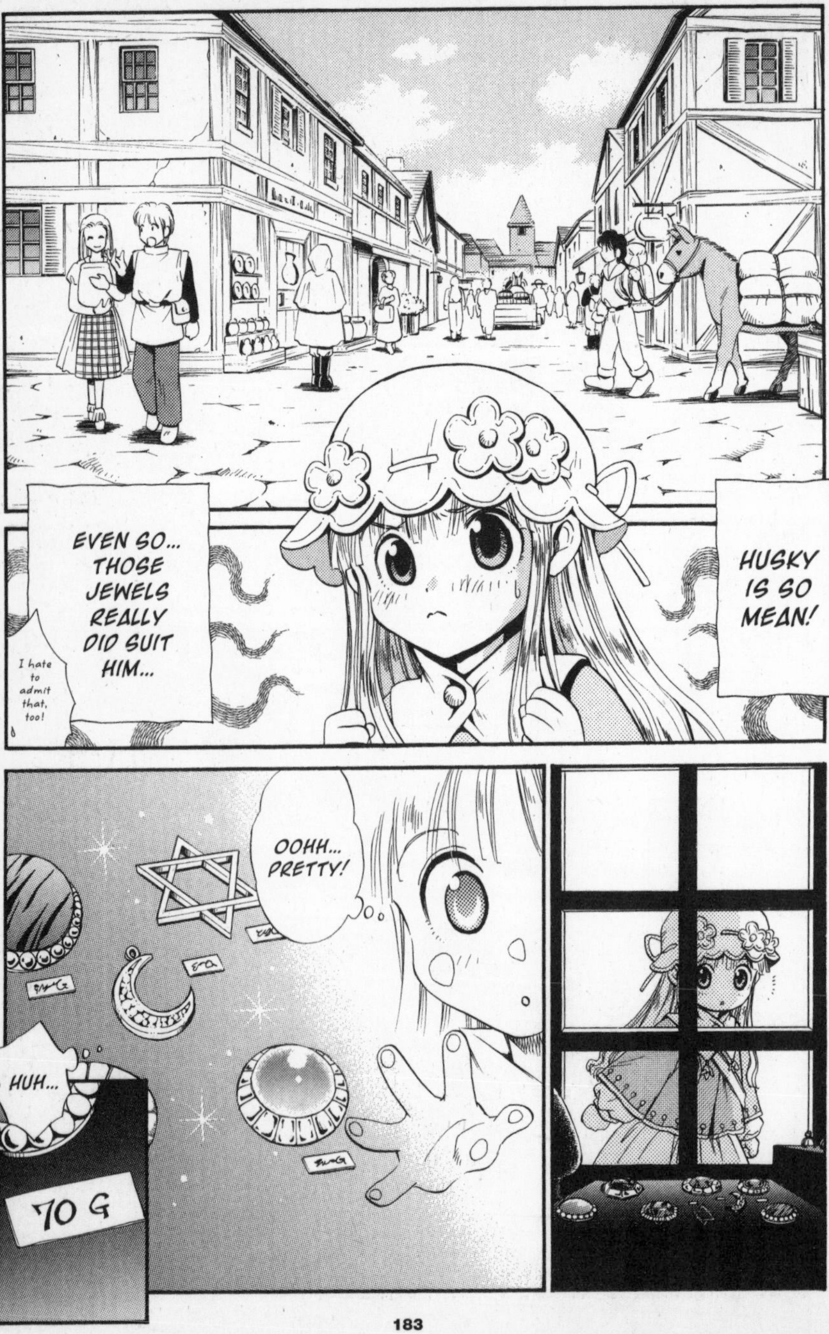
HUSKY IS SO MEAN!
EVEN SO... THOSE JEWELS REALLY DID SUIT HIM...
I hate to admit that, too!
OOHH... PRETTY!
HUH...
70 G

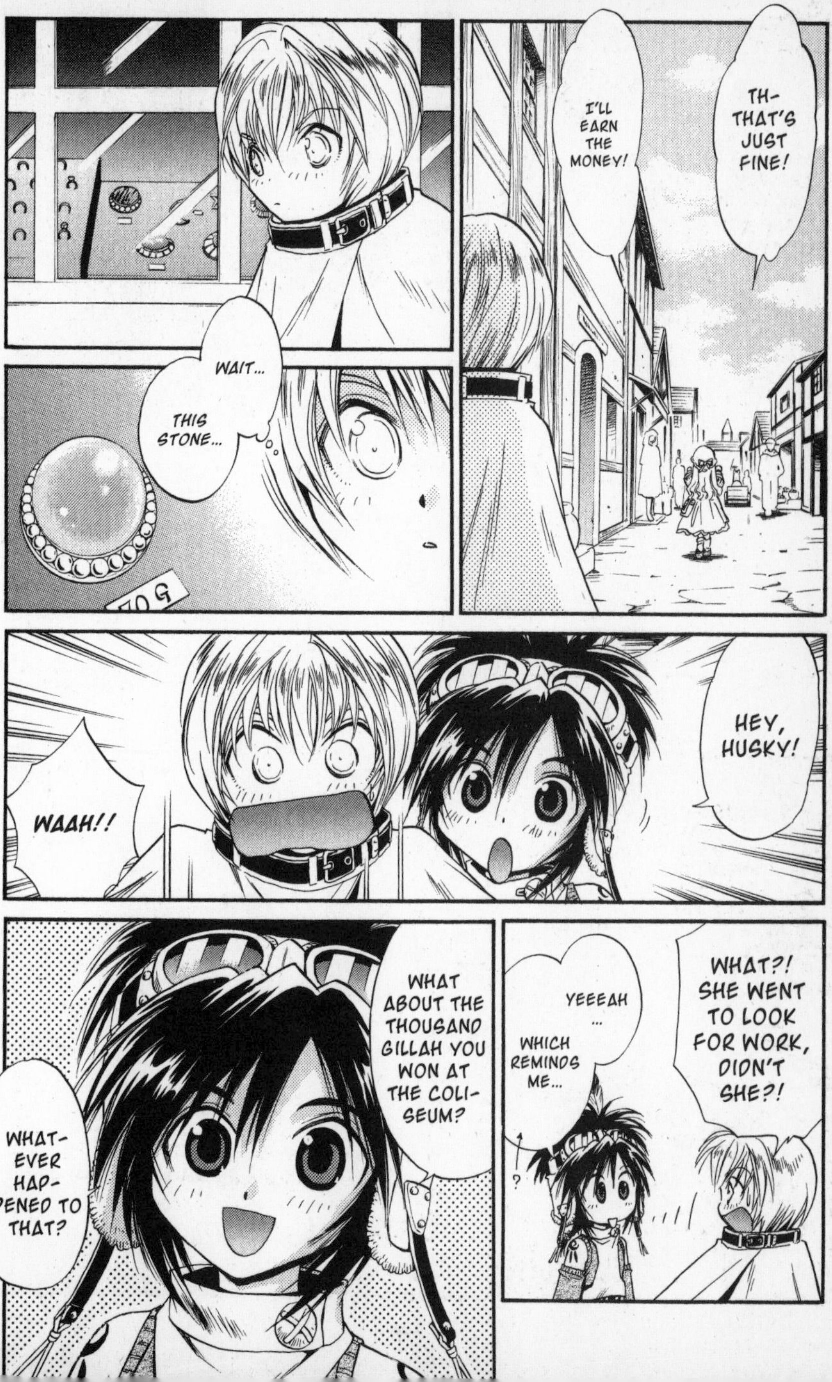
TH-THAT'S JUST FINE!
I'LL EARN THE MONEY!
WAIT...
THIS STONE...
70 G
HEY, HUSKY!
WAAH!!
WHAT?! SHE WENT TO LOOK FOR WORK, DIDN'T SHE?!
YEEEAH ...
WHICH REMINDS ME...
?
WHAT ABOUT THE THOUSAND GILLAH YOU WON AT THE COLISEUM?
WHATEVER HAPPENED TO THAT?

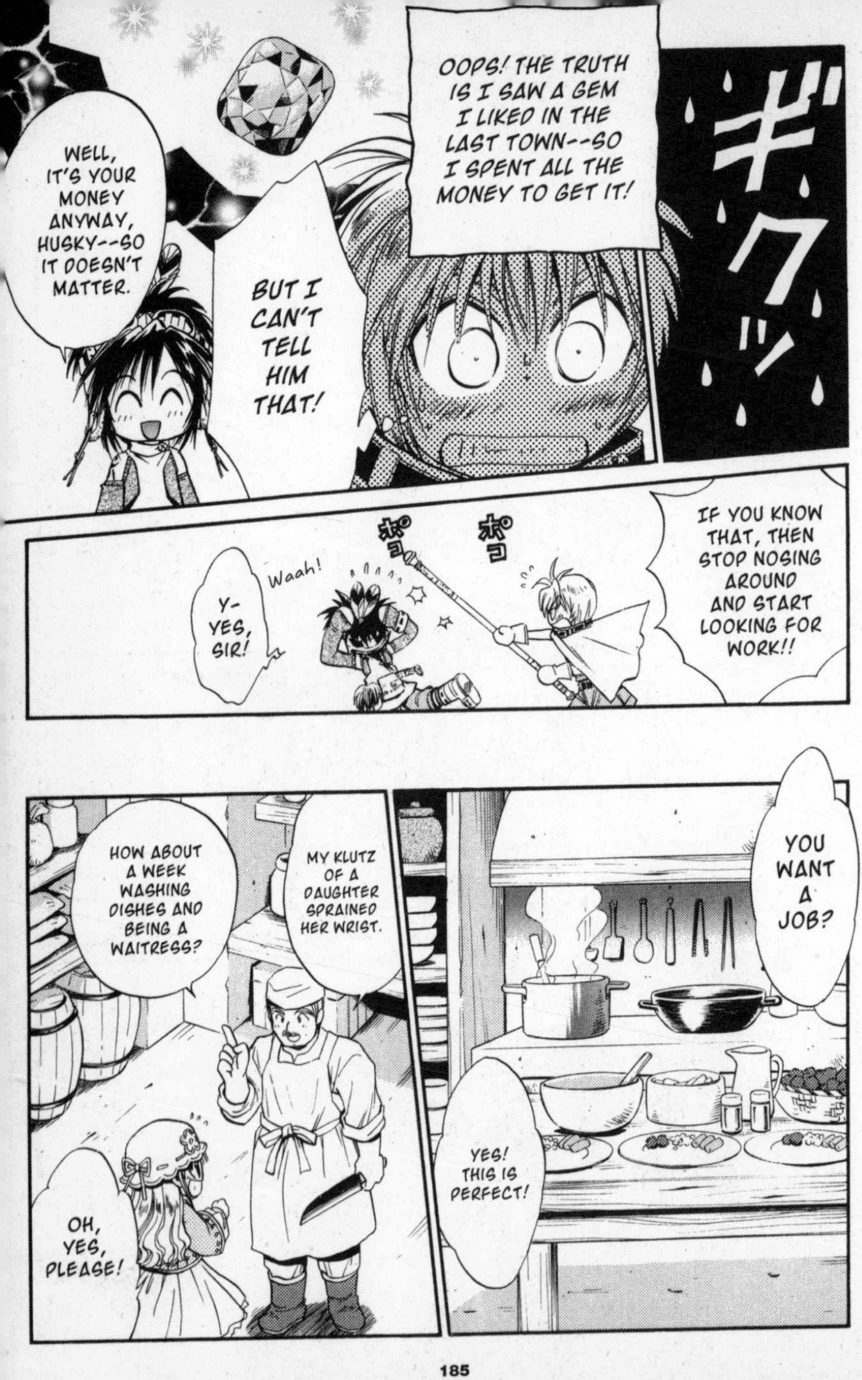
ギクッ
OOPS! THE TRUTH IS I SAW A GEM I LIKED IN THE LAST TOWN--SO I SPENT ALL THE MONEY TO GET IT!
WELL, IT'S YOUR MONEY ANYWAY, HUSKY--SO IT DOESN'T MATTER.
BUT I CAN'T TELL HIM THAT!
IF YOU KNOW THAT, THEN STOP NOSING AROUND AND START LOOKING FOR WORK!!
ポコ
ポコ
Waah!
Y-YES, SIR!
YOU WANT A JOB?
YES! THIS IS PERFECT!
MY KLUTZ OF A DAUGHTER SPRAINED HER WRIST.
HOW ABOUT A WEEK WASHING DISHES AND BEING A WAITRESS?
OH, YES, PLEASE!

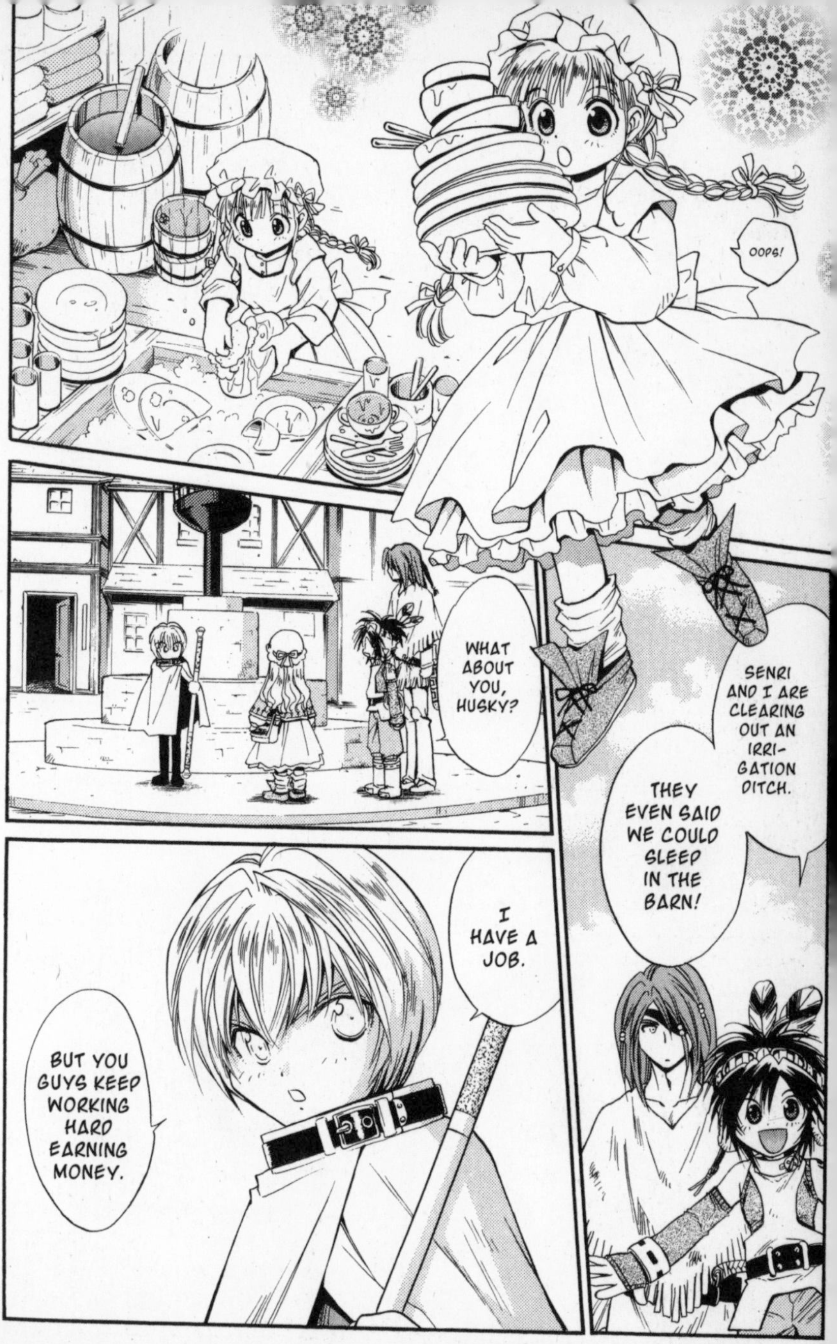
OOPS!
SENRI AND I ARE CLEARING OUT AN IRRI-GATION DITCH.
THEY EVEN SAID WE COULD SLEEP IN THE BARN!
WHAT ABOUT YOU, HUSKY?
I HAVE A JOB.
BUT YOU GUYS KEEP WORKING HARD EARNING MONEY.

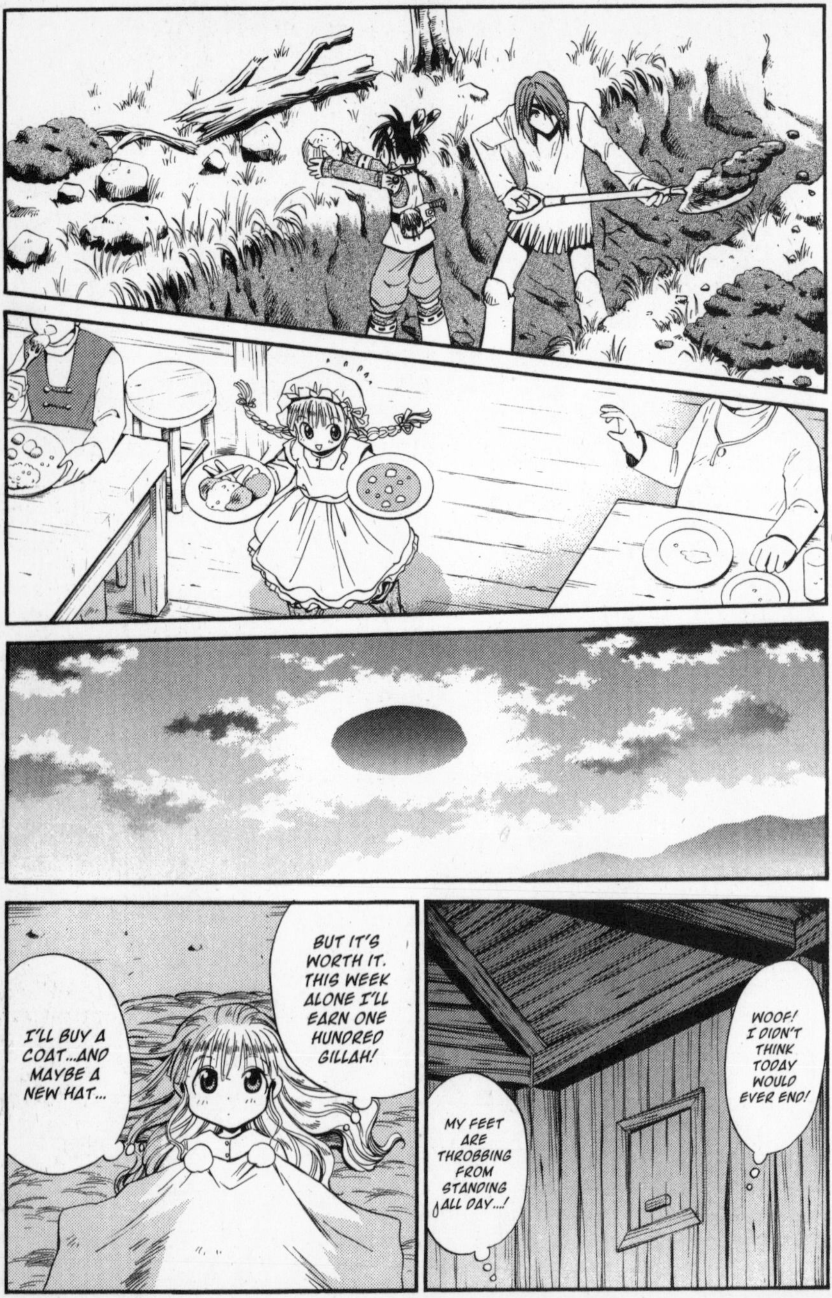
WOOF! I DIDN'T THINK TODAY WOULD EVER END!
MY FEET ARE THROBBING FROM STANDING ALL DAY...!
BUT IT'S WORTH IT. THIS WEEK ALONE I'LL EARN ONE HUNDRED GILLAH!
I'LL BUY A COAT...AND MAYBE A NEW HAT...

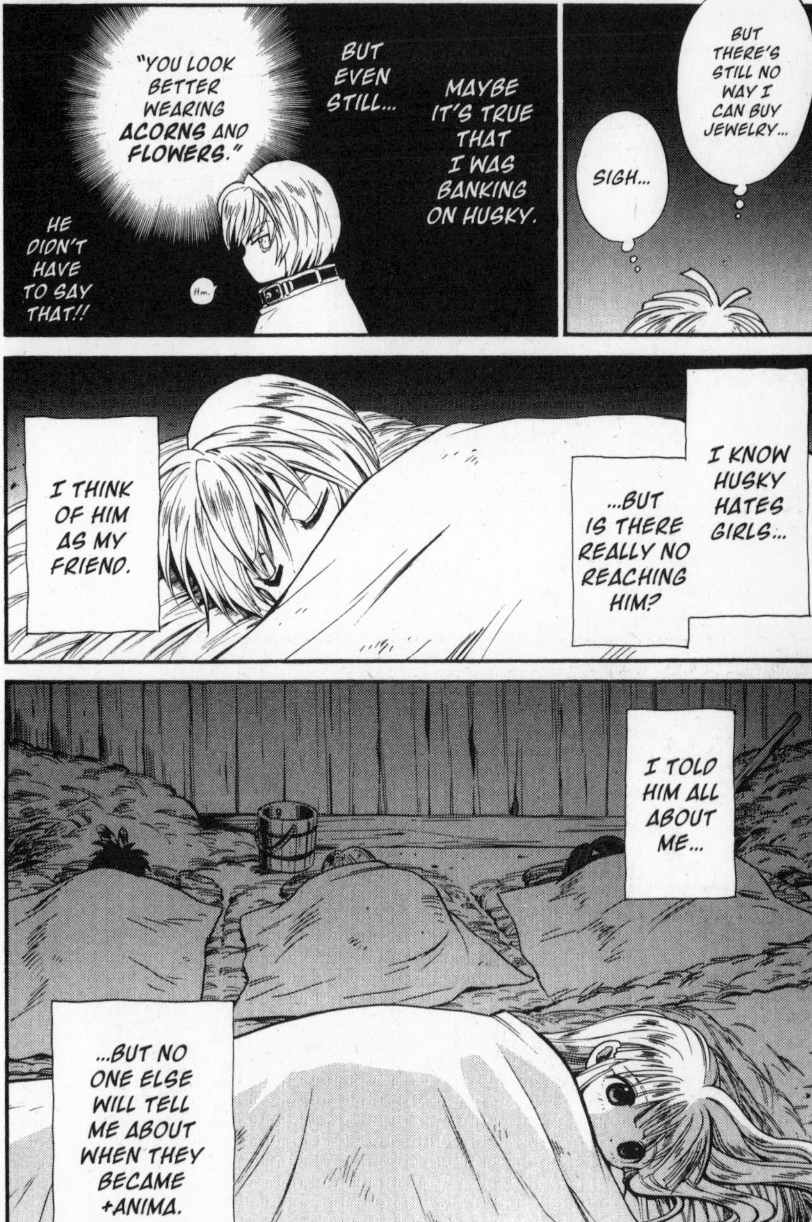
BUT THERE'S STILL NO WAY I CAN BUY JEWELRY...
SIGH...
MAYBE IT'S TRUE THAT I WAS BANKING ON HUSKY.
BUT EVEN STILL...
"YOU LOOK BETTER WEARING ACORNS AND FLOWERS."
Hm.
HE DIDN'T HAVE TO SAY THAT!!
I KNOW HUSKY HATES GIRLS...
...BUT IS THERE REALLY NO REACHING HIM?
I THINK OF HIM AS MY FRIEND.
I TOLD HIM ALL ABOUT ME...
...BUT NO ONE ELSE WILL TELL ME ABOUT WHEN THEY BECAME +ANIMA.

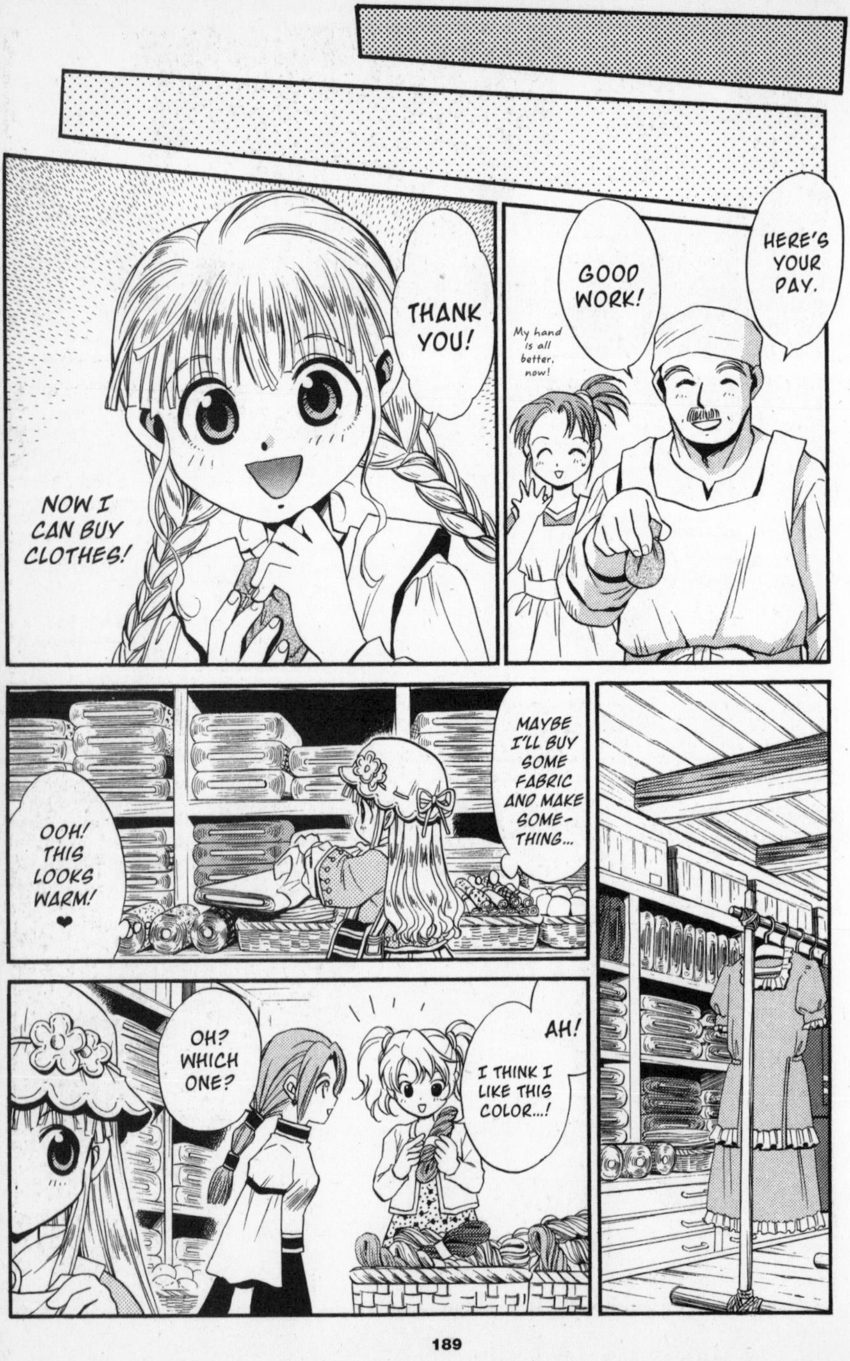
HERE'S YOUR PAY.
GOOD WORK!
My hand is all better, now!
THANK YOU!
NOW I CAN BUY CLOTHES!
MAYBE I'LL BUY SOME FABRIC AND MAKE SOME-THING...
OOH! THIS LOOKS WARM! ❤
AH!
I THINK I LIKE THIS COLOR...!
OH? WHICH ONE?

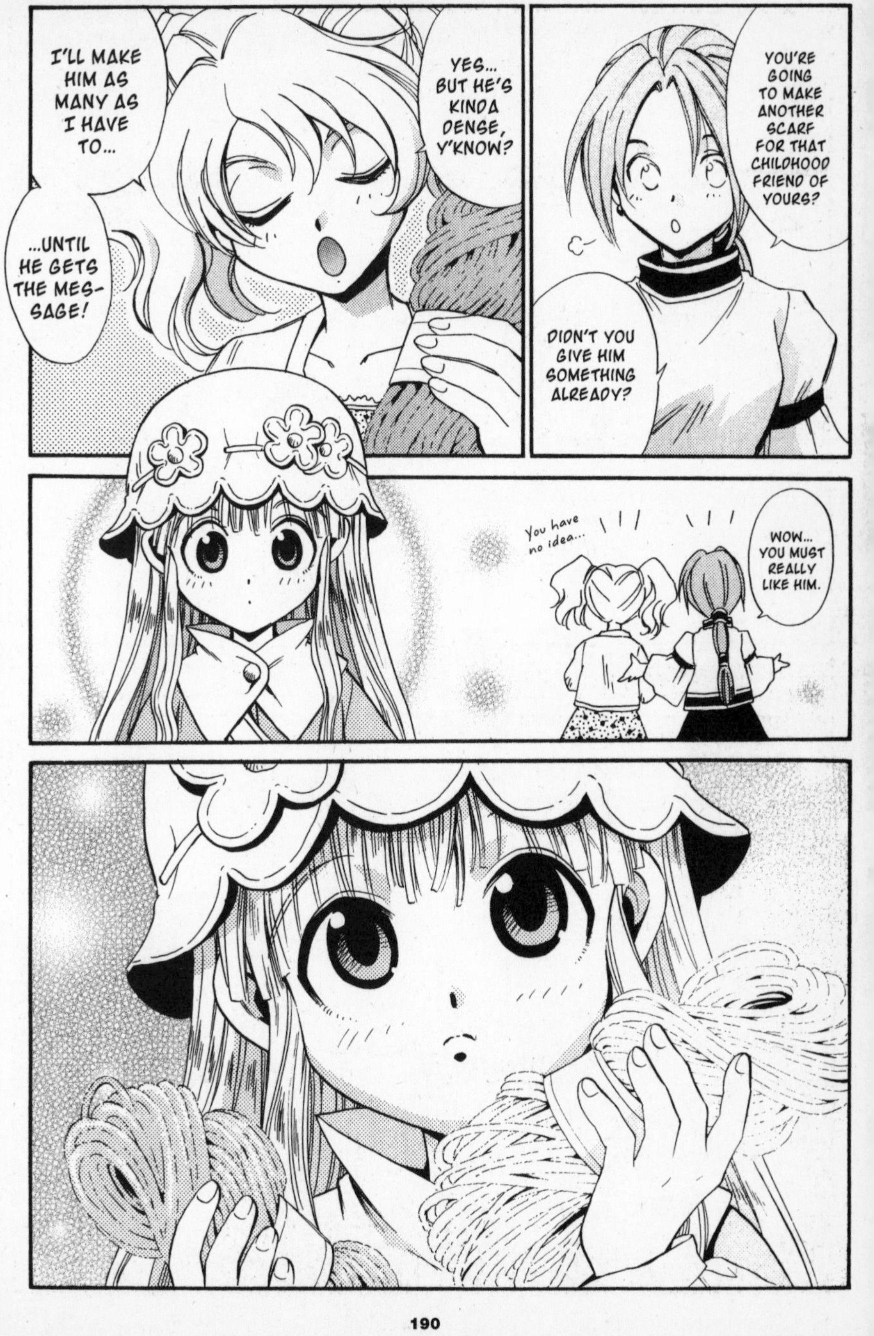
YOU'RE GOING TO MAKE ANOTHER SCARF FOR THAT CHILDHOOD FRIEND OF YOURS?
DIDN'T YOU GIVE HIM SOMETHING ALREADY?
YES... BUT HE'S KINDA DENSE, Y'KNOW?
I'LL MAKE HIM AS MANY AS I HAVE TO...
...UNTIL HE GETS THE MES-SAGE!
WOW... YOU MUST REALLY LIKE HIM.
You have no idea...

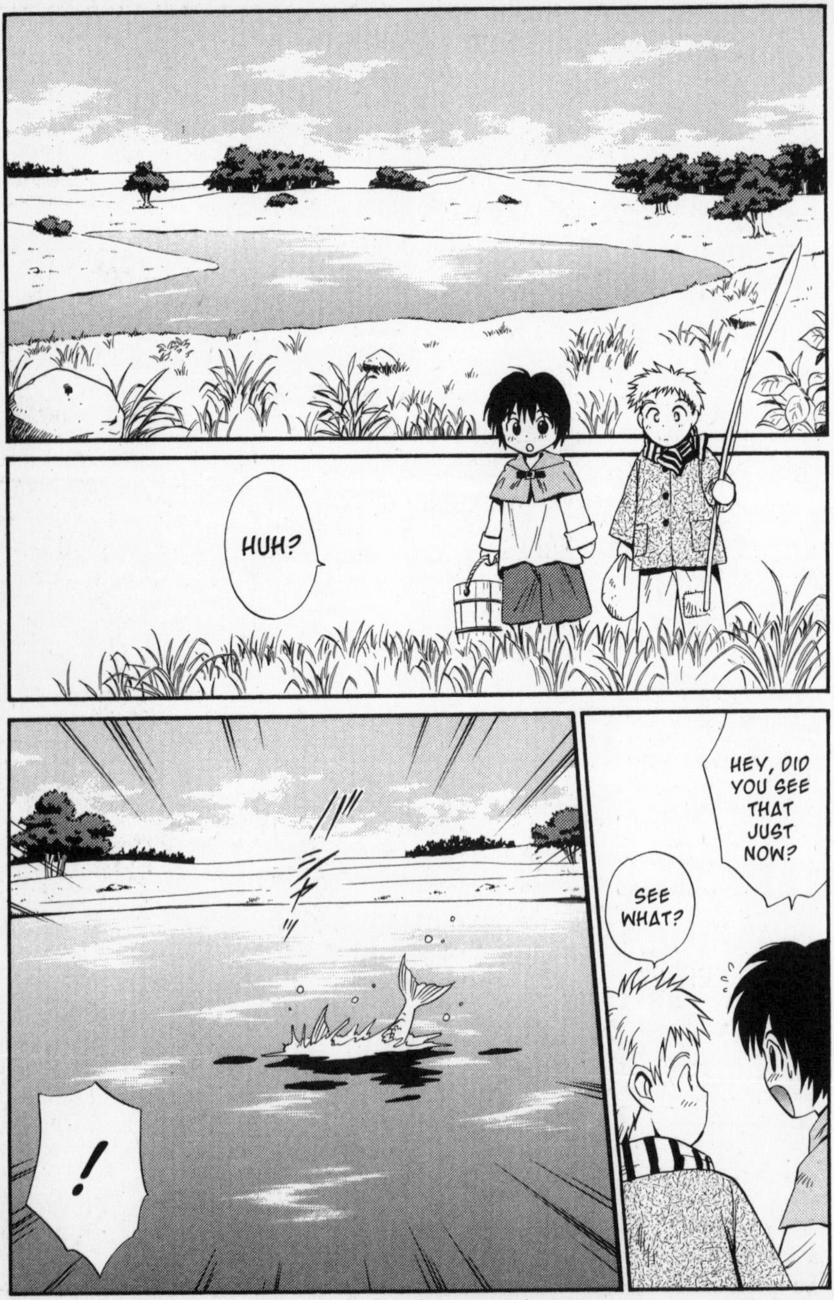
HUH?
HEY, DID YOU SEE THAT JUST NOW?
SEE WHAT?
!

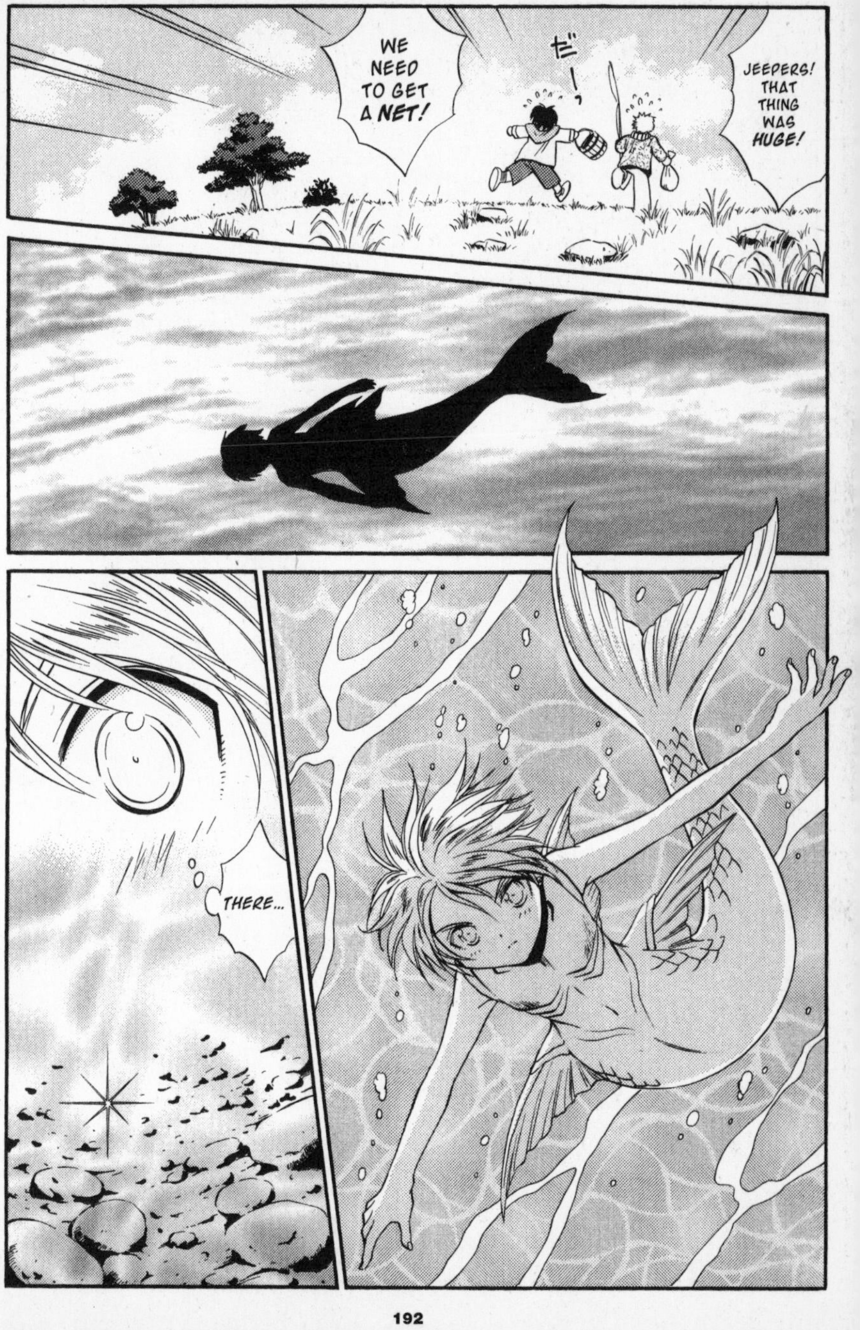
JEEPERS! THAT THING WAS HUGE!
だー
WE NEED TO GET A NET!
THERE...

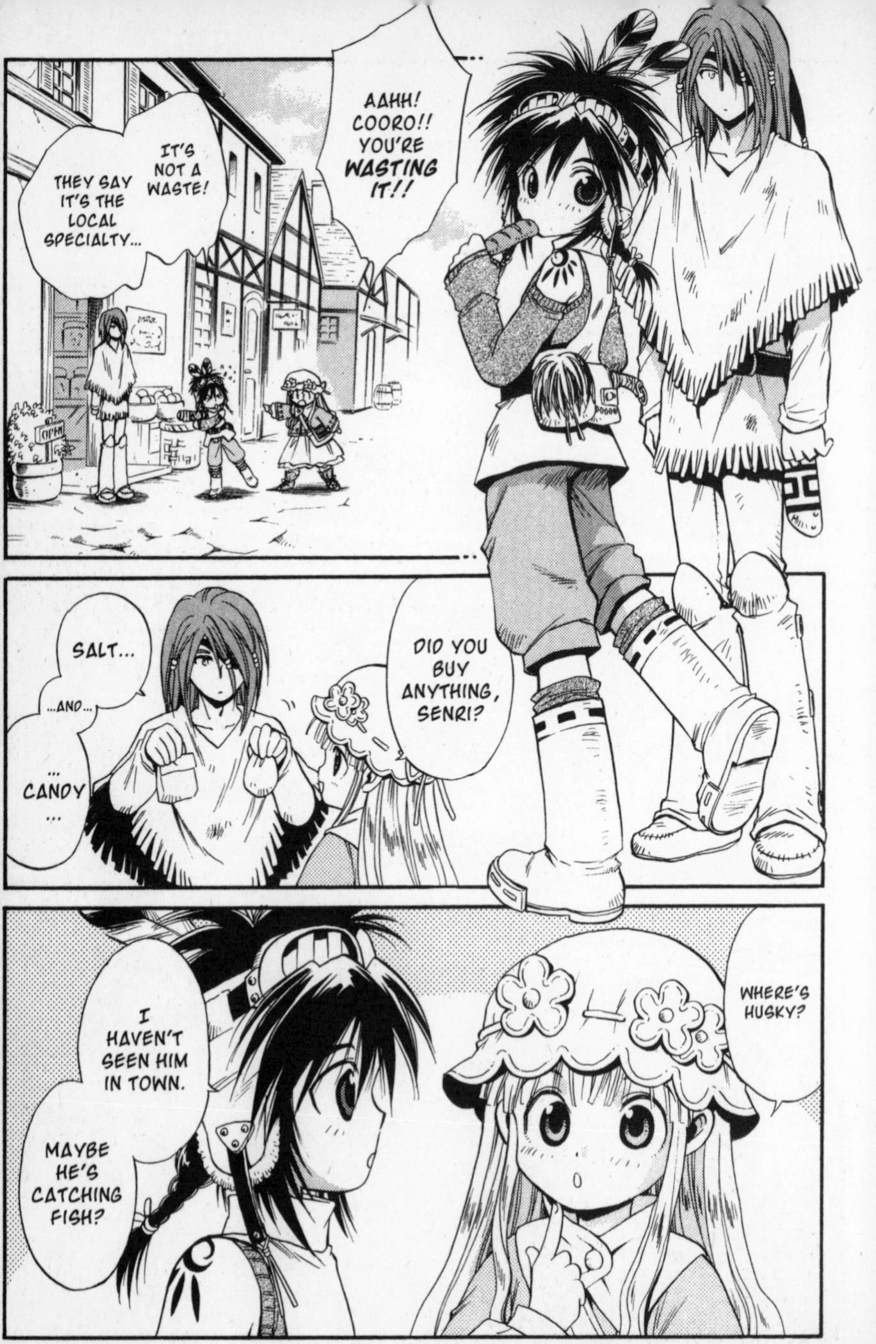
AAHH! COORO!! YOU'RE **WASTING** IT!!
IT'S NOT A WASTE!
THEY SAY IT'S THE LOCAL SPECIALTY...
DID YOU BUY ANYTHING, SENRI?
SALT...
...AND...
... CANDY ...
WHERE'S HUSKY?
I HAVEN'T SEEN HIM IN TOWN.
MAYBE HE'S CATCHING FISH?

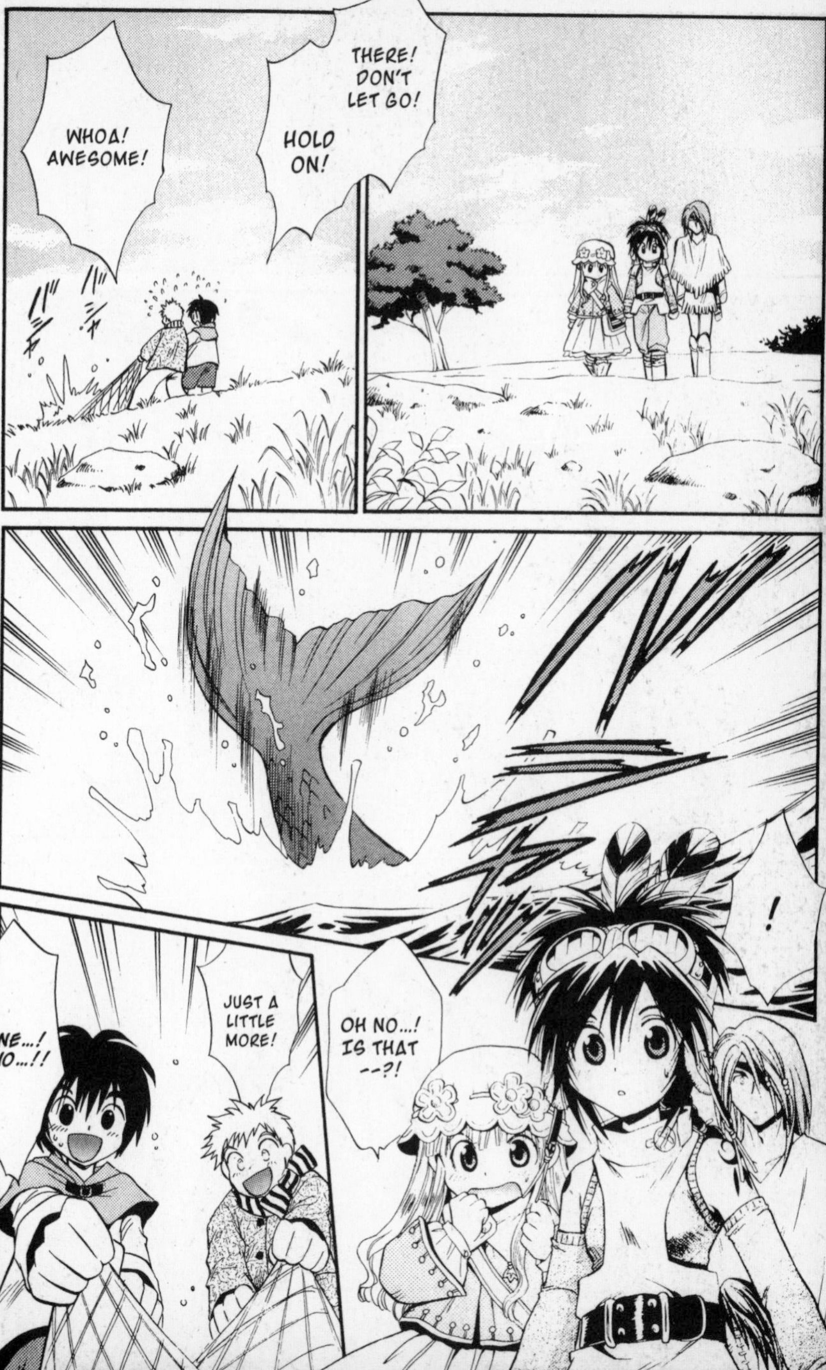
THERE! DON'T LET GO!
HOLD ON!
WHOA! AWESOME!
!
OH NO...! IS THAT --?!
JUST A LITTLE MORE!
ONE...! TWO...!!

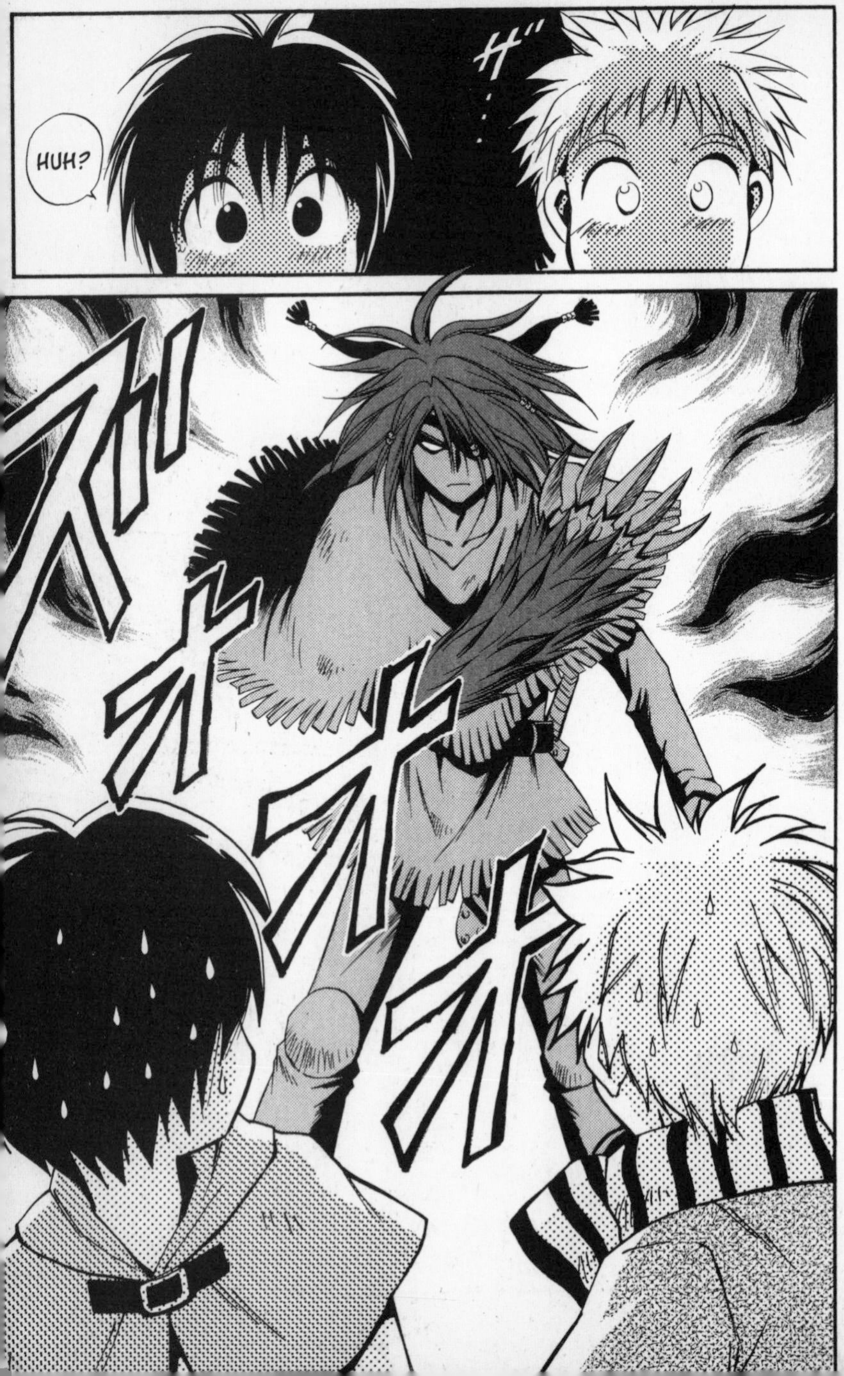
HUH?

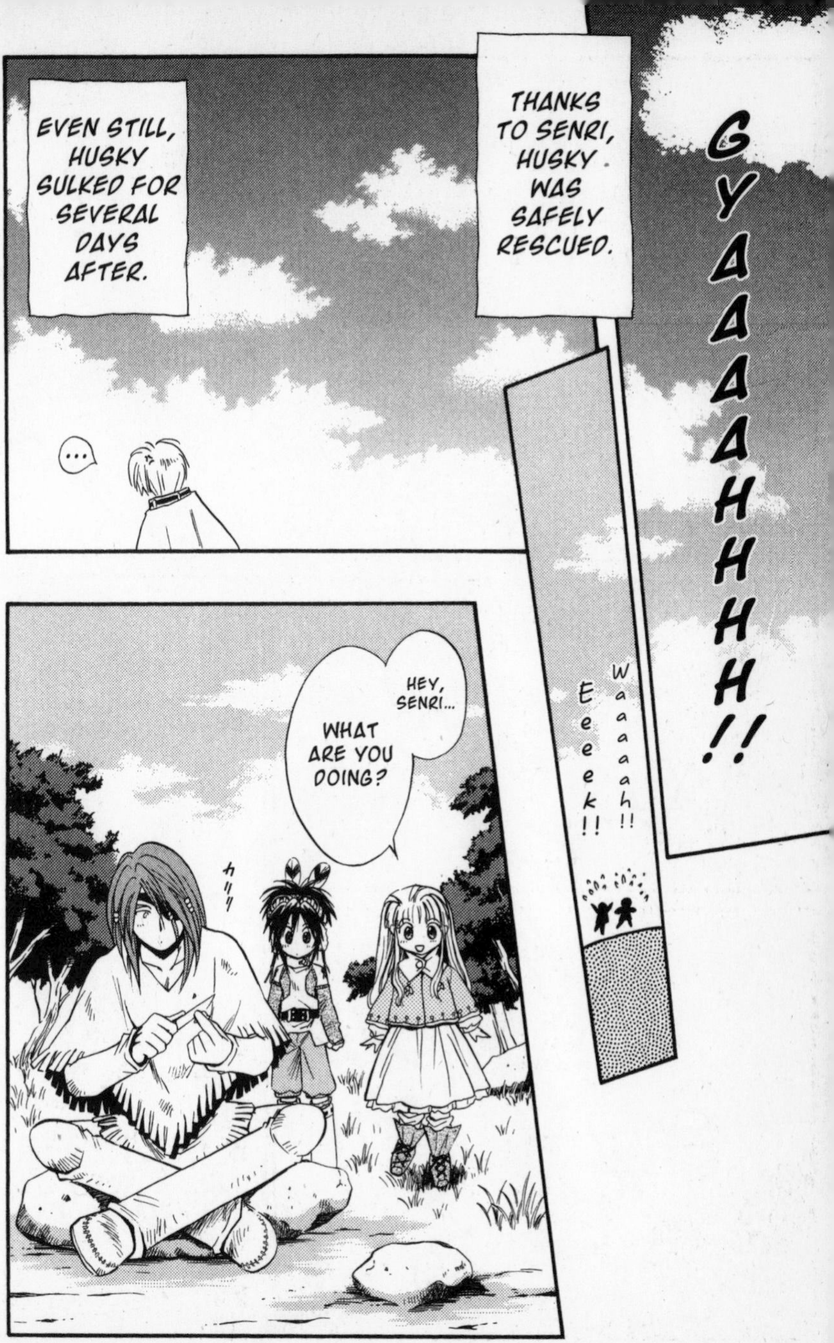
GYAAAAAHHHH!!
Waaaaaah!!
Eeeeek!!
THANKS TO SENRI, HUSKY WAS SAFELY RESCUED.
EVEN STILL, HUSKY SULKED FOR SEVERAL DAYS AFTER.
...
HEY, SENRI...
WHAT ARE YOU DOING?

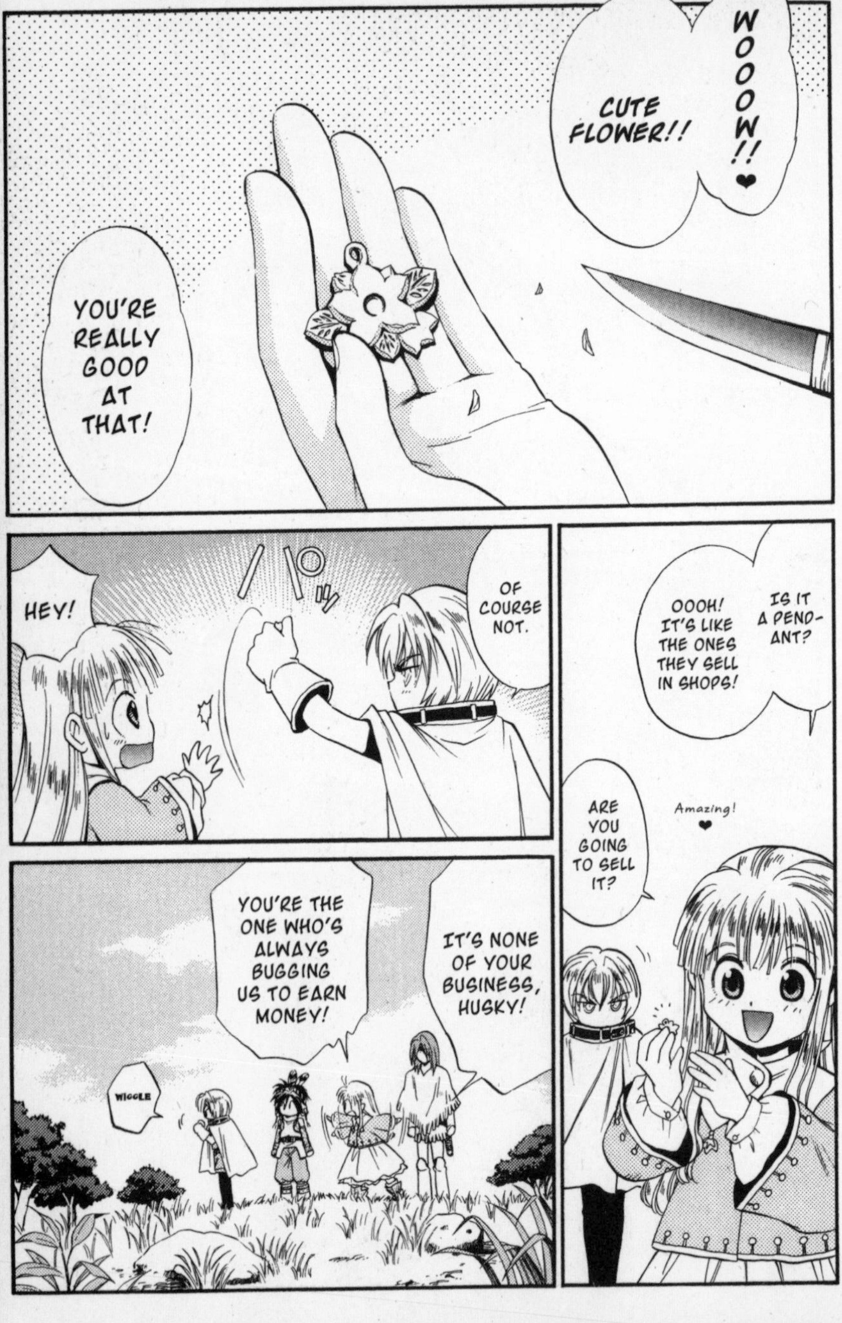
WOOOW!! ❤
CUTE FLOWER!!
YOU'RE REALLY GOOD AT THAT!
IS IT A PEND-ANT?
OOOH! IT'S LIKE THE ONES THEY SELL IN SHOPS!
Amazing! ❤
ARE YOU GOING TO SELL IT?
OF COURSE NOT.
HEY!
IT'S NONE OF YOUR BUSINESS, HUSKY!
YOU'RE THE ONE WHO'S ALWAYS BUGGING US TO EARN MONEY!
WIGGLE

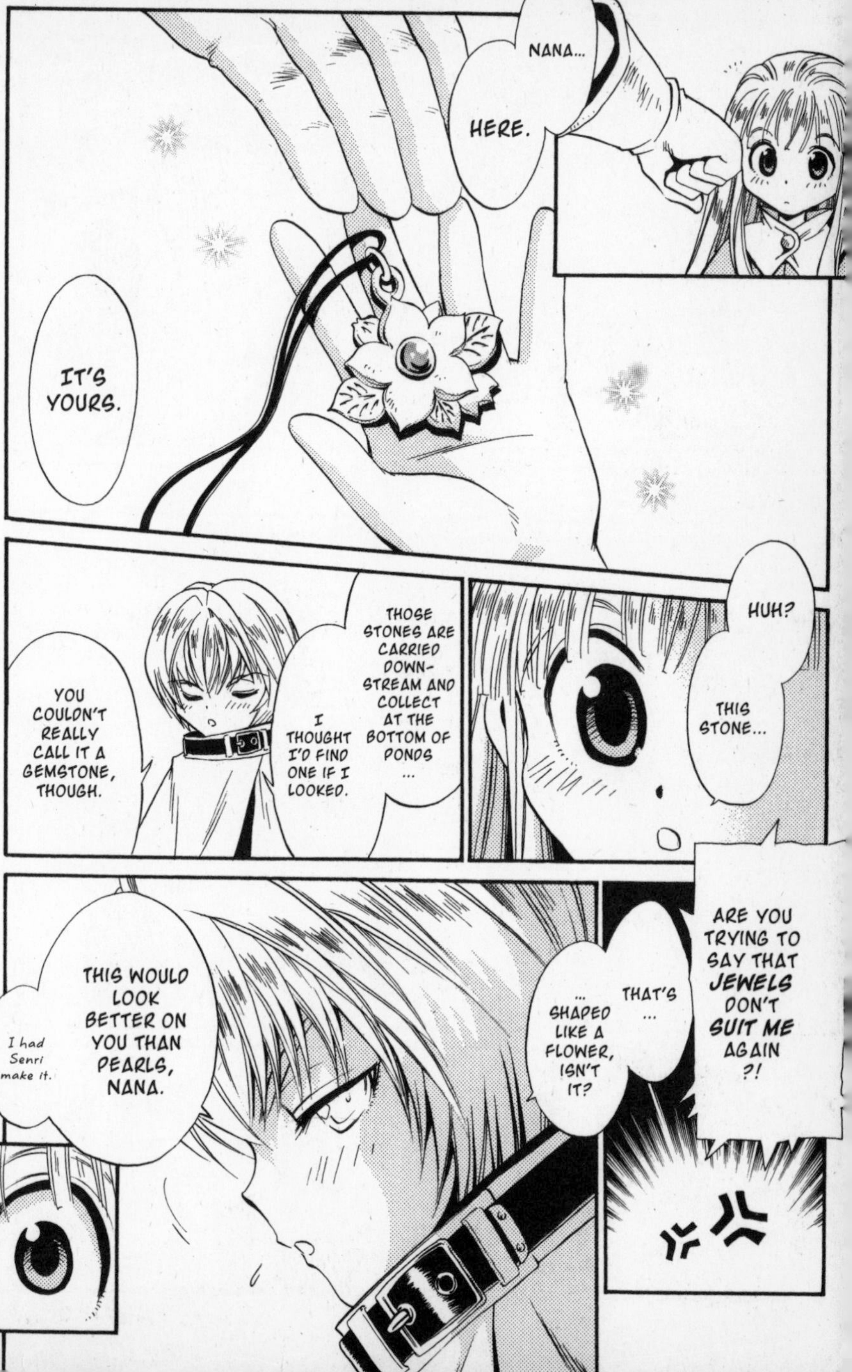
NANA...
HERE.
IT'S YOURS.
HUH?
THIS STONE...
THOSE STONES ARE CARRIED DOWN-STREAM AND COLLECT AT THE BOTTOM OF PONDS ...
I THOUGHT I'D FIND ONE IF I LOOKED.
YOU COULDN'T REALLY CALL IT A GEMSTONE, THOUGH.
ARE YOU TRYING TO SAY THAT JEWELS DON'T SUIT ME AGAIN ?!
THAT'S ...
... SHAPED LIKE A FLOWER, ISN'T IT?
THIS WOULD LOOK BETTER ON YOU THAN PEARLS, NANA.
I had Senri make it.

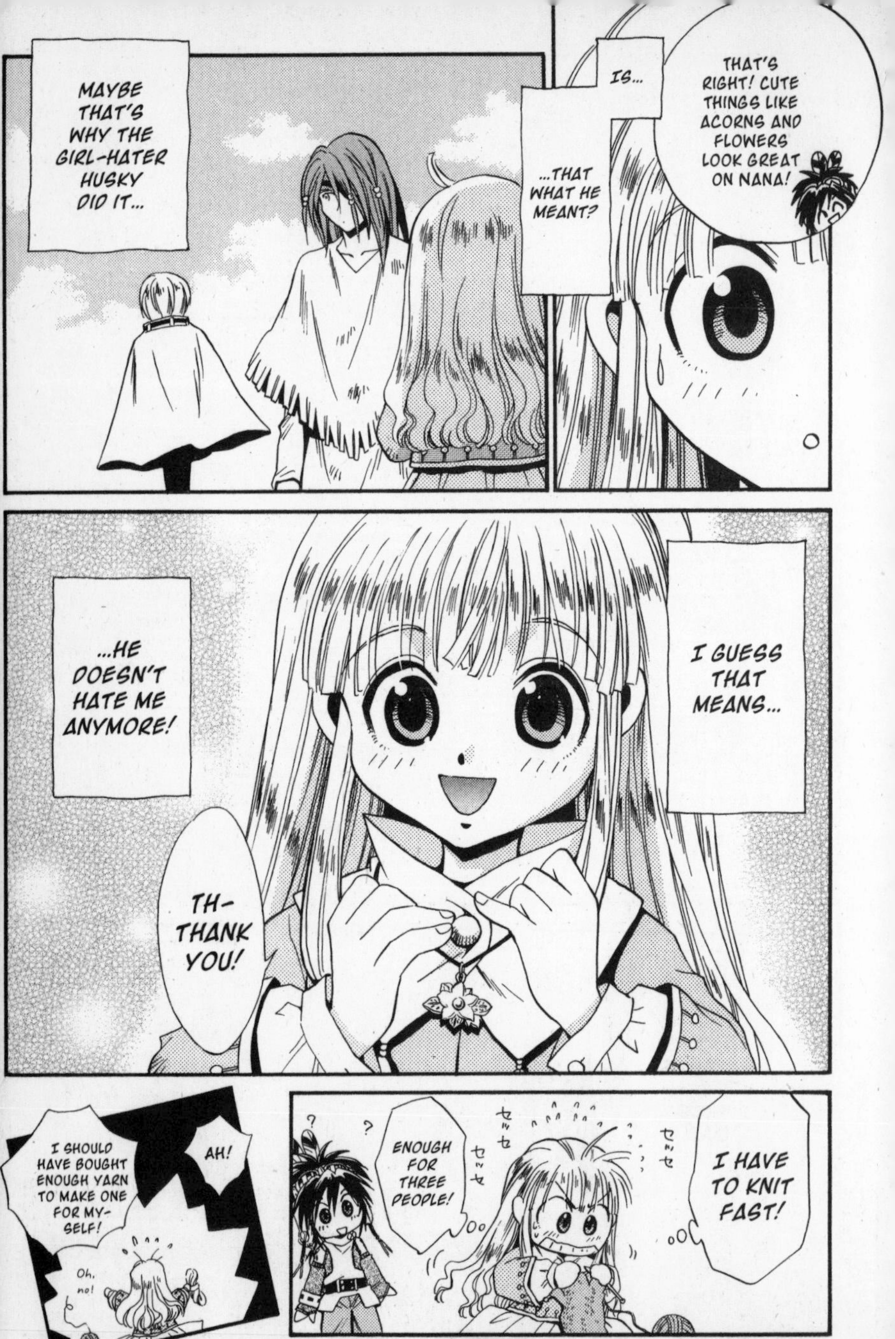
THAT'S RIGHT! CUTE THINGS LIKE ACORNS AND FLOWERS LOOK GREAT ON NANA!
IS...
...THAT WHAT HE MEANT?
MAYBE THAT'S WHY THE GIRL-HATER HUSKY DID IT...
I GUESS THAT MEANS...
...HE DOESN'T HATE ME ANYMORE!
TH- THANK YOU!
I HAVE TO KNIT FAST!
セッセ
セッセ
セッセ
ENOUGH FOR THREE PEOPLE!
AH!
I SHOULD HAVE BOUGHT ENOUGH YARN TO MAKE ONE FOR MY-SELF!
Oh, no!

To be continued...

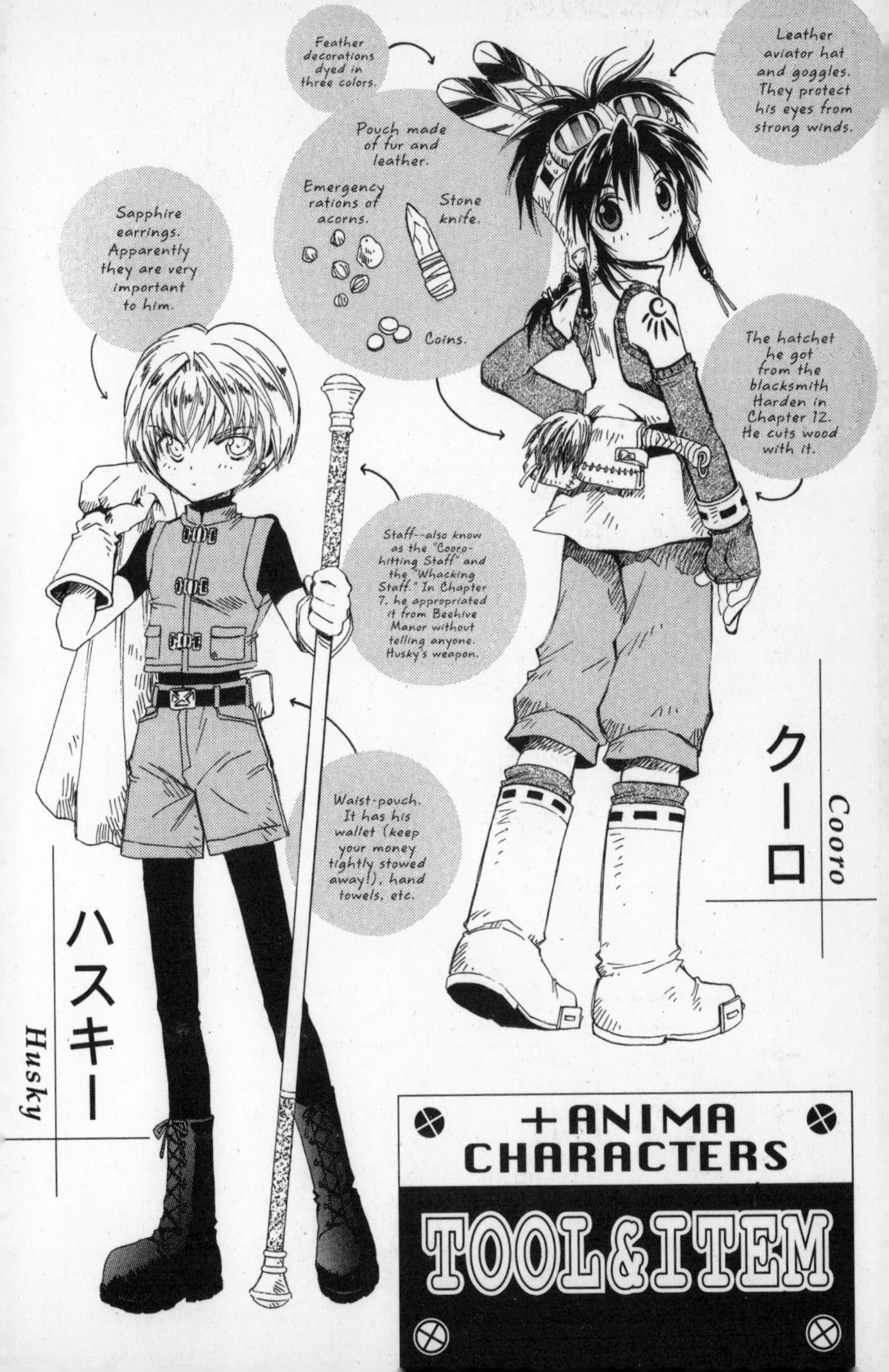

+ANIMA CHARACTERS
TOOL&ITEM
クーロ
Cooro
Leather aviator hat and goggles. They protect his eyes from strong winds.
Feather decorations dyed in three colors.
Pouch made of fur and leather.
Emergency rations of acorns.
Stone knife.
Coins.
The hatchet he got from the blacksmith Harden in Chapter 12. He cuts wood with it.
ハスキー
Husky
Sapphire earrings. Apparently they are very important to him.
Staff--also know as the "Cooro-hitting Staff" and the "Whacking Staff." In Chapter 7, he appropriated it from Beehive Manor without telling anyone. Husky's weapon.
Waist-pouch. It has his wallet (keep your money tightly stowed away!), hand towels, etc.

+ANIMA CHARACTERS

TOOL&ITEM

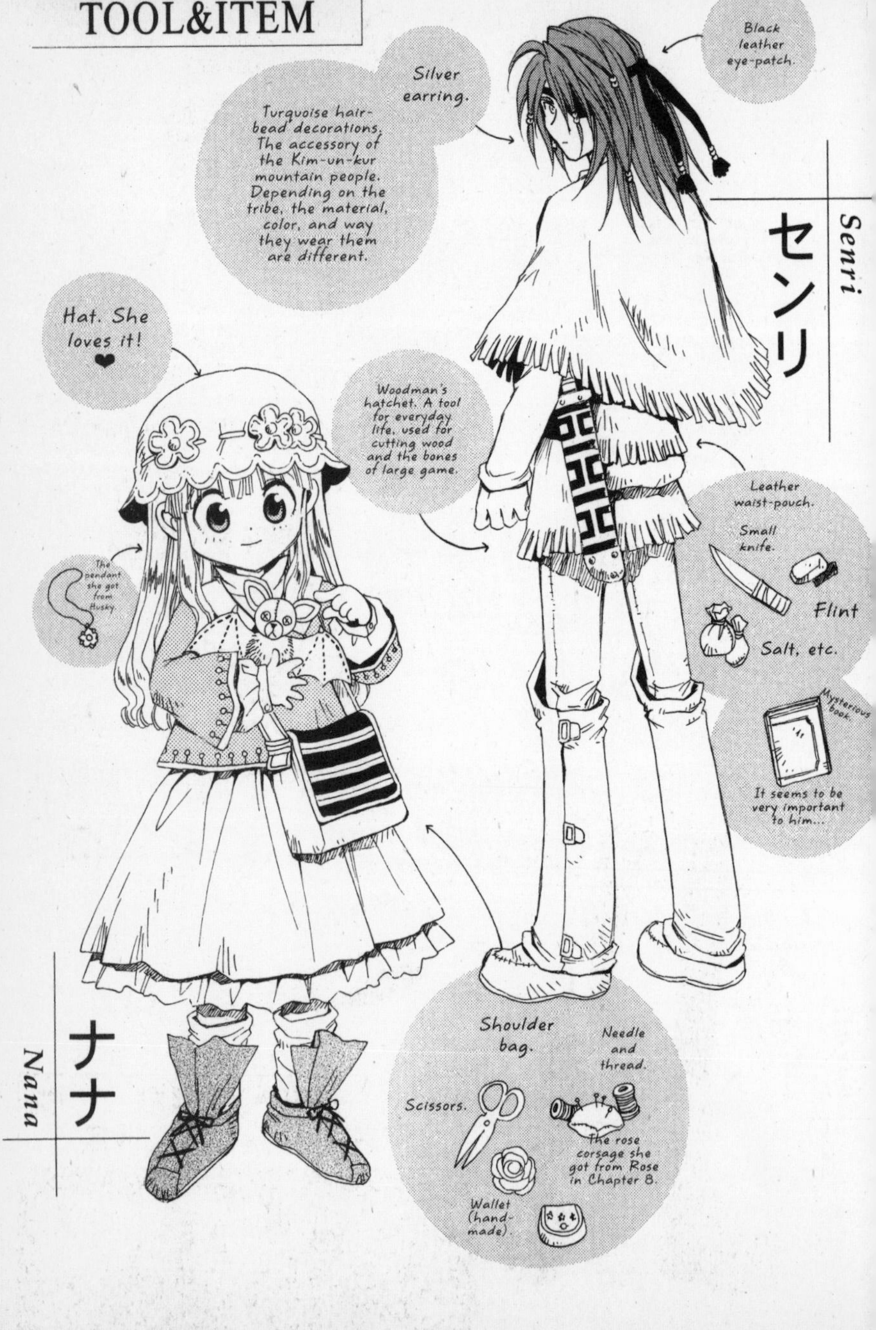
Black leather eye-patch.
Silver earring.
Turquoise hair-bead decorations. The accessory of the Kim-un-kur mountain people. Depending on the tribe, the material, color, and way they wear them are different.
Senri
センリ
Hat. She loves it! ❤
Woodman's hatchet. A tool for everyday life, used for cutting wood and the bones of large game.
Leather waist-pouch.
Small knife.
Flint
Salt, etc.
The pendant she got from Husky.
Mysterious book.
It seems to be very important to him...
Shoulder bag.
Needle and thread.
Scissors.
The rose corsage she got from Rose in Chapter 8.
Wallet (hand-made).
ナナ
Nana

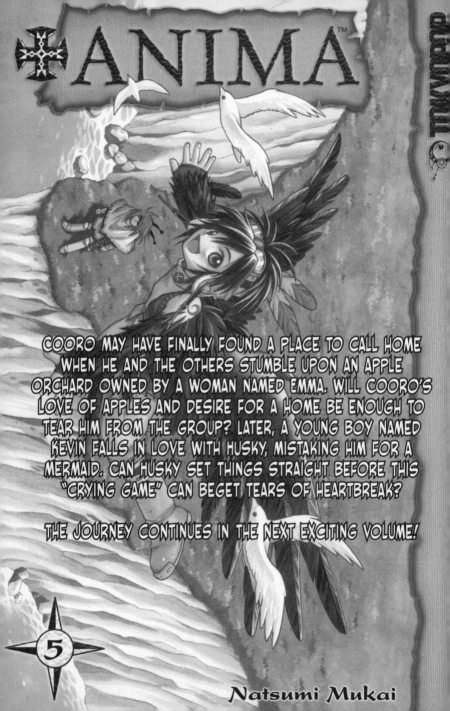

+ANIMA

COORO MAY HAVE FINALLY FOUND A PLACE TO CALL HOME WHEN HE AND THE OTHERS STUMBLE UPON AN APPLE ORCHARD OWNED BY A WOMAN NAMED EMMA. WILL COORO'S LOVE OF APPLES AND DESIRE FOR A HOME BE ENOUGH TO TEAR HIM FROM THE GROUP? LATER, A YOUNG BOY NAMED KEVIN FALLS IN LOVE WITH HUSKY, MISTAKING HIM FOR A MERMAID. CAN HUSKY SET THINGS STRAIGHT BEFORE THIS "CRYING GAME" CAN BEGET TEARS OF HEARTBREAK?

THE JOURNEY CONTINUES IN THE NEXT EXCITING VOLUME!

5

Natsumi Mukai

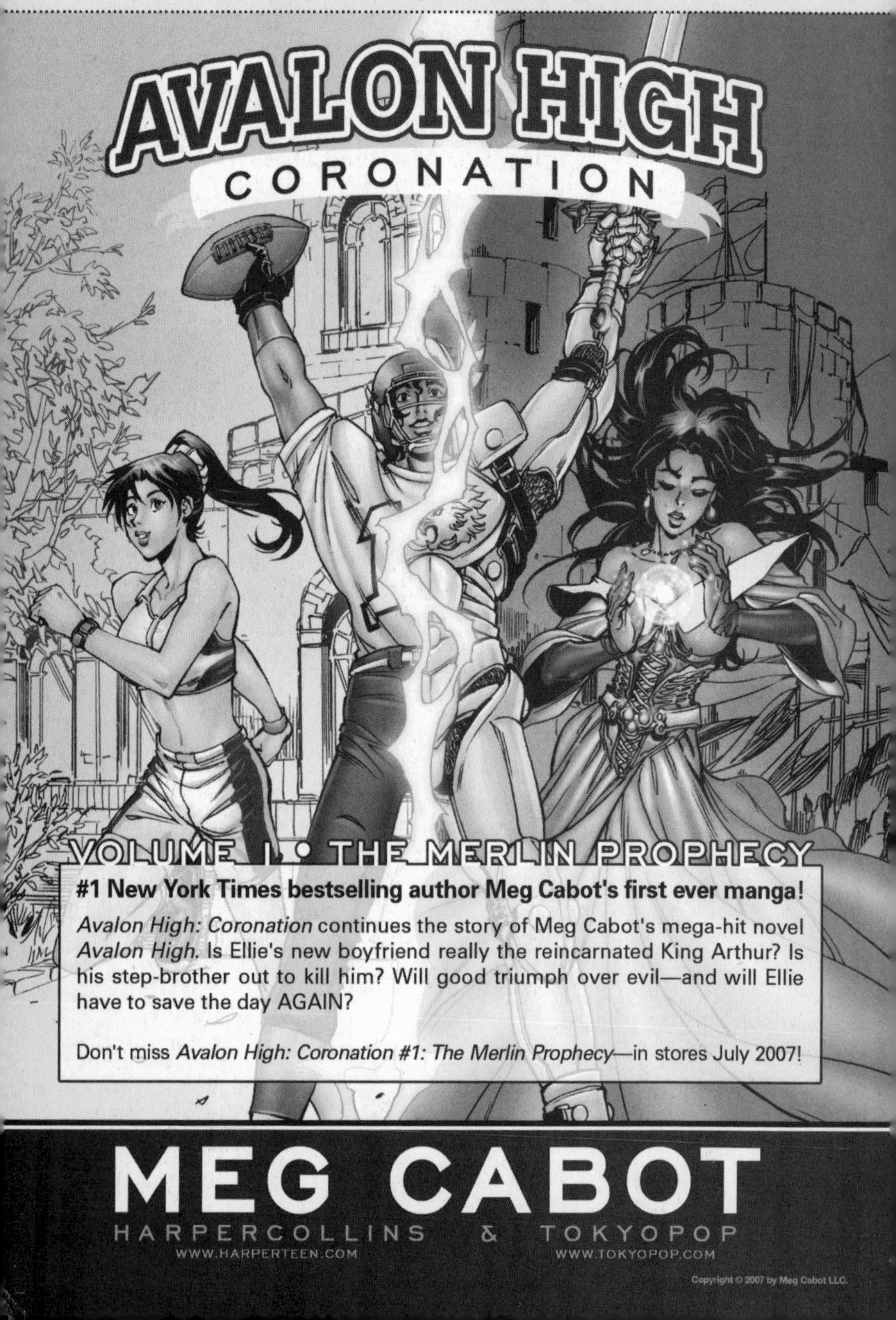
AVALON HIGH
CORONATION
VOLUME 1 • THE MERLIN PROPHECY

#1 New York Times bestselling author Meg Cabot's first ever manga!

Avalon High: Coronation continues the story of Meg Cabot's mega-hit novel *Avalon High*. Is Ellie's new boyfriend really the reincarnated King Arthur? Is his step-brother out to kill him? Will good triumph over evil—and will Ellie have to save the day AGAIN?

Don't miss *Avalon High: Coronation #1: The Merlin Prophecy*—in stores July 2007!

MEG CABOT

HARPERCOLLINS & TOKYOPOP

WWW.HARPERTEEN.COM WWW.TOKYOPOP.COM

P9-BIJ-412

STOP!

This is the back of the book.
You wouldn't want to spoil a great ending!

This book is printed "manga-style," in the authentic Japanese right-to-left format. Since none of the artwork has been flipped or altered, readers get to experience the story just as the creator intended. You've been asking for it, so TOKYOPOP® delivered: authentic, hot-off-the-press, and far more fun!

DIRECTIONS

If this is your first time reading manga-style, here's a quick guide to help you understand how it works.

It's easy... just start in the top right panel and follow the numbers. Have fun, and look for more 100% authentic manga from TOKYOPOP®!

漫画革命

THE MANGA REVOLUTION · LEADING